# The Image of Peter the Great
# in Russian History and Thought

*Peter I*, painting by V. A. Serov (Tretyakov State Gallery, Moscow) Sovfoto

# The Image of Peter the Great
# in Russian History and Thought

NICHOLAS V. RIASANOVSKY

OXFORD UNIVERSITY PRESS
New York   Oxford

Oxford University Press

Oxford  New York  Toronto
Delhi  Bombay  Calcutta  Madras  Karachi
Petaling Jaya  Singapore  Hong Kong  Tokyo
Nairobi  Dar es Salaam  Cape Town
Melbourne  Auckland

and associated companies in

Berlin  Ibadan

First published in 1985 by Oxford University Press, Inc.,
200 Madison Avenue, New York, New York 10016

First issued as an Oxford University Press paperback, 1992

Oxford is a registered trademark of Oxford University Press

Library of Congress Cataloging in Publication Data

Riasanovsky, Nicholas Valentine, 1923–
The image of Peter the Great in Russian history and
thought.

Bibliography: p.
Includes index.
1. Peter I, Emperor of Russia, 1672–1725—Influence.
2. Peter I, Emperor of Russia, 1672–1725, in fiction,
drama, poetry, etc.  3. Peter I, Emperor of Russia, 1672–
1725—Personality.  4. Soviet Union, 1917–1984—Intellectual life.
I. Title.
DK132.R53   1984      947'.05'0924      83-25157
ISBN 0-19-503456-2
ISBN 0-19-507480-7 (pbk)

9 8 7 6 5 4 3 2

Printed in the United States of America
on acid-free paper

To my teachers

# Preface

Every nation has its gods and its myths. One's evaluation of their importance depends closely on one's estimate of the significance of symbols, ideology, and psychology in nationalism. Although historical parallels are inexact, the central and rich Petrine theme in modern Russian history and thought has been compared to that of the Reformation in Germany; and it can be matched with the American Revolution and the French Revolution in their respective countries. I wrote this book because I have been especially interested in the Russian topic and because it has not so far received a general treatment. A study in intellectual history, in a broad sense, the work easily fell into four parts—four chapters as I eventually designated them—in accord with the four main successive intellectual climates in modern Russia. Of course, each part could readily become a book itself, or there was the possibility of writing two volumes instead of one or four, and of other compromises. I decided, however, on a single volume not only because it was in at least some obvious ways more manageable, but also and especially because I wanted to concentrate on the consecutive evolution of the image of Peter the Great through time, not on the comprehensive coverage of its presence in a given period. For the same reason of concentration and brevity, together with that of my rapidly diminishing competence in adjacent fields, I pursued, with but a few exceptions, Petrine images only in words, not in illustration, painting, sculpture, or music. Nor did I generally include images drawn by foreigners because they belonged to other milieus and were parts of other stories, although, as a student of B. H. Sumner, I am quite aware of non-Russian contributions to Petrine scholarship. An image, by definition, is not a summary, although even a book on images may have to rely heavily on summarizing. I did try to quote and to present authentic images at least in part where possible; also, to retain as much of the original Russian in my English translation as I could. Repetition was not treated as a disaster to be always avoided; and the pace of the narrative, slow at times, much faster in certain places, was related—I would like to believe—to the evolution of the Petrine image itself.

The reader should be warned about certain things this book was not intended to be. It is not a study of Peter the Great or his reign, but of their Russian images. Nor is it a historiographical essay meant to delineate the progressive development of our knowledge of the Petrine period and the present state of that knowledge. Images, to repeat, have their own historical value, which is related imperfectly at best to their scholarly validity: in the present work the poet Derzhavin and the novelist Aleksei Nikolaevich Tolstoi take up considerable space, and Professor Reinhard Wittram, a fine German Petrine specialist, none. But even as an investigation of images, my study represents only one approach. Others may legitimately concentrate on the psychoanalytic or comparative aspects of the problem, or they may try to elucidate, for example, the Petrine impulse to Russian cultural creativity. I can only say that I found my investigation rich and full. Besides, it is usually unwise to mix genres.

As at the end of my other books, I find myself deeply indebted to many institutions and people. First, I have to mention the University of California in Berkeley, where I am the Sidney Hellman Ehrman Professor of European History: I am grateful to the university's library, to the university sabbatical policy, to a number of advantages connected with my chair, and to much else. Next I want to express my appreciation for an I.R.E.X. grant to the Soviet Union and, in the same breath, for the way I was received and helped by my Soviet colleagues in the course of my work in Moscow, Leningrad, and the Baltic republics in the autumn and December of 1979. My hosts, the Institute of Russian History of the Academy of Sciences in Moscow, the Institute of Russian Literature of the Academy of Sciences (*Pushkinskii Dom*) in Leningrad, as well as several Baltic hosts and still other institutions with which I was not formally connected, contributed enormously to my stay in the U.S.S.R. and to this book. Of the libraries, I am especially indebted to the great Lenin and Saltykov-Shchedrin collections, in particular to their rare book, that is, in my case, eighteenth-century, sections. But I profited also from many other Soviet libraries. As to people, I want to thank Dr. L. A. Nikiforov, who guided my steps in Moscow, and, together with him, numerous other Soviet Petrine scholars on whom I imposed for advice, discussion, and even argument. I shall always remember the late Academician Mikhail Pavlovich Alekseev, already gravely ill, coming to my presentation of research in *Pushkinskii Dom,* which lasted several hours.

Besides *Pushkinskii Dom,* I must thank the Canadian Association of Slavists, the Western Slavic Conference, and Southern Methodist University for arranging for me to speak on parts of the present work and must express my personal gratitude to all participants in the sessions in question. Similarly, I want to thank all the students in my seminar on "The Image of Peter the Great in Russian History and Thought" whose papers are listed in the bibliography. Very special thanks are due to my invaluable research assistant, Mr. Maciej Siekierski, and to my secretary, Mrs. Dorothy Shannon. The manuscript was read by Professors Terence Emmons of Stanford University, Ralph T. Fisher, Jr., of the University of Illinois, and Ladis K. D. Kristof of Portland State University and also by my Berkeley colleagues Professors Hugh McLean, Martin Malia, Robert Middlekauff, Wolfgang Sauer, Frederic Wakeman, and Reginald Zelnik.

Professors Gary Marker of the State University of New York in Stony Brook and Karen Rasmussen of Indiana University at South Bend read the first chapter. I am in debt to them all in more ways than one. However, and obviously, errors and weaknesses remaining after all that reading have to be results of my own obtuseness.

And I want to acknowledge the unfailing support and help—now for almost thirty years—of my wife, Arlene.

*Berkeley, California*                                                        N.V.R.
*July, 1984*

# Contents

*The Image of Peter the Great*
*in Russian History and Thought*

# I

# The Image of Peter the Great in the Russian Enlightenment, 1700–1826

> Your amazing deeds are your trophies. Entire Russia is your statue, reshaped by your expert skill, as pictured not in vain in your emblem; and the entire world is your poet, and the preacher of your glory.
>
> Feofan Prokopovich[1]

1

Images have lives of their own, sometimes over centuries and even millennia of human history. Remembrance and praise of the hero have functioned as a secular surrogate for immortality in many societies and civilizations, including our Western civilization at least from the time of the *Iliad*. Not all images are positive. Destroyers have stayed in man's memory along with creators, scourges with saints; Attila probably left a greater resonance in the world than Louis IX. Moreover, in spite of the human preference for black and white, images have come down also in other colors; in fact, they seem to reflect the totality of human experience. I remember the shudder of recognition when introduced to a person whose last name was Pilate. Disturbingly for the historian, images do not have to correspond to reality: witness Horst Wessel as the incarnation of a regenerated Germany or the unbelievable content and career of Stalin's "cult of personality." Yet even these wayward examples were by no means merely exercises in abstract imagination. Although Horst Wessel himself apparently was not at all what Nazis wanted Germans to be, he came much nearer to representing faithfully many of the Nazis and, on the whole, was not such an inappropriate symbol for the total catastrophe of 1945. As to Stalin in life and the Stalin of the cult, the connection was a complex one indeed: direct, reverse, perhaps dialectical—appropriately for that preacher of the dialectic—and in any case in need of a special study. By contrast, most images stay closer to reality, emphasizing genuine character traits, accomplishments, and historical roles of their

---

[1] Feofan Prokopovich, *Sochineniia* (Moscow and Leningrad, 1961), 144. In this case and in general, the translation is my own. For interesting contemporary English translations of Feofan Prokopovich and other Petrine sources, see especially James Cracraft, ed., *For God and Peter the Great: The Works of Thomas Consett, 1723–1729* (New York, 1982).

heroes. Even when imagination soars and propaganda proliferates, as they so often must, there remains something of an authentic base as a point of departure. It is this strong grounding in the person and in historical reality that strikes the student eager to investigate the image of Peter the Great in Russian history and thought.

Peter I was an impressive individual. Almost seven feet tall and powerfully built, the tsar possessed astonishing physical strength and vigor. Stories spread of his ability to bend silver talers with his fingers, roll up a silver plate, or cut with a knife a piece of cloth in the air. Moreover, he appeared to be in a constant state of restless activity, taking on himself tasks normally performed by several men. Few Russians could keep up with their monarch in his many occupations. Indeed, as he walked with rapid giant strides, they had to run even to continue conversation. Handsome, in spite of a nervous twitching of his face, domineering, utterly terrifying in anger, the tsar was an overwhelming presence for his contemporaries.

In addition to his extraordinary physical attributes, Peter the Great exhibited some remarkable qualities of mind and character. The ruler had an insatiable intellectual curiosity coupled with an amazing ability to learn. He proceeded to participate personally in all kinds of state matters, technical and special as well as general, becoming deeply involved in diplomacy, administration, justice, finance, commerce, industry, education, and practically everything else besides. To this day historians keep uncovering further evidence of Peter I's direct management of Russian affairs.[2] In his reforms, the tsar invariably valued expert advice, but he remained generally independent in thought and did not hesitate to adapt projects to circumstances. Personally brave, deeply interested in the army and in love with the navy, although by no means a conventional militarist in his attitude and orientation, Peter the Great also developed into an accomplished military and naval commander. He studied the professions of soldier and sailor from the bottom up, serving first in the ranks and learning the use of each weapon before promoting himself to his first post as an officer. The monarch attained the rank of full general after the victory of Poltava and of full admiral after the successful conclusion of the Great Northern War. In addition, the sovereign found time to learn some twenty different trades and prided himself on his ability to make almost anything, from a ship to a pair of shoes. With his own hands he pulled the teeth of his courtiers and cut off their beards. Lacking a regular education and an autodidact all his life, Peter I nevertheless learned to speak Dutch and German and to manage to some extent in several other languages. He even considered introducing Dutch as the official tongue of his state! The sovereign's ungrammatical Russian

---

[2] As one example, see G. A. Nekrasov, *Russko-shvedskie otnosheniia i politika velikikh derzhav v 1721–1726 g. g.* (Moscow, 1964). I would like to refer here also to my conversations with Dr. Nekrasov.

had concreteness and power, and it becomes more compelling the more one reads it. Characteristically, the ruler wanted to be everywhere and see everything for himself, traveling indefatigably around his vast realm as no Muscovite monarch had ever done. In a still more unprecedented manner he went twice to the West to learn, in 1697–1698 and in 1717. Peter I's mind can best be described as active and practical, able quickly to grasp problems and devise solutions, if not to construct theories.

As to character, the tsar impressed those around him in particular by his unbending will, determination, and dedication. They observed how he recovered quickly from even the worst defeats and how he regarded every obstacle as an invitation to further exertion and achievement. Historians too noted the amazing self-confidence and directness of a man who, during decades of extremely difficult, disparate, and even desperate situations, never doubted in the main what he was doing, nor his right and obligation to do it. To be sure, this confidence related to the conscious not the subconscious level, to the external not the internal world. Internally Peter the Great was constantly at the boiling point, possibly on the verge of a breakdown or madness; all his life he struggled against his emotions, rage especially, but repeatedly lost that struggle. His cruelty, drunkenness, and a strangely dissolute style of life can probably only in part be explained by the standards of the age and adventitious circumstances (just as there is some evidence that the tsar's celebrated and historically significant love of the sea succeeded an original water phobia). But in the world of political action and historical record, very few major actors played their roles with more confidence, consistency, and clarity of purpose. Peter I's image of himself was thus the first and, as it turned out, a basic and seminal one of the remarkable ruler.

Yet in some ways it is not an easy one to reconstruct, at least not beyond the obvious. This obvious, to repeat, was constant, driving, obsessive activity in almost every field of endeavor. Above all, Peter the Great was a tremendous worker. Contemporaries as well as later commentators recognized this fully. Ivan Pososhkov, the first Russian economist and a collaborator of the tsar who acquired a fine appreciation both of the sovereign's reforms and of the obstacles in their way, expressed the matter in a famous image: "the Great Monarch" exercising every effort was pulling uphill with some ten assistants, but millions were pushing downhill.[3] Or—a century later—in the words of Pushkin known to all educated Russians:

> Now an academician, now a hero,
> Now a seafarer, now a carpenter,
> He, with an all-encompassing soul,
> Was on the throne an eternal worker.[4]

[3] Ivan Pososhkov, *Sochineniia* (Moscow, 1842), 95.

[4] A. S. Pushkin, *Izbrannye proizvedeniia* (2 vols., Leningrad, 1961), I, 189 ("Stances," 1826). Pushkin's image of Peter the Great will be discussed in the first section of Chapter 2.

Again, several decades after Pushkin, perhaps the best and most important Russian historian, Sergei Soloviev, chose as a leitmotif of his public
lectures on Peter the Great the ruler's own reference to himself in an
early letter from Pereiaslavl, where he was engaged in shipbuilding, to
his mother: "occupied in work" (*v rabote prebyvaiushchii*).[5]

Devoted to his work and proud of it, Peter I judged others in the same
manner. The emphasis on work and achievement permeated the reforms
of the reign, whether the Table of Ranks, on which state service in modern Russia was to be based; the law of succession to the throne; the law
of inheritance of the gentry estates; or other legislation, including the
Spiritual Regulation, which reorganized the church. By means of and
beyond all specific measures, Peter the Great made a continuous, almost
superhuman effort to obtain appropriate service from all his subjects, in
particular from the members of the gentry, whom he wanted to start
that service at the bottom (e.g., as privates in the army) and advance only
according to merit. And it was the same emphasis on knowledge, ability,
and work—on getting things done—that accounted for the extraordinary
motley group of assistants who gathered around the ruler.[6]

Intensely practical and pragmatic, usually overwhelmed with work and
frequently facing crisis, Peter the Great and his collaborators moved from
one immediate task to the next with little occasion to think beyond tomorrow. The Great Northern War dominated the reign, but associated—
at times catastrophic—financial and economic problems, a series of rebellions inside the country, diplomacy and war with Turkey, and even
the issue of Tsarevich Alexis and the succession to the throne could be
equally pressing. For many participants, "the epoch of Peter the Great"
must have been one grueling ordeal, with personal and national survival
possibly at stake to help supply the energy. For later generations, the
character of the times is reflected in the greatest documentary collection
for that age, the so-called *Letters and Papers of Emperor Peter the Great*.[7]

[5] S. M. Soloviev, *Publichnye chteniia o Petre Velikom* (Moscow, 1872), esp. p. 32.
Soloviev's image of Peter the Great will be discussed in the first section of Chapter 3.

[6] As told by Kliuchevskii: "Peter collected the necessary men everywhere, without
worrying about rank and origin, and they came to him from different directions and all
possible conditions: one arrived as a cabin-boy on a Portuguese ship, as was the case of
the chief of police of the new capital, de Vière; another had herded swine in Lithuania,
as was rumored about the first Procurator-General of the Senate, Iaguzhinskii; a third
had worked as a clerk in a small store, as in the instance of Vice-Chancellor Shafirov; a
fourth had been a Russian house serf, as in the case of the Vice-Governor of Archangel,
the inventor of stamped paper, Kurbatov; a fifth, that is, Ostermann, was the son of a
Westphalian pastor. And all these men, together with Prince Menshikov, who, the story
went, had once sold pies in the streets of Moscow, met in Peter's society with the remnants of the Russian boyar nobility" (V. O. Kliuchevskii, *Ocherki i rechi. Vtoroi
sbornik statei* [Petrograd, 1918], 461). The study "Peter the Great Amidst His Collaborators" ("Petr Velikii sredi svoikh sotrudnikov") occupies pp. 454–495 of the volume.
Kliuchevskii's image of Peter the Great will be discussed in the second section of
Chapter 3.

[7] *Pisma i bumagi Imperatora Petra Velikogo* (12 vols. in 19 books, Moscow and Leningrad, 1887–1977). The publication has advanced only through the year 1712.

The first entry for the year 1709 begins: "The Narva and the Pskov garrisons must be supplied with provisions this winter, and there must always be in each garrison provisions for five thousand men for two years."[8] The second states: "This moment your judgment was brought to me and, therefore, while I consider it, do not order to proceed with the executions; order, however, to be ready for that, and you with the commanders come here."[9] One could go on and on.

Yet hectic hard work, central to the life of Peter the Great and to his image of himself—as well as to many other contemporary and subsequent images of him—did not exhaust the image. At the very least, questions would arise about the reasons for that work, about its proximate and eventual purpose, about the relationship among different activities, about the likelihood of success. And, in effect, Peter the Great had these and other such questions in mind, and they were highly relevant to his image of himself.

Most students of Peter the Great and his reign emphasize that he turned against the Muscovite past, toward the new world of the West; but they frequently underestimate the passion and the psychological power of this reaction and commitment. The past meant for the monarch ignorance, prejudice, inefficiency, and corruption—in political terms, weakness and defeat; in the West resided knowledge, reason, and salvation. Peter I's "Westernism" is all the more noteworthy because he did not admire blindly but always tried to separate, in the West as at home, the wheat from the chaff and because he remained a dedicated Russian patriot. Negative impressions of palace torpor and intrigue, an unusual boyhood spent in large part in the foreign suburb of Moscow and in independent self-discovery, and an insatiable curiosity to learn and do novel things were some of the factors that combined to make Tsar Alexis's son violently reject the old and enthusiastically grasp the new. The absolute ruler was never happier than when building a ship or learning another trade, and his favored companions were foreign specialists of all sorts. Indeed, the informal and unrestrained atmosphere of the foreign suburb, with its smoking, drinking, lovemaking, rough good humor, conglomerate of tongues, and especially its profusion and variety of technical experts, became an enduring part of the emperor's life. Later he was to say that if he were not the ruler of Russia, he would want to be an English admiral. As to Peter the Great's frightful hatreds, characteristically they were directed against the *streltsy* or against the clique surrounding the heir apparent Alexis, not against foreigners in or out of Russia, not even against the Swedes. At times his hatreds seemed to extend to all opponents of change. A legitimate, complex, and extensive

---

[8] *Ibid.*, IX (1950), 9.

[9] *Ibid.*, 10. The case concerned looting of the civilian population by the military. Characteristically, Peter the Great ordered severe punishment, especially of the officers involved.

debate has ensued among scholars as to whether objectively Peter the Great's reforms were radical or gradualist; but subjectively the remarkable tsar was a revolutionary.

Revolutions, however, are difficult to accomplish, all the more so when the purpose is to replace darkness with light. Peter I's entire life became an intense effort to make his country catch up with the West, to modernize it as later scholars would put it. The realities of the Great Northern War helped to underscore the ruler's repeatedly stated conviction that procrastination meant death. It is in this context that one must understand the concept of devoted service, which the sovereign believed to be fundamental to his own behavior and which he tried so hard to impose on his subjects.

Peter the Great was an absolute ruler in theory and in practice. He certainly considered himself an autocrat, and his view was supported and developed by such political writers as Feofan Prokopovich in his *Justice of the Monarch's Will.*[10] More important, he acted like one of the memorable autocrats of history. An uncompromising character and a violent temper accentuated further his decisiveness and the plenitude of his power. Still, important changes from the uncodified principles and the more tangible attitudes and mores of Muscovite tsardom emerged. Most significant was the separation of the ruler as a person from the state, in fact, a subordination of his private person to the state, and a new utilitarian rationale for the ruler's behavior. Professor Nicholas Pavlenko, a leading present-day Soviet specialist on Peter I, has emphasized that the concept of the common good, *obshchee blago,* was first advanced in 1702, in a ukase concerned with inviting foreign specialists into Russian service, and that it became increasingly prominent thereafter. Pavlenko believed that a growing stress on the interests of the country as distinct from those of the person of the ruler can be detected in the recurrent official Russian justifications of the Great Northern War.[11] And, to repeat, the monarch practiced and preached, above all, service, service to the state for the common good. Revealingly, when reorganizing the army, he crossed out "the interests of His Tsarist Maj-

[10] *Pravda Voli Monarshei.* I used the 1788 reprinting in Feodor Tumanskii, *Sobranie raznykh zapisok i sochinenii, sluzhashchikh k dostavleniiu polnogo svedeniia o zhizni i deianiiakh Gosudaria Imperatora Petra Velikogo* (Part 10, St. Petersburg, 1788), 123–243. See also esp. Feofan Prokopovich, "A Sermon on the Tsar's Power and Honor, as Established in the World by God Himself, and on How People Must Honor Tsars and Obey Them; Who Are Those Who Oppose Them and What Sin They Commit," *Sochineniia,* 76–93, 467 fns. But Feofan Prokopovich's authorship of *Justice* is by no means certain. See particularly the latest investigation, which assigns the authorship to Condoidi, a Greek archimandrite in Russia: James Cracraft, "Did Feofan Prokopovich Really Write *Pravda Voli Monarshei?*" *Slavic Review,* vol. 40, no. 2 (Summer 1981), 173–193.

[11] N. I. Pavlenko, "Petr I. (K izucheniiu sotsialno-politicheskikh vzgliadov)," in N. I. Pavlenko, responsible ed.; L. A. Nikiforov, M. Ia. Volkov, eds., *Rossiia v period reform Petra I* (Moscow, 1973), 40–102, esp. 60–62. For Pavlenko's full account of the emperor, see N. Pavlenko, *Petr Pervyi* (Moscow, 1976).

esty" as the object of military devotion and substituted "the interests of the state."[12] Or, to quote from Peter the Great's celebrated address to his troops immediately preceding the battle of Poltava:

Let the Russian host know that that hour has come that places the fortunes of our entire Fatherland in their hands: either to perish utterly or for Russia to be reborn in a better condition. And let them not think that they were armed and put forth for Peter, but for the state entrusted to Peter, for their kin, for the Russian people. . . .

As to Peter, they should know clearly that his life is not dear to him, provided only that Russia lives, Russian piety, glory, and well-being.[13]

Not surprisingly, Peter I drew a sharp distinction between his own resources, which he considered limited to the salaries he earned in his various functions, and the possessions of the state. Not surprisingly, too, he ordered his subjects not to use derogatory diminutive names when signing addresses to the sovereign, not to kneel in front of him, not to take hats off when passing the palace. "What will be the difference between God and the tsar"—he would say—"if both are paid equal honors? Less obsequiousness, more effort in the service, and a greater faithfulness to me and the state: this is the honor that belongs to the tsar."[14]

In spite of the colossal demands of his self-assigned task, Peter the Great on the whole looked confidently to the future. A part of that confidence stemmed, no doubt, from his own energetic optimism; a part reflected the affirmative and hopeful outlook of the age. The tsar expected reason to accomplish the transformation of Russia. It was reason that made the Russian sovereign prize experts, whether Leibniz or a shipwright, and utilize them as much as possible, for they usually had reason on their side. It was reason that even made him at times, defying his own temperament, listen to dissenting or contrary advice and admit his mistakes. As the monarch jotted down once on a piece of paper: "Thinking is above all virtues because without reason every virtue is empty."[15] Peter the Great's hectic, disjointed, at times desperate reordering of Russia was nevertheless also meant to be a tribute to reason and to result eventually in its triumph in the entire land.

Applied to the monarch's subjects, reliance on reason meant explanation and education. It has been noted that, in his all-pervasive, minute regulation of the lives of his people, the sovereign almost invariably supplied the reasons for his legislation. *Ponezhe* or *dlia togo,* that is, "because," became the hallmark of his edicts.[16] To be sure, he also stated appropriate punishment for each transgression, but this only added further point to the didacticism of his efforts. From the first translated book

---

[12] B. H. Sumner, *Peter the Great and the Emergence of Russia* (London, 1950), 59–60.
[13] Pavlenko, *Petr Pervyi,* 169.
[14] Soloviev, *op. cit.,* 83.
[15] Pavlenko, *Petr Pervyi,* 315.
[16] *Ibid.,* 315–316, with some examples of these reasons.

of manners, the so-called *Mirror for Youth*,[17] the new Russian publishing industry devoted special attention to teaching its readers how to behave. More formal education was of central importance. Again, the ruler worked feverishly himself, whether simplifying the Russian alphabet, establishing the School of Mathematics and Navigation, or organizing the Academy of Sciences. "For learning is good and fundamental, and as it were the root, the seed, and first principle of all that is good and useful in church and state."[18]

Peter the Great was a man of action rather than a man of thought; a practitioner, not a theoretician. He was also something of a visionary. With grandeur and optimism, themselves typical of the age, he foresaw the image of a modern, powerful, prosperous, and educated country; and it was to the realization of that image that he dedicated his life.

2

Whereas Peter the Great's image of himself can be logically considered the first and basic image of the reforming ruler, many other such images inevitably appeared during the monarch's life. In fact, the Petrine canon was fully formed at the time of the emperor's death; and, although it was to grow and change in subsequent decades and centuries, the early formulations proved remarkably lasting, both in general and in detail, as well as strikingly influential on later appraisals.

The reformer's image of himself, although idealized and oversimplified, corresponded in certain important ways to reality—or at least to one logical interpretation of reality. On the whole, it was enthusiastically taken up, championed, and propagated by his collaborators. Without changing its basic content, they added to it extravagant praise, adulation, at times veneration—qualities absent from the monarch's own simple and pragmatic view of his activities. Yet the roles of genre (sermons are different from administrative commands), occasion, and sheer flattery aside, that glorification had, again, a firm grounding in historical reality: the admirers were, in effect, acclaiming not only their remarkable leader and his deeds, but also themselves and their own work, even their very existence as a conscious group in modernizing Russia. That fundamental link between Peter the Great on the one hand and the modern Russian government and educated public on the other was to be a dominant factor in Russian intellectual life in the eighteenth century and beyond. One understands how Archbishop Feofan Prokopovich, statesman and foremost preacher and ideologist of the reign, began his celebrated funeral sermon, "What is this? What have we lived to witness, oh Russians?

---

[17] *Iunosti chestnoe zertsalo ili pokazanie k zhiteiskomu obkhozhdeniiu. Sobrannoe ot raznykh Avtorov. Napechatasia poveleniem Tsarskago Velichestva, v Sanktpiterburkhe Leta Gospodnia 1717, Fevralia 4 dnia.* A facsimile edition of the *Mirror* was published in Moscow in 1976.

[18] Peter the Great as translated in Sumner, *op. cit.*, 149.

What do we see? What are we doing? We are burying Peter the Great!" and then could not continue, while he cried and the congregation howled and howled its grief.[19]

Images of Peter the Great—or at least representations if not fully developed images—abounded in the panegyrical literature and decorative architecture and art so prominent at the time. The reformer abolished most of the Muscovite ceremonial, but he delighted in huge celebrations of important events, especially military and naval victories. These frequently combined poetry, school plays (produced particularly at the Slavonic-Greek-Latin Academy), complex military reviews (sometimes with prisoners), fireworks, distribution of food and drink to the people, and very elaborate triumphal arches and other appropriate decor. Although the sovereign preferred to march in a parade in the uniform of the Preobrazhenskii regiment, leaving higher functions, such as receiving the review to others, notably Prince Fedor Romodanovskii, even styled "caesar," he was depicted in painting and sculpture as Jupiter, Mars, Hercules (victor over the Swedish lion), and, of course, Neptune. He was also pictured as a hero of antiquity, an Agamemnon or an Alexander the Great. Panegyrical literature used, too, such Biblical images as David killing Goliath, Moses liberating his people, Samson defeating, once more, the lion. Even old Kievan princes, St. Vladimir and Iaroslav the Wise, made their appearance. Alexander Menshikov and other associates of the ruler sometimes accompanied their monarch in his various disguises.[20]

A greater and more historically significant celebration than usual followed the final victory over Sweden and the Treaty of Nystad. On that occasion, on October 22, 1721, State Chancellor Count Gabriel Golovkin (made state chancellor in 1709 on the battlefield of Poltava) offered in the name of the Senate to Peter I the titles of "Emperor," "Great" and

---

[19] Feofan Prokopovich, *Sochineniia*, 126. The sermon occupies pp. 126–129; and the editorial notes to it, pp. 472–473 of the volume.

[20] As introduction to the panegyrical literature and art of the reign, see *Panegiricheskaia literatura petrovskogo vremeni* (Moscow, 1979). The texts in the volume include detailed descriptions and explanations of two magnificent triumphal arches, "Torzhestvennaia vrata, vvodiashchaia v khram bezsmertnye slavy" (135–149), and Iosif Turoboiskii's "Preslavnoe torzhestvo svoboditelia Livonii" (150–180). Russians objected to classical mythology as pagan, thus providing further incentive for Petrine propagandists to explicate and defend what they were doing. For the tradition of festivals in imperial Russia in the eighteenth century, see, for example, the catalog of a Hermitage exhibition, *Feierverki i illiuminatsii v grafike XVIII veka* (Leningrad, 1978). Recent work in the field of decorations, medals, and military emblems, all greatly affected by the reign and relevant to its ideology, includes George Vilinbakhov's expert articles: G. V. Vilinbakhov, "K istorii uchrezhdeniia ordena Andreia Pervozvannogo i evoliutsii ego znaka," *Sbornik russkoi kultury i iskusstva petrovskogo vremeni* (Leningrad, 1977), 144–158; "Emblema na rotnom znameni Sankt-Peterburgskogo Polka 1712 goda," *Soobshcheniia Gosudarstvennogo Ermitazha*, XLIV (Leningrad, 1979), 32–34. On coins, as well as medals, see esp. the bilingual publication *Medals and Coins of the Age of Peter the Great. From the Hermitage Collection / Medali i monety Petrovskogo vremeni. Iz kollektsii Gosudarstvennogo Ermitazha* (Leningrad, 1974).

"Father of the Fatherland." As motivation for the offer, he spoke of the ruler's achievement as follows: "We, your faithful subjects, have been thrust from the darkness of ignorance onto the stage of glory of the entire world, promoted, so to speak from nonbeing into being, and included in the society of political peoples."[21] An attenuated form of this promotion from nonbeing into being, namely the image of Peter the Great as a sculptor shaping Russia with his tools into a statue of his own making, became quasi-official in formal rhetoric and was reflected in the emperor's seal, his flag, and even the dress of his heavily caparisoned horse as it walked in the funeral procession.[22]

Longer-lasting than fireworks, richer in material and argument than proclamations or festive poems, sermons are 'of special interest to a student of the early images of Peter the Great. Preached, often in the presence of the ruler, by Archbishop Feofan Prokopovich, Bishop Gabriel Buzhinskii, Metropolitan Stephen Iavorskii, in many ways the leading cleric of the reign—who, however, came to disagree with the sovereign on church matters and thus deviated from the main body of his supporters—Archimandrite Feofilakt Lopatinskii, and others, they presented a striking quasi-official view of Peter the Great and his works, justified them both in general and in particular, and taught Russians perfect obedience and support. As Feofan Prokopovich restated grandly the monarch's own vision of his reign as a move from darkness into the light, a leap from backwardness to a new prominence and parity with the West:

Be it not remembered for shame, because it is true, the opinion we elicited from, the value we were assigned by foreign peoples formerly: by political peoples we were considered barbarians, by the proud and the majestic the despised ones, by the learned the ignorant, by the predatory a desirable catch, by all shiftless, insulted from all sides. . . . But now what is it that our most luminous monarch has accomplished by courage, wisdom, justice, by correcting and teaching the fatherland, not only for himself but also for the entire Russian people? This, that those who abhorred us as rude assiduously seek our fraternity; those who dishonored us glorify us; those who threatened us are afraid and tremble; those who despised us are not ashamed to serve us; many European crowned heads are not only willing to ally with Peter, our monarch, but do not consider it dishonorable to give him precedence: they have repealed their opinion, they have repealed their narratives about us, they have erased their antiquated little stories, they have begun both to speak and to write about us differently. Russia has raised her head, bright, beautiful, strong, loved by friends, feared by enemies.[23]

Peter the Great's own role in the transformation was all-important: "By your labors we rest, by your campaigns we stand unshakable, by your

[21] Quoted from V. Mavrodin, *Petr Pervyi* (Leningrad, 1948), 250.

[22] The funeral was described in precise detail in [Feofan Prokopovich], *Kratkaia povest o smerti Petra Velikogo Imperatora Rossiiskogo*. In the St. Petersburg 1819 edition the description occupies pp. 25–39.

[23] Feofan Prokopovich, *Sochineniia,* 46.

(yes, this is what I mean to say) many deaths we are alive."[24] Feofan Pro-kopovich, as already indicated, liked especially the image of Peter I as sculptor and Russia as his statue. Another preacher, Feofilakt Lopatin-skii, depicted the reforming ruler as architect.[25]

In discussing Peter the Great's achievement, orators often stressed his versatility as well as his heroic effort and personal participation in every-thing. As Feofan Prokopovich put it, combining historical fact, classical and Biblical learning, and his own imagination:

It would have been amazing had one sovereign accomplished one thing and an-other the other: as Romans praise their first two tsars, Romulus and Numa, that one by war and the other by peace strengthened the fatherland, or as in sacred history David by arms and Solomon by politics created a blessed well-being for Israel. But in our case both this and that, and, in addition, in countless and varied circumstances, were achieved by Peter alone. For us he is Romulus, and Numa, and David, and Solomon—Peter alone.[26]

Or, as expressed in the solemn eulogy of Gabriel Buzhinskii, in a sermon marking the first anniversary of the monarch's death:

*Greater love hath no man than this, that a man lay down his life for his friends.* In this love *Peter* is a true imitator of Christ the Lord, not sparing his dearest life for his fatherland, for his friends in the faith in Christ, and, by the scepter God had given him, his subjects, not sparing his life in labors and deeds, in cold and in heat, in travels and in seafaring, in land journeys full of tribulations and in much heavier and more calamitous storms at sea; not sparing his life in battles, where he was in a situation when an enemy bullet pierced the hat on his most precious head; not sparing his life in seafaring, where once he was in such a storm on the Baltic Sea that all hope of salvation was gone; all this he suffered for the fatherland, laying down his life for his friends.[27]

The preachers gave their unstinting support to the ruler and the state, against every enemy and in all circumstances. Using the splendid ecclesi-astical vocabulary available for such purposes, they denounced and anath-ematized Mazepa and other "traitors" or lamented the unbelievable "ingratitude" and evil behavior of Tsarevich Alexis. Feofan Prokopovich, to repeat, became through his various writings and orations probably the leading ideologist of the Petrine autocracy and of his reign in general. Gabriel Buzhinskii, who served for a number of years as, in effect, the head chaplain of the Russian navy, in his turn, argued as follows in a sermon pronounced aboard ship, commemorating the victory of Hangö

24 *Ibid.*, 67.
25 See Feofilakt Lopatinskii's sermon "Slovo o bogodarovannom mire," *Panegiriches-kaia literatura petrovskogo vremeni*, 255–264.
26 Feofan Prokopovich, *Sochineniia*, 137.
27 Gavriil Buzhinskii, *Polnoe sobranie pouchitelnykh slov, skazyvannykh v vysochai-shem prisutstvii gosudaria imperatora Petra Velikogo* (Moscow, [1784]), 252–253. Italics are in the original. The sermon occupies pp. 224–263. It was delivered "in the presence of Peter the Great" only in the sense that it was pronounced by his tomb.

and dealing with such topics as military service, just wars, and the soldier's or sailor's role and fate.

Contrary to the Anabaptists, the Socinians, and other assorted heretics, force and wars had their proper place in human affairs. These critics, in effect, disregarded overwhelming scriptural evidence against their claims and cited what passages they did cite out of context, in particular without distinguishing the private from the public. Thus, in the injunction to love one's enemies, they failed to realize that "these words must be understood as referring to loving one's own private and particular enemies, not the enemies of the entire society."[28] Just wars did exist, and of those wars "God Himself is both the beginner and the supporter, and He alone grants victories and triumph."[29] They were marked by certain signs: fighting not for no reason but because of great need; fighting on orders of lawful authorities, which distinguished just wars from rebellions; fighting because of a rightful claim of injury; fighting in defense and for survival. The Old Testament was full of just wars and of the divine support of them. Even in the New Testament, Christ, while ordering Peter not to use his sword and thus commit merely a private murder, never told warriors to cease being warriors, for instance, when he cured a centurion's son. "The Russian crown started a true, just, and rightful war for its vestments torn unjustly by the Swedish lion, for the numerous lands and provinces grabbed by it, and God, the highest Judge, took the crown under His righteous protection."[30] As to the Russian soldiers and sailors who went into battle:

Rejoice, then, you too, and exult, Russian flag-officers, captains, and the entire Christian host, who for the fatherland and for your Sovereign do not protect your health and do not spare your life: for you a martyr's crown has been prepared; you, having abandoned all worldly attachments, will be rewarded a hundredfold in the heavenly kingdom and will inherit life eternal. Sweet for you is death for the fatherland, but rewards eternally sweet, which the eye can not see, the ear can not hear, and the heart can not feel, have been prepared for you. There, with those warriors, Theodore Stratilatos, which means military commander, Andrew Stratilatos, George, Dimitrios, Sebastian, and others without number, you will receive the crown of victory.[31]

Feofan Prokopovich used more down-to-earth language in justifying Peter the Great's creation of the navy:

We shall not find a single village in the world that is located by a river or a lake and does not have boats. How is it possible then for such a glorious and mighty monarchy, which stretches around southern and northern seas, not to have ships—this would be shameful and deserving reproach even if there were no particular need for them. We stand over water and watch how merchants come to

---

28 *Ibid.,* 80. The sermon covers pp. 68–106.
29 *Ibid.,* 87.
30 *Ibid.,* 97.
31 *Ibid.,* 105–106.

us and leave us, but ourselves cannot do that. Word for word, as in poetic tales, a certain Tantalus is standing in water, but experiences thirst. And that is why even our sea is not ours.[32]

Moreover, without a fleet the shores themselves were not safe. A maritime enemy could strike suddenly; even when the authorities were forewarned, the point of the enemy's attack could not be foreseen; and he was free to withdraw at will without the possibility of pursuit. Gabriel Buzhinskii, on his part, referred to Cosimo de' Medici for the assertion that a state relying on land forces alone was similar to a bird trying to fly on one wing. By contrast, history was full of examples of the success of sea power. Themistocles used a navy to excellent effect; according to Polybius, Rome defeated Carthage once it had acquired navigation; distant territories could be quickly conquered by sea long before land forces reached them. Yet the naval chaplain, too, thought of trade as much as of war when he spoke of a fleet: "What an abundance of everything prevails there, where you have ports, and, just the opposite, what a shortage of everything, even the necessities, is noticeable in those settlements that are distant from the sea, or are entirely deprived of a sea connection."[33] Indeed, Feofan Prokopovich cited St. Basil the Great to insist that God had divided the fruits of the earth among different lands so they would have to cooperate economically, and He had provided water for effective communication: those objecting to the fleet were thus opposing God's plan for humanity.[34] In addition to justifying and glorifying the Great Northern War, the army, and the navy, the preachers applied their talents to many other aspects of Peter the Great's activity—witness Gabriel Buzhinskii's remarkable defense of the building of St. Petersburg, which will be presented later in this chapter.

The preachers not only taught a proper understanding of Peter the Great and of various aspects of his reign, but they also supplied significant detail. Together with the official pageantry and certain writings of the reign, they helped to establish the iconography, so to speak, of the image of the ruler, an iconography that has survived in large part to our day. Thus the hat on Peter's head shot through in the battle of Poltava—and already cited in this chapter in Gabriel Buzhinskii's eulogy on the first anniversary of the sovereign's death—became an almost indispensable symbol of that decisive engagement, of Peter the Great's heroism, and of his direct military leadership. ". . . you were not frightened by the very fires of Mars, by most obvious death, you have shown to the world such courage as has nowhere been heard, nowhere described. The very hat on the thrice-crowned head shot through by the enemy pro-

[32] Feofan Prokopovich, *Sochineniia*, 107. "A Laudatory Sermon about the Russian Fleet and about the Victory Obtained on July 27 by Russian Galleys over Swedish Ships" occupies pp. 103–112, and 468–469 fns.

[33] Gavriil Buzhinskii, *op. cit.*, 21–22.

[34] Feofan Prokopovich, *Sochineniia*, 107.

claims this courage louder than any trumpets and will proclaim it for ages and ages."[35] Similarly, Peter I's honorific brief appointment (after all, he was a monarch) in August 1716 as the commander of joint fleets of Russia, Holland, Denmark, and Great Britain became an abiding symbol of the new prominence and acceptance of Russia as a major power—and was included, for instance, in Professor Nicholas Pavlenko's brief list of "fundamental dates in the life and the activity of Peter the First" in a book published in 1976.[36] As Gabriel Buzhinskii expatiated on the matter of the joint command:

. . . but what boggles the mind, what is totally unheard of, but for God Who arranges everything so wisely, is this assumption of the honor of Admiral over three ancient and glorious fleets of different states; for, having lowered their flags in front of the Russian state standard on the ship named *Ingermanland,* in front of our victorious Emperor who was present there in person and who had been honored by them with the title of *Admiral,* they rendered him proper obeisance and respect.[37]

Examples of significant Petrine details that became, in a sense, canonical while Peter I was still alive could be readily multiplied.

The sermonizers, however, differed from many later admirers of Peter the Great in laying stress on the religious nature and the Christian virtues and behavior of their hero. They ascribed to him not only a willingness to sacrifice his life for his people, but also a profound faith, a trusting reliance on God, kindness, mercy, and humility. They argued that he did not like war and had turned to it only as the last resort. Rather disingenuously they even utilized a complex diplomatic game to claim that Charles XII himself, shortly before he died, came finally to admire Peter the Great, "began to love him and, disdaining all others, with him alone wanted not only to make peace, but also to unite in a friendly alliance."[38] This conversion of his greatest enemy could well constitute a conclusive testimony to the Russian ruler's character and Christian merit.

Whereas Petrine sermons were generally permeated with this Christian emphasis, it found probably its most concentrated expression in a special brief work that Feofan Prokopovich wrote about the death of Peter the Great and that became basic to later accounts of the demise of the reforming tsar:

[35] Gavriil Buzhinskii, *op. cit.,* 11. Feofan Prokopovich declared: "Oh precious hat! Not valuable because of its material, but because of the damage done to it more valuable than all the crowns, all tsar's utensils! Historians who describe the Russian state write that on no European sovereign can one see as precious a crown as on the Russian monarch. But from now on no longer the crown but this tsar's hat you should consider and describe with amazement" (Feofan Prokopovich, *Sochineniia,* 57).

[36] Pavlenko, *Petr Pervyi,* 382.

[37] Gavriil Buzhinskii, *op. cit.,* 24. Italics in the original. A commemorative medal was struck for the occasion with Peter the Great's bust and the inscription "Master of the four [fleets]."

[38] Feofan Prokopovich, *Sochineniia,* 134.

And when the Sovereign was tormented by a most severe and uncomfortable illness, it was thought that he could barely respond by signs to religious consolation, but it was then that he showed a very strong and vivid feeling of piety. For when one of the consolers mentioned the death of Christ and what it obtained for us, and began to say that the time had come when for his own good he should think only of what he used formerly to tell to others (because he had spoken often enough to others about the blessed exculpation of sinners through Christ), immediately, as if excited, he made an effort to get up and, raised slightly by his assistants, he lifted his eyes and his arms, as best he could, and with a parched tongue, his speech confused, pronounced the following words: "yes, that is the only thing that quenches my thirst, the only thing that brings me joy" . . .

However, when a consoler would approach him, which would be done periodically, and would remind him of the vanity of the world, of the coming eternal blessedness and the price for which it had been purchased, the blood of the Son of God, he would force himself, as if having gained strength, to try to get up and to make with his hand the sign of the cross, or to point toward heaven, and, what was very remarkable, to change his groans into an exclamation of gladness and to look joyful in the face, and he would attempt to embrace the consoler. In the meantime the Archimandrite of the Holy Trinity Monastery arrived and addressed the Sovereign to inquire whether he would allow an additional administering of the Holy Eucharist, and, if he would allow it, he was to raise his hand so to indicate; immediately he raised his hand, and he partook additionally of the Holy Eucharist. And after that the consolers, taking turns, did not cease to console and to confirm him; and he, similarly, did not cease to indicate by signs his assent.[39]

Religion could sometimes aid politics, for instance, in enjoining obedience to the sovereign or in mobilizing support for Peter the Great's wars against Turkey. More fundamentally, the strong religious element in the sermons stemmed from the nature of the genre itself, the orators, and the occasion, as well as the general requirements in addressing an officially Orthodox ruler and government and a devoutly Orthodox people. Feofan Prokopovich's preaching in particular can be considered a study in the transition from the old Muscovite to the new modernizing Russia.[40] Nor, it should be added, was the religious element necessarily inappropriate in the creation of the image of Peter the Great.[41]

[39] Feofan Prokopovich, *Kratkaia povest* . . . , 13–16.

[40] For interesting recent comment on "the change of the type of the writer in the Petrine epoch," see A. M. Panchenko, "O smene pisatelskogo tipa v petrovskuiu epokhu," *Problemy literaturnogo razvitiia v Rossii pervoi treti XVIII veka, XVIII vek, Sbornik* 9 (Leningrad, 1974), 112–128.

For the unique background of the image of the Russian ruler, certain Western parallels, and other related matters, see especially Michael Cherniavsky, *Tsar and People* (New Haven, 1961), and the writings of Professor Stephen L. Baehr: "From History to National Myth: *Translatio imperii* in Eighteenth-Century Russia," *The Russian Review*, vol. 37, no. 1 (January 1978), pp. 1–13; "In the Re-beginning: Rebirth, Renewal and *Renovatio* in Eighteenth-Century Russia," *Russia and the West in the Eighteenth Century*, ed. A. G. Cross (Newtonville, Mass., 1983), pp. 152–166; and "In the Image and

3

Although eighteenth-century images of Peter the Great could be affected by the Muscovite tradition and even by Christian hagiography, their basic content derived from the Age of Reason. Whatever one thinks of that major weltanschauung of our Western civilization or of its ultimate appropriateness for Russia, Peter I belonged to it by belief, word, and deed. It was the optimistic faith in reason, in the possibility and feasibility of reasonable solutions to human problems that constituted the leading inspiration of the age and also, as we have seen, of the Russian reformer. The enemies were ignorance, prejudice, stagnation, the barbaric past. Salvation could be found only in education, enlightenment, work.

Peter the Great was thus a true enlightened despot. That he has not generally been so called is to be explained by the facts that that appellation has been usually reserved for the second half of the eighteenth century, that the Russian history of the period has not been sufficiently studied in the European context, and that the crudity and cruelty of the reformer, as well as the barbarism of his surroundings, have stood in the way of a full recognition of his place among the elect of the age. Yet if Enlightenment meant bringing light, as understood at the time, into darkness, no other ruler of the period could compete in the scope, decisiveness, and irreversibility of his actions with the Russian emperor. Peter the Great not only performed impressively as an enlightened despot, but also bequeathed enlightened despotism to his successors. This legacy was expressed indelibly in his image.

The Western Enlightenment recognized Peter the Great. That recognition began during his life, marked by such events as his becoming a member of the French Academy of Science—another canonical detail in the image of Peter the Great (after the tsar corrected the academicians

---

Likeness: The 'Political Icon' in Seventeenth and Eighteenth Century Russia," which I read in manuscript and for which I particularly thank the author.

41 The Russian tsar was, apparently, a sincerely and strongly religious man, who often referred to the presence of God in his daily life, for example, in the dangers and fortunes of war. I know of no evidence contradicting Feofan Prokopovich's hagiographic depiction of his death. Also, he liked very much to attend church services, frequently singing in the choir or reading the epistle (e.g., count such activities during his three relatively brief visits to the Russian far north, in 1692, 1694, and 1702, narrated in *O Vysochaishikh prishestviiakh Velikogo Gosudaria, Tsaria i Velikogo Kniazia Petra Alekseevicha, vseia Velikiia i Malyia i Belyia Rossii Samoderzhtsa* [Moscow, 1783]). The difficulty with this assessment of Peter the Great as simply and thoroughly religious is not his struggle against the ecclesiastical establishment and his church reform—reformers can also be religious—nor even his enthusiasm for the secular world and a secularization of Russian life and culture, but his notorious blasphemous debauchery. I find explanations that the blasphemy was meant against the Catholic Church, but not the Orthodox, or against superstition, but not true religion, insufficient, but I have no solution to offer. The best treatment of the subject and its historiography can be found in Mr. Paul Hollingsworth's seminar paper listed in my bibliography and as yet unpublished.

concerning the exact geography of the Caspian shoreline). It could be considered finally achieved with the publication, at long last, in 1759–1763 of Voltaire's two-volume *History of the Russian Empire under Peter the Great.*[42] Ordered by the Russian government, which supplied historical materials, *Peter the Great* is not one of Voltaire's immortal works, although it proved to be one of the more troublesome as the philosophe's Russian patrons despaired over his ignorant and cavalier treatment of Russia and over his independence. Nevertheless, it accomplished its purpose of setting the Russian monarch firmly in the European Enlightenment.

As Voltaire put it, "Nothing is left for human attention except striking revolutions that have changed the mores and laws of great states; and it is under this rubric that the history of *Peter the Great* deserves to be known."[43] The Russian ruler was a legislator by no means inferior to Solon or Lycurgus.[44] His sweeping and many-sided reforms proved to be remarkably successful:

The arts that he transplanted with his own hands into the lands, some of which were at the time savage, by bearing fruit gave testimony to his genius and eternalized his memory; they appear today native to the lands to which he had brought them. Law, police, politics, military discipline, the navy, commerce, manufactures, the sciences, the fine arts, all have been perfected according to his intentions. . . .[45]

The results of Peter the Great's efforts indeed justified the costs, sometimes in most striking ways. The pacifistically inclined Voltaire wrote: "Whereas there is not a single example among our modern nations of any war compensating by a little good the evil that it had caused, the day of Poltava led to happiness for the largest empire on earth."[46] The tragic condemnation and death of Tsarevich Alexis could also be vindicated by referring to a higher purpose. ". . . *Peter* was more king than father, and he sacrificed his own son to the interests of the founder and the legislator and to those of the nation, which, without this unfortunate severity, would have fallen back into the condition out of which he had pulled it."[47] And, in general, except for the author's personal style, obvious discomfort with Russia and things Russian, and explicit anticleri-

[42] *Histoire de l'empire de Russie sous Pierre le Grand,* par l'Auteur de l'histoire de Charles XII, tome premier MDCCLIX, tome second MDCCLXIII. On the writing of the work, see esp. E. Shmurlo, *Volter i ego kniga o Petre Velikom* (Prague, 1929).
[43] [Voltaire], *Histoire de l'empire . . . ,* I, pp. XXV–XXVI. Italics in the original.
[44] *Ibid.,* XXVIII–XXIX.
[45] [Voltaire], *op. cit.,* II, 269–270.
[46] *Ibid.,* I, 279.
[47] *Ibid.,* I, 183. Italics in the original. Voltaire had explained earlier that, in contrast to the Prince of Wales, a Russian heir to the throne was not free to travel where he pleased, and that "A criminal thought without any consequence cannot be punished in either England or France; it can in Russia (*ibid.,* 173).

calism, Voltaire's work read very much like those of the reformer's Russian apologists.[48]

Although Western images of Peter the Great are not the subject of this study, it is important for an appreciation of the Russian intellectual scene to realize that Voltaire developed what came to be, in the Age of Reason, a dominant view of Peter the Great and Russia. Of course, Western Europe produced its critics of the Russian reformer and reform, too, figures as prominent as Rousseau, Mably, Raynal, or Condillac. But perhaps the main body of the philosophes, represented by Diderot, D'Alembert and the *Encyclopédie,* joined Voltaire in extolling the Russian sovereign and in directly linking him and his work to the culminating glory of Catherine the Great's reign. In the words of a French scholar:

With Voltaire, Europe saw that this immense land, peopled by ignorant and bruitish muzhiks, "had given birth to Peter the Great, tsar legislator and reformer," that next it placed at its head a "new Semiramis," Catherine, whose writings and codes were admired by all; the philosophes wept as they read these laws, laws so beautiful that it was the duty of all the sovereigns of the world to take them as their example. Within a few decades Russia steps out of its historical and intellectual "nonbeing," provides for itself "rational, harmonious" laws and becomes for Western intellectuals a kind of model state, which attracts the eyes of all the theoreticians in politics and philosophy. The "Muscovy" of 1700 has transformed itself into an "enlightened" empire, into a country of "Light," into an example.[49]

Voltaire had already written that "the Russians came late, and, having introduced in their country the arts already fully perfected, it transpired that they made more progress in fifty years than any nation had made by itself in five hundred."[50] Diderot and others took up this suggestion—to be repeated so often in later times—that it was the very newness of Russian participation in history and culture that augured so well for the future development of Russia. Imprisoned by its own past, the Age of Reason looked with hope at the unencumbered giant who was validating and would continue to validate its most cherished beliefs. No wonder that there occurred what its closest student called "the Russian mirage

---

[48] For anticlericalism, see the blaming of "the priests and the monks" for the Tsarevich Alexis tragedy ([Voltaire], *op. cit.,* II, 185–186) or the favorable comparison of the Russian monarch to Louis XIV, allegedly in Peter the Great's own words, on the point that he made his clergy obey him whereas the French king was subjugated by his (*ibid.,* 221–222). To be sure, the great bulk of Voltaire's history was a dry factual narrative rather than an ideological treatise, in which respect it again resembled Russian histories of Peter the Great and his reign produced in the eighteenth century and later, including Feofan Prokopovich's own account, Feofan Prokopovich, *Istoriia Petra Velikogo ot rozhdeniia ego do Poltavskoi batalii i vziatiia v plen ostalnykh shvedskikh voisk pri Perevolochne vkliuchitelno* (St. Petersburg, 1773).

[49] F. de Labriolle, "Le prosveščenie russe et les lumières en France (1760–1798)," *Revue des études slaves,* 45 (1966), 75–91, quoted from p. 75.

[50] [Voltaire], *op. cit.,* I, 51–52.

in France in the eighteenth century."[51] To repeat, Peter the Great's reforms and the evolution of Russia fitted well, and especially seemed to fit well, the views of the Enlightenment.

Although the Russian Enlightenment is a generally accepted concept, there is no consensus as to when the Age of Reason established itself in Russia, nor how long it lasted there. In trying to identify it, specialists have ranged from the second half of the sixteenth century to the first quarter of the nineteenth and the Decembrists, not to mention what has been sometimes described as the "neo-Enlightenment" of the 1860s and the years following.

Characteristically, a symposium on "the problems of the Russian Enlightenment in eighteenth-century literature" offered different opinions.[52] In the opening presentation, the distinguished specialist P. N. Berkov provided an overelaborate scheme based on his formulation of two closely related, yet distinct, concepts referring to the Enlightenment, *prosvetitelstvo* and *Prosveshchenie*.[53] In his view, the reign of Peter the Great constituted the second period of the Russian *prosvetitelstvo,* which had begun in the seventeenth century with such intellectuals as Simeon of Polotsk and Sylvester Medvedev, as well as the first period of Russian enlightened despotism.[54] Berkov's outline reflected the general tendency in Soviet scholarship to push the Russian Enlightenment—once confined by most specialists to the reign of Catherine the Great—further back,[55] and it displayed nuance and a certain sophistication. But it lacked the directness and power of I. Z. Serman's interpretation of the Russian Enlightenment based squarely on Peter the Great and his reforms. In his

[51] A. Lortholary, *Le Mirage russe en France au XVIII^e siècle* (Paris, n.d.).

[52] *Problemy russkogo Prosveshcheniia v literature XVIII veka* (Moscow and Leningrad, 1961).

[53] P. N. Berkov, "Osnovnye voprosy izucheniia russkogo prosvetitelstva," *ibid.,* 5–27.

[54] The concept of enlightened despotism intrinsically related to that of the Enlightenment proved to be similarly controversial in its application to Russia, particularly as far as its boundaries in time were concerned. While I fully share Berkov's view of Peter the Great as an enlightened despot, other opinions have been offered for consideration. For one of the better discussions, see N. M. Druzhinin, "Prosveshchennyi absoliutizm v Rossii," in N. M. Druzhinin, N. I. Pavlenko and L. V. Cherepnin, eds., *Absoliutizm v. Rossii (XVII–XVIII vv.)* (Moscow, 1964), 428–459. Druzhinin skillfully presents Catherine the Great's rule as part and parcel of European enlightened despotism. He is unwilling, however, to extend this concept to the reign of Peter the Great, although he is fully aware of the many enlightened ideas and measures of the reformer, essentially because, in his opinion, the Russian economy was not ready for it until the second half of the century. Druzhinin also excludes the rule of Alexander I from enlightened despotism on the ground that it went beyond it in its constitutional appeal before finally turning to reaction. For my treatment of that problem and my view of the Russian Enlightenment in general, see the first two chapters (pp. 1–100) of Nicholas V. Riasanovsky, *A Parting of Ways: Government and the Educated Public in Russia, 1801–1855* (Oxford, 1976).

[55] Cf. Z. I. Gershkovich's contribution to the symposium, "Concerning the methodological principles of the study of the Russian Englightenment" ("O metodologicheskikh printsipakh izucheniia russkogo prosvetitelstva"), 151–157, especially p. 153.

treatment of "the Enlightenment and Russian literature in the first half of the eighteenth century," the second contribution to the symposium, Serman asserted:

Even a minimally attentive study of the ideology and works of Kantemir, Trediakovskii, Lomonosov, Sumarokov, and other literary-public figures of the period 1730–1750 . . . convinces one that their entire activity was based on ideological foundations that had been created earlier, that is, in the Petrine epoch, and in large part by Peter I himself and by his associates. By their practical-concrete content the Petrine reforms gave birth to ideas new in Russian ideological life. Already by 1720 the concept of a break made by Peter in the history of the country, of two Russias, "the old" and "the new," captures completely the minds of the contemporaries and becomes the starting point for all Russian ideological constructions of the first half of the eighteenth century. Already in 1716 Feofan Prokopovich declared: "So, what was Russia formerly, in such a recent past, and what is it now?" Following him, Kantemir, Trediakovskii, Tatishchev, Lomonosov, Sumarokov in their social-political reasoning invariably began with the idea of the decisive influence exercised by the person and the activity of Peter the Great on the entire course of Russian history at the end of the seventeenth and the first half of the eighteenth century.[56]

A view of the Russian Enlightenment centered on Peter the Great is bound to be attractive to a student of the image of the reforming emperor. And it also finds its justification in the broader context of Russian history.

Glorifying Peter the Great thus became a main theme—even the main theme as the glorifiers extended it, in what was for them a natural manner, into attacks on the old Russian ignorance and prejudices, a championing of education, or an exaltation of Catherine the Great—of the intellectuals of the Russian Enlightenment. The reformer's image of himself as a dedicated warrior struggling with every ounce of energy to drag his country from darkness into the light, an image that was developed and canonized, so to speak, by such contemporaries of his as Feofan Prokopovich and Gabriel Buzhinskii and that found a marvelous applicability and resonance in the fundamental ideology of the Age of Reason, shone as the gospel of the epoch. Not surprisingly, eighteenth-century Russian historians, poets, playwrights, publicists, scholars, teachers, and other intellectuals vied with one another in affirming and extolling it. Not surprisingly too, the gravest danger for them came to be, in the words of the foremost student of the phenomenon, an endlessly repetitive "vicious circle of eulogy without content."[57]

[56] I. Z. Serman, "Prosvetitelstvo i russkaia literatura pervoi poloviny XVIII veka," *Problemy russkogo Prosveshcheniia* . . . , 28–44; quoted from p. 32.
[57] E. Shmurlo, *Petr Velikii v otsenke sovremennikov i potomstva* (St. Petersburg, 1912), 62. For Shmurlo's contribution to the study of the image of Peter the Great, see pp. 202–203 below.

4

The years following the death of Peter the Great, however, proved to be damaging to the reformer's work, if not necessarily to his image. There was a reaction against the extreme harshness of his reign and even, in part, against its direction. Symbolized by a brief restoration of Moscow as the Russian capital, the reaction threatened to undo some of the first emperor's most cherished accomplishments. More ominous still than any contravention of Peter I's laws and measures was the inability of his successors to carry them out effectively. Especially, without Peter the Great, it quickly became impossible to exact full service from the gentry, to propound the principle of position and reward strictly according to merit. So-called gentry emancipation developed into a major trend of the century. In the affairs of the country indecision, confusion, and conflict replaced the former firm, if at times very difficult, direction. Historians have written at length about the dissolute incompetence of Catherine I, the extreme youth of Peter II and the intrigues surrounding him, and the hateful, "antinational" rule of the favorite Biron and "the German party" during the decade 1730–1740, when Empress Anne reigned in Russia. Yet the contrast between Peter the Great and his heirs should not be exaggerated, and, more specifically, they should not be presented as two equal and antithetical forces. After all, the two persons, Catherine I and Alexander Menshikov, who in their different positions and ways took over from the deceased monarch the charge of the state were probably more his creatures than anyone else in the entire empire: a semiliterate Livonian peasant girl, who became Peter I's mistress, wife, Empress, and finally sovereign of Russia, and an even less literate hungry boy who, reportedly, began as a pie vendor or a groom to rise to fabulous riches, to titles such as Generalissimus (the only other two in Russian history were to be Suvorov and Stalin), Prince in Russia, and Prince of the Holy Roman Empire, and, more importantly, to being almost the monarch's alter ego and participating in a very wide range of his activity. Anne's "German party," in its turn, was a direct result of Peter the Great's German orientation and policy, and it featured such able "fledglings of Peter's nest" as Count Andrew Ostermann and Count Burkhard Münnich. In any case, in 1741 Empress Elizabeth ascended the Russian throne to reaffirm most explicitly the continuity of Peter the Great's work and the direct link between herself and her father.

The fact that the figure of Peter the Great dominated his ineffectual successors in the government of Russia did not, of course, mean that their view of him was confined to "eulogy without content." Contrary to the impression given by Professor Shmurlo's study of the subject, and quite naturally so, it was the early, not the late, eighteenth-century estimates of the reformer that contained realism and variety, although unfortunately few of them have been preserved, even in part. Often, apparently, they combined admiration, even adoration, with terror. Such successors of Peter I on the imperial throne as his wife, his grandson, his niece, or his daughter were bound to have personal or familial impressions of him other than Feofan Prokopovich's quasi-official iconic image. The leading statesmen of the period, the men who actually governed Russia, also took as their point of departure in judging the reformer their own experiences during his reign and their knowledge of Russian problems, not panegyrical poetry or funeral orations. One wonders what Menshikov himself thought of Peter the Great at the end of it all in his exile in the wilderness. It would seem that a particularly intelligent, as well as critical, estimate of Peter the Great and his work belonged to Prince Dmitrii Golitsyn (1665–1737), a Petrine statesman and a leading member of the Supreme Secret Council, which in effect ruled Russia from 1726 to 1730. Other critics, too, could readily be found. In fact, what was lacking in the judgments of Peter the Great by this well-informed top personnel of the Russian state was not realism, not even criticism, but a different basic ideology. Dmitrii Golitsyn's sharp strictures referred, in the words of a specialist, "only to the excesses of the reformer" and not to his main activity.[58] Others had an even less independent position from which to mount an attack on the man who turned Muscovy westward. In truth, in Russia at the time the only really alternative views of the world resided among the dark masses, Old Believers and Orthodox, and among the unreconstructed monks, priests, and nuns—to whom a note will be given at the end of this chapter.

One political and intellectual novelty of the immediate post-Petrine years deserves mention nevertheless: Russian constitutionalism. According to most specialists, Muscovy, in spite of the omnipresence of the boyar *duma,* the periodical activities of the *zemskie sobory,* various developments during the Time of Troubles, and the weakness and dependence of some of its rulers, knew only autocracy as a political principle, although many Muscovites came to realize, no doubt, that some of their neighbors, notably the Poles, were governed in a very different manner. In a sense, modern constitutionalism became part of Russian thinking once Peter the Great turned to the West, for it long had been part of European political ideology and practice, just as the Russian reformer's own emphatic enlightened despotism constituted another political alternative in the Western world. The new richness of Russian political thought and life could be considered a tribute to the efficacy of the change brought about by the first emperor. Not inappropriately, such a supporter of Peter the Great and of the Russian monarchy as the his-

---

[58] M. D., "Golitsyn, Dmitrii Mikhailovich," *Entsiklopedicheskii Slovar* (Brockhaus-Efron), vol. IX, book 17 (St. Petersburg, 1893), 48–49; quoted from p. 49. Cf. N. P. Pavlov-Silvanskii, "Mneniia verkhovnikov o reformakh Petra Velikogo," *Ocherki po russkoi istorii XVIII-XIX vv* (St. Petersburg, 1910), 373–401.

torian and administrator Vasilii Tatishchev also believed that that monarchy would profit from the establishment of a senate of twenty-one members and an assembly of one hundred, with elections held for high offices. Much later the Westernizers and the liberals in general wanted to extend the legacy of Peter the Great precisely in the direction of constitutionalism and faithful emulation of Western political progression. Yet in the years immediately after the death of the reformer, Russian constitutionalism, especially in the oligarchic variant that the Supreme Secret Council managed to impose upon Empress Anne briefly in 1730, represented also an aristocratic reaction against the first emperor.[59] And it can be vaguely and broadly linked to the persistent criticism of Peter the Great as a willful tyrant that we shall encounter repeatedly in this study. But, whatever its exact nature, Russian eighteenth-century constitutionalism proved to be abortive, and it did not supplant, or apparently even affect, the triumphant image of a crowned reformer bringing light into the Russian darkness.

That image kept gaining in strength, stature, and scope as the Enlightenment spread in the empire. The preachers followed Feofan Prokopovich in emphasizing the thesis of two Russias and the incomparable accomplishment of Peter the Great in transforming his native land from one into the other. Shmurlo noted that their voices rose higher with the advent of Elizabeth to the throne. The reforming emperor was the sower, the resurrector of Russia from her lethargic sleep, or, again, the stupendous sculptor. "Have we forgotten how Peter the Great found us similar to a tree in a forest, crooked, stubby, stout, yellowed, rough, not suitable for any purpose, and how with his own hands he made us into beautiful statues and, besides, statues with souls?" "All agree on one thing: that Russia owes her entire better condition to Peter the Great. It is the voice of the whole people that only that which is bad among us is not Peter's." Hieromonk Gideon Krinovskii declared at Empress Elizabeth's coronation:

And now I address you, o Russia! Do you remember in what condition you were a few years ago? Do your troops armed with pole-axes and spears come to mind? A navy composed of fishing boats; a merchantry confined almost entirely within the Russian borders? Are you carrying again in thought traces of those unspeakable injuries, which the Swedish lion inflicted with his beastly claws in your torn insides? Finally, do you recollect that not only among other European peoples because of the coarseness of your inhabitants, but even among barbarians themselves, perhaps because of carelessness and unskilled actions in war, you were

---

[59] For key documents *re* the crisis of 1730, in English, see Marc Raeff, *Plans for Political Reform in Imperial Russia, 1730–1905* (Englewood Cliffs, N.J., 1966), 41–52. The latest study of the subject is remarkably favorable to Dmitrii Golitsyn and the constitutionalists: Vadim Borisovich Vilinbakhov, "Pir byl gotov, no . . . ." (the title reproduces the first part of Dmitrii Golitsyn's celebrated Biblical remark that the feast, i.e., the constitution, was ready, but the guests were unworthy of it). I would like to thank the author for letting me read his work in manuscript.

treated with extreme disdain and ridicule? And for that reason you begged by praying day and night, in front of the altar of God's mercy to man, you begged that He bestow upon you such a tsar as would make up your countless defects, correct the bad, wreak just vengeance on the enemies, and instill in all peoples better thoughts about you. And the Lord listened to you, responded to your tears, and did not scorn your sighs: He placed on your throne Peter, Great both in name and in deeds.[60]

Historians joined preachers, having, as usual, more to say, even if sometimes in a less inspired manner. Feofan Prokopovich, as we saw, belonged to both groups. Yet, even preceding Feofan Prokopovich, modern Russian historical writing can be considered to begin with the official *History of the Swedish War* produced under the supervision and with important participation of Peter the Great himself. An impressive piece of work, which tended to expand in scope with time, it remained, unfortunately, unfinished and unpublished.[61] Other Russian historians of the first decades of the eighteenth century, ranging from the "premodern" and generally unreliable Peter Krekshin (1684–1763) to Vasilii Tatishchev (1686–1750), usually described as the first modern Russian historian, were also deeply interested in Peter the Great and his reign. Although Tatishchev's huge *magnum opus,* his *Russian History,* did not advance beyond the Time of Troubles, the historian made his attitude toward the reforming ruler perfectly clear in his introduction, as well as on other occasions. The work was inspired by

the desire to render proper gratitude to His Imperial Majesty Peter the Great, who is worthy of eternal glory and memory, for the high kindness he had shown me, and to contribute to the glory and honor of my dear fatherland.

As to the kindnesses on the part of His Majesty to me, I do not have the space here to describe them in detail, and, moreover, the sorrow of the loss interferes with my remembering, but to put it briefly: everything that I possess, ranks, honor, an estate, and, above all else, reason, I possess solely because of the kindness of His Majesty, for had he not sent me to foreign lands, had he not used me in important affairs, had he not encouraged me with his kindness, I could not have obtained any of these things. And although my desire to express gratitude can add no more to the glory and honor of His Majesty than two pennies to the treasures of Solomon's temple or a drop of water as it falls into the sea, my desire to do so is boundless, and it is greater than the entire treasure of Solomon and the full waters of the river Ob.[62]

Until Ivan Golikov's voluminous efforts in the last quarter of the eighteenth century, Russian literature was more prolific than the emerg-

[60] Shmurlo, *Petr Velikii* . . . , 40–41.

[61] For a recent and very high evaluation of both *History of the Swedish War* and Peter the Great as historian, see T. S. Maikova, "Petr I i 'Gistoriia Sveiskoi voiny,'" *Rossiia v period reform Petra I,* 103–132. Among other things, Maikova considers Peter I to be the founder of Russian military history. The article includes a bibliographic discussion.

[62] V. N. Tatishchev, *Istoriia Rossiskaia,* vol. I (Moscow and Leningrad, 1962), 86–87.

ing modern Russian historiography in celebrating Peter the Great. Almost every writer of note of the Russian Enlightenment, from Peter I's own time and into the nineteenth century, dealt with the reforming emperor and participated in the general eulogy of him. Literary hacks proved to be equally industrious, if less memorable. A student of the subject even discovers numerous pieces, mostly poems, about Peter the Great, the authors of which are not known. The ode in particular, it might be added, became a vehicle for extolling enlightened despotism, Peter the Great, and especially Catherine the Great.

"The originator of modern Russian belles lettres," Prince Antioch Kantemir (1709–1744), a young friend of Feofan Prokopovich, contributed a famous lament on the death of the reforming emperor, *Petrida*, a long panegyrical poem where the author had the Creator decide that the earth was unworthy of carrying Peter the Great on its surface, but where, incidentally, he also gave the correct diagnosis of the sovereign's death from uremia, by contrast with a later legend of pneumonia caught when saving some soldiers from drowning or the recurrent suspicions of syphilis.[63] More important for Russian literature and intellectual history, probably the most valuable products of Kantemir's many-sided literary career, his satires, expressed faithfully Peter the Great's and Feofan Prokopovich's thesis of two Russias, emphasized education, and put their hope in enlightened despotism, in the new role of the government as against the stagnant and ignorant upper classes and the retrograde clergy—the reforming emperor himself could hardly have stated his beliefs better. And it was in the context of that vision that Kantemir acted out his life in reformed Russia and abroad. "Kantemir's love of learning had a utilitarian character in the spirit of Peter the Great: he valued both learning itself and his own literary activity only to the extent to which they could advance Russia toward well-being, and the Russian people toward happiness. This determines, in the main, the importance of Kantemir as a public figure and a writer."[64] Kantemir's mentality and pattern of literary activity were basic to the age, in Russia as elsewhere. Major and minor figures of the Russian Enlightenment were to differ in talent and accomplishment, but usually not in orientation or inspiration. Most of them could have said, with Tatishchev, that their reason, their mind, belonged to Peter the Great.

Whereas Feofan Prokopovich and Tatishchev were Peter the Great's

---

[63] Antiokh Kantemir, "Petrida ili opisanie stikhotvornoe smerti Petra Velikogo, Imperatora Vserossiiskogo," *Sobranie stikhotvorenii* (Leningrad, 1956), 241–247; the unworthiness is proclaimed on p. 243. I am indebted to a discussion with Professor N. I. Pavlenko for an expert analysis of the causes and circumstances of the death of Peter I.

[64] R. Sementkovskii, "Kantemir (kn. Antiokh Dmitrievich)," *Entsiklopedicheskii Slovar* (Brockhaus-Efron), Vol. XIV, Book 27 (St. Petersburg, 1895), 314–317, quoted from p. 315. For a discussion of Kantemir's views on education, in the framework of the European Enlightenment, see M. Erhard, "La Satire 'De l'éducation' de A. D. Kantemir," *Revue des études slaves*, XXXVIII (1961), 73–79.

younger contemporaries and Kantemir became a noted writer in the years immediately following the first emperor's death, Alexander Sumarokov (1718–1777) stood out as a prominent representative of the literary generation that came into its own in mid-century. "The father of Russian drama" produced also poetry, satires, orations, and still other forms of literature. Thus he glorified the reformer of Russia in a variety of genres. Sumarokov's laudation of Peter the Great lacked the personal explosive emotional impact to be found in Feofan Prokopovich's and Gabriel Buzhinskii's sermons or even Tatishchev's introductory acknowledgment to his *History*. Probably for that reason Sumarokov could on occasion take a kinder view of pre-Petrine Russia and generally be more flexible than his predecessors. But he certainly supported the established scheme of Russian history and by no means moderated the praise of the creator of modern Russia. To the contrary, that praise kept expanding, if anything, in the writings of Sumarokov and of others of his generation as well as continually gaining in perspective.

Sumarokov's best known piece on Peter the Great is his "Russian Bethlehem," a page of prose followed by eight lines of verse. The prose is devoted to a bogus derivation of the name of the village of Kolomenskoe, where Peter I was born, from the Colonna family of Rome. But it ends with an invocation of the birth of Peter the Great, "the founder of our well-being, father of the fatherland, the honor of his people, a terror to his enemies, and an adornment of humankind," and a paraphrase "permissible in a certain sense (*v nekotorom razume*)" of St. Matthew the Evangelist's address to Bethlehem. After that, the verse reads:

> Russian Bethlehem: the Kolomenskoe village,
> Which brought Peter into the World!
> You are the source and the beginning of our happiness;
> In you Russian glory began to shine.
> The infant, whom you saw swaddled,
> Europe saw on city walls,
> And Oceanus surrendered to him his waters.
> Peoples of the entire earth trembled in front of him.[65]

In a much longer poem, an ode "On the Victories of Lord Emperor Peter the Great," Sumarokov defined the real problem when praising the surpassing Russian ruler and the effective limit to such praise:

> Do not resound, icy waves,
> Do not storm, northern wind,
> Harken, people of all the lands,
> *Peter* is bringing verses to my mind.
> Planets, what were your positions,
> When you greeted *Peter* into the world?

[65] Aleksandr Petrovich Sumarokov, "Rossiiskii Vifleem," *Polnoe sobranie vsekh sochinenii* (Moscow, 1787), vol. (*Chast*) VI, 302–303.

From the beginning of the first age
Nature never saw
Such a Man.

It is not appropriate in Christianity
To revere creatures as Gods;
But if still during paganism
Such a Tsar had occurred,
As soon as his fame had spread
The entire universe would have been shaken
By his most marvelous deeds:
Fame, like an unsilenceable trumpet,
Would have proclaimed God, not Tsar,
That Warrior, who ascended the throne.[66]

As to the course of Russian history, Sumarokov presented it perhaps most strikingly in his "Laudatory Oration about Lord Emperor Peter the Great, Composed for the Name Day of Her Imperial Majesty [Elizabeth] in 1759":[67]

Until the time of *Peter* the Great, Russia was not enlightened either by a clear understanding of things, by most useful knowledge, or by a profound learning; our mind was drowned in the darkness of ignorance; sparks of sharp wit would go out and would not have the strength to flame again. The noxious darkness of the mind was attractive, and the useful light seemed burdensome. Peter was born. His infancy came. The rosy dawn, the forerunner of the sun, appeared on the somber horizon. Truth rejoiced and prejudice was gripped by fear. . . . *Peter* the Great became man, the sun rose, and the darkness of ignorance scattered.[68]

Time confirmed the reformer's work in an astounding manner: "Who among the not farsighted people could fail to judge as little the first house in Petersburg, the first naval vessel, *Peter* the Great's first army composed of children? The little town of Romulus became the ruler of all the world, *Peter*'s tiny hut became Northern Rome, *Peter*'s skiff became the father of a great navy, *Peter*'s mock army became the terror of the most powerful enemies of Russia."[69] The orator intoned in a Biblical

66 Aleksandr Petrovich Sumarokov, "Na pobedy Gosudaria Imperatora Petra Velikogo," *op. cit.*, vo. (*Chast*) II, 3–12, quoted from pp. 3–4. In this and in subseqent quotations from Sumarokov, "Peter" is in capitals in the original. In addition to full-fledged poems, Sumarokov specialized in Petrine "inscriptions." Shmurlo lists eight of them: three to a statue of Peter the Great, and one each to a marker on the Poltava field, and to Peter the Great's skiff, little house, likeness and portrait (Shmurlo, *Petr Velikii*, p. 46 of the note pagination). Actually, there were more. Cf. e.g., a nine-line inscription commemorating Catherine the Great's naval victory over Turkey, the last three lines of which read: "Declares Peter, Looking at the Russian fleet: This is Peter's Labor." Sumarokov's inscriptions (*nadpisi*) were gathered in Sumarokov, *op. cit.*, I, 265–284, quoted from p. 280.

67 Aleksandr Petrovich Sumarokov, "Slovo Pokhvalnoe o Gosudare Imperatore Petre Velikom, sochinennoe ko dniu Tezoimenitstva Eia Imperatorskogo Velichestva 1759 goda," *op. cit.*, II, 219–228.

68 Sumarokov, *op. cit.*, II, 221.

69 *Ibid.*, 225.

manner: "May our tongues stick to our throats if we do not remember you when we speak about the well-being of our fatherland."[70] If Sumarokov were less in the thrall of the reforming emperor than Feofan Prokopovich or Tatishchev had been, it was only in the sense that they could not have even imagined forgetting Peter the Great.

Sumarokov, however, was not the loudest glorifier of Peter the Great in the middle of the eighteenth century. That position belonged by right to Michael Lomonosov (1711–1765), an outstanding poet, a pioneer grammarian, an important literary scholar, and a historian, but also a chemist, a physicist, an astronomer, a meterologist, a geologist, a mineralogist, a metallurgist, a specialist in navigation, a geographer, and an economist, as well as a master of various crafts and a tireless inventor. In other words, Lomonosov was a genius and also a universal scholar of the type still possible and present in the European Age of Reason, which Peter the Great's turn Westward brought to Russia. Lomonosov's overwhelming praise of the reforming ruler stemmed from a number of factors. Most important was the established image of the first emperor itself—with which we are now acquainted—which demanded eulogy. Lomonosov's own sovereign, Empress Elizabeth, very prominent in his writing, further compelled it: Peter the Great and Elizabeth, father and daughter, were extolled together in ceaseless repetition. But there were, apparently, more personal factors, too. Lomonosov came from a peasant family of the Russian far north and his progression to Marburg University to the Imperial Academy of Sciences and to everything else he accomplished appeared like a realization, almost a fairy tale realization, of Peter the Great's projects and dreams. Moreover, during his none-too-long life the encyclopedic scholar managed to advance those projects and dreams, that is, the cause of modern Russian culture, more than any other individual of his generation, and probably many generations, and he was aware of this. Lomonosov's praise of the reformer, in spite of its extraordinary bombast, did not ring essentially false the way so much other such praise did. It should be added that as a poet Lomonosov created best in the solemn style, notably when he dealt with the vastness and the glory of the universe.

Lomonosov's treatment of Peter the Great is a rich subject. As the distinguished scholar put it when providing an example of a figure of speech in a work devoted to rhetoric: "Although great Peter has been snatched from our vision, he remains nevertheless always present in our hearts."[71] Lomonosov referred to the reformer in a wide variety of writings, from poetry, particularly odes but also other poetic forms, and orations to notes on the first volume of Voltaire's *History of the Russian*

[70] *Ibid.*, 227.
[71] M. V. Lomonosov, *Polnoe sobranie sochinenii.* Vol. VII, *Trudy po filologii, 1737–1758 gg.* (Moscow and Leningrad, 1952), 207.

*Empire under Peter the Great*,[72] for he was connected on the Russian side with the production of that history, and from a series of pieces specifically on the topic of the first emperor to extremely numerous mentions in passing. The index of a single volume of his collected works, the one covering poetry and orations, contains 267 page references to Peter I.[73] Yet Lomonosov's fundamental appraisal of Peter the Great was simple and straightforward, as well as comprehensive, and, of course, very much in line with the established image. It found probably its best expression in the justly famous "Laudatory Oration to Lord Emperor Peter the Great of the Blessed Memory, Pronounced on the Twenty-Sixth Day of April of the Year 1755,"[74] at a public session of the Imperial Academy of Sciences.

The oration began with an emotional and extensive treatment of Elizabeth and of her coming to the throne of Russia, always emphasizing the direct Petrine connection, and a briefer eulogy of the child Paul, the imperial heir. Then the speaker turned to the central theme, the transformation of the country by Peter the Great. Quite appropriately, he paid special attention to knowledge, the acquiring of new skills, travel to the West, and learning there:

Our most wise Monarch foresaw that it was strictly necessary for His great intentions that knowledge of all kinds spread in the fatherland and that people skilled in the high sciences and also artists and craftsmen multiply there. . . . Then the wide gates of great Russia opened; then across borders and through ports, like flow and ebb that occur in the vast Ocean, now sons of Russia departing to obtain competence in different sciences and arts, now foreigners arriving with different skills, books and instruments, flowed in ceaseless motion. Then the Mathematical and Physical science, formerly considered magic and sorcery, received reverent respect from the consecrated Person of Peter, already dressed in porphyry, crowned with laurels, and elevated to a Monarchical throne. What good the sciences and the arts of all sorts, surrounded by this radiance of majesty, brought us is proved by the overabundant mass of our multivaried satisfactions, which our ancestors, before the great Enlightener of Russia, not only had lacked, but of which in many cases they even had had no idea.[75]

Russia began to produce herself what had formerly been imported and even to supply other lands with her products. Russians learned modern warfare as well as commerce. Peter the Great's powerful and labor-loving hands uncovered the natural resources of the country. "The brave Rus-

---

[72] Lomonosov, *op. cit.*, VI, *Trudy po russkoi istorii, obshchestvenno-ekonomischeskim voprosam i geografii, 1747–1765 gg.* (1952), 357–364, and the notes of the editors of Lomonosov's volume on pp. 592–594.

[73] Lomonosov, *op. cit.*, VIII, *Poeziia, oratorskaia proza, nadpisi, 1732–1764 gg.* (1959), 1233–1234. A third of these references is to editorial comments.

[74] *Ibid.*, 584–612, editorial notes pp. 1044–1056; the Russian title is "Slovo pokhvalnoe blazhennyia pamiati Gosudariu Imperatoru Petru Velikomu, govorennoe aprelia 26 dnia 1755 goda."

[75] *Ibid.*, 591–592.

sian host turns against the enemy weapons produced from Russian mountains by Russian hands."[76]

The reformer's creation of a modern army and his victory over Charles
XII and Sweden were phenomenal achievements, which the orator could
trace only very briefly. Characteristically and significantly, as a legacy to
his successors, the first emperor insisted in the hour of victory that the
army be maintained, that it never be neglected. The navy, like the army.
Again, Peter the Great built it himself, studying abroad, working with
his own hands. "I bring you as witnesses, great Russian rivers, I turn
to you, happy shores, consecrated by Peter's steps and watered by his
sweat."[77] And, once more, he brought it to the pinnacle of power and
success. "Supreme on land, incomparable on water in military might and
glory, such was our Great Defender!"[78]

To establish and activate such a great naval and land force, in addition to build
new cities, fortresses, ports, to connect rivers by great canals, to fortify boundary
defenses with earthen walls, to fight a long war, to engage in such frequent and
distant campaigns, to erect public and private buildings in the style of the new
architecture, to find specialists and to utilize all other means to spread learning
and the arts, to maintain new court and civil officials—what a great treasury
was necessary for that, and anyone can see and realize clearly that the income
of Peter's Ancestors could not be sufficient for it. Because of that, our most wise
Sovereign made extreme efforts to multiply internal and external state collections, without ruining the people. And because of His inborn reason He saw to
it that not only a great profit to the treasury would follow but also the general
calm and safety of His subjects would be established by the single measure, for
at that time the number of the entire Russian people and the habitation of
every person had not yet been ascertained, willfulness had not been suppressed, no
one was forbidden to settle where he pleased or move about as he pleased, streets
were full of shambles and homeless misery, highways and great rivers were not
infrequently closed by the violence of thieves and by whole regiments of murderous bandits, who devastated not only villages but even towns. The most wise
hero transformed harm into benefit, laziness into diligence, devastators into
defenders, when he calculated the number of His subjects, fixed everyone in his
habitation, and imposed a light but definite tax, which multiplied and established a set amount of internal state revenues and the number of men to be
drafted, multiplied diligence and strict military training. Many, who in former
circumstances would have remained noxious robbers, He forced to be ready to
die for the fatherland.[79]

Peter the Great brought prosperity to Russia, financing the difficult war
without falling in debt. He founded the Ruling Senate, the Holy Synod,
and other state institutions and agencies. The orator deemed it best to

[76] *Ibid.*, 592.
[77] *Ibid.*, 660.
[78] *Ibid.*, 602.
[79] *Ibid.*, 602–603. Lomonosov's discussion of Peter the Great's reforms is remarkable
as an early statement of the thesis of financial determinism, as an all-out defense of
the poll tax, and for other reasons.

rely on the knowledge of his audience, for he could not list everything. Indeed, if a Russian were to be absent during Peter the Great's reforms and then return to his fatherland

he would have seen a new knowledge and skills in the people, a new dress and manners, a new architecture with improvements for homes, a new construction of fortresses, a new navy and army; he would have noticed not only a change in all that, but even in the flow of the rivers and the boundaries of the seas, and what would he have thought then? He could not have helped but decide that he had wandered for many centuries, or that it all had been accomplished in such a short time by the joint effort of mankind, or by the creative hand of the Supreme Being, or, finally, that it was all a mirage, a vision in a dream.[80]

Moreover, the Russian emperor accomplished everything under most difficult circumstances and in spite of powerful and determined enemies both at home and abroad. Throughout he acted as a true selfless hero. And at the same time he managed to be simple, accessible, kind, close to his people. Lomonosov was coming to his conclusion:

I am in the field under fire, I am in judicial sessions in the midst of difficult discussions, I am in different arts and crafts among multiple and varied contraptions, I am at the building of cities, ports, canals, among a countless multitude of people, I am in spirit among the groaning of the waves of the White, the Black, the Baltic, the Caspian Sea and of the Ocean itself. Everywhere I see Peter the Great, in sweat, in dust, in smoke, in flame—and I can not convince myself that a single Peter is everywhere, not many, and that this is one short life and not a thousand years. To whom shall I compare the Great Sovereign? I see in antiquity and in modern times rulers called great. And in truth, they are great in relation to others. However, they are small before Peter. One conquered many states, but left his fatherland without care. Another defeated an enemy already styled great, but on both sides shed the blood of his citizens for his own ambition alone and, instead of a triumph, heard the cry and the sobs of his fatherland. A third is adorned by many virtues, but, instead of erecting one, could not support the weight of a falling state. A fourth was a warrior on land, but was afraid of the sea. A fifth dominated the sea, but did not dare to reach the shore. A sixth loved the sciences, but was afraid of the naked sword. A seventh was not afraid of iron, water, or fire, but lacked the human property and heritage of reason. I shall use no examples, except for Rome. But even that is not sufficient. What the Neposes, the Scipios, the Marcelluses, the Reguluses, the Metelluses, the Catos, the Sullas accomplished in the two hundred and fifty years between the first Punic War and Augustus, Peter the Great did in the brief time of His life. To whom, then, shall I liken our Hero? I have often thought, what is like He, Who by an almighty wave of His hand rules the sky, the earth, and the sea: His spirit blows—and waters flow; He touches mountains—and they rise. But there is a limit assigned to human thoughts! They can not comprehend Divinity! Usually He is pictured in human form. Well then, if a man similar to God, according to our understanding, must indeed be found, I know of no other than Peter the Great.[81]

[80] *Ibid.*, 604.
[81] *Ibid.*, 610–611.

Or, in verse, in an ode for the name day of the future Peter III, in the words of Minerva and Mars:

> He was God, He was your God, Russia,
> He assumed in you corporeal forms,
> Having descended to you from on high;
> Among Heroes, above the stars
> He is now shining in eternity,
> Looking joyfully at His Grandson.[82]

5

Catherine II, also known as Catherine the Great, ascended the Russian throne in the summer of 1762, when "His Grandson," her husband, Emperor Peter III, was overthrown and killed in a palace coup. Brutish, stupid, and generally hopelessly inadequate as a person and as a ruler of Russia, Peter III contributed only another brief chapter to the long story of deficient sovereigns who followed the first emperor. The reformer, if indeed he had been looking down from on high, had little reason to be joyful. But what followed was different and unexpected: Catherine II, a German woman without a legal claim to the crown and, at least initially, without strong personal standing or support, proceeded to rule the realm for over a third of a century, from 1762 to 1796, and to raise it to new heights in terms of expansion, war, diplomacy, and cultural progress, in terms of the Enlightenment itself. Moreover, for the first time since Peter the Great a Russian monarch made a deep personal impress on the development of Russia and, notably, on its intellectual and cultural evolution. It should be added that Peter III followed, apparently quite sincerely, Elizabeth in emphasizing the direct link with Peter I and his absolute devotion to the person and policies of his ancestor, even when his government was changing those policies. The attitude of Catherine the Great was more complicated in this as in so many other matters.[83]

Many factors must be kept carefully in mind in trying to reconstruct Catherine II's image of Peter the Great and her treatment of her illustrious predecessor throughout her long reign. A princess from Anhalt-Zerbst, the most famous Russian empress had originally, in contrast to all other modern Russian rulers, no connection with the reigning Romanov dynasty and, indeed, no connection at all with Russia. Her pietis-

---

[82] *Ibid.*, 109. The ode, "Oda na den tezoimenitstva Ego Imperatorskogo Vysochestva Gosudaria Velikago Kniazia Petra Feodorovicha 1743 goda," occupies pp. 103–110 of the volume.

[83] The fullest treatment of the subject is to be found in Professor Karen Rasmussen's unpublished doctoral dissertation, which I directed: Karen Malvey Rasmussen, "Catherine II and Peter I: The Idea of a Just Monarch," University of California, Berkeley, California, November 1973. Professor Rasmussen summarized her views in an important article: Karen Rasmussen, "Catherine II and the Image of Peter I," *Slavic Review*, vol. 37, no. 1 (March 1978), 51–69.

tic references to "Our Most Beloved Grandfather" meant, of course, the grandfather of her husband, Peter III, who was killed in the coup that brought her to power. Free of direct links to Peter the Great and his family, Catherine II was also free, in a much broader sense, of any relationship to Muscovy. In particular, she lacked totally the explosive hatred of the old order, which had been so prominent in the lives and work of the reformer himself and of his associates and which was still present in Kantemir and in Lomonosov. The German ruler on the Russian throne even came to admire, in her search for worthy predecessors, the very Muscovite Tsar Alexis—and later St. Vladimir of Kiev. Yet this absence of a certain kind of personal involvement did not result in a weakening of interest. To the contrary, the first crowned intellectual in modern Russia, Catherine the Great spent a lifetime trying to understand Peter the Great, in terms of the Enlightenment to which she entirely belonged, to interpret him, to live with him. Her efforts would deserve notice even if she were not an autocrat imposing her will on a huge empire for a third of a century. Other factors, especially those of character and political style, entered the picture. One was the empress's enormous vanity, which, it would seem, made Peter the Great and his work an immediate and persistent challenge, both in general and in detail, to her sense of her own worth and accomplishment. Other relevant traits included Catherine II's duplicity, hypocrisy, and rare gift for propaganda. On the topic of Peter the Great, as on other significant topics, it is at times difficult to establish what it was that Catherine the Great believed and whether she believed anything at all.

Yet a study and interpretation of the evidence can suggest a complex pattern. First, and most important, the empress started from an ardent cult of Peter the Great—which was discussed in the preceding sections of this chapter—and she never explicitly repudiated it. Whatever her shifts of emphasis, reservations, and criticisms; whatever especially her private comments or at times her revealing silence for that matter, the overwhelming established public image of the reformer continued to dominate the Russian intellectual scene. In fact, Catherine II herself contributed and had others contribute to that image. Nor was the connection between her and the first emperor ignored. Falconet's celebrated statue known as *The Bronze Horseman,* with its inscription "To Peter I, Catherine II," unveiled in 1782, is only one illustration of the official ideology. And, according to the Prince de Ligne, the empress allowed no criticism of Peter the Great in her presence.[84] In the true Enlightenment tradition, Catherine II emphasized the role of the reformer as the benefactor of his subjects, the monarch who worked for their well-being, for the common good. But she was also very much impressed by his military successes on land and on water. Not inappropriately, military standards captured

---

[84] Rasmussen, "Catherine II and the Image of Peter I," 57.

from the Turks were brought to Peter the Great's tomb. It was especially during the First Turkish War, 1768–1774, that the empress kept referring to her martial predecessor. Beyond that, however, she seemed to be interested in everything Peter the Great had done at all times.

Catherine's close attention to the first emperor led also to criticisms, which, apparently, deepened with the passage of years. Although the empress might have discovered the critical approach early in her favorite Montesquieu, who considered Peter the Great a tyrant, most of her observations were, no doubt, her own, based on her constant rethinking of the role of the reformer, especially after she came to occupy his throne and deal directly with many of his measures and problems. Concerned especially with the ideal of the just legislator, central to the concept of enlightened despotism and even to the political thought of the Age of Reason in general, Catherine II found Peter the Great sadly wanting. His laws, in particular his penal code, were essentially the old, backward, and cruel *Ulozhenie* of 1649, and he failed to make them more modern and humane. In fact, he tended to emphasize punishment and to rule by fear rather than through love and approbation of his subjects. Although the enlightened German empress approved the direction of the Russian ruler's reforms, his desire that the old world be replaced by the new, he himself, in her perspective—originally the perspective of the French Enlightenment in the German principality of Anhalt-Zerbst—belonged too much to that old world.[85]

And, as already mentioned, Peter the Great was a formidable rival, Catherine the Great's only possible competitor, she came to be convinced, for the honor of being the greatest ruler of Russia. The empress's preoccupation with that rivalry is beyond doubt, although the pertinent evidence has to be analyzed with care. Little can be concluded from the mere fact that Catherine II always promoted herself, that she tended to occupy center stage, to push Peter the Great into the background, to receive the highest praise. That was simply the prerogative, indeed the proper due, of a reigning monarch. Sumarokov and Lomonosov too eulogized Empress Elizabeth even at greater lengths than her father. Probably more relevant is the argument from silence, from omission. Professor Rasmussen studied carefully the references to Peter the Great in the Catherinian legislation and in other materials connected with the reign to discover periods when Peter the Great did not appear, even when such appearance would have been most appropriate. Deliberate suppression seems likely. Paradoxically—in commonsense logic, not in terms of depth psychology—another relevant line of reasoning points to the frequent and varied references to Peter I by Catherine II. These references were often not simple pairings of the reigning sovereign and a particularly illustrious predecessor in terms of affirmation, continuity,

---

[85] As its title suggests, Professor Rasmussen's dissertation treats the concept of the enlightened legislator as central to Catherine II's view of Peter I and of herself.

and achievement, a common practice in monarchies beautifully exemplified by Empress Elizabeth's treatment of her father, but rather determined efforts to indicate that Catherine the Great did better than Peter the Great, whether in legislation, culture, or land and sea campaigns and battles. The very last available comment of the empress about the emperor, written in 1796, consisted of the boast that her conquest of Baku had eclipsed his.[86]

To sum up, the image of Peter the Great remained central in the official ideology and public thought of Catherinian Russia. Nor was that image substantially changed. It came to be linked, however, to the newly proclaimed glory of Catherine the Great. To be sure, the first emperor's image had always been linked to that of his reigning successor. Yet such heirs as the reformer's beloved wife Catherine I or even his indolent daughter Elizabeth were so inconsequential that they could only hope to gain strength from their relation to the first emperor without contributing anything of their own. Catherine II was different. The new pairing aimed to capitalize on Peter the Great's immense prestige, to underline his importance, for indeed there would have been no Catherinian Russia without him, but at the same time to assign a still higher place in Russian history to the desperately ambitious empress. Its daring classical formulation can be found, for instance, in Ivan Betskii's address to the throne, quite early in the reign: "Peter the Great created men in Russia; Your Highness has given them souls."[87] The formula accounted for Peter the Great and, in fact, assigned an awesome importance to him—for who was he who could create men?—yet it placed Catherine the Great still higher. It even provided an explanation and a justification for the crudity and the harshness of the reformer's measures, natural and unavoidable at the time, although personally distasteful to the philosophic empress and no longer required in her truly enlightened age. We shall see in a later section of this chapter that defending the first emperor and his activity in terms of the standards and needs of his epoch became a flourishing industry among the intellectuals of the empire in the second half of the eighteenth century. With the formula, modern Russian history presented two stages, the Petrine and the Catherinian, the second building on the first but also rising above it. Voltaire, who caught on skillfully to what was wanted, wrote to the Russian empress of Peter the Great and Catherine the Greater.[88]

It would be an exaggeration, however, to claim that Catherine II tamed, so to speak, the image of Peter I and made it simply serve her

[86] Rasmussen, "Catherine II and the Image of Peter I," 57.

[87] *Polnoe sobranie zakonov*, XVIII, no. 12.597 (August 11, 1767), 292, column 1.

[88] "En attendant, madame, permettez-moi de baiser la statue de Pierre-le-Grand, et le bas de la robe de Catherine plus grande" (the letter of December 16, 1774, in W. F. Reddaway, ed., *Documents of Catherine the Great: The Correspondence with Voltaire and the "Instruction" of 1767 in the English Text of 1768* [Cambridge, 1931], 203–205, quoted from p. 204).

own purposes. Although the remarkable propaganda of the willful empress even achieved some long-range successes, including those among
certain twentieth-century historians, she was the weaker figure in the new
coupling. After her death the image of the first emperor uncoupled itself, and we shall have to follow its progress through Russian history
without its would-be companion. Personally, too, the empress could not
settle her accounts with her celebrated predecessor. Professor Rasmussen
even concluded that late in her reign she underwent another change toward him, this time in the direction of a greater admiration and acceptance. The main reason was her own failure as legislator, certainly earlier
with the Legislative Commission, but in effect throughout her rule. It was
in relation to the concept of the enlightened legislator that Catherine II
had constructed her main criticisms of the reformer and postulated her
superiority over him: by the end of her reign she could see that that
superiority was largely imaginary. It is quite possible that it was at the
time of her death that Catherine the Great had the deepest appreciation
of Peter the Great as well as of the obstacles in his path.

6

The Catherinian version of the Petrine cult pervaded the expanding intellectual and cultural life of Russia of the last third of the eighteenth
century. For instance, Sumarokov, who, as we saw, praised the first emperor so well in the days of Elizabeth, adapted his work gracefully to the
new mode. His inscription to the statue of Peter the Great read:

> This bronze delineates the features of the face
> Of *Peter* the Great, Father of the Fatherland,
> He created this city, he organized the navy and the army;
> He raised Russia by means of Heroic deeds.
> As a sign of gratitude to him on the part of all of Russia
> *Catherine* erected this image.
> But if *Peter* were to rise from the dead in Russia now, again,
> He would erect a more beautiful monument to *Catherine*.
> *Peter* defeated internal and external enemies,
> He spread his sway on sea and on land,
> Having brought glory to the Russians he rewarded them with riches.
> *Peter* gave us existence, *Catherine* the soul.[89]

A younger writer, Michael Kheraskov (1733–1807), a disciple of Sumarokov, presented the same formula in a poem included in his "Numa or
Flourishing Rome," a splendid expression of the Enlightenment doctrine
of the philosopher ruler, bringing light into darkness, replacing savagery
with civilization, and in turn receiving the true reward of such rulers,

[89] Sumarokov, *op. cit.*, I, 268. The names of the sovereigns were in capitals in the
original.

the enthusiastic love of their subjects. Numa, Kheraskov discovered, was followed generally by unworthy monarchs. Fortunately:

> But in late times there rises like a cedar
> Above all Tsars the lawgiver *Peter:*
> He works, He keeps vigil, He revivifies Russia,
> He shows new skies and a new world;
> He gives light to the minds, sensibility to the hearts;
> He brought glory to His subjects and became immortal Himself.
> After him comes more beautiful than a lily of paradise
> *Catherine* who is flourishing in front of our eyes.

The empress utilized every hour of her rule to extend grace to her subjects, to enlighten them, to bring them peace and restful quiet. "To the temple of happiness She found a path and with joy led her subjects thither." To conclude:

> I shall never fail in my respect to those sacred words:
> *Peter* gave bodies to the Russians, *Catherine* their souls.[90]

The two supreme sovereigns did not have to be praised necessarily in the same poem. Gabriel Derzhavin (1743–1816), the poetic genius of the age, has justly been called Catherine the Great's official bard: he constantly eulogized, at length, skillfully, at times brilliantly, the insatiably vain empress and such prominent Russians of her reign as Potemkin and Suvorov. But he also wrote some remarkable verses on Peter the Great, very much in line with the established cult. It can be said that Derzhavin's total oeuvre expressed richly and faithfully the Catherinian synthetic view of Russian enlightened despotism and despots, even if no single piece of his presented the synthesis as starkly and sharply as the above-cited poems of Sumarokov and of Kheraskov. Whereas Derzhavin's laudation of Catherine II lies—mercifully—outside the purview of this study, his encomium of Peter I deserves notice. In particular, his ode "To Peter the Great," written in 1776, may well be the best presentation of the dominant image of the reforming emperor in Russia as the country entered the last quarter of the eighteenth century, fifty years after the reformer's death.

> Russia, clothed in glory,
> Wherever it turns its gaze,
> Everywhere, with exultant joy,
> Sees Peter's work.
>> Carry the voices to heaven, o wind:
>> You are immortal, great Peter!
>
> He, conquering our ancient darkness,
> Established the sciences in the midnight land;

90 [Kheraskov, Mikhail Matveevich], "Stikhi ot izdatelia," *Numa ili Protsvetaiushchii Rim* (Moscow, 1768), 177–180.

Lighting a torch in blackness,
He also poured into us good morals and manners.
　　Carry the voices to heaven, o wind:
　　You are immortal, great Peter!

　Like God, with great foresight,
He encompassed everything in his gaze,
Like a slave, with unheard of devotion,
He executed everything himself.
　　Carry the voices to heaven, o wind:
　　You are immortal, great Peter!

　He went across lands and across seas,
He learned himself in order to teach us;
He sought to converse with tsars
In order later to surprise all of them.
　　Carry the voices to heaven, o wind:
　　You are immortal, great Peter!

　Hands born for the scepter
He extended to inappropriate labor;
To this day there reverberate in the world the sounds
Of his axe striking.
　　Carry the voices to heaven, o wind:
　　You are immortal, great Peter!

　His games of an infant
Gave birth to thunderstorms in the end;
But in the midst of martial glory
He remained father of the fatherland.
　　Carry the voices to heaven, o wind:
　　You are immortal, great Peter!

　Hiding the rays of majesty,
He served as a simple warrior;
Teaching the art to the commanders,
He himself led regiments into battle.
　　Carry the voices to heaven, o wind:
　　You are immortal, great Peter!

　The universe was frightened by his valor,
When he smote his enemies;
The universe was consoled by his kindness,
When he entertained prisoners.
　　Carry the voices to heaven, o wind:
　　You are immortal, great Peter!

　Master of half the world,
A hero in the field and on the seas,
He did not disdain giving an accounting
Of his activities to his servants.
　　Carry the voices to heaven, o wind:
　　You are immortal, great Peter!

Laurel crowns, triumphs, chariots
He established not for himself:
Distinction, the sparkle of purple
He assigned as reward for merit.
> Carry the voices to heaven, o wind:
> You are immortal, great Peter!

He was firm in his faith and obedient to it;
He was a singer himself in front of the altar,
In evil and in good fortune he was generous,
Without flattery a friend of his friends.
> Carry the voices to heaven, o wind:
> You are immortal, great Peter!

He returned crowns to monarchs,
He wrote laws for subjects;
What millions should be doing,
He in his own person gave example to all.
> Carry the voices to heaven, o wind:
> You are immortal, great Peter!

He ground water through the mountains
He planted cities on swamps;
He brought prosperity to his peoples,
He linked the West with the East.
> Carry the voices to heaven, o wind:
> You are immortal, great Peter!

Loving the edicts of truth, he
Preserved justice without hypocrisy;
To this day his useful laws
Lead to well-being.
> Carry the voices to heaven, o wind:
> You are immortal, great Peter!

To this day the universe is amazed
By the greatness of his miracles;
The mind of the very wise can not comprehend it,
Could it be that God came down to us from heaven?
> Carry the voices to heaven, o wind:
> You are immortal, great Peter!

O Russians, shining with glory!
O clan and assembly of heroes!
Be grateful to Peter,
May your chorus to him forever resound!
> Carry the voices to heaven, o wind:
> You are immortal, great Peter![91]

In another poem about Peter the Great, written at the same time—
Falconet had begun making his statue of *The Bronze Horseman,* and

[91] G. R. Derzhavin, "Petru Velikomu," *Sochineniia Derzhavina s obiasnitelnymi primechaniiami* (4 vols., St. Petersburg, 1895), I, 10–12, and notes on p. 210.

praise of the first emperor was particularly in order—Derzhavin reflected more closely the sensibility of Catherine the Great herself and of a certain "progressive" part of the high Enlightenment. Whereas "To Peter the Great" restated grandly and powerfully, as we have seen, the fundamental Russian image of Peter the Great in the Age of Reason, entirely in the tradition of Feofan Prokopovich, Lomonosov, and other earlier extollers of the reformer, "Peter the Great's Monument" concentrated more narrowly on the first emperor's virtue. It contrasted the Russian monarch to the tyrants of history, eulogized his role of father to his country, and stressed virtue, not immortality, in its cadenced refrain.[92]

To go beyond Derzhavin and quote Professor Shmurlo's summary:

In the footsteps of first-class poets there follow, of course, second-class ones: on the lips of one of them Peter the Great is "the most marvelous hero"; according to the words of another, Peter's deeds are so extraordinary that descendants will consider them as invention; a third exclaims, "The Russian began to shine only through Peter!" and so forth. The poets are seconded from the pulpits by the preachers; Metropolitan Plato, a brilliant orator, says, as if copying Nepliuev: "No matter at what we direct our gaze, everything owes its origin to him, everything is a fruit of his reason and enlightenment. . . . Whatever we see, whatever we imagine, Peter either invented it or consolidated it or founded it or provided the occasion for the above." To another ecclesiastical orator there appears "Russia reborn through him [Peter] and, so to speak, raised from universal nullity, having frightened in its very babyhood its enemies both on land and on sea." Finally, even a dry geography textbook, it too, as soon as it touched on Peter, immediately raised its tone and referred to the crowned reformer as "the very greatest of all Russian sovereigns who have so far existed," one who bestowed "an entirely new appearance on his empire."[93]

Publication of relevant sources and historical studies of Peter the Great and his reign also expanded in Russia in the last third of the eighteenth

---

[92] G. R. Derzhavin, "Monument Petra Velikogo," *op. cit.,* I, 13–14, note on p. 210. Derzhavin became a courtier as well as a poet, and even a statesman, serving as the first Russian minister of justice after Alexander I established ministries. In his official capacity he had to deal with the first emperor's legacy in other than highly poetic and eulogistic terms. But he, apparently, remained an admirer of Peter the Great along statist and conservative lines, which culminated later in the doctrine of official nationality, to be discussed in the next chapter.

To obtain something of a balance to the outrageous praise of the hero filling this chapter, as well as to return, perhaps, to the deepest roots of such praise, we may find it useful to remember Derzhavin's "last verses":

> The river of time in its urgent course
> Carries away all the works of human beings
> And drowns in the abyss of oblivion
> Peoples, tsardoms, and tsars.
> And even if something remains
> Through the sounds of a lyre or a trumpet,
> It will be swallowed by the gullet of eternity
> And will not escape the common fate!

(Derzhavin, *op. cit.,* III, 131).

[93] Shmurlo, *Petr Velikii* . . . , 61–62. Ellipsis in Shmurlo.

century. Whereas rather little had been done along these lines before the time of Catherine II, the field was transformed by the immense labors of Ivan Golikov (1735–1801). A merchant by origin and occupation, poorly educated, Golikov became as a youth fascinated by the first emperor, and this fascination grew with the years. The result of the lifelong absorption was a series of twelve volumes of the *Acts of Peter the Great, the Wise Reformer of Russia, Gathered from Reliable Sources and Arranged Year by Year,* which came out in 1788–1789, and another series of eighteen volumes of the *Addition* to the *Acts,* published in 1790–1797, as well as several smaller related pieces.[94] Golikov's treatment of Peter the Great had some obvious limitations. As the author himself stated the matter in his Preface to the first volume of the *Acts,* he had reached the decision:

to devote the rest of my days not to a cunning, but to a simple, zealous description, moved by gratitude, of the great, overwhelming, glorious, and resounding, but at the same time salutary for Russia, immortal deeds of His.

Offering to my kind countrymen the first volumes of these deeds, in order to avoid incorrect judgments of my work, I find it necessary to repeat something that I already confessed more than once above: I am an uneducated man, and I am therefore ignorant of any rules of criticism and unskilled in the historical style; I am not at all a historian, and even less so a pragmatic historian; I am only a gatherer into one of *Peter's* acts and a grateful narrator of them. For which reason may my readers on their part be well enough disposed not to demand more than can be demanded from me; not to search in my narration for scholarly-deep-philological analyses of every act of *Peter* the Great; and accordingly not to blame me for the fact that my style will often resemble more the panegyrical than the historical. I confess in advance this defect, if, judging on the basis of what I said above about myself, it can be called a defect.[95]

Yet Golikov's study of Peter the Great could be considered a major success in more ways than one. The determination of the author to present admiringly every move of the first emperor bore remarkable results. The *Acts* and the *Addition* to the *Acts* offered the Russian reader an extremely rich, full, and detailed consecutive account of the reformer and his momentous reign. The "simplicity" of the approach added to the coherence and power of the image. Golikov strove for a complete recon-

---

[94] Ivan Golikov, *Deianiia Petra Velikogo, mudrogo preobrazovatelia Rossii, sobrannye iz dostovernykh istochnikov i raspolozhennye po godam* (12 vols., Moscow, 1788–1789); *Dopolnenie k Deianiiam Petra Velikogo, mudrogo preobrazovatelia Rossii* (18 vols., Moscow, 1790–1797). Of Golikov's lesser works, I found especially interesting a comparison of "traits and acts" of Constantine the Great with those of Peter the Great, together with the events of their reigns, written on the basis of compilations made by the learned priest Peter Alekseev (Petr Alekseevich Alekseev, 1727–1801): Ivan Ivanovich Golikov, *Sravnenie svoistv i del Konstantina Velikogo, pervogo iz rimskikh khristianskogo imperatora, s svoistvami i delami Petra Velikogo, pervogo vserossiiskogo imperatora, i proizshestvii, v tsarstvovanie oboikh sikh monarkhov sluchivshikhsia* (2 vols. in one, Moscow, 1810).

[95] Golikov, *Deianiia,* I, p. IX. The Preface, Predislovie, occupies pp. III–X.

struction of the glorious Petrine past, championing narrative totality and unity in a field that had been dominated by highly fragmented recollections of, and commentary on, such individual episodes as the monarch's celebrated first journey to the West, the building of the navy, and the battle of Poltava or by very general oratorical and poetic eulogies. Golikov's many volumes, combining primary sources with a painstaking secondary account, became basic texts from which to learn Petrine history. Moreover—a very important point for a student of the image of Peter the Great—Golikov belonged intrinsically and entirely to the continuous Enlightenment cult of the Russian reformer discussed throughout this chapter. In a reading of his works, it is often difficult to believe that he was not himself a contemporary of the first emperor, so direct and immediate are the sovereign's presence and Golikov's praise of him. And, in fact, Golikov tried his best to witness Peter the Great and his reign, listening from his boyhood to personal accounts, gathering a splendid library of relevant books and manuscripts, working in the archives. Ivan Nepliuev (1693–1773), whose examination in the naval service in 1720 the first emperor attended and reportedly approved with the words "this fellow will be of use (*v etom malom budet tolk*),"[96] putting him in command of all ships being built in St. Petersburg, and who later became a diplomat, the founder of Orenburg and generally a prominent statesman, was, apparently, a particularly important personal link between the reformer and the historian. But there were many others, admirals, statesmen, merchants. Not surprisingly, Golikov not only gave a fine expression to the image of Peter the Great of his contemporaries and predecessors, but also did much to impose that image on later generations of Russians. His pioneering works became basic, popular, and highly influential with readers as well as with later writers on the subject.[97]

Golikov was not alone. While he published some 1500 letters of Peter the Great in the last three volumes of the *Acts,* as well as numerous other documents elsewhere, another investigator, Theodore Tumanskii—whose publication of Feofan Prokopovich's *Justice of the Monarch's Will* was cited earlier in this chapter—produced a ten-volume *Collection of Different Notes and Works Serving to Provide Full Knowledge about the Life and the Acts of Lord Emperor Peter the Great.*[98] Tumanskii's own study

96 V. R-v., "Nepliuev (Ivan Ivanovich)," *Entsiklopedicheskii Slovar* (Brockhaus-Efron), vol. XXA, book 40 (St. Petersburg, 1897), 887.

97 Shmurlo, the authority on the subject, is generally convincing in his emphasis on the magnitude of Golikov's impact, including the penetration of the provinces and even the claim that rich, educated landlords had a set of *Acts* on each one of their many estates. He exaggerates, however, the importance of Golikov in presenting the reformer's momentous reign as a total break with the past. After all, this had been the view of the first emperor himself, of his entourage, and of his admirers from Feofan Prokopovich on down; beyond personalities, it was the fundamental view of the Enlightenment: light brought into darkness. See Shmurlo, *Petr Velikii . . .* , 93–95.

98 F. Tumanskii, *Sobranie raznykh zapisok i sochinenii sluzhashchikh k dostavleniiu polnogo svedeniia o zhizni i deianiiakh Gosudaria Imperatora Petra Velikogo* (10 vols., St. Petersburg, 1787–1788).

of the reformer, however, never went beyond a single volume and the year 1682, apparently because he found the subject preempted by Golikov.[99] The well-known German scholar in Russian service, Gerhard Müller (Miller), renowned for his early study of Siberia, was appointed historiographer in 1748 and edited and published many important Russian historical sources, including some from Peter the Great's reign, before he died in 1783. Unfortunately, Müller's projected history of the first emperor did not materialize beyond the beginning, which appeared in the form of several articles. The greatest publisher of the age and a central figure of the Russian Enlightenment, Nicholas Novikov, similarly included Petrine materials in his numerous publications. Some other Russians also contributed, for instance, when in 1774 Count Peter Sheremetev published Peter the Great's letters to his father, Count Boris Sheremetev, the commander of the Russian armies in the Great Northern War. The government, Catherine II herself in particular, promoted this interest in the Petrine age. The empress even appointed a commission to publish "the letters and papers" of Peter the Great, which, however, produced no results. In addition to Golikov, Tumanskii, and Müller, a few other historians in the Catherinian age began themselves to write on the first emperor or aspects of his reign. Also, several foreign books on the topic were translated into Russian. In sum, by the end of the eighteenth century, scholars had started making important contributions to the subject, and image, of Peter the Great dominated throughout the Enlightenment by orators and didactic poets.

7

From the reign of Catherine I through that of Catherine II, from Feofan Prokopovich's sermons through Golikov's writings, the image of Peter the Great dominated the Russian scene. True, one may speak instead of a cluster of images. There was Peter the Great the Enlightener, who introduced light into darkness, transforming nonbeing into being. There was Peter the Great the Educator, perhaps the very same personage only seen at closer range, who went himself to study in the West in order to teach his subjects, who sent them there to learn, who established schools in Russia. There was Peter the Great the Lawgiver, who issued progressive laws and regulations for the development and happiness of his country. There was always Peter the Great the Worker, who did everything himself and who labored every minute of his life. That Peter the Great undertook the most ordinary tasks, repairing fishing nets or making shoes. By contrast, Peter the Great the Titan, a godlike avatar of the first emperor, constructed canals to change the river network in Russia and erected cities upon swamps. There was Peter the Great the dauntless

[99] F. Tumanskii, *Polnoe opisanie deianii Ego Velichestva Gosudaria Imperatora Petra Velikogo*, vol. I (St. Petersburg, 1788).

Hero of Poltava, Peter the Great the Founder of the Russian Navy and, related but by no means identical, Peter the Great the victorious Naval Commander. There were other Peters the Great besides.

Yet, united by the sensibility of the Age of Reason and the concept of that age of the ideal ruler, all Peters the Great complemented one another or at least coexisted without getting unduly in one another's way. A Lomonosov or a Derzhavin had no difficulty at all in moving from one of them to the next. In that sense at least a single synthetic Enlightenment image of the first emperor did exist. To be sure, certain adjustments had to be made. Thus, although Peter the Great was and remained the supreme hero of Poltava attracting endless praise in that role, Russian writers also strove to demonstrate—with some justice—that he was not a militarist, that he fought only for excellent reasons and when forced to do so, that he was in fact the opposite of his opponent, the savage Swedish warrior Charles XII. As we saw, Voltaire himself had argued that whereas all other modern wars produced only evil, the day of Poltava led to happiness for the largest empire on earth. The taste of the Age of Reason, especially in the last part of the eighteenth century, contributed also to the emphasis on Peter the Great as the lawgiver, although, as Catherine II discovered, that probably had not been his strongest point. Again, late Enlightenment preferences led to the stress on the first emperor's humane virtues as well as on the rapturous love of his subjects for their benefactor. But these claims did not replace the established aspects or functions of the image, remaining rather like frosting, or froth, on its surface. They seem strangely akin, perhaps like pale reflections, to the earliest sermons dealing with Peter the Great, where preachers lauded his achievements beyond compare yet also insisted on humility and other Christian requirements.

The narrow and dogmatic structuring and content of the Russian Enlightenment image of Peter the Great can be seen particularly well in the defense of that image. For, in spite of its overwhelming dominance in the Russian empire, the image needed a constant defense, a continuous apologetics. It was threatened on the one hand by the facts of history, which failed to match the Enlightment ideal, and on the other by foreign opinion. From the start, the enormous exertion and pain of the reformer's reign had to be justified, in general and especially in detail, and the problem of justification remained with the admiring and ideologically committed succeeding generations. As to evaluations from the outside, the first major dispute concerned the Great Northern War and the effort of the Russians to vindicate their part in it. Then and later, foreigners criticized, and Russians talked back. Golikov devoted the first 136 pages of the *Acts,* the "Introduction," to a refutation of a denunciatory book by a Swedish officer and a prisoner of war in Russia, Philipp Johann von Stralenberg, published in German in Stockholm in 1730. Other Russian writers of the Enlightenment usually took less than a hundred pages to make their point, but throughout the century they remained extremely sensitive to foreign criticism. They were sensitive also to foreign praise of the first emperor, frequently reproducing such praise verbatim and at length in their own works. The Western Age of Reason affirmed, as we know, in the words of Voltaire and others the glorious role and legacy of the Russian sovereign. But it also produced influential critics of Peter the Great. Montesquieu, as already mentioned, considered him a tyrant. Rousseau had the temerity to declare that his reforms did not fit the Russian character, the Russian people. Other critical voices also reached Russia.

The task was, then, to present Peter the Great, in terms of the Age of Reason, as perfect in behavior and supreme in accomplishment or at least as close to that as possible. Significant aspects of the reformer's life were in question. For example, the monarch's penchant for doing everything himself, for being constantly engaged in varied and hard work, an intrinsic part of his image from its inception, came to be criticized not only as improper for a sovereign but also as deplorably wasteful, taking time away from much more important affairs—Peter the Great's most famous critic along these lines was, a little later, Napoleon. The defense rose to the occasion. Feofan Prokopovich, eager to justify the very un-Muscovite behavior of his ruler, had already pointed out that the reformer worked with his own hands only to set an example, to get others going. Later the argument was developed by a variety of writers. In backward Russia, contrary to advanced states, everything had to be explained from the beginning; everything had to be demonstrated. Moreover, superstition and prejudices stood in the way of learning. The sovereign's personal and direct participation in a given activity was the best way to destroy them. It was especially in that sense that the monarch's celebrated early voyage to study everything in the West opened Western knowledge to other Russians. Again, the sovereign's own advancement through the ranks, from the bottom up, was the best way to buttress promotion according to merit. Even more broadly, contended Golikov, Peter the Great's magnificent example of hard and varied labor meant that in Russia all who worked would be satisfied with their function and would perform it enthusiastically. He quoted Sumarokov:

> You assumed the last rank, and reigning you served,
> Your laws you confirmed by your own example.[100]

We have already heard Derzhavin:

> What millions should be doing,
> He in his own person gave example to all.

And Derzhavin's refrain:

[100] Golikov, "Vvedeniie," *Deiania*, I, 1–136, quoted from p. 20.

> Carry the voices to heaven, o wind:
> You are immortal, great Peter.[101]

Could reason ask more?

The first emperor's heroic bravery created problems. The most glorious, hallowed hat of Poltava, shot through by a Swedish bullet, itself needed justification because it suggested that the behavior of its wearer had been less than fully rational. Moreover, Peter the Great had risked his life recklessly not only at the critical moment of the decisive battle but throughout the war, or rather wars, both on land and on sea. In this difficult case the defense assumed a high tone and delivered an argument that was suggestive rather than entirely explicit and that was not likely to influence skeptics, although it was certainly meant to be effective with the bulk of the Russian public and perhaps with many foreigners too. As early preachers expounded at length and as other apologists repeated throughout the century, Peter the Great's miraculous survival at Poltava, and indeed also through all other dangers, was an unmistakable sign of Providence, of divine protection. The deeply religious sovereign felt the divine hand, which gave him strength and courage whenever needed. Thus he emerged victorious, as well as safe and sound, out of fire and water, and it was rash for outsiders to question the arrangement between monarch and God.

More troublesome on the whole than heroism were certain practices of the reign, such as the forcible change of dress or the cutting of beards, which appeared ridiculous, crude, cruel, or simply unnecessary to some enlightened foreigners and even Russians. Again, explanations were ready. As Sumarokov put it, *"Peter* the Great would not have had the least need to change the dress or to shave beards, if old dress had not covered old obstinacy, while the beard had not multiplied pride in base heads."[102] Significantly, he made this comment after describing the murderous violence of the superstitious and barbarous *streltsy*. Or, in the words of Golikov: ". . . every foreigner, because of his external attire alone, seemed to them worthy of contempt. And it is this last fact that motivated the great sovereign to liken them themselves in external appearance to the foreigners whom they despised; and it was for that purpose that he ordered them to shave beards and to wear German dress, imposing on those who objected to that order only a light monetary fine."[103]

It was especially important to dispel accusations of primitive crudity and cruelty directed at the reformer. Hence Golikov's extraordinary defense of the memorable cudgel, which Peter the Great used to punish those in his entourage, very much including the virtual second-in-command, the able but corrupt Prince Alexander Menshikov:

[101] See note 91.
[102] Sumarokov, *op. cit.*, II, 222.
[103] Golikov, "Vvedenie," 61.

And in any case in the punishments, which sometimes occurred with a stick from his own hands, one can observe both that temperament most prone to anger and together with it the inseparable presence of the spirit and grace, all of which can be proved by the following: (1) the fact that even in extreme rage he was careful not to touch the head; (2) the fact that those punishments were always in proportion to the crime and never passed beyond the boundaries of moderation; (3) the fact that insofar as those subject to punishment were either his orderlies or high-ranking persons whom he needed because of their abilities, he did not want to disgrace them or to lower respect for them among the people by some public punishments, but punished them secretly by his own hand, so that it was almost impossible for anyone to learn about it; (4) the fact that these punishments took place only when the guilty would not admit his crimes or misbehavior; (5) the fact that even in that case he would, after several blows, already ease off and bring matters to an admission that in justice the punishment had been earned; and (6) the fact that when the punishment did not correspond to the crime, he begged forgiveness from the punished, promising to make an appropriate adjustment in the future were he to become guilty of any transgression, and always kept that promise, all the while without depriving him of his favor. All this I heard from certain of those very punished, who, for the reasons given above, considered what had transpired not as an act of his rage but as an act of fatherly punishment.[104]

One had not only to understand the appropriateness and advantages of Peter the Great's ways, but also to allow for the conditions and standards of the age. Golikov was convinced that those who accused Peter the Great of "excessive severity and anger" sinned doubly, against justice, for they forgot his acts of kindness, but also in a more complicated manner:

They sin against reason, for judging times past according to the present time and acts of those days that seem to them rude and cruel, they do not take into account the mental set, the manners, the customs, the upbringing, and the conditions of those times; for what was then necessary, that very thing is not at all needed now: then one felt a stick less than one now feels a cruel word or just a severe look. . . . Move, then, readers, in your thoughts to those times, and you will see *Peter* the Great fighting not so much against external enemies as against internal wild fanaticism, superstition, and ancient prejudices, which served as a strong opposition and obstacle to all his undertakings, and in consideration of that will you not justify that great sovereign, when he, exhausted so to speak, was forced sometimes to tame those monsters by severity.[105]

Ascribing the painful aspects of Peter the Great's life and reign, cruelty in particular, to the conditions and standards of the time became widespread. In a sense, the Catherinian postulation of the two phases of the Russian Enlightenment, the Petrine and the Catherinian, made it part of official ideology, for the second phase differed from the first precisely in being more humane, more civilized.

104 Golikov, *Sravnenie* . . . , II, 45–46.
105 Golikov, "Vvedenie," 124–126, quoted from pp. 125–126.

Both rationalizing the first emperor's behavior and pleading for him the circumstances of the period had to be repeatedly applied to the problem of violence and cruelty in Peter the Great's reign because of the pervasive nature of that problem. Simple omission or understatement was at times inadequate. As Feofan Prokopovich put it so well, referring to the tragedy of Tsarevich Alexis, more specifically his "rebellion" against his father: "How can one speak about such things, but then how can one be silent about them!"[106] Golikov's own two-volume comparison of Peter the Great with Constantine the Great had as a leitmotif the Russian monarch's explosive temper, in particular his proneness to anger, which, however, he controlled and balanced with his virtues—much as when wielding the cudgel—thus avoiding injustice in personal relations and damage to state interests, whereas the Byzantine ruler failed to restrain himself. Later Peter the Great was to be compared along the same lines to Ivan the Terrible.

Of the many painful episodes in Peter the Great's reign, perhaps two especially exercised the abilities of his apologists: the frightful punishment of the rebellious *streltsy* in 1698 and the judgment, condemnation to death, and death in prison of Tsarevich Alexis, Peter's son by his first wife, in 1718. The massacre of the *streltsy,* in which the reformer participated most actively in person and forced many in his entourage to participate, was treated in a simple manner. The entire emphasis—often well-supported by the facts—was placed on the terrible crimes of the *streltsy* and on the danger that they presented to the realm. Presumably, therefore, no punishment of them could be excessive or deserving of criticism. As Lomonosov explained matters:

He is not burdened by the execution of the *streltsy.* Imagine for yourself and think, what zeal for justice, compassion for his subjects, and his own danger were telling him in his heart: "Innocent blood has been shed in the houses and streets of Moscow, widows cry, orphans weep, raped women and maidens howl, my relatives were deprived of life in my house in front of my eyes, and sharp weapons were pointed at my heart. I was preserved by God. I suffered, dodged. I wandered outside the city. Now they have cut short my useful journey, arming openly against the fatherland. If I do not wreak vengeance for all of this and do not prevent by executions the ultimate disaster, I can already see in advance squares filled with corpses, houses being looted, churches being destroyed, Moscow swept by flames on all sides, and my dear fatherland brought down in smoke and ashes. God will make me respond for all these disasters, tears, blood." Looking at that ultimate justice forced Him to be severe.[107]

For the Petrine apologists at least, Tsarevich Alexis proved to be more troublesome than the *streltsy.* In contrast to the official image of these special troops, the tsarevich made a poor candidate for evil incarnate. He was, after all, Peter the Great's own son, a deeply beloved son the apolo-

---

106 Feofan Prokopovich, *Sochineniia,* 121.
107 Lomonosov, *op. cit.,* VIII, 608–609.

gists insisted. His so-called rebellion was of a remarkably passive kind; Voltaire, it will be remembered, had to explain to his readers that, unlike the Prince of Wales, a Russian heir to the throne was not free to travel where he pleased, and that, contrary to the situation in England or France, a mere criminal thought without any consequences could be punished in Russia. The first emperor's condemnations of his son were interspersed with pardons and reconciliations, quite possibly to the very last. The exact circumstances of the tsarevich's death remain unknown; the official proclamation cited shock at the death verdict and sudden illness. Tsarevich Alexis was given a fine burial, which his father attended.

The complexity and the strangeness of the case, as well as its significance, because, of course, it was directly related to the issue of succession to the Russian throne, made it all the more important that the official version be fully, clearly, and carefully presented. This had already been done at the time, with the publication of certain documents, and—documents, narration, and explanation put together—it became part of the Petrine canon. The canonical account emphasized the sovereign's profound love for his son and his effort to bring him up properly and to make him his worthy successor. Alexis, however, refused to cooperate, rebuffing his father's approaches and neglecting the opportunities offered him. Instead he relied on the evil advice of obscurantists and enemies of Peter the Great and his reforms—in a sense a reincarnation or, less dramatically, a continuation of the *streltsy*. These fiends wished death to the emperor and annihilation of his work. A conspiracy thus, in fact, existed, even if it did not manifest itself by precipitate action. Alexis's own decision remained crucial. Unfortunately, he stubbornly declined to reform, in spite of all his father's attempts. Hence his renunciation of his claims to the throne in preference to reforming, his criminal escape to Hapsburg lands, his return to a promised pardon provided he revealed all his associates and their activities, his cunning failure to do so, further investigation exposing the extent of the conspiracy, the verdict of capital punishment by all 127 secular notables of the empire whom Peter the Great asked to pass judgment—churchmen answered more vaguely, recognizing the supreme guilt of a son who had turned against his father, but citing Scriptural examples of pardon—and the sudden death of Alexis, who had been questioned and tortured, in prison two days later. Utilizing effectively the reformer's own words, the apologists waxed eloquent on the subject of this ultimate example of civic virtue, a father sacrificing his son to the interests of the fatherland, of the state, of the people. One could contrast the Russian solution triumphantly to the failure of Marcus Aurelius with Commodus and even suggest that it had the supreme merit of eventually bringing Catherine the Great to the Russian throne. Nicholas I remembered the episode later, when he had troubles with his own son and heir; and in general it became part of the established image of Peter the Great. But the apologists also emphasized sentimental aspects of the story, such as the first emperor's love for his son, and Alexis's alleged final repentance and call for his father. The entire topic of Tsarevich Alexis was promising to the glorifiers of Peter the Great, but at the same time, obviously, very delicate and even dangerous.[108]

The problem of the reformer's debauchery also had to be handled, although it required on the whole less attention than that of cruelty. The techniques utilized were much the same. In addition to the usual omission and understatement, there were occasional rationalizations—leisure, conviviality, coming to know people—and pleas to judge that particular topic in proportion to Peter the Great's other activities and, especially, according to the standards of his age. At times one reads about "old-fashioned Russian" parties where joy reigned supreme and where even state affairs could sometimes be successfully conducted, but where, unfortunately, people drank too much. As a rule one reads nothing at all.

Important though it was, the problem of cruelty in Peter the Great's reign could be considered only one element of a larger issue, the total cost of that reign to the people of Russia. The first emperor's temperament aside, his policies, right or wrong, exacted a huge toll. Contemporaries, needless to say, were aware of this. The ardent and strident laudation of the Russian role in the Great Northern War had among its main purposes a vindication of all the losses and suffering brought about by that war and a mobilization of the country to prosecute the hostilities. But some other undertakings of the reformer, too, made heavy demands and needed apologists. For example, in a powerful sermon entitled "In Praise of St. Petersburg and Its Founder, Lord Emperor Peter the Great" Gabriel Buzhinskii argued as follows in defense of the building of the new capital, in spite of the frightful cost of the project in human lives.[109] The vipers who spewed their hatred against the city failed to recognize its already apparent advantages and "fruits" as well as the fact that Peter the Great was building for the future. Furthermore, "consider, what beginning is not hard, what first journey is not difficult? . . . All cities had calamities at their foundation and incomparable labors."[110]

And if it is the death of many people that you pity, look at the greatest cities, and this is what you are going to find in them: whether in misery or in prosperity, whether at work or at leisure, one's end waits for everyone. When all-

[108] Skillful apology was all the more desirable because, to repeat Feofan Prokopovich, "how can one be silent about such things?" And indeed the standard version of the Alexis story was continuously reiterated in the Russian writings on Peter the Great in the eighteenth century and after. As one fine example of this, see Golikov, *Sravnenie* . . . , II, 48–88. The latest scholarly and balanced treatment of the subject belongs to Vadim Borisovich Vilinbakhov, whom I want to thank here for having let me read it in manuscript: V. B. Vilinbakhov, "Gosudarevo synoubiistvo."

[109] Gavriil Buzhinskii, "V pokhvalu Sanktpeterburga i ego Osnovatelia, Gosudaria Imperatora Petra Velikogo," *op. cit.*, 1–36.

[110] *Ibid.*, 31.

merciful God in his inscrutable ways assigns a certain death to someone, no person can ever avoid it. There are many who escaped death in battle, in storms at sea, in horrible fires; there are also many who in the midst of festivities, with all the safety and security, ended their lives damnably. Do not lament what you are lamenting; lament instead your sin, which gives birth to death. . . .[111]

Buzhinskii's realistic view of the cost of building St. Petersburg and other realistic judgments of Petrine costs did not last long into the century. The most important reason for the change in the attitude was, of course, the end of the reign: problems that were a pressing necessity for Peter the Great, Buzhinskii, and their contemporaries faded into an increasingly distant and unreal image of an idealized past. But there was also a certain evolution of ideology, not only of vision. The reformer's increasingly secular apologists could no longer utilize, effectively and with conviction, the naval chaplain's religious injunctions. They had to find entirely elsewhere their rationale for the defense and glorification of Peter the Great. And that "elsewhere," the thought of the Catherinian Enlightenment, waxed so high in optimism, self-satisfaction, and rationalistic promise that it made hardly any allowance for costs, let alone tragedy. At the end of the century Golikov wrote the following passage:

To prevent fires in villages and to provide a better life for the peasantry, he issued plans according to which their households were to be constructed; and the execution of this measure was assigned to the Governors and the Voevodas; to be sure, that Great Master in his private journeys throughout the State entered their huts, examined carefully their way of life, tasted their bread and food, talked with them, as father with children, found out their needs and wants, and satisfied them: they paid no more State taxes than 120 kopecks for the State peasants and 70 for the serfs per male soul, and the collection of that small tax was so arranged that they virtually did not feel it; administrators of Governments and Provinces were held most strictly accountable to him for burdening them with additional collections; his ever-vigilant eye observed equally the owners, so that they too would not wear them out by means of extra work or quitrents, and so on and so forth.[112]

111 *Ibid.*, 32–33. For another, and different, defense of the building of St. Petersburg see [Petr Nikiforovich Krekshin], *Kratkoe opisanie slavnykh i dostopamiatnykh del Imperatora Petra Velikogo, ego znamenitykh pobed i puteshestvii v raznye Evropeiskie Gosudarstva so mnogimi vazhnymi i liubopytnymi dostoinymi proizshestviiami, predstavlennoe razgovorami v tsarstve mertvykh General-Feldmarshala i kavalera Rossiiskikh i Maltiiskikh ordenov Grafa Borisa Petrovicha Sheremeteva, boiarina Fedora Alekseevicha Golovina i samogo sego Velikogo Imperatora so Rossiiskim Tsarem Ioannom Vasilevichem, s Shvedskim Korolem Karlom XII, Izrailskim Tsarem Solomonom i Grecheskim Tsarem Aleksandrom* (St. Petersburg, 1788), 48–50. Krekshin (1684–1763) served under Peter the Great and became one of the first historians as well as an unconditional admirer of his sovereign. A believer in legends and tales and archaic in style, he did little for history, but made nevertheless a contribution to the Petrine cult. Of a number of interesting passages in the book here cited, see, for example, Peter the Great's explanation to Ivan the Terrible of how the title of "emperor" is superior to that of "tsar" (p. 56; cf. p. 97).
112 Golikov, *Sravnenie* . . . , II, 115.

Breathtakingly, the entire financial burden of the Petrine rule became a secondary part of a sentence dealing with fire prevention. And that was all, in a book by a man who had spent a lifetime studying Peter the Great and his reign. One is reminded of Catherine the Great's correspondence with Voltaire, in which the empress explained that her wars and other undertakings really cost nothing and that Russian peasants had become so prosperous that they could always afford a chicken for dinner, but in some areas preferred turkey.

The question of the cost of Peter the Great's reign was, however, to return in later epochs and indeed to serve as a main motif in the historical and ideological debate about the Russian reformer.

The problem of the relationship of the first emperor and his reign to the preceding Russian history, to Muscovite Russia, also presented certain difficulties to the writers of the Russian Enlightenment. From the time of Feofan Prokopovich, they had postulated an absolute contrast between the new and the old, light and darkness, being and nonbeing. This view, as I have tried to indicate, corresponded marvelously to the philosophic outlook of the age as well as to the reformer's own estimate of his task. It became dogma. What troubled some eighteenth-century Russians, however, was not only and perhaps not so much the accuracy of the view—a central issue later in Russian history—as its apparent denigration of the Russian people. If Peter the Great accomplished everything, centuries and centuries of Russian historical life had to be dismissed as nothing. The most devoted glorifiers of the reformer cringed when even well-meaning foreigners congratulated them on their propulsion from total savagery into the Age of Reason.[113] As already noted, Catherine the Great, who had no personal feelings about Muscovy, was willing to see some good in Tsar Alexis and his Russia. A few eighteenth-century writers, such as the poet and historian Basil Ruban, similarly presented the Muscovite legacy as not entirely negative in relation to Peter the Great.[114] Indeed Sumarokov and a number of others who

---

[113] As one example of this cringing, see Golikov cite approvingly and very prominently a British poet making this point, but add gratuitously that in describing most unflatteringly the pre-Petrine Russians "the author means here, of course, only those infected with hypocrisy, fanaticism, and superstition, as were the *streltsy*, the rebels, the rioters, and many of their kind, who hated the monarch for his introduction of the Enlightenment and so forth" (Golikov, *Sravnenie . . .* , II, 239). Actually, "the dispassionate Englishman," as he is referred to in the Russian sources, wrote simply of the subjects the reformer inherited as rude, slow, unfit for war, ignorant, disobedient, uninterested in glory, and avoiding danger, creatures only called humans, but in their characteristics more beasts than articulate beings. Cf. Iv . . . N.kh.n [Ivan Vasilievich Nekhachin], *Iadro istorii gosudaria Petra Velikogo pervogo Imperatora Vserossiiskogo s prisovokupleniem opisaniia Monumenta, vozdvignutogo v pamiat semy Ottsu Otechestva Ekaterinoiu II Velikoiu i s kratkoiu Istorieiu syna Ego, tsarevicha Alekseia Petrovicha* ([Moscow], 1794), 414–416.

[114] [Vasilii Grigorievich] Ruban, *Nachertanie, podaiushchee poniatie o dostoslavnom tsarstvovanii Petra Velikogo, s priobshcheniem khronologicheskoi rospisi glavneishikh del i prikliuchenii zhizni sego velikogo gosudaria* (St. Petersburg, 1778). Ruban (1742–1792), a mediocre writer but a fine exponent of the Catherinian glorification of Peter

praised the reformer beyond all measure nevertheless claimed on occasion that the Russian historical past was not inferior to those of Western nations and that there was no ground at all for any Russian diffidence vis-à-vis the West. The growth of Russian historiography was also making a nihilistic view of pre-Petrine Russia increasingly untenable. By the end of the century there was developing a "national" reaction to the classical Enlightenment image of Peter the Great, which we shall consider in the next section of this chapter.

8

The unity, dominance, and power of the image of Peter the Great in eighteenth-century Russia corresponded closely to the hegemony of the ideology and culture of the Age of Reason in the reformed realm of the tsars. Yet, as the continuous defense of the image indicated, there were challenges to be met abroad and even at home. Within the philosophy of the Enlightenment, a certain shift in emphasis, that is, from abstract reason and enlightened benevolence to human rights and participation in governance—popular or at least aristocratic or otherwise elite—could well threaten the image. Other and growing tendencies, such as wounded national pride or a penchant for the historic past, not effectively provided for in the reigning creed of the epoch, were equally disturbing. In fact, already in the eighteenth century a few educated Russians went far enough in these different directions not to be simply included among the devotees of the established cult of the first emperor but to deserve special notice.

One of them was Princess Catherine Dashkova (1743–1810), an early associate of Catherine the Great and a prominent figure in her reign and in the Russian Enlightenment. In a single table conversation with Prince Kaunitz, the Austrian chancellor and apparently an admirer of Peter the Great in the standard manner, Dashkova managed to bring up pell-mell most of the arguments used against the first emperor throughout the century.[115] She began by denying the chancellor's statement that Peter I had been the creator of Russia. Indeed that was an invention of foreigners, whom the ruler had invited to his country and who thus pretended to claim part in the alleged creation. The Russians had conquered the kingdoms of Kazan, Astrakhan, and Siberia and had defeated

the Great was known best for his "inscription" to the stone foundation of *The Bronze Horseman*: Vasilii Ruban, *Nadpisi k Kamniu Gromu, nakhodiashchemusia v Sankt-peterburge, v podnozhii konnogo, vylitogo litsepodobiia dostoslavnogo imperatora Petra Velikogo* (St. Petersburg, 1782). A single sheet with a German translation by I. C. Schildt on the opposite side.

115 E. R. Dashkova, "Mon histoire," *Bumagi kniagini E. R. Dashkovoi. Arkhiv kniazia Vorontsova*, vol. XXI (Moscow, 1881), 1–365; the conversation is reproduced on pp. 219–222. Princess Dashkova was born Countess Vorontsova.

the supreme warriors of the Golden Horde before Peter I or his ancestors ascended the Russian throne. The arts flourished in ancient Russia as some paintings in monasteries still attested whereas priceless churches with their mosaics were destroyed in Khan Batyi's invasion. Ancient Russian historians produced more works than those of all the rest of Europe. As to Kaunitz's argument that the reforming emperor had brought Russia close to Europe, a great empire as rich and powerful as Russia did not have to be brought anywhere: if well-governed, she was bound to attract others to her instead. Previous lack of knowledge of Russia in the West proved only European ignorance and carelessness. To be sure, one had to be fair to Emperor Peter I. He had been a man of genius, a man of action, a striver for perfection, but he had lacked totally education, and he had allowed his violent passions to dominate his reason.

Quick-tempered, brutal, and despotic, he treated all without distinction like slaves who had to bear everything; his ignorance prevented him from seeing that some innovations that he had introduced by force would have introduced themselves peacefully given time, contacts, commerce, and the example of other nations. He would not have destroyed the most worthy character of our ancestors, had he not valued foreigners so much above the Russians. He would not have weakened the power and the respect due to laws, had he not changed them so often, and even those that were his own. He sapped the foundations of the rules and the code of his father; he replaced them with despotic laws, only to annul some of those in turn.[116]

In short, Peter I took away almost entirely the liberties and the privileges of both the nobles and the servants. He established the most despotic form of government, military government. Attracted by the conceit of being a creator, he pushed the building of St. Petersburg by most tyrannical means: thousands of workers perished in the swamps, and nobles were obliged to provide men for construction and to have their own brick houses built, according to the specifications of the monarch, in the new capital, whether they needed them or not. He established an admiralty and the docks on the low Neva, so that ships had to be brought at great expense to Kronshtadt to complete the construction. By contrast Catherine the Great built more and better and without the use of force. The chancellor's remark that it was good to see a sovereign work long and hard himself had to be a joke:

for you know better than I that the time of a sovereign must not be taken by an execution of the motions of a simple laborer. Peter I was in a position to attract into his service not only carpenters and construction workers but also admirals. He failed in his duty and in his handling of the operations and the major needs of the state by remaining in Saardam to become a carpenter and to mutilate the Russian language by means of Dutch endings and terminology, which abound in

116 *Ibid.*, 220–221.

his edicts and in everything related to the navy.[117] He had no unavoidable need whatsoever to send nobles to foreign countries to learn the skills of a gardener, a smith, a miner, etc., etc.: every noble would gladly have given him three or several of his subjects to have them learn these occupations.[118]

Understandably, at that point Kaunitz changed the topic of conversation. Dashkova, on her part, remained faithful to her views. As she described her bitterness many years later, after the death of Catherine the Great:

> How very indignant I was to hear that the circle of persons surrounding the emperor, though internally divided, unanimously denigrated the reign of Catherine II, and that it was inculcated in the young monarch that a woman could never govern an empire! By contrast, Peter I was raised to heaven, that brilliant tyrant, that ignoramus, who sacrificed good institutions, the laws, the rights and the privileges of his subjects to an ambition to change everything, without distinguishing the useful, the good, and the bad, and whom foreign writers, ignorant or dishonest, proclaimed the creator of a great empire, which, long before him, had played a greater role than it was to play in his reign![119]

The princess was so indignant and argued so hard with those around her, including her equally famous brother Simon, ambassador to Great Britain and statesman, that she was taken ill.

Dashkova's ideology, like her conversation, consisted, it would seem, of different things. One is struck by the wounded national pride, which led her to claim more historical manuscripts for Russia than could be found in "all the rest of Europe" and which made it increasingly difficult for her, and for many of her countrymen and women, to regard Peter the Great simply as a demigod who had brought his people from savagery into civilization. The princess also represented well the continuous aristocratic dissatisfaction with the reformer and his measures, the reaction of those who had to build willy-nilly brick houses in St. Petersburg and, in addition, contribute serfs to the erection of the new capital. She reiterated sharply the criticism that the first emperor had not acted like a true sovereign or even an aristocrat: he had done the work of common laborers himself and had forced his nobles into unseemly occupations and positions. But Dashkova's main charge against Peter the Great, that he was a cruel, crude, and ignorant tyrant, reflected the thought and the standards of the Western Enlightenment, which she knew very well. Fluent in foreign languages since her childhod, a sojourner in the West for some ten years, where she sought the company of philosophes and writers—Voltaire, Diderot, or Adam Smith—and determined to be progressive, the princess easily shared a point of view that made the Russian

---

117 Dashkova was the president of the Russian Academy, a favorite project of hers approved by Catherine the Great, one of its aims having been improvement of the Russian language. Appropriately for the time, Dashkova, the protectress of Russian, wrote her own memoirs in French.

118 *Ibid.*, 222.

119 *Ibid.*, 361.

reformer look less than civilized and his system less than humane and rational.

This, so to speak, Left Russian critique of Peter the Great had a much firmer foundation in the thought of the one outstanding Russian radical of the age, Alexander Radishchev (1749–1802). And indeed, the admirer of Mably and other writers of the later and more egalitarian and radical phase of the Western Enlightenment, whom he read especially during his education at the University of Leipzig, the author of an explosive denunciation of serfdom in Russia, *A Journey from St. Petersburg to Moscow,* and eventually a republican by conviction could hardly be expected to remain a docile devotee of the established Petrine cult. Yet two factors complicate the issue: a paucity of sources, for little by Radishchev on Peter the Great has come down to us, and Radishchev's enormously high regard for the first Russian emperor and his historical role. In fact, much of what we do have from Radishchev fits perfectly the standard cult. In "A Letter to a Friend Living in Tobolsk," an interesting description of the ceremony of the unveiling of Falconet's *The Bronze Horseman* in 1782, Radishchev speculated as follows about the meaning of the statue:

The steepness of the mountain represents the obstacles that *Peter* faced when he was carrying out his intentions; the snake lying in his path is insidiousness and malice aiming at his death for introducing the new ways; ancient dress, the animal skin, and the entire simple apparel of the horse and the rider are simple and rude manners and the absence of enlightenment, which *Peter* found in the people whom he decided to reform; the head crowned with the laurels denotes that he was victor first, rather than lawgiver; the manly and powerful appearance indicates the firmness of the reformer; the extended arm, protecting as Diderot described it, shows that the hero, having overcome all strong vices opposing his intention, gives his protection to all, who are called his children. Here, my dear friend, is a weak depiction of what I feel as I look at the representation of *Peter.*[120]

And Radishchev added that had the first Russian emperor never defeated Charles XII or done other things, he could still be called great because he had been "the first to give motion and direction to this enormous mass, which, like a primary element, had remained inactive."[121] In a late poem, "The Eighteenth Century," Radishchev presented, again in the established manner, Peter the Great and Catherine the Great as the two dominant figures of the century ("ice fields of fallacy, many thousands of years old, melted") and linked them directly to the great successes and promise of the new reign of Alexander I.[122]

By contrast, Radishchev's criticism of the reformer has to be scraped

---

[120] A. N. Radishchev, "Pismo k drugu, zhitelstvuiushchemu v Tobolske, po dolgu zvaniia svoego," *Polnoe sobranie sochinenii* (Moscow, 1907), vol. I, 67–75, quoted from p. 73.

[121] *Ibid.,* 74–75.

[122] A. N. Radishchev, "Osmnadtsatoe stoletie," *op. cit.,* 462–464, quoted from p. 462.

together bit by bit. The radical did write in the last sentence of the letter to his friend in Tobolsk that Peter the Great could have been still more glorious and could have raised himself and his country still higher had he established individual freedom, adding sadly that a ruler never surrenders willingly any of his power.[123] A few other adverse or qualifying comments could be discovered in Radishchev's "scattered notes" and elsewhere. It was on such a basis that scholars, particularly Soviet scholars much concerned with Radishchev as a founder and martyr of the radical and revolutionary trend in Russian history, have tried to explicate "the elements of a dialectical approach" in his evaluation of the first emperor combining an appreciation of the reformer's historical role with appropriate radical criticism.[124]

Whereas Radishchev and, in part, Dashkova criticized the Russian Enlightenment image of Peter the Great on the basis of certain more radical views of the Western Enlightenment, the bulk of the criticism of that image in Russia came from what can be vaguely described as patriotic and national sentiments supported by an increasing awareness of the pre-Petrine Russian past. Dashkova, of course, represented that approach too, and so to an extent did Catherine the Great. In fact, as already noted, understandably if illogically, even extreme proponents of the dichotomy between Petrine light and pre-Petrine darkness changed their argument sometimes when explaining their country to foreigners. Historical interest and knowledge also contributed to change. Shmurlo draws special attention to "Thoughts about Russia, or Some Comments concerning the Civil and the Moral Condition of the Russians prior to the Reign of Peter the Great," written by an unknown Russian nobleman in French abroad at the time of the French Revolution, for its positive general presentation of Muscovy.[125] Nor was that the only attempt at a reconsideration.

The ablest and the most important Russian historian of the second half of the eighteenth century, Ivan Boltin (1735–1792), distinguished himself by his scholarly rigor, precision, and good sense, as well as an ability to pursue his aim relentlessly over hundreds of pages. His devastating, two-volume, minute critique of N.-G. Le Clerc's "Histoire physique, morale, civile et politique de la Russie ancienne et moderne" set many historical points straight, including some dealing with Peter the Great, and has been highly considered ever since both for its scholarship and for its patriotism.[126] Boltin wrote within the general ideology of the Russian

123 Radishchev, "Pismo k drugu . . . ," 75.
124 For two of the better explications, see G. P. Makogonenko, *Radishchev i ego vremia* (Moscow, 1956), esp. pp. 590–595; and S. A. Pokrovskii, *Gosudarstvennopravovye vzgliady Radishcheva* (Moscow, 1956), esp. pp. 64–65. "Elementy dialekticheskogo podkhoda" is used by Pokrovskii on p. 64.
125 Shmurlo, *Petr Velikii . . .* , 69–72, notes pp. 88–91.
126 Ivan Boltin, *Primechaniia na Istoriiu drevniia i nyneshniia Rossii g. Leklerka* (2 vols., St. Petersburg, 1788).

Enlightenment with its overwhelming emphasis on the reforming emperor.[127] Yet, being a careful historian, he provided a realistic treatment
of Muscovite Russia rather than a caricature, and he was interested in
continuity as well as in change. Moreover, Boltin was capable of far-
reaching criticisms of some of Peter the Great's measures. The most frequently quoted critical passage reads as follows:

When we began to send our youth abroad and to entrust their education to
foreigners, our morals entirely changed; together with the supposed enlightenment, there came into our hearts new prejudices, new passions, weaknesses, and
desires that had remained unknown to our ancestors. These extinguished in us our
love for the fatherland, destroyed our attachment to the faith of our fathers and
to their ways. Thus we forgot the old, before mastering the new, and while
losing our identity, did not become what we wished to be. All this arose out of
hastiness and impatience. We wanted to accomplish in a few years that which
required centuries and began to build the house of our enlightenment on sand
before having laid firm foundations.[128]

Boltin explained, to be sure, that though the original Petrine policy of
sending unprepared youths abroad proved to be a disaster, young men
returning in a worse condition than the one in which they had departed,
the contemporary Catherinian provision of a good upbringing in Russia
prior to the journey and other measures of the empress benefited the
country greatly.

At the very time Boltin published his lengthy commentary on Le
Clerc's history of Russia, with its critique of the reformer's education
abroad program, a rival historian, writer, and prominent intellectual and
political figure, Prince Michael Shcherbatov (1733–1790), developed similar critical ideas into the main thesis of his negative and pessimistic
treatise "On the Corruption of Morals in Russia."[129] The case of Shcherbatov was, however, a complex one, and it testified as much to the power
and scope of the Enlightenment image of Peter the Great as to a certain
challenge to that image.

Like other Russian writers of the age, Shcherbatov had enthusiastically
praised the first emperor in prose and poetry. Moreover, as a historian,
he undertook the assignment of arranging and publishing the reformer's
papers. His judgment of his subject was stated notably, sharply, and
polemically in his "Consideration of the Vices and the Absolute Power
of Peter the Great," an outstanding example of the "defensive" literature

127 See for example, section 44 of the second volume: "Peter was both a victor and a
hero, both a founder of the sciences and a protector of scholars."
128 I changed slightly the translation of the passage in Hans Rogger, *National Consciousness in Eighteenth-Century Russia* (Cambridge, Mass., 1960), 68. Professor Rogger's
book provides a fine account of "national" and related trends at the time, perhaps
somewhat exaggerating them because of the focus of the study.
129 Prince M. M. Shcherbatov, "O povrezhdenii nravov v Rossii," *Russkaia Starina*
(July 1870), 13–56 (August 1870), 99–116, vol. III (1871), 673–688.

discussed in the preceding section of this chapter.[130] It was Shcherbatov, too, who, unsatisfied with the general vague praise of how much the reformer had advanced Russia, calculated in a special study the measure of that advancement to be 130 years; that is, without Peter the Great, the country would have reached its condition of 1762 in 1892, and that only under most favorable circumstances.[131] Interestingly, though most of his literary activity fell into the reign of Catherine the Great, the versatile author did not share the Catherinian view of the Russian Enlightenment: the two stages, with the Catherinian surpassing the Petrine. Rather, he regarded the first emperor as the one true creator of enlightened Russia, from a realm of darkness, whereas his successors inherited from him only the secondary task of improving and refining.[132] That view made Shcherbatov a poor admirer of the Semiramis of the North, but it emphasized even further his devotion to Peter the Great.

And yet the historian parted company with the reformer, or at least that is the explicit and unmistakable message of Shcherbatov's late survey of "The Corruption of Morals in Russia." Shcherbatov was not happy with the world in which he was tightly enveloped. Moralist first, he observed bitterly what he considered to be a precipitous decline in the standards of behavior at the court and in the high society to which he belonged. Moreover, he felt that the disease was spreading as well as becoming more pronounced. By the time Shcherbatov wrote "On the Corruption . . ." he had given his critique a historical explanation and structure that distinguished it from the literary sallies against Gallomania and the glib moral preaching very common in the reign of Catherine the Great. The root cause of the disease, the historian discovered, was the triumph of luxury and voluptuousness as a direct result of Peter the Great's reorientation of Russian life. It led to the corruption of both public and private morals, the courts and administration as well as family life. Old probity and decency ceded their place to the evil new ways. Shcherbatov's study was a narrative history, almost a conventional chronicle, except that its elements were not battles and diplomatic agreements,

130 Prince M. M. Shcherbatov, "Rassmotrenie o porokakh i samovlastii Petra Velikogo. Beseda," *Chteniia v Imperatorskom Obshchestve Istorii i Drevnostei Rossiiskikh pri Moskovskom universitete* (Moscow, January–March 1860), vol. I, 5–22.

131 Prince M. M. Shcherbatov, "Primernoe vremiaishchislitelnoe polozhenie, vo skolko by let, pri blagopoluchneishkikh obstoiatelstvakh, mogla Rossiia sama soboiu, bez samovlastiia Petra Velikogo, doiti do togo sostoianiia, v kakom ona nyne est, v rassuzhdenii proshveshcheniia i slavy," *Chteniia v Imperatorskom Obshchestve Istorii i Drevnostei Rossiiskikh pri Moskovskom universitete* (Moscow, January–March 1860), vol. I, part 1, 23–28. A rough English translation would be: "An approximate chronological calculation as to the number of years in which, under the most favorable circumstances, Russia could reach by itself, without the absolute power of Peter the Great, that condition in regard to enlightenment and glory in which it is at present."

132 See esp. Prince M. M. Shcherbatov, "Otvet grazhdanina na rech, govorennuiu E. I. V. Ober-Prokurorom Senata Nekliudovym, po prichine torzhestva Shvedskogo mira, 1790 sentiabria, 5 chisla," *op. cit.*, III, part 5, 41–49.

but the appearance of the silver plate, the nature and cost of carriages, or separations between husbands and wives. The moralist recognized that Peter the Great had not been given to luxury himself, and he criticized his personal behavior only moderately; nevertheless, the long-term nefarious impact of his reforms was staggering. Also, although Shcherbatov concentrated almost his entire attention on the rulers and the high officials and aristocrats surrounding them, he made it clear that that elite group influenced the country in a decisive manner, both directly and through imitation by others. In addition, one of the historian's few comments about the common people was perhaps even more devastating than his main line of exposition. Shcherbatov wrote:

It is laudable that Peter the Great wanted to destroy superstition in religion, for, in truth, superstition means abusing rather than venerating God and religion; because it is sacrilege to assign to God acts improper to Him . . .

But when did he do that? When the people was still unenlightened; and thus, taking superstition away from an unenlightened people, he was taking away their belief in the divine law itself . . . Thus cutting down superstitions injured the most fundamental parts of faith; superstition declined, but faith declined also; the slavish fear of hell disappeared, but the love of God and of His holy law disappeared too; and morals, corrected by faith in the absence of another enlightenment and having lost that support, began to turn into debauchery.[133]

Shcherbatov's thought had never been notable for its consistency. Still, the glaring contradiction between his general enthusiastic, thorough, elaborate, and carefully considered praise of the reformer and the new sweeping critique, between the Russian Enlightenment image of Peter the Great and the message of "On the Corruption . . . ," must have cried for a resolution. The issue was put to rest by the historian's death shortly after the completion of his iconoclastic work.

Shcherbatov's carping moralistic attack on the historical role of the first emperor could be readily considered subjective and narrow. Examining the tableware of the boyars or their desserts would hardly rival the glorious vision of a realm of darkness transformed into that of light. When not regarded simply as personal, the prince's dissatisfaction and criticisms have often been linked to exclusive aristocratic concerns, very prominent on the whole in Shcherbatov's work and life as well as in the content of the piece in question. Rudely but not surprisingly, the editor of the 1870 edition of "On the Corruption . . ." referred to "peculiarities to the point of absurdity, to the point of a complete obscurantism of views and conclusions."[134] And, as already indicated, Shcherbatov wrote

133 Shcherbatov, "O povrezhdenii . . . ," 36–37. Shcherbatov referred specifically to the first emperor's struggle against certain kinds of alleged miracles, his orders to the armed forces (approved by the Holy Synod and Orthodox patriarchs) to eat meat when necessary during Lenten fasting, and, again, to the cutting of beards.
134 Ibid., 15.

in the course of his life much more in praise than in condemnation of
Peter the Great and died without having drawn the balance. Even when
mounting his major assault, he began by qualifying the Petrine change
as "needed but, perhaps, excessive."[135] Nevertheless, "On the Corruption
of Morals in Russia" deserves the serious attention of a student of the
Russian image of Peter the Great. The gist of the moralist's criticism of
the reformer in that work was not that the first emperor had not been
enlightened enough or that he needed Catherine the Great to accomplish
what he had merely started and not even that he had made a particular
mistake or mistakes, but rather that, unexpectedly, the new turning itself
proved to be a disaster. This approach to Peter the Great and his reforms, directly opposed to the letter and spirit of the Russian Enlightenment, was to become prominent in subsequent periods of Russian history.[136]

9

In Russia, the Enlightenment continued beyond the death of Catherine
the Great, more furtively in the brief reign of Paul I, 1796–1801, more
openly and confidently during the much longer rule of his son and successor, Alexander I, 1801–1825. Whether because of the intellectual retardation of Russia compared to the West, the special attraction of the
ideology of the Age of Reason for the Russian government and the Russian educated public, or other factors, that ideology, with its attendant
images, was to last long in the realm of the tsars. True, Paul I, reacting
against his mother, Catherine the Great, who had kept him for decades
from ascending the throne, as well as against the French Revolution,
instituted repressive measures, restricting further Russian intellectual
and cultural life, already badly crippled during the last years of Catherine II. Still, a brief span of extravagant autocracy, with no new orientation to offer and no change in the fundamental intellectual climate in
the country, was not sufficient to destroy the Russian Enlightenment.
Indeed, although he was in fact a petty and even virtually unbearable
tyrant, Paul I thought of himself, and with some justification, as an
enlightened despot guiding his country by reason to the common good.
By contrast, Alexander I seemed to be everything the educated Russians

135 *Ibid.*, 26.
136 The best treatment of Shcherbatov's views on Peter the Great is to be found in
the following booklet: V. E. Valdenberg, *Shcherbatov o Petre Velikom* (St. Petersburg,
1903). See also Marc Raeff, "State and Nobility in the Ideology of M. M. Shcherbatov,"
*The American Slavic and East European Review*, vol. XIX, no. 3 (October 1960), 363–
379, where the author presents effectively the total impact of the reformer on Shcherbatov, aside from the narrower problem of the reformer's image, as shown, for example, in Shcherbatov's utopia "Voyage to the Land of Ophir." Incidentally, that
utopia contains a thinly veiled critique of St. Petersburg, that is, a costly capital set
upon swamps in a far corner of the state and keeping the ruler and the ruling group
away from the people.

wanted, and his assumption of rule was accompanied by an extraordinary general elation. The monolithic unity of the government and the educated public in Russia was probably never stronger, nor the belief in Enlightenment and enlightened despotism firmer, than in that remarkable year of 1801. And, although the liberal promise of the reign went unfulfilled, with reaction replacing progressive beginnings, Enlightenment thought, vocabulary, and images remained at least one alternative for the emperor as long as he lived, as well as for some of his assistants and for the Russian educated public. Climatic vacillations ceased, and new weather settled in firmly only after the death of "the enigmatic tsar" and the suppression of the Decembrist rebellion.[137]

That Peter the Great dominated Russian eighteenth-century political life and thought was demonstrated, once again, by the case of Paul I. Whereas Catherine the Great, as we have seen, was both deeply involved personally with the image of the reformer and made a comprehensive, careful, and clever use of it in her own propagandistic version of the Russian Enlightenment, Grand Duke Paul, in opposition, simply cultivated a still stronger and more direct emphasis on the first emperor, while disregarding, in fact hating, the claims of his mother. A "Petrine" ideology was confronted by a "more Petrine" one. Expounded by the Catherinian statesman and tutor of Grand Duke Paul, Count Nikita Panin, and certain other figures in the grand duke's entourage and ardently adopted by the grand duke, this "return to Peter the Great" became official doctrine when Catherine II died in 1796,[138] In a sense, it was a return to Empress Elizabeth. Just as that monarch declared herself to be the direct and exact continuer of the work of Peter the Great, postulating the simple formula "father-daughter," so at the end of the century the straight line of continuity was made to proceed from Peter I to Paul I. A visitor to Leningrad can still admire a statue of Peter the Great in front of Paul I's palace with its succinct inscription: "To great-grandfather great-grandson" (*Pradedu pravnuk*).

Alexander I was different. He might well have been the first imperial ruler of Russia—not counting, of course, the infant Ivan VI—not deeply concerned personally with the image of Peter the Great. One is reminded of Derzhavin's "river of time in its urgent course," or one could speculate that the new sovereign's theoretical penchant for constitutions as well as his faith in the Holy Alliance and his mysticism or quasi-mysticism in general found no ready points of contact with the activities or the image of the reformer of Russia. It is undeniable that, as a person, Alexander I was very different from Peter I. Nevertheless, there was certainly no repudiation of the official cult of the first emperor. We know that, as

[137] I stated my views on Alexander I more fully in my already mentioned book on *A Parting of Ways*. See esp. the chapter on the reign of Alexander I, pp. 54–100.

[138] See particularly David Ransel, *The Politics of Catherinian Russia: The Panin Party* (New Haven, 1975).

grand duke, Alexander subscribed to Golikov's exposition of the reformer's acts;[139] that, as ruler, he was at times reminded of Peter the Great, his image, and the associated problems and criticisms. For example, in 1806 the monarch wrote as follows in a letter to his close associate, Admiral Paul Chichagov:

Can I help it that education in our country is still so far behind? And, until a need develops for parents to pay more attention to it, were I not to obtain aid from well-known foreigners of proven talent, the number of capable people, already so small, would diminish further to a considerable extent. What would Peter the First have done, had he not employed foreigners? At the same time I feel that this is an evil, but this evil is the lesser of the two, for can we postpone events until our nationals become masters of every function that they have to perform? I am saying all this only to demonstrate to you that at the present moment it is impossible to establish it as a principle not to employ foreigners.[140]

Beyond specific references, it is reasonable to assume that the image of the first emperor was generally present to those who governed Russia in the first quarter of the nineteenth century, as it had been in the eighteenth. That image was soon to be reemphasized again, as well as narrowed in scope, by another crowned worshipper of Peter the Great, Alexander's brother and successor, Nicholas I.

Like the ruling circles, the Russian educated public, including its more critical and oppositional members, continued to be interested in the reformer. This was notably true of the so-called Decembrist movement, which assembled for a period of years a considerable number of educated and able privileged young Russians trying to understand the nature and the historical course of their country and even to do something about it. Brought up in the Russian Enlightenment, future Decembrists encountered and often assimilated the Russian Enlightenment image of Peter the Great. But, frequently fluent in French and acquainted directly with the West, they also expressed splendidly in their ideas and actions the late Western Enlightenment and the momentous years of revolutionary thought and practice—and constitution-making—that followed the fall of the Bastille. Their own constitutions, as well as their rebellion, went, certainly, beyond any reliance on an enlightened despot, which, however, did not necessarily mean that the Decembrists turned against the man who had initiated change in Russia. As if the ideological and historical relations between the young revolutionaries and the first emperor were not already complex enough, they were further affected by the rising patriotic and national spirit in the Decembrist midst and by many individual circumstances of different members of the movement.

139 I am indebted for this information to Professor Gary Marker.

140 Quoted from N. K. Shilder (Schilder), *Imperator Aleksandr pervyi, ego zhizn i tsarstvovanie* (St. Petersburg, 1904), II, 351. This letter from one Russian to another concerning the need to employ foreigners was written in French.

In general, see Shmurlo, *Petr Velikii v russkoi literature*, 37–43, for the continuation of the Enlightenment image of Peter the Great in the reign of Alexander I.

The result was a complex and sometimes contradictory commentary on Peter the Great, his reign, and his historical role, with no specific evaluation shared by all members of the Decembrist movement. Still, certain patterns of judgment emerged. First and perhaps foremost, the Russian Enlightenment image of the reformer, light brought into darkness, progress replacing stagnation, reason conquering superstition, retained a powerful hold on the Decembrists. Many members of the group were enthusiastic admirers of the first emperor, their admiration exhibiting in certain cases a deeply personal and emotional character so often encountered among earlier Russian intellectuals. At the same time, some Decembrists at least also knew well what they were talking about. The historian of the historical views of the Decembrists, S. S. Volk, emphasized that two of his protagonists, Alexander Kornilovich (1800–1834), and Nicholas Bestuzhev (1791–1855), qualified as historians of the Petrine age.[141] Kornilovich collected historical materials and produced a series of articles and papers on such topics as "The First Balls in Russia," "Entertainment at the Russian Court under Peter I," and "Russian Manners at the Time of Peter the Great." In the well-established tradition, he depicted the first emperor in his daily life as a tireless worker, simple, and accessible to all. Interestingly, Kornilovich's study of Tsarevich Alexis—which has not come down to us—was denied publication, although the author had written it "to refute slander and to show that the judging of the tsarevich was alone sufficient for Peter's immortality."[142] Bestuzhev, a brilliant graduate of the naval cadet school and subsequently a teacher there for a number of years, was appointed in 1822 as the official historiographer of the Russian navy and assigned the task of writing its history. Broadly conceived and rich, that history remained, unfortunately, unfinished and largely unpublished.[143] Although devoted supporters of Peter the Great, Kornilovich and Bestuzhev were less rigid and narrow in their approach to Petrine history than, for example, Golikov. The painter of manners was concerned with the seventeenth century, as well as with the Petrine period, and can even be considered an early exponent of the idea of a transition from the one to the other rather than of a break between the two. His articles included a study entitled "Information about the Successes of Manufacturing in Russia and Especially in the Reign of Tsar Aleksei Mikhailovich." The naval historian, for his part, combined his firm allegiance to Peter the Great with realistic accounts of the tremendous burden of his reign, of unbearable taxes that made peasants escape to the borderlands, of the human costs of the building of St. Petersburg or of the navy in Voronezh, where mortality stopped construction.

[141] See the section on "Dekabristy o Petre I i ego preobrazovaniiakh. Otsenka osnovnykh sobytii russkoi istorii XVIII veka" in S. S. Volk, *Istoricheskie vzgliady dekabristov* (Moscow and Leningrad, 1958), 395–421, esp. pp. 395–413.
[142] Quoted from *ibid.*, 395. Kornilovich's articles were republished in A. O. Kornilovich, *Sochineniia i pisma* (Moscow and Leningrad, 1957), 148–203.
[143] In my comments on it, I am relying on Volk, *op. cit.*, 403–408.

Some other Decembrists took a generally negative view of the first emperor and his historical role, repeating most of the arguments of the earlier critics of the reformer, with special attention to the issue of tyranny, to the charge that the reformer was an enemy of freedom. Peter the Great was accused of being a barbarian, his actions characterized by cruelty and overall inhumanity. Imitative rather than creative, he inaugurated a process that led to a wholesale borrowing from the West of even useless and noxious things. Moreover, the Russian people had little or nothing to show for the effort: they had borne the entire cost of the new policies, but they remained serfs, ignorant, poverty-stricken, and legally unprotected. Even the military achievements of the Russian empire had to be tempered with the realization of the horrible condition and treatment of its soldiers, of which the Decembrists, as enlightened officers, were especially conscious. Most important, the reformer established a total tyranny, destroying the elements of freedom that had existed in Muscovy and bidding to bring everything and everyone under his complete control. The figure of Mazepa, so prominent in Conrad Ryleev's poetry, constituted one Decembrist protest against the tyranny.[144] That Peter the Great was a difficult and divisive subject among the Decembrists can be seen from the desperate efforts of some members of the group to form a balanced view of him, from major shifts of opinion of others, and, of course, from passionate arguments among the participants in the movement. When the Decembrist and prominent intellectual Nicholas Turgenev, who himself had switched from an overwhelming admiration of the reformer to a condemnation of him as a tyrant, made his attack, Nicholas Bestuzhev responded, "I am out of my mind in love with that tyrant."[145]

The Decembrist treatment of Peter the Great reflected the range of the Enlightenment opinion of the first Russian emperor and thus served as a fitting culmination and conclusion, logically as well as chronologically, to his depiction in Russia for over a century. Suggestive beyond its own time, it also indicated the ambivalence and difficulties that Russian radicals and revolutionaries were to experience repeatedly as they tried to take their measure of the remarkable reformer.

Whereas the bulk of the Decembrist criticism of Peter the Great was made from the point of view of the Enlightenment Left, Nicholas Karam-

144 On the complicated problem of Ryleev's Mazepa, see esp. A. E. Khodorov, "Ukrainskie siuzhety poezii K. F. Ryleeva," *Literaturnoe nasledie dekabristov*, edited by V. G. Bazanov and V. E. Vatsuro (Leningrad, 1975), 121–141. The following article in this useful joint volume is devoted to Kornilovich: I. Z. Serman, "Aleksandr Kornilovich kak istorik i pisatel," 142–164. For a different Decembrist approach to Mazepa, see Kornilovich's unfinished "Zhizneopisanie Mazepy" ("A Biography of Mazepa"): Kornilovich, *op. cit.*, 203–207.

145 Quoted from: Volk, *op. cit.*, 413. Nicholas Turgenev (1789–1871), too, did not adhere firmly to his negative view of Peter the Great, but rather kept returning in the course of his long life to a belief in the desirability of appropriate "Petrine" change for Russia; it was in that spirit that he welcomed Alexander II's "great reforms."

zin (1766–1826), a writer and a historian of the first rank in importance, became the major Russian critic of the reformer in the first quarter of the nineteenth century from the position of the new Right, largely disappointed in the Age of Reason and in the French Revolution associated with it. Karamzin's complaints bore strong resemblance to Shcherbatov's earlier lament.

The inaugurator of "sentimentalism" in Russian literature also came out of the Russian Enlightenment and, in fact, was one of its leading figures at the end of Catherine the Great's reign. Accordingly, until about the turn of the century, he accepted faithfully and completely the Russian Enlightenment image of the reformer, and he championed it both in general and in detail with his accustomed literary skill. In 1790, Karamzin wrote in his celebrated "Letters of a Russian Traveler":

In the center of a large square, adorned with dense paths and surrounded on all sides by splendid houses, stands a bronze statue of Louis XIV on a marble pedestal. This monument is of the same size as that of our Russian Peter, though these two heroes are hardly equal in greatness of soul and deeds. Louis' subjects made their ruler renowned; Peter made his subjects renowned. The former only partly furthered the progress of enlightenment; the latter appeared on man's horizon, like a radiant god of light, and dispelled the intense gloom around him. During Louis' reign thousands of industrious Frenchmen were obliged to leave their native land; Peter attracted accomplished and useful foreigners to his country. The former I respect as a strong ruler; the latter I revere as a great man, a hero, a benefactor of mankind, as my own benefactor!

At this time let me say that I consider it to have been a splendid, a matchless idea to place the statue of Peter the Great on rough-hewn stone, for this stone is a striking symbol of the condition of Russia before the time of its transformer. No less pleasing to me is the brief, forceful, and meaningful inscription: "To Peter the First / Catherine the Second." I did not read the inscription on the monument of the French king.[146]

Karamzin added, appropriately, "the lines in which the poet Thomson glorified our unforgettable emperor," who "His stubborn country tamed— her rocks, her fens / Her floods, her seas, her ill-submitting sons. . . . Then cities rise amid th'illumined waste." Indeed, in the words of Thomson: "What cannot active government perform / New-moulding man?"

Somewhat later in his travels, thinking of Levesque, whom he had just met, and of Levesque's *History of Russia*, which he considered defective but the best available, the Russian writer commented, "We had our Charlemagne—Vladimir; our Louis XI—Tsar Ivan; our Cromwell—Godunov; and in addition a sovereign unlike any other anywhere—Peter the

[146] N. M. Karamzin, *Letters of a Russian Traveler, 1789–1790*, translated and abridged by Florence Jonas (New York, 1957), 174–175. See my review of this English version in *The American Slavic and East European Review*, vol. XVII, no. 4 (December 1958), 545–546.

Great.''[147] Levesque and others were wrong in belittling the reformer, in condemning him as an imitator. Russia had to borrow from the West all kinds of things, big and small. Karamzin even produced a notable pragmatic defense of the cutting of beards.[148] The universal light of the Age of Reason made Peter the Great's role and policies perfectly clear and perfectly praiseworthy:

The Germans, French, and English were at least six centuries ahead of the Russians. Peter moved us with his mighty hand, and in a few years we have almost caught up with them. All the doleful jeremiads about the change in the Russian character, the loss of the Russian moral physiognomy, are either nothing but jesting or proceed from unsound thinking. We are not like our bearded ancestors—so much the better! Outer and inner coarseness, ignorance, laziness, boredom were the lot of even those in the highest ranks. All paths to refining the mind and satisfying the noble spirit were opened to us. The purely national is nothing next to the all-human. The main thing is to be human beings, not Slavs. Whatever is good for all mankind can not be bad for Russians, and whatever the English or Germans have invented for the use and benefit of man is mine, for I am a man![149]

And as late as 1798, Karamzin was planning a panegyric to Peter the Great, which, however, he never produced.[150]

147 Karamzin, *Letters* . . . , 218.
148 *Ibid.*, 220:

A beard belongs to the state of savagery. Not to shave is the same as not paring one's nails. A beard protects only a small part of the face from the cold, and how uncomfortable it is in the summertime when it is very hot! How uncomfortable in winter, too, to carry around frost, snow, and icicles on one's face! Is it not better to have a fur collar, which warms not only the chin but the entire face as well? To select the best in all things is the mark of an enlightened mind. And Peter the Great wanted to enlighten the mind in all respects. Our sovereign declared war on our ancient customs, firstly, because they were coarse, unworthy of his age, and secondly, because they hindered the introduction of other foreign innovations, even more important and more useful. It was necessary to wring the neck, as it were, of the ingrained Russian obstinacy, to make us flexible, capable of learning and of borrowing.

149 *Ibid.*, 220–221.
150 Karamzin not only praised the first emperor repeatedly, but also followed very closely the shifts in the form of the official cult. He greeted Paul I's accession to the throne in 1796 with an ode, which proclaimed: "Peter the First was the beginning of everything; / But with Paul the First there arose shining / In Russia the happiness of people. / Forever, forever inseparable, / Forever will be revered / These two names of tsars!" (N. M. Karamzin, "Oda na sluchai prisiagi moskovskikh zhitelei Ego Imperatorskomu Velichestvu Pavlu Pervomu, Samoderzhtsu Vserossiiskomu," *Polnoe sobranie stikhotvorenii* [Moscow and Leningrad, 1966], 185–190, quoted from p. 189). When Paul I's overthrow and murder in 1801 separated the two names, Karamzin reacted by writing an ode to the accession of the new ruler, Alexander I, and joined in the general acclaim of the new sovereign and reign. Catherine the Great returned as part of the imperial cult, and Paul I disappeared. Karamzin composed "A Historical Laudatory Oration to Empress Catherine II" and observed the revised table of ranks with reference to the reformer: "The name of *Peter* and of *Catherine* will forever shine at the head of the history of reason and enlightenment in Russia; but what they could not accomplish, that is being done by Alexander, who has the happiness of reigning after them, and in the nineteenth century. Heaven left for *him* the glory and the oppor-

A combination of interrelated factors led to a transformation of Karamzin's opinion of the first Russian emperor and of that emperor's historical role. Extremely important, although elusive, was the already-mentioned phenomenon of wounded national pride, which made it increasingly difficult for educated Russians—and many other educated Europeans—to accept foreign cultural leadership and to be satisfied with imitation, no matter how successful. A matter of vanity and personal pique on one level, it suggested, more deeply, a breakdown in the universal standards and cosmopolitan ideology of the Enlightenment. Karamzin, as we just saw, met the national challenge head on, but in the long run it proved to be too powerful. The French Revolution and the reign of Napoleon also raised major questions as to what the Age of Reason really meant and where it led. Karamzin has frequently been cited as the outstanding example of the reaction of Russian intellectuals against the momentous events in France, and in general this treatment of him is correct, provided one remembers that even the sharpest turnings usually leave much of a person's intellectual past intact. Moreover, Karamzin became a historian. Interested in history for many years and deploring the fact that the Russian historical record had not been effectively presented, he decided in 1803 to dedicate himself thenceforth to Russian history. Granted by the government the title and the salaried position of historiographer, Karamzin abandoned other activities and devoted the rest of his life, until he died in the middle of his historical work in late spring 1826, to his monumental, but graceful and most readable, *History of the Russian State* (*Istoriia gosudarstva rossiiskogo*). Eight volumes of that *History* came out in 1816; the ninth, in 1821; and the tenth and the eleventh, in 1824; finally, the twelfth volume appeared posthumously in 1826. Karamzin was, thus, both writing history and reacting to recent and contemporary developments when in the second half of his creative life he came to pass a novel judgment on Peter the Great.

Unfortunately, Karamzin's magnum opus—like Shcherbatov's history, which served Karamzin as an important source—never reached Peter the Great, ending abruptly in the Time of Troubles. (In the sixth volume there was a brief comparison between Ivan III and Peter the Great favorable to the former.) The historian, however, did present a summary account of his new views on the reformer and the reformer's impact on Russia in the historical introduction of his major piece of political writing, "A Memoir on Ancient and Modern Russia," a private memorandum which he submitted in 1810 for Alexander I's attention.

At this point Peter appeared. In his childhood, the license of the lords, the impudence of the *streltsy,* and the ambition of Sophia had reminded Russia of the unhappy times of boyar troubles. But deep inside of him the youth already had

---

tunity of crowning their immortal work" (*Vestnik Evropy*, no. 5, March 1803; quoted from p. 51).

the makings of a great man, and he seized hold of the helm of state with a mighty hand. He strove toward his destination through storms and billows. He reached it—and everything changed! . . .

Posterity has praised passionately this immortal sovereign for his personal merits as well as for his glorious achievements. He was magnanimous and perspicacious; he had an unshakable will, vigor, and a virtually inexhaustible supply of energy. He reorganized and increased the army, he achieved a brilliant victory over a skillful and courageous enemy, he conquered Livonia, he founded the fleet, built ports, promulgated many wise laws, improved commerce and mining, established factories, schools, the academy, and, finally, he won for Russia a position of eminence in the political system of Europe. And speaking of his magnificent gifts, shall we forget the gift that is perhaps the most important of all in an autocrat: that of knowing how to use people according to their ability?[151]

Still, there was no need for Russians to follow ignorant foreigners and proclaim the first emperor the founder of Russian political greatness:

Shall we forget the princes of Moscow, Ivan I, Ivan III, who may be said to have built a powerful state out of nothing, and—what is of equal importance—to have established in it firm monarchical authority? Peter found the means to achieve greatness—the foundation for it had been laid by the Moscow princes.[152]

Moreover, Peter the Great's glorious reign had its pernicious side:

Let us not go into his personal vices. But his passion for foreign customs surely exceeded the bounds of reason. Peter was unable to realize that the national spirit constitutes the moral strength of states, which is as indispensable to their stability as is physical might. This national spirit, together with the faith, had saved Russia in the days of the Pretenders. It is nothing else than respect for our national dignity. By uprooting ancient customs, by exposing them to ridicule, by causing them to appear stupid, by praising and introducing foreign elements, the sovereign of the Russians humbled Russian hearts. Does humiliation predispose a man and a citizen to great deeds? The love of the fatherland is bolstered by those national peculiarities that the cosmopolite considers harmless, and thoughtful statesmen beneficial. Enlightenment is commendable, but what does it consist of? The knowledge of things that bring prosperity; arts, crafts, and sciences have no other value. The Russian dress, food, and beards did not inter- fere with the founding of schools. Two states may stand on the same level of civil enlightenment although their customs differ. One state may borrow from another useful knowledge without borrowing its manners. These manners may change naturally, but to prescribe statutes for them is an act of violence, which is illegal also for an autocratic monarch. The people, in their original covenant with the king, had told them: "Guard our safety abroad and at home, punish criminals, sacrifice a part to save the whole." They had not said: "Fight the

151 *Karamzin's Memoir on Ancient and Modern Russia,* a translation and analysis by Richard Pipes (New York, 1966), quoted from pp. 120–121. The section on Peter the Great occupies pp. 120–127. See also Professor Pipes's perceptive essay on "The Back- ground and Growth of Karamzin's Political Ideas down to 1810," 3–92.

152 *Ibid.,* 121. Note how creation "out of nothing" is here shifted to earlier Muscovite rulers.

innocent inclinations and tastes of our domestic life." In this realm, the sovereign may equitably act only by example, not by decree.

Human life is short, and the rooting of new customs takes time. Peter confined his reform to the gentry. Until his reign all Russians, from the plow to the throne, had been alike insofar as they shared certain features of external appearance and of customs. After Peter, the higher classes separated themselves from the lower ones, and the Russian peasant, burgher, and merchant began to treat the Russian gentry as Germans, thus weakening the spirit of brotherly national unity binding the estates of the realm.[153]

The reformer abolished glorious and revered old titles and institutions, replacing them with foreign ones, which made no sense to his people. "Imitation became for Russians a matter of honor and pride."[154] Family customs changed, and family links declined. Reformed Russians excelled their ancestors in knowledge and in some ways even in morality.

However, it must be admitted that what we gained in social virtues we lost in civic virtues. Does the name of a Russian carry for us today the same inscrutable force that it had in the past? No wonder. In the reigns of Michael and of his son, our ancestors, while assimilating many advantages that were to be found in foreign customs, never lost the conviction that an Orthodox Russian was the most perfect citizen and *Holy Rus* the foremost state in the world. Let this be called a delusion. Yet how much it did to strengthen patriotism and the moral fibre of the country! Would we have today the audacity, after having spent over a century in the school of foreigners, to boast of our civic pride? Once upon a time we used to call all other Europeans *infidels;* now we call them brothers. For whom was it easier to conquer Russia—for *infidels* or for *brothers?* That is, whom was she likely to resist better? Was it conceivable in the reigns of Michael and Fedor for a Russian lord, who owed everything to his fatherland, gaily to abandon his tsar forever in order to sit in Paris, London, or Vienna and calmly read in newspapers of the perils confronting our country? We became citizens of the world but ceased in certain respects to be the citizens of Russia. The fault is Peter's.

He was undeniably great. But he could have exalted himself still higher, had he found the means to enlighten Russians without corrupting their civic virtues.[155]

. . . without trying to transform Russia into Holland. Opposition led to repression:

The Secret Chancery of the Preobrazhenskoe operated day and night. Tortures and executions were the means used to accomplish our country's celebrated reform. Many perished for no other crime than the defense of the honor of Russian caftans and beards, which they refused to give up, and for the sake of which they dared to reproach the monarch. These unfortunates felt that by depriving them of their ancient habits Peter was depriving them of the fatherland itself.[156]

[153] *Ibid.,* 121–122.
[154] *Ibid.,* 123.
[155] *Ibid.,* 123–124.
[156] *Ibid.,* 124.

Jealously protecting his unlimited autocracy, Peter the Great abolished the patriarchate and brought the church under his control, although it had never bid for power but represented simply an independent moral voice; subordinated and in part secularized, the church lost much of its authority among the people, depriving the country of a valuable resource in time of crisis. Yet another "glaring mistake" of Peter the Great was "his founding a new capital on the northern frontier of the state, amid muddy billows, in places condemned by nature to barrenness and want . . . Truly, Petersburg is founded *on tears and corpses.*"[157]

Still and all, there could be no turning back:

But a great man demonstrates his greatness with his very errors. They are diffi-cult, if not impossible, to undo, for he creates the good and the bad alike for-ever. Russia was launched on her new course with a mighty hand; we shall never return to bygone times![158]

In particular, the Supreme Secret Council, or any other kind of oligarchy, was not a viable alternative:

And could Russia at this time have dispensed with monarchy, after she had changed her time-sanctioned customs, and undergone internal disorders as a re-sult of her new, important reforms, which, by dissociating the customs of the gentry from those of the people, had weakened spiritual authority? Autocracy became more essential than ever for the preservation of order.[159]

Eight years later in an address to the Russian Academy, Karamzin re-turned to the topic of the irreversibility of the change produced by Peter the Great, this time in the field closest to the speaker, Russian literature:

Having transformed the fatherland with his mighty arm, Peter the Great made us similar to other Europeans. Complaints are useless. The link between the minds of the ancient and of the modern Russians was cut forever. We do not want to imitate foreigners, but we do write as they write: because we live, as they live; we read, what they read; we have the same models of intellect and taste; we participate in the general, reciprocal drawing together of peoples, which is a result of their enlightenment itself. *Particular* beautiful qualities, which constitute the nature of the literature *of a people,* cede to general beau-tiful qualities; the first change, the second are eternal. It is good to write for Russians: it is better still to write for all human beings.[160]

And yet the orator's elegant and cadenced declaration apparently did not quite resolve the issue of imitativeness or that of a national literature. In any case, Karamzin proceeded to assert that the concept of "soulless imi-tation" did not apply where an author's own mind or heart was truly en-

157 *Ibid.,* 126.
158 *Ibid.,* 127.
159 *Ibid.*
160 N. M. Karamzin, "Rech, proiznesennaia na torzhestvennom sobranii Imperatorskoi Rossiiskoi Akademii 5 dekabraia 1818 goda," *Izbrannye sochineniia* (Moscow and Lenin-grad, 1964), vol. II, 233–242, quoted from p. 238.

gaged, even if he used the common language of his time. Moreover, Karamzin continued, certain national elements remained after Peter the Great, whether because he had not wanted to destroy them all or because he could not. Russian literature, thus, expressed some "sounds of the Russian heart," a certain "play of the Russian mind," distinctive, if elusive, characteristics, while forming at the same time a part of general European literature.

Like Shcherbatov, Karamzin lamented what he considered to be a tragic decline of Russian private morals and especially civic virtue as a result of the change—Westernization, if you will—introduced into the country by Peter the Great. The transformation, the critics contended, went too fast and too far, thus unsettling the moral equilibrium of the Russians. The weakness of the critique consisted in the facts that its authors themselves belonged entirely to the Russian Enlightenment and that they had little or nothing new to offer as a counterweight to the well-established positions, values, and advantages of the Petrine cult. Karamzin deserves full credit for wrestling honestly with the problems of the Petrine progress and its dangers, in particular in the fields dearest to him, Russian literature and Russian education in general. Yet it is certainly a far-reaching reflection on the intellectual climate of the time that that champion of autocracy, the gentry, and tradition, eventually something of a patron saint of the Russian Right, was a lover of the republican form of government—under ideal, not Russian, conditions—and assailed Peter the Great in the name of the "bounds of reason" and even of the correct reading of the alleged original compact between a ruler and his people. Still and to conclude, one should not underestimate Karamzin. He surmounted his own original unquestioning admiration to launch a serious moral and historical critique of the Petrine reform, and he, as a writer of Russian history, as well as many of his specific opinions, became influential in a different intellectual climate with subsequent generations of educated Russians, even when the more perceptive of the latter were quick to realize that Karamzin, although interesting and useful, had in fact belonged to a different ideological world.

## A Note on Popular Images of Peter the Great

The ideology of the Enlightenment and the Russian Enlightenment image of Peter the Great dominated the thought of the Russian educated public for over a century. The image and its domination were, however, coterminous with modern education. The great bulk of the Russian people knew none of it, remaining totally unaware of such interesting developments as Voltaire's evaluation of the reformer or even the Catherinian formulation of the Russian Age of Reason. Yet that huge mass of people produced, elaborated, and carried its own image, or rather images, of Peter the Great, as well it might, for it had served, after all, as the ubiquitous chief protagonist of the first emperor's reign. Nevertheless, there is little point in putting together, either synthetically or dialectically, the Petrine images of the Russian educated public and those of the people, because they do not combine. Although contacts between the two worlds obviously did exist, as when a leading intellectual of the reign, Metropolitan Stephen Iavorskii, wrote against the Old Believers or, more broadly, when the monarch himself and his immediate associates rallied common soldiers and led them into battle, they were remarkably restricted in nature.[161] More important still, even when joined in one way or another, the two sides were activated by different beliefs and values. Some investigators have complained that the Russian masses, the peasants, were more upset by the sovereign's Western dress or smoking than by his continuous demand for an almost superhuman exertion and even death—an inconclusive criticism because the educated classes have not solved the problem of death either, but a good indication of different orientations. Even in form the two worlds were far apart. Oral literature as a genre, more exactly, a series of genres, ranged from historical and realistic description to legends and fairy tales, where Peter the Great might have simply been substituted for Ivan the Terrible or for some magical figure of folk imagination. The precise relevance of a given reference to the first Russian emperor is often impossible to establish. All this does not deny the importance of popular literature on Peter the Great as on other significant topics; it only indicates that it is a separate subject. In this study devoted to the educated public, popular literature is mentioned simply to remind the reader of its contemporaneous existence and, very summarily, of what it had to offer on Peter the Great.

Whereas it took the Russian educated public, as represented by its leading critics Shcherbatov and Karamzin, seventy-five or a hundred years to produce a comprehensive negative evaluation of Peter the Great and his impact on Russia, that evaluation remaining even then ambivalent and strongly qualified and contradicted by its authors' enormous appreciation of the reformer and his work, popular condemnation appeared immediately. Nor should this be surprising: Russian intellectuals had to overcome their own origin in the Petrine reform and the ideology that they largely shared with the first emperor to pronounce decisive judgment against him; the Russian people had no such problem. More than that, as Peter I made his bid to change Russia, one of his major relationships to the unreformed masses—there were other major relationships between the two sides, to be sure, and some of them will be mentioned later in this note—became that of direct antagonism. I emphasized the hatred of

161 I discussed the gulf between the Russian masses, overwhelmingly peasants, and the Russian educated public in Nicholas V. Riasanovsky, "Afterword: The Problem of the Peasant," *The Peasant in Nineteenth-Century Russia*, edited by Wayne S. Vucinich (Stanford, Calif., 1968), 263–284, 306–307. The entire volume is a useful introduction in English to the world of the Russian peasant.

the old, which inspired Peter the Great and many of his associates. Some of the popular response to the reformer returned that hatred with interest. And, as Soviet specialists always remind us, Russia remained a class state with its exploited and largely enserfed population unlikely to rival Sumarokov or Derzhavin in singing hosannas to the Petrine and post-Petrine order of things. Popular opposition and popular rebellions in Peter the Great's reign and later in the century emphasized the point.

Already by the year 1700 and the turn of the century, a legend emerged, with the government trying to extirpate it, that Peter I on the Russian throne was not the true Peter I, but a substitute and, apparently, an un-Russian and evil one. K. V. Chistov[162] and others, attempting to trace the circumstantial origins of this view, cited the sovereign's early avoidance of state affairs and frequent absences, the prominence of foreigners around the ruler, his blasphemous, quasi-ritualistic debauchery, his constant preference for subordinate roles while leaving center stage to Lefort or other associates, a practice baffling to the popular imagination, the unprecedented and mystifying voyage abroad, when the monarch was not listed in his own name in the traveling party and thus, in effect, vanished from the earth abandoning his tsardom, his precipitous return and most violent punishment of the *streltsy*, and so forth. At least three fundamental versions of the legend, with numerous variants, have been recorded: the substitution took place in Peter I's infancy, in fact in the usual variant immediately after birth; the substitution occurred "beyond the seas"; and, the Antichirst substituted himself for Peter I. In the first version, the ruling monarch was most commonly presented as Lefort's son, with the elucidation that Tsar Alexis had demanded a son, and when his wife gave birth to a daughter instead, she exchanged her secretly for a boy born in the Lefort household—incidentally, an impressive way to explain Lefort's special position in the new reign. In the second, the emphasis was on true Peter I's imprisonment abroad, sometimes in a barrel thrown into the sea, and the substitution of a foreign prince to rule Russia. In the third version, the Antichrist had different ways of appearing: in some variants from the beginning, but in others when the true Peter I, who had been on the throne during the earlier part of the reign, was doing penance for his persecution of Old Believers and other sins while buried in a grave. Whatever the version, Holy Russia was ruled, in effect, either by a heretical foreigner or by the Antichrist himself. Utilizing published sources alone, Chistov found for the years 1700–1722 over thirty separate recordings of the substitution legend, coming from different groups of the

---

[162] K. V. Chistov, *Russkie narodnye sotsialnoutopicheskie legendy XVII–XIX vekov* (Moscow, 1967), esp. pp. 96–109. The book is a fascinating, if highly controversial, examination of the Russian popular mind. As one critique of Chistov, see Haruki Wada, "The Inner World of Russian Peasants," *Annals of the Institute of Social Science* (University of Tokyo, 1979), no. 20, 61–94.

Russian population and extending territorially from the far north to the Don and the Ukraine and from Pskov to Siberia.[163]

The identification of Peter the Great as the Antichrist had a touch of genius. For a time at least, it fitted the apocalyptic world vision of the Old Believers as well as his definition as the model enlightened despot suited the proponents of the Russian Enlightenment, and it was equally ably developed. Neither concept, to be sure, was invented for the first Russian emperor, but mutatis mutandis he became a marvelous incarnation of each one. The doctrine of Antichrist goes back to the early years of Christianity; it acquired a new importance in Russia with the major and tragic Old Believer split from the established Orthodox Church in the third quarter of the seventeenth century. For the persecuted Old Believers, Patriarch Nikon and Tsar Alexis had already served as Antichrists before Peter I ascended the throne.[164] In the absence of the reformer, other crowned Antichrists could also probably have been found, but almost certainly not as compelling as the first emperor. It was not so much what the new ruler did to the Old Believers: cruelty and persecution continued, and in the last part of his reign the monarch apparently decided that Old Belief was fundamentally incompatible with his reformed state, but he also proclaimed religious tolerance at one point and imposed special taxes and fines on a large scale rather than more drastic measures. It was rather what Peter I came to represent in their vision of the true faith, Russia, and the world.[165]

The sovereign's unusual, mighty, and striking appearance itself suggested evil power. The foreign dress, the smoking, the novel drinking and eating habits, the pointed clipped whiskers, "like those of a cat," the new uniforms introduced everywhere had something satanic in them. Foreigners were ever-present. The cutting of beards—so recently denounced not only by the Old Believers, but also by Patriarch Hadrian—was a clear violation of the image of God in man, a catastrophic sacrilege. The magic

---

[163] Chistov, *op. cit.*, 99–100. For another stimulating treatment of the perception of Peter the Great as Antichrist, see B. A. Uspenskii, "Historia sub specie semioticae," *Kulturnoe nasledie drevnei Rusi: istoki, stanovlenie traditsii* (Moscow, 1976), 286–292.

[164] Peter I was, of course, Tsar Alexis's son, and the Old Believers were quick to note that he had been born in 1672, that is, six years after the decisive break between them and the established church, and thus after divine grace and legitimacy had departed from the holders of the Russian throne. But there was even a version that Peter I was really the son of Patriarch Nikon, enemy number one of Old Belief. For the present-day existence of that version, see Michael Cherniavsky, "The Old Believers and the New Religion," *Slavic Review*, vol. XXV, no. 1 (March 1966), 1–39, specifically p. 29, fn. 122.

[165] Old Belief, which I am summarizing here so briefly, was divided from the start and proceeded to splinter throughout its history. Usually its various groupings are defined precisely by the extent to which they rejected the state and the established religious forms and practices. At the extreme, Old Believers burned themselves to death in mass conflagrations to escape the sinful world and the Antichrist, and that occurred on a large scale in Peter I's reign. A recurrent issue in scholarship is what wing or how much of the Old Belief a given depiction of the reformer represents.

ruler stole time from God as he changed the calendar and began the year in January, and, similarly, he introduced a new script instead of the old one in which all church books had been written. He brought heretical Western learning into Russia. He sent his lawful wife to a convent and lived with a *chukhonka,* a local Finnic inhabitant, without the benefit of church sacrament. He killed his son. Above all, he extended his control to everything, branding his soldiers—a true mark of the Beast—and "obtaining the number," that is, census data for taxation, from the entire population of Holy Russia. He abolished the patriarchate and took direct command of the church itself. His pagan classical festivals (with "crowns of thorns," i.e. laurel wreaths, which also appeared as part of the ruler's image on his coins) presented him as a divinity and parodied the true religion, whereas his drunken and debauched rites spoke directly of the devil. The convincing picture was filled in with very rich, further, factual detail, elucidated, where necessary, with countless calculations of the number of the Antichrist, 666—mainly by adding the numerical values of letters of names and titles connected with the ruler—and with relevant sacred texts. The Old Believers had no difficulty explaining the first emperor's victories on the battlefield and other successes, for the Antichrist, supported by magic and the forces of hell, was indeed bound to prevail until the final climax. And the Antichrist in the main Christian tradition, it must be emphasized, was not an abstract concept or a void, nor, on the other hand, simply a savage destructive creature, but a very close imitation and caricature of Christ the ruler of the world. His realm was a satanic perversion of the divine order of things. It is this perversion that the Old Believers saw as they looked around and compared Petrine Russia to their idealized image of Muscovy before the time of Peter I or, more precisely, before the time of Nikon—the reformer's blasphemous drunken rites to holy liturgy.

Apocalyptic visions are hard to maintain because the apocalypse has not materialized so far. Yet Old Belief demonstrated a remarkable staying power or, perhaps better, a power of revival throughout the eighteenth century and beyond.[166] The image of Peter the Great as the Antichrist lived on with it. Shmurlo paid detailed attention to such documents as the writings of the fugitive soldier and founder of the sect of runners, Euthymius, Evfimii (1743–1792), including his "Commentary on the Sermons of Hippolyte, the Pope of Rome, concerning the Antichrist" and "About the Ill-fated Last Days and the Signs of Antichrist," where Peter the Great was presented as the third and final Antichrist following Apollyon, who came to rule "the Greek tsardom" in A.D. 1000, and Nikon, who manifested himself 666 years later; to a further development of these views in a passionate pamphlet entitled "The Tale of Antichrist, Who is

---

[166] In English, for some important aspects of Old Belief, see Robert O. Crummey, *The Old Believers and the World of Antichrist: The Vyg Community and the Russian State, 1694–1855* (Madison, Milwaukee and London, 1970).

Peter I"; to Basil Moskvin's "Disquisition of a Wanderer of Tiumen," composed around the 1820s, where the Antichrist appeared in the persons of Tsar Alexis, Patriarch Nikon, and Arsenius the Greek, a strange figure connected with the Nikonian correction of religious texts and practices, which led to the Old Believer split, and was renewed in the person of Peter I, who assumed the telltale title of emperor.[167] The Old Believers interpreted the history of imperial Russia from their own point of view, condemning especially such developments as reigns of women or the erection of *The Bronze Horseman*, an example of a bid for divinity and of idolatry characteristic of the Antichrist. The distinguished specialist in Russian literature and social thought A. N. Pypin published a striking account of "Peter the Great as Antichrist, among the Old Believers," based largely on the cases of the Preobrazhenskii prikaz, Peter I's police, and extending beyond the reformer's reign.[168] P. P. Basnin, in his "Old Believer Legends about Peter the Great," told a remarkable tale of an encounter with Old Believers in the last part of the nineteenth century, over two hundred years after the reformer's birth. The stunning climax comes when the narrator—and the reader—suddenly realizes that his intelligent and able interlocutor is firmly convinced that the true Peter I, who was displaced by the Antichrist, served his penance in the grave and was saved miraculously when he confronted his satanic double, remains under divine protection alive and in hiding, apparently among Old Believers, to reappear at the right time and claim back his own. Other scholars added equally useful, and occasionally even equally gripping, information.[169]

Still, one has to remember that the popular evaluation of Peter the Great was not confined, even in its negative aspects, to the image of the Antichrist. That image, to come back to where we began, was merely one of the three main versions of the substitution legend. The other two, Lefort's son and an intruder from abroad, though in no sense complimentary, at least did not point directly to the prince of darkness. Nor was the Preobrazhenskii prikaz preoccupied only with the Antichrist charge or exclusively with the Old Believers. Obviously, criticism of the reformer and opposition to him had a broader base.[170] Repeated efforts of some

---

167 Shmurlo, *Petr Velikii* . . . , has as its second chapter, "Glas naroda" ("The Voice of the People"), 13–30, popular evaluations of Peter the Great; the reference here is particularly to pp. 19–24.

168 "Petr kak antikhrist, u raskolnikov" constitutes the first part of A. Pypin, "Petr Velikii v narodnom predanii" ("Peter the Great in the Popular Tradition"), *Vestnik Evropy*, St. Petersburg, Year XXXII, Book 8 (August 1897), 640–690.

169 P. P. Basnin, "Raskolnichi legendy o Petre Velikom," *Istoricheskii Vestnik* (St. Petersburg, 1903), vol. XCII, 513–548. For the latest example of the Old Believer denunciation of Peter the Great, see Serge Schmemann, "Deep in Siberia, 3 Centuries of Faith in God," *The New York Times*, November 30, 1982, pp. 1, 7.

170 A major work on the Preobrazhenskii prikaz and its activities is N. B. Golikova, *Politicheskie protsessy pri Petre I. Po materialam Preobrazhenskogo prikaza* (Moscow, 1957).

scholars to reduce the popular critics of the first emperor to Old Believers have, on the whole, failed. At the same time most historians remain convinced that the Petrine program was imposed by a small minority on the reluctant or hostile masses. That reluctance and hostility were
bound to find a rich expression in the popular views of Peter the Great.
Chistov has made the interesting point that the reformer was never pictured as a peasant tsar, one of those recurrent would-be saviors who were
to abolish serfdom and establish justice and well-being in the land. No
pretender ever claimed his name; no popular movement or rebellion
used it as its banner. By contrast—and indeed in direct opposition to the
image of the first emperor—there emerged saviors and pretenders bearing
the name of Aleksei Petrovich, that is, Tsarevich Alexis. The first appeared in 1724, still during the reformer's lifetime. There were at least
six altogether, active at the time of the first emperor's death and especially in the period 1731–1738.[171]

Popular criticism of Peter the Great also found some remarkable pic-
torial representation. Much of that referred, again, to the Antichrist and,
in fact, served as illustrations to the polemical texts of the Old Believers.[172] Other examples, however, can be best described as broad popular satire, and some of these, it would seem, had a wide and continous
appeal.

That was notably true of the celebrated popular print "How the Mice
Were Burying the Cat," which appeared in uncounted editions and a
number of variants over, apparently, a very long period of time.[173] The
picture represents a funeral procession, arranged in four rows or levels,
of some one hundred mice accompanying a disproportionately huge cat
lying on a sled to its resting place. It was only toward the end of the
nineteenth century that D. A. Rovinskii convincingly deciphered the
meaning of the print, utilizing both the picture itself and the abundant
captions, as a satire on Peter the Great.[174] The late cat, Brys or Alabrys,
had been obviously a personage of major importance, and the descriptive
formula applied to it mentions Kazan, Astrakhan, and Siberia in the sequence well-known from the title of the Russian rulers. The departed expired in the same season and on the same days of the month and of the

---

171 Chistov, *op. cit.*, 113–124.

172 See esp. the thirteen marvelous illustrations to Professor Cherniavsky's already-
mentioned article. Figure 7, for example, pictures the Antichrist in the body of Peter
the Great and the uniform of the Preobrazhenskii regiment together with the Antichrist's wife and the Antichrist's baby, who is a carbon copy of his father in appearance and dress, although reduced in size and without the pointed whiskers.

173 For a more accessible, although a little too small, reproduction, see *Istoriia russkogo iskusstva*, edited by I. E. Grabar, V. S. Kemenov, and V. N. Lazarev (Moscow,
1960), vol. V, 411. A large-size reproduction can be found, for example, at the end of
I. Golyshev, *Lubochnaia starinnaia kartinka: "myshi kota pogrebaiut" nekotorye
prezhnie narodnye graviury* (Vladimir, 1878).

174 D. A. Rovinskii, *Russkie narodnye kartinki* (2 vols. in 1, St. Petersburg, 1900), I,
251–271, reproductions on pp. 256, 258, 262. The work was originally published in
1881.

week as Peter I. And there is a reference to a widow, *"chukhonka,* admiral's wife Malania."　The cortege of mice both celebrates the momentous event and reflects the first emperor's reformed Russia. Celebrate they well might, for the deceased had been of a severe character: "when he was among the living, he used to swallow an entire little mouse in one gulp." As to new Russia, the picture satirizes shaving, smoking, dancing, new ways of drinking, a cabriolet (a kind of carriage forbidden before the reformer's time but favored by the reformer), music in the funeral procession—introduced in fact first in Russia at Lefort's funeral and used at that of the sovereign himself. Unfortunately, some members of the funeral party cannot dance all they want because they are cripples or invalids, a likely reference to the cat's martial reign. Moreover, certain mice may represent particular associates of the first emperor, that is, Stephen Iavorskii and the monarch's agent in Balkan affairs, Savva Raguzinskii. Such other specific items, cited in the captions, as the making of the bast shoes and certain geographic nomenclature again seem to refer to the reformer. But even more striking than the rich detail is the effective execution of the overall satirical conception—or perhaps even two conceptions: a parody both of the Russia of Peter the Great and of his own blasphemous parodying of the religious ritual.

Still, hostility and denunciation by no means exhausted the attitude of the Russian people toward Peter the Great. For one thing, even the extreme Old Believer condemnation of the reformer was in a sense ambivalent, corresponding to the ambivalence of the first emperor's position in Russian history: a direct successor to Muscovite rulers and Muscovy, yet a sovereign who turned violently against much of his own past. This ambivalence was reflected, for example, by those Old Believers who professed full allegiance to Peter as tsar, but not as emperor—a title specifically connected to the Antichrist (in fact, from the times of Nero and Caligula). It found expression in the strange legend of two Peters, the authentic one and his satanic double, which we have already encountered more than once. The real Peter of that story, one may recall, had sinned and persecuted Old Believers, but redeemed himself through penance while buried in a grave; he and the impostor looked exactly alike. Related sentiments inspired a touching prayer by a certain simple woman, Alena Efimova, who begged God, all heavenly powers, and even the entire universe that the persecution of the Old Believers stop and all Russian Christians be reunited:

Hear me, holy catholic church with the entire altar of the cherubim and with the gospel and every holy word in that gospel—all remember our tsar Petr Alekseevich. Hear me, holy, catholic, and apostolic church, with all the local icons and honored small images, with all the apostolic books and censers, and with local candles, and the holy shrouds, with stone walls and with iron boards, with different kinds of fruitbearing trees. . . . Oh, I beg you also, beautiful sun, pray to the Heavenly Tsar for Tsar Petr Alekseevich! Oh, young bright crescent moon with the stars! Oh, the sky with the clouds! Oh, mighty clouds with storms and whirlwinds! Oh, birds of the sky and of the earth! Oh, the blue sea, with rivers and minor springs and small lakes! Start praying to the Heavenly Tsar for Tsar Petr Alekseevich, and the fish of the sea, and the cattle of the field, and the animals of the forest, and the fields, and all that comes out of the earth, start praying to the Heavenly Tsar for Tsar Petr Alekseevich![175]

Interestingly, the author of this prayer was married to an apparently rather extreme Old Believer, who rejected icons, whereas she herself belonged in a sense to both worlds, crossing herself with two rather than three fingers, but attending Orthodox church services and trying to promote the praying for Tsar Petr Alekseevich through the Orthodox Church.

Moreover—and now we are turning to the opposite side of the folk perception of Peter the Great—many of the popular sources on the first emperor, far from condemning him or even trying to redeem him and praying for him, take a distinctly approbative view of the ruler and his work. True, no popular positive image emerged to challenge in comprehensiveness and power the figure of the Antichrist. Affirmative depictions of the remarkable tsar were usually limited to some aspect of his activity or even to an incident or a series of incidents. They are no less authentic for all that and should be given their full weight. Attempts to downgrade them by presenting them as instances of specific approval within the framework of a general condemnation are unsupported by evidence—for usually there is no criticism attached to the praise—and unconvincing psychologically.[176]

One area where Peter the Great stood out as a hero from the beginning and forever after was war:

> The action was at Poltava,
> A glorious action, friends.
> We were then fighting the Swede
> Under Peter's banners.

Not only soldiers' songs, but all kinds of popular tales and legends reflected Petrine military events basically in the positive sense.[177] In addition to the usual, and certainly eventual, victory, accounts often stressed the sovereign's personal participation and his closeness to common soldiers. In the "glorious action" of Poltava, "our great emperor" flew "like a hawk" in front of the regiments, himself used a soldier's rifle, himself loaded a cannon.

[175] Pypin, *op. cit.*, 665.

[176] At the other extreme, it has even been claimed that all popular opinion of Peter the Great was positive, save for "religious fanatics." That approach runs the risk of proving either too little or too much: too little, because popular criticism of the reformer extended beyond Old Belief; too much, if "religious fanatics" is to encompass Russian people of that age in general.

[177] A. F. Nekrylova, "Predaniia i legendy, otrazivshie voennye sobytiia petrovskogo vremeni," *Russkaia narodnaia proza. Russkii folklor* (Leningrad, 1972), vol. XIII, 103–110.

A related and overlapping, but also a distinct, focus of popular approval and appreciation of the first emperor centered on his general closeness to the people, for the sovereign joined ordinary Russians not only on the battlefield. A. F. Nekrylova, a specialist on the popular literature of the Russian North, stressed the persistence and the precision of the Petrine tradition in some of that huge territory, for instance, in connection with a road built at top speed through the wilderness to assail enemy troops from the rear. Popular memory retained the inspiring hard labor of the sovereign himself, his encouragement of other workers, and his punishment of slackers, and also how he met peasants, treated them to a kind of liqueur, and baptized their children; how he gave a caftan as a gift to the owner of the house where he stayed, and so forth.

In its form of expression it still remains as if it were the story of a witness. It is remarkable that after more than a century and a half (the road was built in 1702 whereas Mainov's writing the story down belongs to the 1880s) the narrative retained such details, as if the narrator himself witnessed this episode. Probably, a not insignificant role was played here by a solicitous attitude to the memory of Peter I, who was long considered in the North to be "one's own" tsar, who understood the people, who did not disdain common labor, and who could accomplish anything.[178]

Legends told of a giant stepping out of the forest to aid a peasant or a fisherman, who realized only later that his helper had been the Tsar of All the Russias. Popular prints occasionally presented Peter the Great as one of the *bogatyri,* mythical heroes and defenders of the Russian land. Some strains of this positive Petrine tradition proved long-lasting indeed. A scholar of Russian folklore informed me of having heard in person an old peasant woman telling a kolkhoz chairman that Peter the Great would have straightened him out, had the ruler only been still alive.

As the preceding material indicates, the nature and penetration of a popular positive image of the first emperor depended also very much on the region. Nekrylova made the further point that it was especially in such areas as the province of Orel, which retained no concrete historical memories of Peter I, that the most fantastic legends in relation to him developed.[179]

The popular memory of many major events of Peter the Great's reign is not easy to interpret. Some specialists, from Slavophile to Soviet, have complained of a certain dispassionate narrative quality, which refused to take sides or took them seemingly at random and which often presented even the most oppressive aspects and the most horrible occurrences of the reign as natural. The frightful executions of many *streltsy* are in apposition to the generous pardon of a young fellow who fully confessed his guilt. The graphic tragedy of the Don rebellion is paired with the image

178 *Ibid.,* 104.
179 *Ibid.,* 107.

of a benevolent master, who shows understanding and grace to some of the accused. A number of investigators wrote of a popular predilection for Peter the Great or at least of a notable lenience toward him; others, particularly Soviet investigators, insisted that the masses recognized the needs of the country while retaining their critical class stance. And beyond specific historical facts speculation can roam freely. Are the many anecdotal stories of a clever and usually tricky soldier gaining promotion or other success in the Petrine army evidence of new opportunities and of a popular recognition of them, or are they simply an ageless tale with new names?

To conclude, Russian popular tradition and literature contain both negative and positive images of Peter the Great. The negative approach is dominated by the apocalyptic figure of the Antichrist and by a rejection by the Old Believers of the sinful world that surrounds them. But it is not limited to their catastrophic vision. It also includes a more general, if less extreme, worry and protest caused by the reformer's innovations, and it presents, although in a restrained manner and often only in passing, the pressing hardships and the main tragic occurrences of the reign. Positive images deal with particular aspects or even episodes of the first emperor's life and activity. Yet they too produce an enduring picture of a victorious commander remarkably close to his soldiers, of an indefatigable and inspiring worker who never disdained common labor, of a monarch who knew how to solve problems and help people directly. Although I have not made an independent analysis of the sources, I remain skeptical of the claims of the scholars who try to go beyond the identification of the different, often contradictory, strains in the popular images of the first emperor and assert, for instance with Shmurlo and in a much more qualified manner with Chistov,[180] that the positive evaluation replaced the negative, whether because the masses gradually came to appreciate the aims and the achievements of the ruler or for other reasons. Rather, we seem to be faced with rich and continuous separate points of view, many links and elaborations within which have been lost.

Popular evaluations of Peter the Great differed from those of the educated public not only in their form and their content, but also, so to speak, in their focus. For the educated, the Petrine turn to the West meant their own creation "out of nothing," the decisive break in Russian history, and the foundation of the Russian Enlightenment image—and myth—of the reformer. For a century and more, Russian intellectuals found it virtually impossible to escape the power of that image long enough and far enough to take a critical look at it, and the weight of *The Bronze Horseman* has remained immense upon them to the present day—

[180] See the already-mentioned second chapter in Shmurlo, *Petr Velikii . . .* , esp. its concluding pages, and most especially its last paragraph (p. 30); Chistov, *op. cit.*, 94. This point aside, Chistov is not given to exaggerating popular appreciation of the reformer; he errs, if anything, in the opposite direction.

as the rest of this study will try to show. For the Old Believers, the world also broke in two, but earlier, in 1666 or thereabout, at the time of the tragic split, the *raskol*. Even when they endowed the first emperor with the stunning magic and might and the crucial position of the Antichrist, they usually saw him as the second or the third Antichrist, after Patriarch Nikon and Tsar Alexis, sometimes even after Arsenius the Greek. No doubt, Peter I fitted the Antichrist role well. Still, that was a programmed, derivative role for him to which historical reality became entirely subordinate, so that satanic doubles could appear and disappear at will. In the intellectual framework of the Russian Enlightenment, Peter the Great was the central, unique, almost all-important figure; in the world of Old Belief, he represented a magnificent prop, but a prop nevertheless, with the center elsewhere. As to the common Russian people other than the Old Believers, their world remained unbroken. They fought the battles, did most of the work, carried most of the burdens of the reign; they were disturbed by the innovations, attracted and even inspired at times by the ever-active and ubiquitous monarch; they contributed the most both to the Bulavin rebellion and to its suppression. Through it all they saw the world and reacted to it much as they had been doing for centuries and as they were going to do for a long time to come. To repeat, they too were impressed in their own way by the first emperor. Only in their undifferentiated view of history and of human existence—and in full accord with various genre characteristics of popular literature—they easily combined his activities and accomplishments with those of others whereas he himself could be transposed in folktales with Ivan the Terrible and appear in folk prints as Alesha Popovich.

# II

## The Image of Peter the Great in Russia in the Age of Idealistic Philosophy and Romanticism, 1826–1860

> . . . At full height,
> Illumined by the pale moonlight,
> With arm outflung, behind him riding
> See, the bronze horseman comes, bestriding
> The charger, clanging in his flight.
>
> Pushkin[1]

1

The Russian Enlightenment image of Peter the Great had a remarkable unity and clarity. For 125 years it was painted, explicated, and defended according to the canon of the Age of Reason. Even when it was under attack, its proponents knew how to respond and exactly what was at issue. Only toward the end of the period Shcherbatov's and Karamzin's strange nostalgia for pre-Petrine morals and their praise of "natural"—organic, so to speak, although they did not use the word—patriotism seemed to carry the discussion beyond the accepted frame of reference. And Shcherbatov and Karamzin, too, as we know, paid a heavy and fundamental debt to the Enlightenment, indeed to the Russian Enlightenment image of Peter the Great. The image and the arguments changed with the transformation of the intellectual climate. In effect, one can speak of more than a single shift. Opposition to the French Revolution and Napoleon and the ensuing period of Restoration and Reaction led in Europe in general, Russia included, to a questioning of some of the cherished ideals of the Age of Reason and of its overall optimism and belief in human progress. More important still—and going quite beyond any mere moderation of Enlightenment enthusiasms—German idealistic philosophy and romanticism as a whole produced a new vision of the world and of human history, no longer subservient to the principles of utility, of practicability, or of enlightened eighteenth-century reason itself. Peter the Great's image changed with everything else. More precisely, the single Russian En-

[1] A. S. Pushkin, "The Bronze Horseman," Oliver Elton, tr., *Verse from Pushkin and Others* (London, 1935), 152–167, quoted from p. 166.

86

lightenment image of the first emperor eventually split into three separate, major, and incompatible images, associated especially with the proponents of Official Nationality, the Westernizers, and the Slavophiles respectively. Appropriately, the relative roles and prominence of the different expounders of the image also shifted. Whereas in the intellectually unified Age of Reason and in harmony with its literary preferences, the Petrine image had been presented, in the first place, by preachers and didactic poets, in the new divided and controversial intellectual world the theoreticians, the ideologues took the lead. A Feofan Prokopovich or a Sumarokov was replaced by a Chaadaev or an Ivan Kireevskii. Moreover, and as symbolized by the split image, the unity and the solidarity between the Russian intellectuals as a group, more broadly the Russian educated public, and the government, so characteristic of the Russian Enlightenment, finally came to an end.[2]

Yet historical change usually takes considerable time, and it is rarely simple or straightforward. The next major contributor to the image of Peter the Great—and a very important contributor he turned out to be—Pushkin (1799–1837), was still a man of the Enlightenment like all the others we have discussed so far. On the whole the greatest Russian writer, Pushkin followed in his tremendous admiration for Peter the Great, as well as in much else, a century of predecessors. His criticisms of the first emperor, his conflicts with him so to put it, also repeated the arguments we have already encountered, notably among the Decembrists, many of whom were the poet's friends or acquaintances. Still, the main reason for considering Pushkin's treatment of Peter the Great in the context of the new intellectual climate is not simply chronological—the need to terminate the Russian Enlightenment at some point—nor is it meant to emphasize the undeniable change that Pushkin underwent in the post-Decembrist decade. The reason is, rather, that "The Bronze Horseman" is such an extraordinary work. Pushkin's *Hamlet,* it has received about as many interpretations as the story of the Danish prince, and it still remains a riddle.[3] The writing itself, as always with Pushkin, is crystal clear, but this time not the meaning or the message. The magic of the poetry and of the statue itself—which can be explained away by a protagonist's madness, by poetic license, or otherwise, but not forgotten—the strange clashing elements of the story, the very abundance of contradictory interpretations by specialists both in general and in rich detail suggest realms beyond the dry light of the Age of Reason. It seems hopeless to discuss whether "The Bronze Horseman" ran away with Pushkin—as some critics believe *Hamlet* did with Shakespeare—or whether a supreme literary genius can re-

---

[2] See my *A Parting of Ways: Government and the Educated Public in Russia, 1801–1855* (Oxford, 1976).

[3] For a rich and expert but incomplete and already dated summary of the interpretations, see W. A. Lednicki, *Pushkin's Bronze Horseman: The Story of a Masterpiece* (Berkeley and Los Angeles, 1955).

flect, perhaps even foretell, the turbulent world around him much better than he knows it himself.

Pushkin's contribution to the established Russian Enlightenment image of Peter the Great was enormous. To repeat the four lines from the "Stances" of 1826, which became probably the most celebrated description of all of the first emperor:

> Now an academician, now a hero,
> Now a seafarer, now a carpenter,
> He, with an all-encompassing soul,
> Was on the throne an eternal worker.[4]

Or to quote an even more programmatic Age of Reason statement two lines earlier:

> With an autocratic hand
> He daringly sowed enlightenment.

The poem was written in 1826, after Nicholas I's accession to the throne and the Decembrist rebellion. The young poet reminded the young ruler that Peter I's reign had also begun in uprising and executions, but that that monarch had turned it mightily toward glory, civilization, and enlightenment.

> Be, then, proud of the family resemblance;
> Be in everything like your ancestor:
> Like him tireless and firm,
> And, like him, remembering no evil.[5]

The "Stances," written in magnificent verse, thus represented a particularly successful example of that well-developed and traditional special form of Russian literature: a "Petrine" address to the reigning sovereign, stressing the connection between that sovereign and the first emperor and frequently utilizing the occasion to restate the principles of the Enlightenment and to introduce the desiderata for the reign of the reformer's latest successor. Pushkin even managed to include in the last line, quoted earlier, a plea for his Decembrist friends.

Two years later, in 1828, the poet created his celebrated image of Peter the Great the war hero, more exactly, the hero of Poltava. The long poem entitled "Poltava" had as its main characters Hetman Mazepa, who had turned against the Russian ruler and Russia and tried to bring the Ukraine over to the Swedish side, and young Maria, who was tragically in love with him. But it also contained a stunning depiction of the decisive battle itself and of Peter I in that battle.

> Just then, inspired from above,
> There sounded the loud voice of Peter:

[4] A. S. Pushkin, "Stansy" (1826), *Izbrannye proizvedeniia* (2 vols., Leningrad, 1961), I, 189.
[5] *Ibid.*

> "Into action, with God!" From the tent
> Surrounded by a crowd of his favorite assistants
> Peter comes out. His eyes
> Shine. His face is terrifying.
> His movements are rapid. He is magnificent.
> He is all like God's thunder.
> He walks. A steed is brought for him.
> High-spirited and obedient is the faithful steed.
> Sensing the fatal fire,
> It trembles. It moves its eyes askance
> And it dashes in the dust of battle
> Proud of its mighty rider.
>                    • • •
> And then, resounding on the plain,
> A *hurray* thundered afar:
> The regiments saw Peter.
>
> And he galloped in front of the regiments,
> Mighty and joyous like battle.
> He was swallowing the field with his eyes.
> After him, in his wake, dashed in a crowd
> These fledglings of Peter's nest—
> In the changes of earthly fortune,
> In the labors of rule and of war
> His comrades, his sons. . . .[6]

And afterwards:

> Peter is feasting. And proud, and clear,
> And full of glory in his gaze.
> And magnificent is his feast of a tsar.
> Accompanied by the shouts of his army,
> In his tent he regales
> His commanders, foreign commanders,
> He shows kindness to his glorious prisoners,
> And for his teachers
> He raises the toasting drinking cup.[7]

It was from Pushkin's "Poltava" that Russian schoolchildren learned about that momentous battle, by heart, while such phrases as the "fledglings of Peter's nest" (*"ptentsy gnezda Petrova"*), for Peter the Great's assistants, became part of the Russian language.

Pushkin, however, undeterred by success, continued his many-sided and absorbing investigation of the Petrine theme. Already in 1827, a year before "Poltava," he had started writing a historical novel, *Arap*

[6] A. S. Pushkin, "Poltava," *Izbrannye proizvedeniia*, vol. I, 498–543, quoted from pp. 533–534.
[7] *Ibid.*, 536.

*Petra Velikogo* ("Peter the Great's Negro").[8] Meant as a revealing picture
of the reformer and his reforms, of the transition in Russia from the old
world to the new, the novel had as its chief protagonist Pushkin's own
famous black ancestor, the young Abyssinian Ibrahim, befriended by the
Russian monarch. Although, unfortunately, the work advanced little past
the beginning, what we have is both fascinating and informative. Written
in contrast to the "Stances" and "Poltava" in limpid prose rather than resounding verse and, so to speak, in a minor, rather than major, key, the
"Negro" nevertheless belongs equally with the other two pieces in the established tradition of Petrine glorification. It is a strikingly sympathetic
depiction through the eyes of Ibrahim-Pushkin—all the more effectively
so because it is also realistic, occasionally critical, and frequently humorous—of the transformation of Russia under Peter the Great. Without the
bombast so overwhelmingly common in the treatment of the subject, it
reaffirms the ideals of the Enlightenment and the progressive role of the
first emperor. He is presented, if rather briefly, as the true and direct
leader of his country, as indeed "an eternal worker on the throne," but
also as a happy family man and as a sensitive and considerate human being in his relations with other people, in particular with Ibrahim.

But the "Negro," too, proved to be only a stage—and a never completed
one at that—in Pushkin's quest for Peter the Great. The writer's interest
extended beyond published materials and accounts. In 1831, Pushkin received from Nicholas I an appointment as historiographer, with the specific assignment of writing a history of Peter the Great. In 1832 he began
work in archives inaccessible to others. He was still preoccupied with Peter the Great on the very eve of the duel of January 27, 1837, which took
his life.

Thus, Pushkin never wrote his history of Peter the Great. We have
merely his extensive detailed notes, from the year 1835, based on Golikov's work, perhaps half of the notes he made. Given little attention for
a long time, they were finally published in 1938 and have since acquired
a greater prominence.[9] In particular, Elijah Feinberg argued effectively,
as well as passionately, that Pushkin knew and utilized many sources
other than Golikov, that he was both generally much less credulous than
Golikov and corrected some of his particular mistakes, that indeed he had
become a true master of his subject. Feinberg considered Pushkin's notes
to be an advanced stage in the composition of the work, and he discerned
in them both its structure, chapter by chapter, and its argument.[10] Yet,

---

[8] A. S. Pushkin, "Arap Petra Velikogo," in *Izbrannye proizvedeniia*, I, 383–417. For
an extensive commentary emphasizing the literary background and setting, see S. Petrov,
*Russkii istoricheskii roman XIX veka* (Moscow, 1964), ch. I, 13–60.

[9] I used the 1950 edition: Pushkin, *Polnoe sobranie sochinenii* (Moscow, 1950), X,
1–292. The title is "Istoriia Petra" ("History of Peter") on the main title page, but
"Istoriia Petra. Podgotovitelnye teksty" ("History of Peter. Preparatory Texts") on a
subsequent one.

[10] Ilia Feinberg, "Istoriia Petra I," *Nezavershennye raboty Pushkina,* 3d enlarged ed.

although apparently factually correct as a rule, even Feinberg cannot quite produce items that are not there, just as hypothetical chapters are no replacement for actual ones.

But there is no doubt that during the last year of his life Pushkin kept studying, considering, and reconsidering the first emperor. His notes for his history, his correspondence, some of his other writings, and the recollections of his friends all point in the same direction. Certain of the writer's new formulations went well with the old glorification and were sometimes, again, brilliantly put. For instance, in 1834 Pushkin wrote:

Russia entered Europe as a ship when launched—accompanied by the sound of the axe and the thunder of cannons. But wars, undertaken by Peter the Great, were beneficial and fruitful. The success of popular education was a result of the battle of Poltava, and European enlightenment berthed at the shores of the conquered Neva.[11]

Shortly afterwards, however, another evaluative comment, which was to become a special favorite of Soviet scholars, offered a different perspective:

Worthy of wonder is the difference between Peter the Great's state institutions and his temporary ukazes. The former are a product of a broad mind, full of benevolence and wisdom; the latter are cruel, arbitrary, and, it would seem written with a knout. The former were for eternity, or at least for the future; the latter escaped from an impatient despotic landowner.[12]

It is generally believed among scholars that Pushkin, as he studied Peter the Great and his times, became increasingly repelled by the cruelty of the reformer. The knout appeared to be ever-present, from the flogging of the reformer's first wife and the massacre of the *streltsy*—Pushkin repeatedly referred to the year 1698 as "frightening"—to the execution of the empress's thoroughly corrupt lover William Mons in the last year of the reign. It is much less clear what general conclusions, if any, the writer drew from his aversion. To be sure, Pushkin at one time had stood close to the Decembrists and their protest against autocratic tyranny. But he became more conservative after their tragic rebellion; and, besides, the Decembrists themselves, as we know, were, to say the least, ambivalent about Peter the Great: the reactionary despotism against which they staged their uprising could be as easily considered a perversion of the system, aims, and policies of the first emperor as their continuation. The personal factor also entered the picture, although in a highly involved manner that is hard to assess. It concerned Pushkin's painful position at the

---

(Moscow, 1962), 13–242. Feinberg, among other contributions, provides a detailed account of which parts of Pushkin's manuscript were preserved and in what manner.

[11] Quoted from Feinberg, *op. cit.,* 58.

[12] Quoted from *ibid.,* 58–59. On the basis of archival sources, Feinberg restored the original Pushkin text, which should read as quoted; notably it should read "the latter are cruel, arbitrary, and, it would seem, written with a knout," not, as usually given, "not infrequently the latter are cruel, arbitrary, and, it would seem, written with a knout"; ("not infrequently" was introduced by a censor. See *ibid.,* 59, fn. 1).

imperial court and difficult and complex relations with Nicholas I, with the further problem of determining to what extent that monarch was a reincarnation of, or at least a faithful successor to, Peter the Great and to what extent his antipode. Pushkin apparently generalized his unsatisfactory personal condition to claim that it was old aristocratic families such as his that had been displaced in new bureaucratic Russia and that they somehow represented a potentially progressive force found in other social strata elsewhere.

Elements adduced from the beginning of this chapter, as well as many others, went into the creation of Pushkin's "Bronze Horseman," written in October 1833. One can even argue that the strangeness of the piece resulted from the fact that Pushkin's own thought on his subject was at the time in transition. Yet one should also be aware lest this consideration provide another too simple explanation for a remarkably rich, complex, and puzzling masterwork.

"The Bronze Horseman" begins with a long and magnificent introduction, which may well be considered the most brilliant single item in the entire glittering Petrine cult:

> There, by the billows desolate,
> He stood, with mighty thoughts elate,
> And gazed; but in the distance only
> A sorry skiff on the broad spate
> Of Neva drifted seaward, lonely.
> The moss-grown miry banks with rare
> Hovels were dotted here and there
> Where wretched Finns for shelter crowded;
> The murmuring woodlands had no share
> Of sunshine, all in mist beshrouded.
>
> And thus He mused: "From here, indeed
> Shall we strike terror in the Swede;
> And here a city by our labour
> Founded, shall gall our haughty neighbor;
> 'Here cut'—so Nature gives command—
> 'Your window through on Europe; stand
> Firm-footed by the sea, unchanging!'
> Ay, ships of every flag shall come
> By waters they had never swum,
> And we shall revel, freely ranging."
>
> A century—and that city young,
> Gem of the Northern world, amazing,
> From gloomy wood and swamp upsprung,
> Had risen, in pride and splendour blazing.
> Where once, by that low-lying shore,
> In waters never known before
> The Finnish fisherman, sole creature,
> And left forlorn by stepdame Nature,

Cast ragged nets,—today, along
Those shores, astir with life and motion,
Vast shapely palaces in throng
And towers are seen: from every ocean,
From the world's end, the ships come fast,
To reach the loaded quays at last.
The Neva now is clad in granite
With many a bridge to overspan it;
The islands lie beneath a screen
Of gardens deep in dusky green.
To that young capital is drooping
The crest of Moscow on the ground,
A dowager in purple, stooping
Before an empress newly crowned.
I love thee, city of Peter's making;
I love thy harmonies austere,
And Neva's sovran waters breaking
Along her banks of granite sheer;
Thy traceried iron gates; thy sparkling,
Yet moonless, meditative gloom
And thy transparent twilight darkling;
And when I write within my room
Or, lampless, read,—then, sunk in slumber,
The empty throughfares, past number,
Are piled, stand clear upon the night;
The Admiralty spire is bright;
Nor may the darkness mount, to smother
The golden cloudland of the light,
For soon one dawn succeeds another
With barely half-an-hour of night.
I love thy ruthless winter, lowering
With bitter frost and windless air;
The sledges along Neva scouring;
Girls' cheeks—no rose so bright and fair!
The flash and noise of balls, the chatter;
The bachelor's hour of feasting, too;
The cups that foam and hiss and spatter,
The punch that in the bowl burns blue.
I love the warlike animation
On playing-fields of Mars; to see
The troops of foot and horse in station,
And their superb monotony;
Their ordered, undulating muster;
Flags, tattered on the glorious day:
Those brazen helmets in their lustre
Shot through and riddled in the fray.
I love thee, city of soldiers, blowing
Smoke from thy forts; thy booming gun;
—A Northern empress is bestowing

Upon the royal house a son!
Or when, another battle won,
Proud Russia holds her celebration;
Or when the Neva breaking free
Her dark blue ice bears out to sea
And scents the spring, in exultation.

Now, city of Peter, stand thou fast,
Foursquare, like Russia; vaunt thy splendour!
The very element shall surrender
And make her peace with thee at last.
Their ancient bondage and their rancours
The Finnish waves shall bury deep
Nor vex with idle spite that cankers
Our Peter's everlasting sleep!

There was a dreadful time, we keep
Still freshly on our memories painted;
And you, my friends, shall be acquainted
By me, with all that history:
A grievous record it will be.[13]

The poem proper opens with a cold "breath of November" and a tur-
bulence of the Neva. The protagonist, Eugene, described as belonging—
like Pushkin himself—to a formerly distinguished family, but poor and
employed apparently in a routine clerical position, returns from a party
and has difficulty falling asleep as he thinks of his lot and worries about
the bad weather, which, by cutting the bridge connection, might separate
him for a few days from his beloved Parasha. With the coming of the
morning, the storm keeps mounting. Then:

Madder the weather grew, and ever
Higher upswelled the roaring river
And bubbled like a kettle, and whirled
And like a maddened beast was hurled
Swift on the city. All things routed
Fled from its path, and all about it
A sudden space was cleared; the flow
Dashed in the cellars down below;
Canals above their borders spouted.
Behold Petropol floating lie
Like Triton in the deep, waist-high![14]

A stunning further description of the tempest and flood is followed by
the appearance of Alexander I on a palace balcony. The monarch declares resignedly that a tsar cannot control God's elements, gazes sadly at
the disaster, and after that sends his assistants to organize and lead the
rescue of those drowning. Near the palace, on one of the celebrated "sen-

13 A. S. Pushkin, "The Bronze Horseman," Oliver Elton, tr., 153–155.
14 *Ibid.*, 157.

try lions" in the storm sits Eugene, beside himself from fear for Parasha.
And beyond him:

> There, on high,
> With Neva still beneath him churning,
> Unshaken, on Evgeny turning
> His back, and with an arm flung wide,
> Behold the Image sit, and ride
> Upon his brazen horse astride![15]

The Neva finally recedes, like a robber dropping his plunder on the
way. Eugene gets a boatman to take him, daringly, to the area next to
the bay where Parasha lives, only to find utter destruction.

> There is the willow. Surely yonder
> The gate was standing, in the past;
> Now, washt away! No house!—O'ercast
> With care, behold Evgeny wander
> For ever round and round the place,
> And talk aloud, and strike his face
> With his bare hand. A moment after,
> He breaks into a roar of laughter.[16]

Shattered, Eugene keeps wandering in the Petrine city, for weeks, for
months, never returning home. A vagabond:

> He seemed like something miscreated,
> No beast, nor yet of human birth,
> Neither a denizen of earth
> Nor phantom of the dead.[17]

Then, one stormy night:

> Our poor Evgeny woke; and daunted,
> By well-remembered terrors haunted,
> He started sharply, rose in haste,
> And forth upon his wanderings paced;
> —And halted on a sudden, staring
> About him silently, and wearing
> A look of wild alarm and awe.
> Where had he come? for now he saw
> The pillars of that lofty dwelling
> Where, on the perron sentinelling,
> Two lion-figures stand at guard
> Like living things, keep watch and ward
> With lifted paw. Upright and glooming,
> Above the stony barrier looming,
> The Image, with an arm flung wide,
> Sat on his brazen horse astride.

[15] *Ibid.*, 159–16c.
[16] *Ibid.*, 161–162.
[17] *Ibid.*, 163.

And now Evgeny, with a shiver
Of terror, felt his reason clear.
He knew the place, for it was here
The flood had gambolled, here the river
Had surged; here, rioting in their wrath,
The wicked waves had swept a path
And with their tumult had surrounded
Evgeny, lions, square,—and Him
Who, moveless and aloft and dim,
Our city by the sea had founded,
Whose will was Fate. Appalling there
He sat, begirt with mist and air.
What thoughts engrave his brow! what hidden
Power and authority he claims!
What fire in yonder charger flames!
Proud charger, whither art thou ridden,
Where leapest thou? and where, on whom,
Wilt plant thy hoof?—Ah, lord of doom
And potentate, 'twas thus, appearing
Above the void, and in thy hold
A curb of iron, thou sat'st of old
O'er Russia, on her haunches rearing!

About the Image, at its base,
Poor mad Evgeny circled, straining
His wild gaze upward at the face
That once o'er half the world was reigning.
His eye was dimmed, crampt was his breast,
His brow on the cold grill was pressed,
While through his heart a flame was creeping
And in his veins the blood was leaping.
He halted sullenly beneath
The haughty Image, clenched his teeth
And clasped his hands, as though some devil
Possessed him, some dark power of evil,
And shuddered, whispering angrily,
"Ay, architect, with thy creation
Of marvels . . . Ah, beware of me!"
And then, in wild precipitation
He fled.

For now he seemed to see
The awful Emperor, quietly,
With momentary anger burning,
His visage to Evgeny turning!
And rushing through the empty square,
He hears behind him as it were
Thunders that rattle in a chorus,
A gallop ponderous, sonorous,
That shakes the pavement. At full height,
Illumined by the pale moonlight,

> With arm outflung, behind him riding
> See, the bronze horseman comes, bestriding
> The charger, clanging in his flight.
> All night the madman flees; no matter
> Where he may wander at his will,
> Hard on his track with heavy clatter
> There the bronze horseman gallops still.[18]

Thereafter Eugene would pass in the vicinity of *The Bronze Horseman* only doffing his cap and looking down. To conclude the story, Eugene's body is found on a nearby island, on the threshold of a cottage, which was carried onto the island by the recent flood.

The common interpretation of "The Bronze Horseman" as a qualified, even tragic, but also stunningly powerful, affirmation of Peter the Great and his work remains the most convincing. While extending sympathy to the unfortunate Eugene, Pushkin depicted *The Bronze Horseman* as an infinitely majestic, an almost divine figure, the greatness and permanence of whose work the poet affirmed unforgettably in the introduction. The astounding lines dealing with the emperor, not those describing Eugene, were to remain a treasure of Russian verse. Pushkin's tale is a tragedy, but its composite parts are not evenly balanced: above all rises the autocratic state sweeping on to its grand destiny, undeterred by the obstacles of nature, such as swamps and floods, and impervious to the pain, the sorrow, and even the opposition of the individual, exemplified by Eugene's miserable plight and his pathetic rebellion. And yet, to put it very mildly, *The Bronze Horseman* himself is not all made of light, whether of the Age of Reason or of any other kind—although, to be sure, he is seen in the poem essentially through Eugene's eyes whereas the author's own vision in the introduction is luminous and radiant. A number of distinguished commentators argued that Pushkin was, in fact, on Eugene's side, and they presented a negative analysis of the figure of *The Bronze Horseman,* including the defining word for him, *kumir*—really "idol" rather than "image" as translated earlier—which was eliminated by the censorship.[19] Some Soviet specialists likened the poet's perception of Peter the Great and the Petrine state to their own treatment of the subject in terms of an extreme juxtaposition of the positive and the negative elements, an approach that will be discussed at length in the last chapter of this study. Many scholars were reminded of Pushkin's onetime closeness to the Decembrists—who apparently were often on Pushkin's mind, as illustrated strikingly by the repeated doodles on the manuscript of "Poltava" of men hanged—and a number noted that rebellion was represented in the poem not only by Eugene's futile protest, but also by the at

---

18 *Ibid.,* 164–166.

19 See Valerii Briusov's article "Mednyi Vsadnik" as introduction to Pushkin's text in Pushkin's collected works edited by S. A. Vengerov, *Pushkin* (St. Petersburg, 1909), III, 456–472; and W. A. Lednicki's own analysis in his already-mentioned book.

least temporarily victorious waves. It was even suggested that the introduction was added to the poem simply to mislead the censor. Moreover, interpretations continue to proliferate. To cite only two relatively original examples from the 1960s, M. Kharlap claimed that in the poem Pushkin championed Peter the Great, but opposed *The Bronze Horseman,* who represented in effect the later autocracy of Nicholas I, not the illustrious reformer[20] whereas A. Gerbstman insisted that the author supported both Peter the Great and *The Bronze Horseman*—mistakenly considered by Eugene to be his enemy—directing his accusations instead, as revealed by correct and informed reading, against Alexander I: it was his fatalistic attitude toward natural calamities that made that monarch delay even sending help to those in need, an attitude logically leading to the death of Parasha and others whereas Peter the Great personally and relentlessly had fought the elements and indeed had died because of his successful attempt to save drowning soldiers. (The belief that the first emperor died of pneumonia caught during such a rescue was common in Pushkin's time.)[21] The simplicity and lucidity of the Enlightenment were no longer present in "The Bronze Horseman."

Pushkin, as we know, continued his urgent interest in Peter the Great after the creation of *The Bronze Horseman* in October 1833 all the remaining years and months of his life until the fatal duel of January 27, 1837. But he made no final and comprehensive statement on the subject, except perhaps to indicate its gigantic scope and importance. On October 19, 1836, the poet wrote to his good friend, Peter Chaadaev—our next protagonist—who had just stunned the Russian educated public by declaring in print that Russia had no history at all and in truth amounted to nothing:

The awakening of Russia, the development of its power, its movement toward unity (Russian unity, of course) . . . How is that possible, can all this be not history, but only a pale and half-forgotten dream? And Peter the Great, who alone is an entire world history![22]

2

Peter Chaadaev (1794–1856) and Pushkin made the greatest and most lasting contributions of their generation to the Petrine tradition. "An officer of the Hussars"—to quote from Pushkin's well-known verses—like the poet, dealt with the first emperor more than once and from different perspectives. Only he presented his views by means of theoretical formulations, not poetic images. Also, whereas Pushkin can be regarded as es-

[20] M. Kharlap, "O 'Mednom Vsadnike' Pushkina," *Voprosy literatury,* no. 7 (July 1961), 87–101.

[21] A. Gerbstman, "O siuzhete i obrazakh 'Mednogo Vsadnika,'" *Russkaia literatura,* no. 4 (1963), 77–88.

[22] Quoted from: Feinberg, *op. cit.,* 56.

sentially a man of the Enlightenment who wrote a rich and complex work going beyond its bounds and thus indicating the coming of a new and more controversial age, Chaadaev underwent a many-sided and involved explicit intellectual transformation. By the time he offered his first and probably most important contribution, the first "Philosophical Letter," written in 1829 and published because of a censor's mistake in 1836—to which Pushkin lived just long enough to respond—he had abandoned his earlier liberalism of the Enlightenment in favor of French Catholic thought, perhaps especially that of Lamennais in his conservative and ultramontane stage and of German idealistic philosophy, notably Schelling's.[23]

In the first "Philosophical Letter," Chaadaev argued that Russia had no past, no present, and no future.

One of the most deplorable things in our unique civilization is that we are still just beginning to discover truths which are trite elsewhere—even among people less advanced than we are in certain respects. That follows from the fact that we have never advanced along with other people; we are not related to any of the great human families; we belong neither to the West nor to the East, and we possess the traditions of neither. Placed, as it were, outside of the times, we have not been affected by the universal education of mankind. This admirable linking of human ideas throughout the passing centuries, this history of the human spirit which led the human spirit to the position which it occupies in the rest of the world today, had no effect upon us.[24]

This absence of a real historical past was totally deplorable:

For us historical experience does not exist; ages and generations have flowed by fruitlessly for us. It would seem that in our case the general law of humanity has been revoked. Alone in the world, we have given nothing to the world, taken nothing from the world, bestowed not even a single idea upon the fund of human ideas, contributed nothing to the progress of the human spirit, and we have distorted all progressivity which has come to us. Nothing from the first moment of our social existence has emanated from us for man's common good; not one useful idea has germinated in the sterile soil of our fatherland; we have launched no great truth; we have never bothered to conjecture anything ourselves, and we have only adopted deceiving appearances and useless luxury from all the things that others have thought out . . .

One time, a great man wanted to civilize us, and in order to give us a foretaste of enlightenment, he threw us the cloak of civilization: we took up the cloak but

[23] Cf. Professor A. Walicki's expert summary of Chaadaev's sources in *A History of Russian Thought from the Enlightenment to Marxism* (Stanford, 1979), 82; the fifth chapter, devoted to Chaadaev, occupies pp. 81–91. On the intellectual evolution of Chaadaev, as indicated by the two libraries he owned successively, see Raymond T. McNally, *Chaadayev and His Friends. An Intellectual History of Peter Chaadayev and His Russian Contemporaries* (Tallahassee, 1971), 164–198. I discussed the change of the intellectual climate in Russia and Chaadaev in my *Parting of Ways*, 148–176, and I am reproducing some of the discussion here.

[24] Raymond T. McNally, tr. and commentator, *The Major Works of Peter Chaadaev* (Notre Dame and London, 1969), 27. The first "Philosophical Letter" occupies pp. 23–51.

did not so much as touch civilization. Another time, another great Prince, associating us with his glorious mission, led us victoriously from one end of Europe to the other: upon our return from this triumphal march across the most civilized lands in the world, we brought only evil ideas and fatal errors which resulted in an immense calamity which threw us back a half a century. We have something or other in our blood which alienates any real progress. Finally, we lived and do now live simply to serve as some great lesson to far-distant posterity which will become aware of it; today, in spite of what anyone says, we do not amount to a thing in the intellectual order. I can not stop being dumbfounded by this void and this surprising solitude of our social existence.[25]

The great man who tried to civilize Russia was, of course, Peter the Great; the Prince who marched Russians across Europe, Alexander I; the calamity, the Decembrist rebellion. Chaadaev's total dismissal of the Petrine effort and of new Russia together with the old was unprecedented in Russian literature and contributed massively to the shock produced by the first "Philosophical Letter" (as we know, many proponents of the Petrine cult were adept at denigrating and even dismissing Muscovy, but never reformed Russia), although it bore resemblance to the opinions of certain philosophes, such as Rousseau, who believed that Peter I's policies did not suit the Russian people and, therefore, could not succeed, and to the views of some French Catholic thinkers, who stressed Russian isolation and lack of civilization.

Indeed Chaadaev agreed with these thinkers also in postulating a religious basis for history. The secret of Russian sterility, he believed, resided in the schismatic separation of Russia from the universal Christian civilization of the West. Certainly, Russians were Christians, but only in the sense in which Abyssinians were Christians: both were off the main creative, historical road of Christianity. As Chaadaev summed up his philosophy of history and in particular his view of the West:

The entire history of modern society occurs on the level of beliefs. That is the essence of genuine education. Instituted originally on this basis, education advanced only by means of thought. Interests have always followed ideas there and have never preceded them. So, beliefs have always produced interests and never have interests produced beliefs. All political revolutions were in principle simply moral revolutions. Man sought truth and found liberty and happiness. This approach explains the phenomenon of modern society and its civilization; it can not be understood in any other way.[26]

Thus, despite all that is incomplete, vicious, evil, in European society as it stands today, yet it is nonetheless true that God's reign has been realized there in some way, because it contains the principle of indefinite progress and possesses germinally and elementarily all that is needed for God's reign to become established definitely upon earth one day.[27]

25 *Ibid.*, 37–39.
26 *Ibid.*, 44.
27 *Ibid.*, 47.

Russia, to repeat, was outside that society and that progress, a gap in the intellectual order of things.

In the conditions of Nicholas I's police state and in the intellectual climate of a rising romantic nationalism, Chaadaev's remarkable "Letter" produced a shock and a scandal. The Russian educated public, with a few notable exceptions such as Alexander Herzen and Michael Lermontov, reacted sharply against the insolent critic—as exemplified by Pushkin's response already quoted in part. The authorities, on their side, banned the periodical *The Telescope,* banished its editor Nicholas Nadezhdin, dismissed the censor, and officially proclaimed Chaadaev insane. As Count Alexander Benckendorff, the head of the political police, instructed the governor-general of Moscow, mental derangement "was the only reason for writing such nonsense. . . . His Imperial Majesty orders you to entrust an able physician with Mr. Chaadaev's treatment and to instruct the physician to visit Mr. Chaadaev absolutely every morning. . . . His Imperial Majesty wants you to send him a monthly report on Mr. Chaadaev's condition."[28] A year later, sick or sound, Chaadaev changed his views in a piece entitled "The Apology of a Madman."

Again under the epigraph *"Adveniat regnum tuum"*—"Thy kingdom come"—Chaadaev vented his bitterness against his narrow-minded and nearsighted calumniators, who failed to realize both that his letter was truly patriotic and that it possessed the still higher justification of speaking the truth. But the main thrust of the "Apology" was to establish an exit from the nihilistic cul-de-sac of Chaadaev's original formulation. Peter the Great provided the escape.

For the past three hundred years Russia has been aspiring to identify herself with the West, she has been admitting her inferiority to the West, drawing all her ideas, all her teachings, all her joys from the West. For more than a century Russia has done better than that. The greatest of our kings, our glory, our demigod, he who began a new era for us, he to whom we owe our greatness and all the goods which we possess, renounced old Russia a hundred years ago in front of the entire world. With his powerful breath he swept away all our old institutions; he dug out an abyss between our past and our present, and he threw all our traditions into it; he went to make himself the smallest in the West, and he returned the greatest among us; he prostrated himself before the West, and he rose as our master and our legislator; he introduced Western idioms into our idiom; he moulded the letters of our alphabet upon those of the West; he disdained the clothes of our fathers and made us adopt Western dress; he gave his new capital a Western name; he threw away his hereditary title and adopted a Western title; lastly, he renounced his own name and wrote his signature with a Western name. Since that time, our eyes constantly turned toward the West, and we did nothing but inhale the emanations which came to us from there and nourish ourselves on them. As for our princes, who were always in advance of the nation, who always dragged us along the road of perfection in spite of ourselves, who always towed the country behind them, without the

28 *Ibid.,* 225. I have slightly altered Professor McNally's translation.

country doing anything at all, they themselves imposed Western customs, language and luxury upon us. We learned how to read from Western books, we learned how to speak from Westerners; as for our own history, it is the West, which taught it to us; we drew everything from the West, we translated the whole West and were finally happy in resembling the West and proud when the West counted us among its own.[29]

And it is not just for his nation alone that the great man worked. Providential men are always sent for the entire universe: a nation demands them first, then they are absorbed into humanity, like these great rivers which first fertilize vast countries, and then go on to flow into the ocean. When forsaking royal majesty and his land, he went to conceal himself in the lowest ranks of civilized people; was it not a unique spectacle, which he offered the universe, of a new effort of man's genius to emerge from the narrow sphere of the fatherland, in order to become established in the great sphere of humanity? Such was the lesson which we ought to have gleaned from it! We really did profit from it, and up to this day we have marched along the road which the great emperor mapped out for us. Our immense development is nothing but the fruition of this vast thought. . . . So, he liberated us from all these precedents which encumber historical societies and impede their development; he opened our intelligence to all great and beautiful ideas existing among men; he handed us over totally to the West, such as the centuries have made it, and he gave us all its history for a history, all its future for a future.[30]

And, in what became Chaadaev's most celebrated sentence: "In his hand Peter the Great found only a blank sheet of paper, and he wrote on it: Europe and the West; since then we belonged to Europe and to the West."[31]

Russia, thus, entered history. Moreover, once it became part of the West, Russia found itself in a remarkably advantageous position. Chaadaev argued, in effect, several connected arguments. Russia possessed the freshness and enthusiasm of the newcomer, and it was unencumbered by the interests, traditions, and prejudices of the past. Besides, as a conscious and voluntary participant in the development of humanity, it could plan and measure its steps and move steadily and advisedly toward its goal. Chaadaev—who was, after all, a transitional figure—wrote at times as a philosophe championing reason and at others as a romantic intellectual profoundly aware of the crucial importance of the understanding of the self and of history for the accomplishment of destiny.

I love my country in the way that Peter the Great taught me to love it . . . I think that if we have come after the others, it is in order to do better than the others, in order not to fall into their superstitions, into their blindnesses, into their infatuations. To reduce us to repeating the long series of follies and calamities which nations less favored than ours had to undergo would be, in my opinion, a strange misunderstanding of the role which has been allotted to us. I find

[29] *Ibid.*, 201–203; "The Apology of a Madman" is on pp. 199–218.
[30] *Ibid.*, 203–204.
[31] *Ibid.*, 205.

that our situation is a fortunate one, provided that we know how to evaluate it, and that the ability to contemplate and to judge the world from the heights of a thought freed from unbridled passions, from miserable interests which encroach upon it, is a lovely privilege. There is more: I have the inner conviction that we are called upon to resolve most of the problems in the social order, to accomplish most of the ideas which arose in the old societies, to make a pronouncement about those very grave questions which preoccupy humanity. I have often said, and I love to repeat it, that by the very force of circumstances we have been constituted as a genuine jury for countless trials being handled before the great tribunals of the world . . .

In our land, there are none of these passionate interests, these already-formed opinions, these inveterate prejudices: we approach each new truth with virgin minds. In our institutions, spontaneous works of our princes, in our customs which possess just a century of existence, in our opinions which still seek to become fixed upon the most significant things, nothing opposes the good things which Providence destines for humanity. It is enough for a sovereign will to be pronounced among us, in order to have all our opinions disappear, to have all our beliefs waver, to have all our minds open up to the new thought offered them. . . . History is no longer ours, it is true, but science is ours; we could not begin the whole work of humanity again, but we can participate in its latest works. The past is no longer within our powers, but the future belongs to us.

There is no possible doubt about it, the world is oppressed by its tradition; let us not envy the world for the limited circle in which it flounders; it is certain that in the heart of all the nations there is a deep feeling of their life of past accomplishments which dominates their present life, an obstinate memory of days gone by which fills their todays. Let them struggle with their inexorable past . . . let us rejoice in the immense advantage of being able to march forward with the awareness of the route which we have to travel, by obeying only the voice of enlightened reason with a deliberate will. Let us realize that for us there exists no absolute necessity, that we are not, thank God, situated on the rapid slope which sweeps the other people towards the destinies of which they are unaware; that it is given to us to measure each step which we make, to reason out each idea which happens to graze our intellect, that we are permitted to aspire to types of prosperity which are vaster than the prosperity of which the most ardent ministers of the religion of progress dream, and that, in order to achieve definite results, we need only a powerful will, like the one which regenerated us recently.[32]

Chaadaev's first "Philosophical Letter" is a study in dissolution. The Russian past, the Russian present, physical reality itself dissolve into nothingness. "I can not stop being dumbfounded by this void and this surprising solitude." To quote one passage among many:

There is no definite sphere of existence for anyone, no good habits, no rule for anything at all; not even a home; nothing which attracts or awakens our endearment or affections, nothing lasting, nothing enduring; everything departs, everything flows away, leaving no traces either without or within ourselves.[33]

32 *Ibid.*, 213–216.
33 *Ibid.*, 28.

The "Letter" is written from "Necropolis," and its crucial and most fre-
quently repeated concept, its focal point, is "nothing." It would seem
that Chaadaev was on the verge of suicide, when he composed his first
"Philosophical Letter." It may be relevant that, in the opinion of many
specialists, he did eventually take his own life.[34] If I am correct, then,
"The Apology of a Madman" was as authentic and as much a product of
Chaadaev's innermost perception and struggle as the first "Philosophical
Letter." Great pressure had been brought to bear on the insolent critic
to change his views: by the authorities certainly and, more powerfully,
by the outraged educated public to which Chaadaev himself belonged.
But the important point was that the turn to Peter the Great gave life to
Russia—and a lease on life to Chaadaev. Will and form stepped forth to
master dissolution and chaos. *The Bronze Horseman* again controlled the
elements.

Chaadaev's preoccupation with Peter the Great did not end with "The
Apology of a Madman." In fact, the closest present-day student of Chaadaev, Professor Raymond McNally, utilized new archival material as
well as some published letters and other sources to postulate a third period—after the letter, and the apology—in Chaadaev's judgment of the reformer that was to last until Chaadaev's death.[35] This time the restless
ideologue came to stress continuity, the legitimate connection between
Peter the Great and the Russian past:

Certainly, that man was indeed a revolution, and I am very far from denying it,
but a revolution brought about, like all revolutions in the world, by the nature
of things. . . . Peter the Great was nothing but an energetic expression of his
country and of his age. Initiated, in spite of itself, to the progressive march of
humanity, Russia had long recognized the superiority of the countries of Europe,
especially as regards military matters; tired of its old routines, bored with its
isolation, its one aspiration was to enter the great family of Christian peoples;
the idea of humanity had already penetrated it through all its pores, and it was
struggling, not without success, against the idea rusting in its soil; finally, at the
moment when the great man called upon to rebuild it ascended the throne, it
asked nothing better than to be rebuilt; he had thus only to add the weight of
his strong will to have the scales tip in his favor.[36]

Because the Petrine reforms emerged logically from the Russian past,
they had full popular support whereas the extent of the opposition to
them within the country was greatly exaggerated by later commentators:

As to the means which he utilized to bring his program to its realization, he
found them most naturally in the instincts, the ways of life and, so to speak, in

[34] On Chaadaev's life, see esp. Charles Quénet, *Tchaadaev et les lettres philosophiques. Contribution à l'étude du mouvement des idées en Russie* (Paris, 1931).

[35] Raymond T. McNally, "Chaadaev's Evaluation of Peter the Great," *Slavic Review*,
vol. XXIII, no. 1 (March 1964), 31–44.

[36] *Ibid.*, 38; the text is not dated, but McNally ascribes it to "around 1843" (p. 32, fn.
4); I translated the original French quoted by McNally.

the physiology itself of the nation of which he was both the most authentic and the most wonderful symbol. Accordingly, his people did not refute him; if it protested, that was done in profound silence, and history never knew anything about it. A military guard drunk with anarchy, the great immersed in their plunder, driven mad by their etiquette of slaves, some rebellious priests, the stupid sectarians: they are no witnesses to the national sentiment. Besides, the kind of opposition he encountered in a part of his people had nothing to do with his reforms, for it had existed from the day of his coming to the throne. I am too good a Russian, I have too high an opinion of my nation to believe that he could have succeeded had he met serious resistance on the part of the country. I know well that certain disciples of the new national school, lost souls of that dear school which fakes so skillfully the great historical school of Europe, will tell you that Russia, acceding to the impulse given by Peter the Great, renounced in effect momentarily its nationality, only to recover it later by I do not know what process unknown to the rest of humanity. But a moment of reflection will make you realize that this is nothing but a presumptuous sentence,[37] borrowed out of turn from that elastic philosophy which is ravaging Germany these days and which believes to have explained everything once it has constructed in its strange jargon a formula. The truth is that Russia abdicated into the hands of Peter the Great its prejudices, its barbarian pride, some remnants of liberty for which it did not care at all, and nothing more, for the very simple reason that a nation can not, under any circumstances, renounce itself wholesale, and even less so in order to provide for itself the extraordinary pleasure of bouncing back one day with a new energy to its own past, a bizarre evolution which human reason can not comprehend, nor human nature accomplish.[38]

One had to recognize the decisive facts that the Slavs were basically a submissive, passive people; that these traits had been also nourished by the ascetic, self-sacrificing spirit of Orthodox Christianity; that such people represented perfect and most congenial material for Peter the Great. Indeed, the entire Russian historical development had been based on the humility and submissiveness of the people: the calling of the Varangians to rule, the ready acceptance of Christianity once the leaders had decided in its favor, the resigned bearing of the Mongol yoke, obedience to Ivan III and Ivan the Terrible, the success of the Petrine reforms. As his correspondence indicates, Chaadaev continued the rest of his life to argue with friends and acquaintances the logic and appropriateness of those reforms. For example, in a letter written in 1846 he insisted again that the Russian people had supported Peter the Great, whereas even the minority opposition had assailed really the ruler's character, not his reforms; otherwise, how could it happen that Russia had not reverted to its old ways when weak monarchs had succeeded the first emperor?[39] In 1854, two years before his death, in another letter, Chaadaev returned to the argument from humility, citing the submission to the Varangians, the

[37] McNally has "phase," which I read as a misprint of "phrase": *ibid.*, 39.
[38] *Ibid.*
[39] *Ibid.*, 41.

adoption of Byzantine Christianity and the Mongol yoke as preparation for the reforms of Peter the Great.[40] Or, in the words of still another passage in the correspondence, aimed at the anti-Petrine nationalists: "If Peter the Great did not come, we might have been today a Swedish province, and where would then have been, I ask you, our dear historical school?"[41]

Chaadaev's unprecedented dismissal of Peter the Great in the "Letter" and his magnificent restoration of him in the "Apology" constituted one of the most remarkable performances in all Russian intellectual history. Nor did the "Apology" merely return matters to where they had been before the "Letter." The point is a very difficult one, yet essential: in spite of all the overwhelming glorification of Peter the Great in the Russian Enlightenment, in spite of all the references to creation out of nothing and to divinity in human form, the Enlightenment vision was checked by practical reason and argued in empirical or quasi-empirical terms; in the new intellectual world of German idealism and Romanticism, which Chaadaev entered and where the Westernizers, the Slavophiles, and other Russians were to advance beyond him, issues became metaphysical and absolute. This meant, *mirabile dictu,* a still greater affirmation than ever before, greater in kind—as well as a greater denunciation—of the first emperor. Chaadaev was a truly seminal thinker. Whereas the "Apology" can be considered the fountainhead of Westernism, the religious historiosophical argument central to Chaadaev's thought—although not his particular religious preferences—led directly to Slavophilism. Even Chaadaev's third, ultimate position, little-known and without the éclat or the impact of the first two, renders further testimony to the paradoxical richness of his mind. Although much of it reads like eighteenth-century apologies for the reformer, certain of its elements anticipate the subsequent historical debate on the relationship between Peter the Great and the Russian past.

3

German idealistic philosophy and romanticism in general were not the only agents of change. Reference has already been made to the ideologies of restoration and reaction raised as banners against the French Revolution and Napoleon. In the Russian case a comprehensive reactionary doctrine was slow to preempt the stage in spite of the efforts of Karamzin and certain other intellectuals, largely because Alexander I could never quite terminate his strange, perhaps perverse, love affair with Enlightenment. It was only after his death, the suppression of the Decembrist rebellion, and the firm establishment of Nicholas I on the Russian throne

40 *Ibid.,* 42.

41 *Ibid.,* 41. Chaadaev also criticized the Russian isolation from other European countries and the Crimean War as a deviation from the Petrine way. *Ibid.,* 42. Cf. Pierre Tchaadaev: *Fragments et pensées diverses (inédits),* présentés par Tsuguo Togawa, *Surabu Kenkyū,* 23, Supplement (1979), 23–36.

that the empire of the tsars joined unreservedly and consistently the European Right. An appropriate government ideology, which came to be known as Official Nationality, was proclaimed still later, on April 2, 1833, by the new minister of education, Serge Uvarov (1786–1855), in his first circular to the officials in charge of the educational districts of the Russian empire.[42] Uvarov wrote to his subordinates:

Our common obligation consists in this, that the education of the people be conducted, according to the Supreme intention of our August Monarch, in the joint spirit of Orthodoxy, autocracy, and nationality. I am convinced that every professor and teacher, being permeated by one and the same feeling of devotion to throne and fatherland, will use all his resources to become a worthy tool of the government and to earn its complete confidence.[43]

The minister proceeded to propound and promote his three cardinal principles throughout the sixteen years during which he remained in charge of public instruction in Russia and to bequeath them to his successors. Not only that. Before long "Orthodoxy, autocracy, and nationality" came to represent much more than Uvarov's attempt at philosophizing, more even than the guiding principles of the Ministry of Education. The formula expanded in application and significance to stand for the Russia of Emperor Nicholas I. Military cadets were enjoined to become "Christians," "loyal subjects," and "Russians" in that order.[44] The entire nation was to rally for "faith, tsar, and fatherland," the phrase used, for instance, in the famous 1848 manifesto defying the revolutionary West.[45] The sovereign himself dedicated his life to the service of Orthodoxy, autocracy, and Russia, and everyone else in the government was compelled to follow the monarch. At the same time a considerable part of the educated Russian public, led by prominent professors, writers, and journalists hoisted the three words as their banner. "Orthodoxy, autocracy, and nationality" were interpreted to mean the past, the present, and the future of Russia, Russian tradition as well as Russian mission, Russian culture as much as Russian politics.

The Petrine cult fitted splendidly into the official ideology. Peter the Great was Russian autocracy incarnate and the ideal model for Nicholas I, his direct successor. Orthodoxy stood next to autocracy—more exactly,

[42] For a full treatment of Official Nationality, see *Nicholas I and Official Nationality in Russia, 1825–1855* (Berkeley and Los Angeles, 1959), on which much of this section is based.

[43] S. S. Uvarov, "Tsirkuliarnoe predlozhenie G. Upravliaiushchego Ministerstvom Narodnogo Prosveshcheniia Nachalstvam Uchebnykh Okrugov 'o vstuplenii v upravlenie Ministerstvom,'" *Zhurnal Ministerstva Narodnogo Prosveshcheniia* (1834), part I, 1.

[44] Quoted from: M. A. Polievktov, *Nikolai I. Biografiia i obzor tsarstvovaniia* (Moscow, 1918), 332.

[45] About the manifesto, see N. K. Shilder (Schilder), "Imperator Nikolai I v 1848 i 1849 godakh," first published in the *Istoricheskii Vestnik* for 1899 and later as an appendix to N. K. Shilder, *Imperator Nikolai Pervyi, ego zhizn i tsarstvovanie* (2 vols., St. Petersburg, 1703), II, 619–639; the text of the manifesto is given on p. 629.

formally ahead of it, in its only appropriate place, the first—in the sermons of Feofan Prokopovich as in the circulars of Uvarov, and it found further expression in the strong personal beliefs of their respective monarchs. "Nationality," to be sure, belonged more to the nineteenth century than to the early eighteenth, but its official interpretation in terms of mass patriotism and of a boundless devotion of the Russian people to their ruler only strengthened the Petrine tradition. Perhaps more striking than the ideological harmony of Official Nationality and of the established image of Peter the Great was the living quality of that image, for it was frequently upheld in the middle of a new century with an immediacy of dedication and passion that belied entirely the distance of 150 years. This was true of government ideologists as well as of more independent thinkers, to be discussed later. Indeed one can speak of a remarkable Petrine revival in Russia.

Nicholas I himself participated fully in the overwhelming and blind veneration of Peter the Great characteristic of Official Nationality. His enthusiasm for the first emperor may have already been stimulated at the age of seven or eight by Golikov's volumes.[46] In any case, it lasted until his death, the monarch admiring his predecessor in an unreserved and almost religious manner. Peter the Great was constantly on Nicholas I's mind: Nicholas I read voraciously about him, referred to him often, and tried to emulate him. Two examples should suffice to illustrate this lifelong devotion. After reading the manuscript of historian Michael Pogodin's play *Peter I,* written in 1831 and full of gushing praise of the first emperor, the monarch wrote the following resolution: *"The person of Emperor Peter the Great must be for every Russian an object of veneration and of love: to bring it onto the stage would be almost sacrilege, and therefore entirely improper. Prohibit the publication."*[47] In 1839 there was a crisis in the imperial family: the heir to the throne, Alexander, would not give up his Polish mistress and agree to a dynastic marriage. On that occasion Nicholas I told his wife in a letter: "But for me the state counts above everything else; and much as I love my children, I love my fatherland much more still. And, if this becomes necessary, there is the example of Peter the Great to show me my duty; and I shall not be too weak to fulfill it."[48] These ominous lines may be attributed to a momentary depression. Yet the appeal to the example of the great predecessor was both characteristic and revealing, perhaps especially so in this dreadful instance. Alexander, however, finally followed the will of his father, thus settling the matter without recourse to the emperor's model of autocracy.

---

[46] Shilder, *Imperator Nikolai Pervyi,* I, 475, fn. 25.

[47] Quoted from: N. P. Barsukov, *Zhizn i trudy M. P. Pogodina* (22 vols., St. Petersburg, 1888–1910), IV, 13.

[48] Quoted from: Theodor Schiemann, *Geschichte Russlands unter Kaiser Nikolaus I* (4 vols., Berlin, 1904–1919), III (1913), 376.

The monarch's associates, and by no means Uvarov alone, shared fully in the cult. Possibly the most striking suggestion was made by Count E. Kankrin, the minister of finance, who was of German origin:

If we consider the matter thoroughly, then, in justice, we must be called not *Russians,* but *Petrovians.* . . . Everything: glory, power, prosperity, and enlightenment, we owe to the Romanov family; and, out of gratitude, we should change our general tribal name of *Slavs* to the name of the creator of the empire and of its well-being. Russia should be called *Petrovia,* and we *Petrovians;* or the empire should be named *Romanovia,* and we—*Romanovites.*[49]

And the ubiquitous journalist and writer Faddei, or Thaddeus, Bulgarin (1789–1859) added his own opinion to the minister's proposal, which he reported: "An unusual idea, but an essentially correct one!"[50]

As in the cases of earlier rulers, special efforts were made to link Nicholas I to Peter the Great. Connections and comparisons of the two emperors were discussed and glorified by numerous literati of the period, ranging from Pushkin and other poets to such historians as Raphael Zotov (1795–1871).[51] In fact, this subject became one of the favorite themes of what may be described as the cheap patriotic press. Similarly, publicists defending Nicholas I and his Russia against foreign criticism considered it their duty to stand up for Peter the Great as well, a task eagerly undertaken, for instance, by the journalist and grammarian Nicholas Grech (1787–1867) in his attempt to refute Marquis de Custine's sensational attack on Russian government and life.[52] Interestingly, scholars of a much later time, quite free from the dogma of Official Nationality, continued to discover significant parallels between the two emperors. M. A. Polievktov, to give one example, stressed the fact that the reign of Nicholas I marked, in Russian history, the high point of absolutism and of its consistent application to government and life—"with the likely exception of the epoch of Peter the Great."[53]

In an age increasingly conscious of history, historians, sometimes doubling as ideologues, played a significant role in the discussion—and cult—of Peter the Great. Official Nationality had more than its share of them, such figures as Professors Michael Pogodin (1800–1875); Stephen Shevyrev

---

49 Quoted from F. Bulgarin, *Vospominaniia* (6 vols., St. Petersburg, 1846–1849), I (1846), 200–201. This was not the only suggestion to rename Russia "Petrovia."

50 *Ibid.,* 201.

51 R. M. Zotov, *Tridtsatiletie Evropy v tsarstvovanie Imperatora Nikolaia I* (2 vols., St. Petersburg, 1857), esp. vol. II, 312–313. We shall return to Zotov as playwright and novelist dealing with Peter the Great and his times.

52 N. I. Grech, *Examen de l'ouvrage de M. le Marquis de Custine intitulé la Russie en 1839* (Paris, 1844), 22–23, 71–74. Custine had stressed the role of the reformer in the creation of modern Russia, which the Frenchman detested. "Here the spirit of Peter the Great dominates the spirit of all men" (Astolphe Marquis de Custine, *La Russie en 1839* [4 vols., Brussels, 1843], II, 23; my reference is to the edition published by Société Belge de Librairie. Hauman et Compagnie; in 1843, and again in Brussels, the same book was also published by Wouters et Compagnie).

53 Polievktov, *op. cit.,* VIII.

(1806–1864) a historian of literature, and Nicholas Ustrialov (1805–1870), to mention the most prominent ones. Pogodin, first to occupy the chair of Russian history, as distinct from general European history, at the University of Moscow, deserves special attention as a leading ideologue of the Right as well as an active scholar. Moreover, though utterly devoted to the principles of Official Nationality, he interpreted them to incorporate certain romantic, nationalistic, and even specifically German idealistic influences of the time whereas his specialization in pre-Petrine Russian history made it impossible for him to dismiss that history altogether, as had been so often done by the proponents of the Petrine cult in the Russian Enlightenment. Pogodin's constant arguments with his associates, as well as with outright opponents, reflect richly the intellectual climate of the period, and they have been remarkably well preserved in such materials as the historian's own prolific writings and N. P. Barsukov's unfinished twenty-two volume biography of Pogodin.

Already in his youth, if not earlier, Pogodin had fallen under the fascination of the first emperor, that "Russian to the highest degree," the "human god."[54] Later, although specializing in an earlier period of Russian history, he taught a course on Peter the Great's reign, collected documents related to it, and wrote on the subject both as historian and as publicist. The reforming monarch even inspired Pogodin to compose the already-mentioned abortive tragedy in verse, *Peter I,* which dealt with the painful story of Tsarevich Alexis and was written as an apotheosis of the great emperor's sense of duty and of his services to Russia.[55]

It is remarkable to what extent Pogodin was emotionally involved in his subject. Thus, he asserted that he had difficulty wrting the second act of his play because he was afraid of his inadequacy and because he could "virtually see" Peter I opening the door and menacing him with his proverbial club. "One shudders even to pronounce this name."[56] Again, the professor told his students that it had proved almost beyond his power to prepare an introductory lecture on the great emperor: "When I stood face to face with this gigantic colossus, my spirit sank. I could not collect my strength to survey at a glance the totality of his actions in order to compose for you an introduction to his history. And, believe me, this is not a piece of rhetoric."[57] Peter the Great also haunted Pogodin on his trips abroad where the historian tried to see the places visited by the

---

[54] See esp. Barsukov, *op. cit.,* I, 56, 211; II, 293. Shevyrev fell under the same spell as Pogodin. For instance, in 1829, at the age of twenty-three, he noted in his diary: "Each evening certainly, and sometimes in the mornings too, I assign it to myself as an unfailing duty to read the life of Peter the Great and everything related to him." And he added the categorical imperative: "Be such a man as Christ; be such a Russian as Peter the Great." The diary was never published. This account with its quotations is from "Shevyrev, Stepan Petrovich," *Russkii biograficheskii slovar* (vol. "Shebanov" to "Shyutts," St. Petersburg, 1911), 19–29, quoted from p. 22; the article is signed "N. Ch."

[55] M. P. Pogodin, *Petr I* (Moscow, 1873).

[56] Barsukov, *op. cit.,* III, 254.

[57] Barsukov, *op. cit.,* V, 181.

emperor. Characteristic was his pilgrimage to the famous little house in Zaandam:

. . . then suddenly my guide exclaimed: "Well, here is the house of your Peter the First!" . . .

My heart contracted, tears came to my eyes, I could hardly breathe as I opened the gate . . .

With a trembling heart I crossed the threshold, for a long time I could not collect my senses. . . . So this is where our Peter lived and worked! So this is where he thought and dreamed about Russia! How pure, how noble he was here! . . .

I bowed to the ground to the Great One and left his sanctuary with a full heart.[58]

Still Pogodin, as well as his friend Shevyrev, knew and loved old Russia too well to be completely uncritical of Peter the Great and of his work. Pogodin tried repeatedly to strike a balance between the old and the new, between the virtues of ancient Russia and the merits of the first emperor's reforms.[59] This task became all the more urgent when the Slavophiles proceeded to mount their attacks on the emperor, and the professor had to meet the charges of his close acquaintances and collaborators. These attempts to compromise, to present "the two sides" of the issue only demonstrate further the extent to which Pogodin remained in Peter the Great's thrall. It was in 1841 and in connection with some discussions with the Slavophiles that Pogodin decided to set down in an authoritative manner his estimate of Peter the Great.[60] In his essay "Peter the Great," he wrote:

The Russia of today, that is, European Russia, diplomatic, political, military, commercial, industrial, scholastic, literary—is a creation of Peter the Great . . . Wherever we look, everywhere we meet this colossal figure, which throws a long shadow over our entire past and even eliminates old history from our field of vision—which at this moment is still stretching, as it were, its arms over us and which, it appears, will never drop out of sight, no matter how far we advance in the future.[61]

After several grandiloquent pages, Pogodin turned to a more mundane exposition of his subject:

58 M. P. Pogodin, *God v chuzhikh kraiakh, 1839* (4 vols., Moscow, 1844), IV, 14–15.

59 An early effort on the part of Pogodin to resolve this problem is recorded in Barsukov, *op. cit.*, I, 211.

60 M. P. Pogodin, "Petr Velikii," *Istoriko-kriticheskie otryvki* (Moscow, 1846), I, 333–363. The essay was originally published in the first number of the *Moskvitianin* (1841). For its background, see Barsukov, *op. cit.*, VI, 5–6. I discussed the relationship between Pogodin, Shevyrev, and the Slavophiles in Nicholas V. Riasanovsky, "Pogodin and Ševyrëv in Russian Intellectual History," *Harvard Slavic Studies*, vol. IV (The Hague, 1957), 149–167, the disjunction emerging precisely on the issues of autocracy and Peter the Great.

61 Pogodin, "Petr Velikii," 335.

Yes, Peter the Great did much for Russia. One looks and does not believe it, one keeps adding and one can not reach the sum. We can not open our eyes, can not make a move, can not turn in any direction without encountering him every-where, at home, in the streets, in church, in court, in the regiment, at a prome-nade—it is always he, always he, every day, every minute, at every step!

We wake up. What day is it today? January 1, 1841—Peter the Great ordered us to count years from the birth of Christ; Peter the Great ordered us to count the months from January.

It is time to dress—our clothing is made according to the fashion established by Peter the First, our uniform according to his model. The cloth is woven in a factory that he created; the wool is shorn from the sheep that he started to raise.

A book strikes our eyes—Peter the Great introduced this script and himself cut out the letters. You begin to read it—this language became a written language, a literary language, at the time of Peter the First, superseding the earlier church language.

Newspapers are brought in—Peter the Great introduced them.

You must buy different things—they all, from the silk neckerchief to the sole of your shoe, will remind you of Peter the Great; some were ordered by him; others were brought into use or improved by him, carried on his ships, into his harbors, on his canals, on his roads.

At dinner, all the courses, from salted herring, through potatoes, which he or-dered grown, to wine made from grapes, which he began to cultivate, will speak to you of Peter the Great.

After dinner you drive out for a visit—this is an *assemblée* of Peter the Great. You meet the ladies there—they were admitted into masculine company by order of Peter the Great.

You receive a rank—according to Peter the Great's Table of Ranks.

The rank gives me gentry status—Peter the Great so arranged it.

I must file a complaint—Peter the Great prescribed its form. It will be received—in front of Peter the Great's Mirror of Justice. It will be acted upon—on the basis of the General Regulation.

You decide to travel abroad—following the example of Peter the Great; you will be received well—Peter the Great placed Russia among the European states and began to instill respect for her, and so on and so on and so on.[62]

In summary, everything in and about contemporary Russia derived from the titanic emperor. He had the key and the lock. Yet, although the importance of the first emperor could not be subjected to doubt, critics had appeared recently to challenge the particular form change took under Peter I and to regret his sharp break with the past. Pogodin went on to reply to these cavilers in no uncertain terms: Peter I's reform was neces-sary if Russia were to survive in the world. This was obviously true as far as the army and the navy were concerned, and this applied also to other fields of state activity that, in addition, were closely linked to the first

---

[62] *Ibid.*, 340–342.

two. "Had Peter not preceded him, would it have been possible for Alexander to fight Napoleon?"[63] Besides, Western enlightenment had been penetrating Russia to an ever-increasing extent before the reformer; the reformer's policies represented, in fact, largely a continuation of those of his predecessors and were to be explained as part of a fundamental historical process. Peter the Great was impulsive and violent at times, but even his outbreaks of temper were usually justifiable. Everything considered, it took remarkable impudence to question the specific measures and directives of the gigantic monarch—"As to me, I would not undertake for anything in the world to offer a different plan of the battle of Poltava, another project of the Treaty of Nystad."[64] True, Russians after Peter the Great proceeded to worship the West and to forget their own nationality. But this had not been the attitude of the reformer himself, and he could no more be blamed for the later aberration than Gutenberg be held responsible for noxious books.

Furthermore, Peter the Great's work was to form an integral part of the glorious Russian synthesis of the future: ancient Russia had possessed enormous riches and gifts, which, however, represented only one half of the total legacy of the ancient world, the Eastern or Greek half; Peter the Great added the remaining Western portion of the inheritance to the treasury of his native land; the third and final epoch was already dawning—it would mark the abandonment of mere imitation of the West and the construction of a new, organic Russian culture on the basis of all the assembled wealth of the past. Pogodin finished his essay—in a traditional way, one might add—with an account of the praise heaped upon Peter the Great by Russians and foreigners alike. The last word belonged to Lomonosov and his claim that if a man like God were to be found, it could be no other than Peter the Great.

Characteristically of Pogodin, even a most extravagant rhetoric could be readily combined with practical suggestions. The historian proposed in his essay that a university chair devoted to Peter the Great be established in Russia, just as there was a Dante chair in Italy.[65] There is little doubt that he would have been eager to occupy the new position himself.

Pogodin's enormously high estimate of Peter the Great was shared by all proponents of the state ideology, the only distinction being that most of them, less learned and less influenced by Romanticism and nationalism than the Moscow University professor, eulogized the first emperor without any reservations or qualifications whatsoever. Their characteristic attitude was expressed, for instance, in N. Atreshkov's essay published in January 1833 in *The Northern Bee*.[66] The essay was aimed at

63 *Ibid.*, 346.
64 *Ibid.*, 350.
65 *Ibid.*, 357.
66 N. Atreshkov, "Nekotorye vozrazheniia kritiku nashchet izmenenii Petrom Velikim natsionalnosti russkikh," *Severnaia Pchela*, nos. 7, 8 (January 10–11, 1833).

those who claimed that Peter the Great's precipitous turn to the West had damaged Russian nationality, and the author wasted no time in assailing his antagonists. After making a certain allowance for criticism by ignorant foreigners, he continued in the following manner:

But you, my countrymen, remember, before you pronounce the blasphemous accusation, that you are talking about Peter, the greatest of geniuses, about Peter, the creator of our glorious fatherland, the sole cause of its might, the source of your well-being and of that of your descendants! Remember that with him you are condemning the foundation and the cornerstone of the building that he erected![67]

Following this broad hint that an attack on Peter the Great might be treason as well as sacrilege, Atreshkov proceeded to disprove to his own satisfaction all the charges against the reforming emperor. In concluding his article, he ran out of comparisons and of words sufficiently strong to praise "divine Peter":

But show me another Peter, founder of the state, lawgiver, general, astronomer, statesman, trader, artist, artisan, and at the same time untouched by any egoism or lust for glory. He renounced for the sake of the enlightenment and the well-being of his subjects all the worldly blessings of a mortal and a monarch. He sacrificed for them his incessant forty-year-long labor, the endurance of constant dangers, and finally his only son. There never was his like. He is the crown of creation, the glory of mankind, the cause of the existence, and the happiness of Russia.[68]

It is understandable why Pogodin, in spite of his own adulation of Peter the Great, sometimes found himself at odds on that subject with certain other proponents of the official view. For example, the historian was angered by Nestor Kukolnik's play *The Orderly* and especially by the following lines in it referring to Peter the Great:

I saw how the Great Anatomist
Split open the decrepit body of Russia,
Changed her rotten insides,
Put together her cleansed members,
Skillfully bandaged her all properly,
Lifted her by the shoulders, put her on her feet,
And—the Muscovite steppe, the China of Europe,
For the marvelous achievements of her monarch,
Is promoted universally to an Empire![69]

But when Pogodin accused Kukolnik of insolent ignorance of pre-Petrine Russia, Bulgarin rose quickly to the defense of the playwright.[70] In the

67 *Ibid.*
68 *Ibid.*
69 N. V. Kukolnik, "Denschchik," *Sochineniia dramaticheskie* (vol. III of his *Sochineniia,* St. Petersburg, 1852), 189–330, quoted from p. 296. Elsewhere in the play Kukolnik made the same point more gracefully: "Great, divine work! Over our dark country Peter is lighting an artificial sun!" (*ibid.,* 288).
70 For the controversy, see *Severnaia Pchela,* no. 78 (April 9, 1852).

opinion of most proponents of Official Nationality, it was impossible to overpraise Peter the Great or his achievements. "In our opinion, in the entire history of mankind there has been nobody like Peter the Great. Compared to him, even Napoleon is a dwarf!"[71] "Everything that has been done following his lead has proved great and useful; everything done contrary to his plans has collapsed of itself!"[72]

Unimportant as an ideologue—because entirely derivative in thought and shunning theoretical discussion—Nicholas Ustrialov was in certain ways more influential as a historian than Pogodin. Moreover, the St. Petersburg professor gave even greater attention to the first emperor than the Moscow one. It was Ustrialov who wrote general histories of Russia, eventually including a depiction of the reign of Nicholas I corrected by that monarch himself, which ranged from a five-volume university course of lectures to brief high school versions and which became standard in the empire. Indeed, no other Russian history high school texts existed until the 1860s. Peter the Great invariably occupied a prominent place in Ustrialov's accounts of Russian history. Unsatisfied, however, with such summary presentation, Ustrialov devoted the last twenty-three years of his life to a comprehensive *History of the Reign of Peter I (Istoriia tsarstvovaniia Petra I)*. Although Nicholas I lived long enough to approve the first volume in manuscript, published work began to come out only after the emperor's death: the first three volumes in 1858, the sixth in 1859, the fourth in 1864; the massive fifth volume dealing with Poltava, although written, was never published, except in the form of a few articles taken from it;[73] the entire huge undertaking remained unfinished.

As a historian, Ustrialov had some undeniable merits. In 1842 he was admitted to work, like Karamzin and Pushkin before him, in the generally closed state archives, and he made good use of his rare opportunity. Though unimaginative and entirely traditional, Ustrialov's account of Peter the Great's reign contains an abundance of useful and appropriate biographical, political, administrative, military, and diplomatic detail. The historian was particularly concerned with a precise exposition and critique of his sources, advancing in that respect far beyond the amateurish and credulous Golikov. Nor was Ustrialov's treatment of the first emperor simply a whitewash. For instance, Ustrialov decided that Tsarevich Alexis had died probably as a result of torture during the investigation, not as officially declared from a stroke, and he so stated in no uncertain terms.[74] Still, a student of the Petrine cult at the time of Official Na-

71 *Ibid.*

72 Bulgarin, *Vospominaniia*, I, 201.

73 *Re* the fifth volume, see esp. Iu. R. Klokman, "Neizdannyi tom 'Istorii tsarstvovaniia Petra Velikogo' N. G. Ustrialova," *Poltava. K 250-letiiu poltavskogo srazheniia. Sbornik statei* (Moscow, 1959), 311–322. Klokman lists the contents of the 684 pages of text and of the 562 pages of appendixes of the volume.

74 N. Ustrialov, *Istoriia tsarstvovaniia Petra Velikogo* (St. Petersburg, 1859), VI, 294. The entire rich volume, subtitled "Tsarevich Aleksei Petrovich," is devoted to Tsarevich Alexis.

tionality is immediately struck by the marvelous congruence of Ustrialov's views with those of Nicholas I and of the emperor's ideologists in general. To cite only a single example, the historian asserted that the entire transformation of Russia was produced:

by the thought of *one* man. When all the estates, all the ranks, secular and ecclesiastical, high and low, wanted to live and think as their fathers and grandfathers had lived and thought, shunned everything new, considered everything foreign noxious, every new concept a heresy, when, in a word, no one wanted change, and everyone was satisfied with his lot, at that time Peter alone formed the idea to bestow upon his state an entirely new life. He entered into a struggle with his entire environment, with the concepts, the opinions, the prejudices, the neighbors, with nature itself; he triumphed over all obstacles, changed the internal arrangements, gave new foundations to foreign policy, woke up popular forces, and as if created a new state.

Ustrialov continued:

Such a rapid transition of the state from one condition into another, obviously a better one, occurred without any perturbation, after a brief internal struggle, precisely because the transformation of the state was the work of the government alone, exclusively: it was divining the needs of the age, it was marching ahead of the people, and, according to its own impulse, with a clear realization of the necessity of change, it was establishing the system of internal organization, determining the rights, opening the ways for industry, introducing the arts and the sciences, softening the mores. The people had merely to follow the directions of the sovereign authority and to thank heaven for its lot: nowhere and never did a government do so much in so brief a period of time for the people as in our fatherland. Having awakened our dormant forces, it placed Russia on the highest rung of power, which was soon reflected in foreign affairs: first our neighbors, Sweden, Poland, Turkey, Persia, experienced Russian strength; after that, all Europe also learned it.[75]

Russian history, Russian autocracy, Russian power, Peter the Great, and, by implication, Nicholas I become one in Ustrialov's synoptic perception. It seems pedantic to remark that the reformer would not have approved the totally passive role assigned to the Russian people by the St. Petersburg historian . . . and by the historian's sovereign.

Nor was Nicholas I's and Ustrialov's estimate of the first emperor limited to government ideologists. A case in point was a four-volume *History of Peter the Great (Istoriia Petra Velikogo)* published in 1843 by Nicholas Polevoi (1796–1846), a prolific and prominent journalist and writer, a patriot, considered progressive in certain respects, perhaps something of a maverick in his views, but not primarily an apologist for the state. At the end of his study, the author came to the following conclusions:

The more his gigantic image recedes from us, the more enormous it becomes, the more obviously everything perishable, everything earthly, everything human

[75] N. Ustrialov, *Russkaia istoriia*, 5th ed. (St. Petersburg, 1855), II, 6–7.

falls off it, and, therefore, there shines in it all the more brightly a heavenly sign revealing "a select of God," and the appellation of *great* already seems to us to be insufficient for him . . .

An epochal world phenomenon, Peter the Great will be possible to comprehend only when the fate of Russia is comprehended and when its place in world history is determined.

The enormous phenomenon of Russia and its separateness from the education of Europe, though it belongs to Europe, its religious, political and moral autochthonous quality, its nationality, the merging of the North with the South, the West with the East, Europe with Asia, its geography, its history, its character, which is able to accept and appropriate everything, while retaining its independence, everything indicates that providence has prepared for Russia a great task in the history of humanity. Centuries built the huge material edifice of Russian strength, and when it was time for Russia to move into Europe, Peter *appeared*, breathed life into matter, closed by his all-powerful will the gap in time and space, and moved an *Asiatic tsardom* into the midst of *European states* . . .

He was born *predestined*, he was realizing a *Divine predestination*, he *could not live differently*, and his great deed was his existence. . . . It is impossible to point to his mistakes because we do not know: could it be that what *seems to be* a mistake to us is necessary for the future, which has not reached us yet, but which he already foresaw . . .

We only sympathize with truth and goodness and aspire toward them, but in a genius they are part of his essence: he can not not be kind and good, as the sun can not not shine, the water can not not move, the flame can not not direct itself upward. Therefore, Peter the Great, like also a few others—very few, let us reiterate—can not be compared to anyone: he is original, like a genius, who breaks all the bounds of transitory human existence.[76]

Polevoi repeated in one of its more extreme forms Feofan Prokopovich's vision of the two Russias:

An Asiatic tsardom, a huge mass of material forces. A tsar recluse in his chambers, under the influences of an oligarchy and of theocracy. An army composed of disorganized mobs, hundreds of thousands retreating from the Crimean Tartars, and elite units ready to stage a rebellion at the word of a conspirator or a wild fanatic. A state surrounded on the outside by powerful enemies, when a courageous king is ruling in Poland and a second Gustavus Adolphus is ascending the Swedish throne; internally, languishing under the yoke of superstition, of ignorance, lacking learning, enlightenment, education. A people, which regards a foreigner as a cursed infidel. A commerce that is a penurious satisfaction of needs or a monopoly of the noble and the rich. There is no naval force because Russia is cut off from all the seas, except the Caspian, which is useless to it. The crudeness of education manifests itself in the way of life of the people, which is subject to the vices of semieducated societies. Women are slaves of their fathers and their husbands. In the very structure of the state the administration is a

---

[76] Nikolai Polevoi, *Istoriia Petra Velikogo* (4 vols., St. Petersburg, 1843), IV, 303–307. The chapter entitled "Peter the Great as Tsar, Man and a Select of Fate. Conclusion" (*"Petr Velikii, kak tsar, chelovek i izbrannik sudeb. Zakliuchenie"*) occupies pp. 301–344.

confusion of judicial forms and of the arbitrariness of judges. The Ukraine and the Don retain their rights in a hostile manner. Siberia is merely a place of exile and of procuring sables for the tsar.

And what do you have, then, after *forty* years?

You see a European state, permeated by an urge for mental education. A tsar, surrounded by a majestic court, by serried ranks of officials, by a powerful brave army, by a mighty, numerous navy on three seas. The neighbors, Sweden and Poland, have been destroyed. Having recently stepped over the Caucasian range, Russia is prepared to punish the pride of distant China, prepared to start once more a war against Turkey and to open for itself the way to the Black Sea, while already possessing the Baltic and the Caspian. There are Russian ships on the distant Pacific Ocean; they will soon reach the shores of America and the borders of Japan. Russia is in alliance with entire Europe, which has already seen closely the Russian tsar, his army, and his fleet. Russian ambassadors are at European courts, and ambassadors of European monarchs at the Russian court. Other sovereigns of Europe become relatives of the tsar, and he is one of the movers of European politics, which will soon depend on the Russian decision. Inside the country rebellion has been wiped out. Parts of the state are fused into one by the will of the tsar. Everything is vivified by learning, by education, by enlightenment, by commerce, which already extends to all of Europe and which is set to penetrate Asia and to reach across the seas to India. Internal communications, paths, roads, canals are laid everywhere. Russia possesses commercial Riga and ancient Revel. Superstition and fanaticism have been deprived of their strength. The might and the authority of theocracy do not exist. Education has entered the life of the people. Thousands of Russians had already been in foreign lands. Thousands of foreigners had already brought their sciences, their knowledge, their industries to the Russians. Laws are being organized into a symmetrical system. *Law*, not the arbitrariness of a judge or a clerk, presides in the courts.[77]

The author described and praised the first emperor in the established manner, fulsomely and without reservations:

*The useful* was always his aim, and only because of that aim he studied history, geography, theology, and knew many crafts and mechanical arts.[78]

In private, family life the virtues of a man and of a Christian were joined in Peter the Great. He was a kind son, a tender brother, a loving husband, a child-loving father, a good master of his house, a quiet family man, a faithful friend. A kindhearted simplicity could be observed in his home life, occupations, habits. His piety was sincere and deep, and it was combined with a hatred of superstition. He knew superbly the Holy Writ, knew by heart the church services, loved to sing and read in church. He was ready to forgive the mistakes and the faults of the guilty.[79]

[77] *Ibid.*, 330–333. Elsewhere in his work, Polevoi allowed much more for the Russian turning to the West prior to Peter the Great, although, to be sure, he considered that turning merely preliminary and entirely insufficient (see esp. I, 141–144).

[78] Polevoi, *op. cit.*, IV, 310–311.

[79] *Ibid.*, 312.

In his case, everything moved immediately from *thought* into *realization*.[80]

Later writers often failed to do the titanic ruler justice.[81]

In conclusion, the author raised the important issue of whether Peter the Great had finished his undertakings:

He *finished* them because nothing, neither the oligarchy after his death nor the forty years that passed between his time and the reign of Catherine II, budged, shook, or destroyed the foundations that he had established. He *did not finish* them because they had no end, and he lived by the life of the entire past, the entire present, and the entire future existence of Russia . . .

Bow in front of Peter the Great, Russian people, and revere his sacred memory![82]

Polevoi's History of *Peter the Great* appeared in 1843, and it paid a certain tribute to the Romantic intellectual climate of the age. For example, to refer back, in his concluding summary, Polevoi presented the first emperor as, especially, a genius, rather than a pragmatic statesman or a Grecian sage and lawgiver. More importantly, the author insisted that the Petrine achievement could be fully understood only in the context of the Russian world mission and after the future accomplishment of that mission. Still, on the whole, Polevoi's image of the first emperor indicated overwhelming continuity, not change. The author faithfully repeated earlier writers and even often treated their legacy in a particularly rigid and narrow manner. Such important and revealing elements of the reign as the story of Tsarevich Alexis were presented entirely from the established, official point of view. Traditional apologetics reigned supreme. But it is also worth noting that Polevoi's image of Peter the Great, with its strictly maintained religious and moral tones and its emphasis on such factors as "awesome justice" and power, stood very close to the political ideal of Nicholas I and Official Nationality, suggesting both the broad penetration of such views at the time in the Russian educated public and their thorough grounding in the Russian past.

Fiction joined journalism and history in painting a highly positive, quasi-official image of Peter the Great. The special case of Pushkin aside— and even the most radical or the most esoteric reading of Pushkin must recognize at least some of the major contributions he made to the established depiction of the first emperor—writers of fiction usually aimed simply to entertain, but their treatment of their subject fitted as a rule nicely, if not necessarily in any important way, the official view. Perhaps the oldest, simplest, most widespread, and most popular form of the

80 *Ibid.*, 321.

81 In particular: "One cannot but be surprised that Russian military writers have not up to now revealed and demonstrated to us the gifts of Peter the Great as a military commander" (*ibid.*, 323), a lacuna in the Petrine historiography that has been filled since, in particular by Soviet specialists.

82 *Ibid.*, 341–342.

Petrine prose literature was the anecdote or the story relating an incident connected with the emperor, his immediate assistants, or at least his times. Common throughout the eighteenth century and especially richly represented in Golikov's massive volumes, the genre continued to thrive in the nineteenth century. In the reign of Nicholas I, it led to such works as Peter Furman's (1809–1856) *Prince Iakov Fedorovich Dolgorukii (Kniaz Iakov Fedorovich Dolgorukii)*; Constantine Masalskii's (1802–1861) "The Black Casket" ("Chernyi iashchik"); or Nestor Kukolnik's (1809–1868) "The New Year" ("Novyi god"), "The Sentinel" ("Chasovoi"), "The Tale of the Blue and the Green Cloth" ("Skazanie o sinem i zelenom sukne"), and others. Typically, the first emperor righted injustices, reunited lovers, and arranged for military promotion or educational advancement. Kukolnik's mediocre stories from the age of Peter the Great not only proved successful in their author's lifetime, but were republished as late as the 1880s in a large popular edition. It will be remembered that it was Kukolnik's Petrine play, *The Orderly (Denshchik)*, which infuriated Pogodin by comparing Muscovite Russia to a cadaver—nevertheless, it did strike the right patriotic note in the days of the Crimean War and was well received by the public.

However, some writers went beyond even extended ancedotes. The historical novel was flourishing at the time in Europe, and both leading Russian practitioners of the new form, Ivan Lazhechnikov (1792–1869) and Michael Zagoskin (1789–1852), as well as a number of their colleagues, wrote historical novels from the reign of Peter the Great. Lazhechnikov's *The Last Recruit (Poslednii novik)*, 1833, stressed the theme of patriotism; presented the extraordinary story of Catherine I; and featured her, Peter the Great, and Menshikov, as well as a number of entirely fictional characters. Zagoskin turned to Petrine themes late in his highly successful career as a novelist, producing *The Brynsk Forest (Brynskii les)* in 1846 and *The Russians at the Beginning of the Eighteenth Century (Russkie v nachale osmnadtsatogo stoletiia)* in 1848. The first novel dealt with the *streltsy* and the old Believers, but managed a happy ending. The second centered on the disastrous Prut campaign of 1711, salvaging again personal happiness for its fictional young protagonists utterly loyal to Peter the Great and his work.

As we have had repeated occasion to observe, a writer on Peter the Great did not have to confine himself to a single genre. One more example of versatility was provided by Raphael Zotov (1795–1871), whom we encountered as a historian comparing Nicholas I to Peter the Great, but who also treated the first emperor in a play and again in a historical novel. The play is sufficiently described by its title: *The Shipbuilder from Zaandam: or, His Name Is Ineffable (Saardamskii korabelnyi master, ili net imeni emu)*. The novel was summarized as follows by Professor Xenia Gasiorowska:

*The Mysterious Monk.* 1834. A novel set mostly in 1682–1701, but with the denouement at Poltava in 1709; it includes plots against Peter by Streltsy and Mazepa's treason. A mysterious foundling, Grisha, is raised by Prince Khovansky and the mysterious monk of the title, Iona, who proves to be Hetman Doroshenko (a historical personage). Doroshenko is in love with Mazepa's (fictional) daughter Elena, wife of Prince Khovansky and mother of Grisha. Grisha saves Peter's life and as a reward marries Masha, the widow of Peter's protégé. A typical "historical" novel of the period.[83]

The doctrine of Official Nationality represented not only the views of Nicholas I and his government, but also, broadly speaking, the convictions of a large part of the Russian educated public of the time. Not surprisingly, its proponents were not an entirely homogeneous body. As I argued at length elsewhere, the main ideological cleavage ran between the purely dynastic, traditional, and reactionary orientation of the emperor and most of his immediate assistants, and the more ambitious Romantic beliefs of such intellectuals of the Right as Professors Pogodin and Shevyrev. In terms of the image of Peter the Great, the division was not a crucial one. Those on the Romantic wing allowed more for pre-Petrine Russia and had greater future expectations, somewhat along Polevoi's lines, than their dynastic counterparts. But all agreed in a resounding affirmation of the stupendous beneficial importance of Peter the Great and his autocracy for Russia. In doing so, they, of course, restated and reemphasized the already very well-established view. There were clear and fundamental connections between Feofan Prokopovich's orations or Gabriel Buzhinskii's sermon on military service and just wars and the cherished Petrine beliefs of the proponents of Official Nationality. Nor were intermediate links missing. Indeed, government and Rightist intellectuals of the second quarter of the nineteenth century loved to repeat the bombastic pronouncements of Lomonosov, of Derzhavin, and of so many others, and to join their voices to the never-ending praise of the Petrine autocracy. In a sense, the continuity was complete.

And yet there was also an important change. The Official Nationality perspective recognized in full the authority and power of Peter the Great, in large part even his achievement, but not the dynamic nature of his reign nor his ceaseless pursuit of the West. Catherine the Great could still imagine herself as the intellectual leader of enlightened Europe and thus as both a true and a superior disciple of the reformer. No such thoughts occurred to Nicholas I. The image of the reformer, as well as everything else, had to be fitted instead into a defensive and static view. In the process something was lost inevitably. And it was precisely that

[83] Xenia Gasiorowska, *The Image of Peter the Great in Russian Fiction* (Madison, Wis., 1979), 190. The Russian title of Zotov's novel was *Tainstvennyi monakh.* Professor Gasiorowska's informative book is extremely useful to a student of the Russian image of Peter the Great; as indicated earlier, the author even provides "plot summaries" of the fiction in question (186–190).

something, the urge West, progress, promise, that the new intellectuals to be known as the Westernizers put at the center of their rival image of Peter the Great.

4

Thus, the image of Peter the Great of the Westernizers, like that of the proponents of Official Nationality, issued directly from the fundamental Petrine perception of the Russian Age of Reason. It could even claim to represent the full development of perhaps the most basic element of that perception: Peter the Great as the enlightener in the true and complete meaning of that word. But it also expressed—and on the whole much more than depictions by government apologists—new Romantic and German idealistic trends of thought. The kind of metaphysical theorizing introduced into Russia by Chaadaev became standard coin among the Westernizers, and, in particular, it provided the frame of reference for the celebrated controversy between the Westernizers and the Slavophiles.

To be more exact, Chaadaev had been preceded by the so-called Lovers of Wisdom (*liubomudry*), a group of some twelve young men, who in 1823 formed the first Russian philosophic circle and published the first Russian philosophic review, *Mnemosyne*. Prince Vladimir Odoevskii (1803–1869) presided, the poet Dimitrii Venevitinov (1805–1827) served as secretary, and the members included such future proponents of Official Nationality as Pogodin and Shevyrev, and such future Slavophiles as Ivan Kireevskii, Peter Kireevskii, and Alexander Koshelev. The Lovers of Wisdom devoted themselves to a study of Schelling and of German idealistic philosophy in general. They disbanded their circle after the Decembrist rebellion in order not to attract attention. Venevitinov, the gifted "poet of thought," who died at the age of twenty-one and who was preoccupied with the aesthetic theories of the Romanticists and with such subjects as man as the microcosm, the organic theory of nationality and nations, and the return to original harmony on a new conscious level through creative effort, left some far-reaching comments on the relationship between his native country and the West. The poet had the highest appreciation of the West, but he was deeply perturbed by the imitative nature of Russian culture and went so far as to condemn all Russian literature as imitation. He even urged that Russia withdraw from contact with the West and develop a true culture of its own on the basis of a real awareness of the self and organic creativity.

Odoevskii, however, went beyond Venevitinov's defensive attitude, and he has been praised as the first Russian to make a critical philosophic appraisal of Western culture and to formulate on this basis a doctrine of Russian messiahship. Of special interest here is Odoevskii's *Russian Nights* (*Russkie nochi*), a work strongly influenced by Schelling, conceived in the twenties, written in the thirties, but published in a complete form only in 1844, in the first volume of its author's collected works. The West, Odoevskii argued, had accomplished marvelous things, but it had lost its balance and its harmony and was in the throes of a most dangerous crisis caused by its inability to resolve the antinomy of man and society, of the private and the public. This failure had led to the perversion of science and art, to the loss of love and faith. Fortunately, salvation was possible. Throughout the history of the world such crises had been surmounted by the appearance of a savior, of a new, fresh people destined to show again to humanity the true path from which it had deviated. For the West the savior was Russia. In the time of Napoleon, Russia had already saved the body of Europe; this was a symbol of the more difficult task yet to be accomplished, the salvation of the soul of Europe. History had prepared Russia for its glorious mission: before Peter the Great, Russia had been distinguished by its enormous size, gigantic strength, and versatile spirit, but it lacked organization and Western learning; Peter the Great had added the latter elements, and thus Russia attained a harmonious development unknown in the West. Russia was an organic society that knew no struggle between the people and the government, preserved the principles of love and unity, and believed in the happiness of all and everyone. The Russian spirit was characterized by a particular versatility, universality, and inclusiveness on which a truly harmonious life could be founded. Odoevskii's benevolent Romantic idealism reflected faithfully the earlier and less exclusive stage of European Romanticism. It also enabled him to resolve in a strikingly integrated, inclusive, and optimistic manner the problem of the role of Peter the Great in Russian, and even world, history.[84]

But the views of the Lovers of Wisdom were relatively little-known and perhaps, in terms of the Russian intellectual development, premature. It was Chaadaev's explosive contributions to the historiosophical interpretation of Russian destiny that set the stage for the Slavophiles, the Westernizers, and their great debate. Paradoxical extremism prevailed over Odoevskii's synthesizing and conciliatory approach.

A coterie of friends that began gathering around Nicholas Stankevich (1813–1840) in the winter of 1831–1832 has been generally considered the first Westernizer circle. The original half a dozen young men were joined a little later by several more, including Vissarion Belinskii (1811–1848) and the future Slavophile Constantine Aksakov (1817–1860), and in 1835 by Michael Bakunin (1814–1876), Michael Katkov (1818–1887), and Basil Botkin (1810–1869). Still later Timothy Granovskii (1813–1855) and the writer Ivan Turgenev (1818–1883) were associated with the group. The

---

84 V. F. Odoevskii, *Russkie nochi* (Moscow, 1913). The standard work on Odoevskii remains P. N. Sakulin's *Iz istorii russkogo idealizma. Kniaz V. Odoevskii* (Moscow, 1913). Parts of Pogodin's depiction of old Russia and of its relationship to Peter the Great, presented in the immediately preceding section, were very close to Odoevskii's position, as were some of the Slavophile opinions concerning the virtues of the Russians and the crisis of the West.

circle was most active from 1833 to 1837 until Stankevich's departure from Russia; 1839, when Belinskii left Moscow for St. Petersburg, has been cited as the terminal date of its effective existence. In the words of the latest literary historian of Stankevich: "The circle was a loosely organized intellectual fraternity with literary and philosophical interests. Its members met irregularly to read romantic literature—their own and others'—to discuss ideas, and to explore the philosophy of Schelling, Kant, Fichte, and Hegel."[85] Or as Stankevich himself put it, as late as 1838:

Art is becoming divinity for me, and I keep repeating one thing: friendship . . . and art! That is the world in which man must live, if he does not want to be like an animal! that is the beneficial sphere in which he must reside to be worthy of himself! that is the fire with which he must warm and cleanse his soul![86]

Perhaps not surprisingly, although the Stankevich circle left a permanent impress in Russian intellectual history as the crucible from which so many remarkable thinkers came and as a continuous influence on all their subsequent development, it did not contribute markedly to historical discussion, let alone to the image of Peter the Great as such.[87] It was only after Chaadaev's sweeping performance and the emergence of Slavophilism in 1839 that the Westernizers began to concentrate, in their turn, on historical, more precisely historiosophical, themes. By that time, too, the former members of the Stankevich circle were going increasingly in their own separate directions, thus contributing considerable variety, as well as occasional brilliance, to Russian thought.

Belinskii was one of the most important of these intellectual travelers. The man who became the most significant and influential Russian literary critic of all times did not have the advantages of a rich cultural background and began his ideological career rather hesitantly in the Stankevich circle, where he learned Romantic philosophy and aesthetics from his more accomplished and cosmopolitan associates. In contrast to Stankevich, however, Belinskii was passionately concerned with the world around him and indeed determined to bring together the ideal and the real. As the circle disintegrated in the late 1830s, he joined Bakunin in a foolhardy attempt to read Hegel and especially Hegel's celebrated assertion that what was real was rational and what was rational was real, so as to identify the real world with the ideal world, apotheosize the Russia of Nicholas I, and eliminate idealism as a separate and alienating category. To be sure, the apotheosis did not last long, certainly not

85 Edward J. Brown, *Stankevich and His Moscow Circle* (Stanford, 1966), 4.

86 Quoted from: S. Mashinskii, "Stankevich i ego kruzhok," *Istoriia literatury*, no. 5 (1964), 125–148, 135.

87 Revealingly, there is no reference to Peter the Great in a volume of Stankevich's correspondence that contains 346 letters as well as fragments of the author's diary, namely, N. V. Stankevich, *Perepiska 1830–1840* (Moscow, 1914).

beyond 1840. But, very importantly for our purposes, the critic's belief in Peter the Great survived his disillusionment with contemporary Russian autocracy and accompanied him on his stridently radical course. For Belinskii saw the reformer as enlightenment, progress, and the true destiny of Russia. His remarkably clear, firm, and comprehensive Westernizer vision combined the rational faith of the Enlightenment, always close to Belinskii's heart, with the newer Romantic conceptualizing and theorizing.

Belinskii's correspondence attests to his intellectual and emotional devotion to Peter the Great. In 1837 he wrote, after commenting on France:

> The destiny of Russia is an entirely different matter. If you want to understand its destiny, read the history of Peter the Great—it will explain to you everything. No people had such a sovereign. All great sovereigns of other peoples are below Peter, all of them were expressions of the lives of their peoples and merely executed the will of their peoples, when performing great work; in one word, all of them were under the influence of their peoples. Peter, to the contrary, departed from his own people; he did not educate it, but he reeducated it, he did not create it, but he recreated it.[88]

The letter was written when Belinskii believed in the Russian government, and he proceeded to explain that Peter the Great represented conclusive proof that Russia was to receive a civic polity and freedom from its tsars, following upon the reformer's work, not by any internal process. Yet ten years later, only a few months before his death, and having become in the meantime the greatest radical voice in the land, the critic had apparently an even deeper faith in the first emperor: "As to me, Peter is my philosophy, my religion, my revelation in everything that pertains to Russia."[89] And in a still later letter: "Russia needs a new Peter the Great."[90]

Literary criticism was both Belinskii's passion and his means of livelihood, and the great bulk of his work has come down to us in the form of book reviews. Fortunately, the genre allowed considerable general discussion and digression, making it possible to reconstruct the critic's opinions, including his opinions on Peter the Great, from his evaluations of at times quite unlikely books. Most significantly, in his literary criticism, as in his correspondence, Belinskii emphasized the overwhelming importance of the reformer for modern Russia. In doing that, he followed the main line of the Russian Enlightenment, adding to it such newer characteristics as repeated references to the first emperor as a genius in the Romantic sense and the assertion that "Peter was the full expression of the Russian spirit."[91]

88 V. G. Belinskii, *Pisma*, E. A. Liatskii, ed. (3 vols., St. Petersburg, 1914), I, 91.
89 Belinskii, *op. cit.*, III, 300.
90 *Ibid.*, 339.
91 V. G. Belinskii, *Sobranie sochinenii v trekh tomakh* (3 vols., Moscow, 1948), F. M. Golovenchenko, general ed., vol. II, *Stati i retsenzii, 1841–1845*, S. P. Bychkov, ed., 517.

Although Peter the Great wrote and published nothing, which Catherine II did, he is nevertheless as much the creator of Russian literature, as of Russian civilization, Russian enlightenment, Russian greatness and glory, in one word, the creator of new Russia. To write a history of Russian literature without saying a word about Peter the Great is the same as to write about the origin of the world without saying a word about the creator of the world.[92]

Moreover:

The name of Peter the Great must be the moral point in which are concentrated all the feelings, all the convictions, all the hopes, the pride, the veneration, and the adoration of all Russians: Peter the Great is not only the creator of the past and the present greatness of Russia, but he will also remain forever as the guiding star of the Russian people, thanks to which Russia will always follow its present path to the high goal of moral, human, and political perfection.[93]

Literary works devoted to Peter the Great offered the critic, of course, special opportunities to write on one of his favorite subjects, as exemplified tellingly by his treatment of "The Bronze Horseman." Here is how Belinskii explained, in 1846, the meaning of Pushkin's remarkable poem:

In this poem we observe the sad lot of an individual, suffering as it were as a result of the selection of the location for the new capital, where so many people perished, and our heart shattered by sympathy is ready to rebel together with the unfortunate one; but suddenly our gaze, falling upon the statue of the cause of our glory, is lowered, and in holy tremor, as if conscious of a heavy sin, it dashes away, thinking that it hears behind it.

> Thunders that rattle in a chorus,
> A gallop ponderous, sonorous,
> That shakes the pavement.

We understand in our abashed soul that not arbitrariness but rational will is incarnate in this *Bronze Horseman,* who, from his unshakable height, his arm outstretched, is as if admiring the city. . . . And we imagine that, amid the chaos and the darkness of this destruction, there emerges from his bronze lips the creating "Let there be!" and the outstretched arm proudly orders the raging elements to subside. . . . And with a humble heart we acknowledge the triumph of the general over the particular, without renouncing our sympathy for the suffering of that particular. . . . At the sight of the giant rising proudly and unshakably in the midst of general ruin and destruction and as if symbolically realizing in himself the indestructibility of his creation, we recognize, although not without a shudder of the heart, that this bronze giant could not protect the destiny of individuals as he was securing the destiny of the people and the state, that historical necessity is on his side, and that his look at us is already his justification. . . . Yes, this poem is an apotheosis of Peter the Great, the most daring, the most grand that could enter the head of a poet entirely worthy of being the bard of the great reformer of Russia . . .[94]

92 *Ibid.,* 364–365.
93 Belinskii, *Sobranie sochinenii,* vol. III, *Stati i retsenzii, 1843–1848,* V. I. Kuleshov, ed., 413.
94 *Ibid.,* 608; all the breaks are Belinskii's. Belinskii's prestige in the Soviet Union is

Yet even the discussion of "The Bronze Horseman" occupied only several pages, and, in general, in spite of frequent references to the reformer, Belinskii's works lacked an extended and sustained treatment of the Petrine theme. The critic came perhaps closest to such a treatment in a relatively early essay, two parts of which were published in *The Notes of the Fatherland (Otechestvennye Zapiski)* in 1841, but which was disfigured by the censorship and remained unfinished. The occasion for the essay was the appearance of books to be reviewed: the second edition of the first thirteen volumes of Golikov's famous account of the first emperor, a translation of a three-volume German work on Peter the Great, and the publication of Gregory Kotoshikhin's remarkable and devastatingly negative description of Muscovy.[95]

Russians, Belinskii declared, paid insufficient attention to Peter the Great precisely because they were not as yet properly concerned with the interests of humanity at large, to which the reformer belonged as much as he belonged to Russia. "Peter the Great is the greatest phenomenon not only of our history, but also of the history of all mankind; he is the divinity that called us to life, breathing a living soul into the body of old Russia, colossal but plunged in deathly slumber."[96] Yet Russians did not seem to care, with Golikov representing the major exception, and in turn being neglected by his compatriots. Russian scholars wasted their efforts on minute topics from the ancient Russian past, although that past had no world historical significance: it was only with Peter the Great that Russia entered world history. The importance of the Petrine reforms lay in the true Europeanization of Russia, in making Russia European in more than simply the geographical sense. The opposite of Europe was Asia. "Asia is the land of the so-called natural immediacy; Europe is the land of consciousness. Asia is the land of contemplation; Europe, of will and reason."[97] An Asiatic, like an infant, lived by direct primitive emotion. Tradition and fatalism ruled social institutions and relations. The individual was of no importance and had no rights. Human life had no

---

so great that his view—and this passage in particular—represents an obstacle to different Soviet interpretations of Pushkin's controversial poem. To counter the celebrated critic, it has been argued notably that he knew only the censored version of "The Bronze Horseman." See, e.g., P. Mezentsev, "Poema Pushkina 'Mednyi vsadnik' (k voprosu ob ideinom soderzhanii)," *Russkaia literatura*, no. 2 (1958), 56–68.

95 The review of "*Deianiia Petra Velikogo, mudrogo preobrazovatelia Rossii, sobrannye iz dostovernykh istochnikov i raspolozhennye po godam, Sochinenie I. I. Golikova.* Izdanie vtoroe. Moskva. 1837–1840. Tomy I–XIII. *Istoriia Petra Velikogo.* Sochinenie Veniamina Bergmana. Perevel s nemetskogo Egor Aladin. Vtoroe, szhatoe (kompaktnoe) izdanie, ispravlennoe i umnozhennoe. S.-Peterburg. 1840. Tri toma. *O Rossii v tsarstvovanie Aleksiia Mikhailovicha.* Sovremennoe sochinenie Grigoriia Koshikhina. S.-Peterburg, 1840," in V. G. Belinskii, *Polnoe sobranie sochinenii*, S. A. Vengerov, ed. (12 vols., St. Petersburg, 1903), VI, 118–143, 179–198, editorial notes pp. 573–575, 585–586. The second installment refers only to the first two works in its title. See p. 586 for the impact of the censorship.

96 *Ibid.*, 119.

97 *Ibid.*, 124.

greater value than that of cattle. Even family ties had no compelling strength in establishing moral behavior, for men were absolute masters over their women, parents sold their children, and a Moslem ruler could upon his accession to the throne execute all his brothers, just as a tiger could devour his own young.

Immobility and petrification are linked to Asia, as the soul is to the body. Just as it was several thousands of years before Christ, so it is now, and so it will remain forever, unless Europe cracks the foundations of its natural condition and transforms it by means of Christianity. There is no science and no art in Asia; there is, instead of them, tradition and custom.[98]

By contrast:

Variety in life, noble relations between the sexes, refined manners, art, science, a subjugation of the blind forces of nature, victory over matter, a triumph of the spirit, respect for the individual, sacredness of human rights, in one word, everything that makes man proud of his human dignity, makes him consider himself the ruler of the world, the favorite son of divine grace and a participant in it—all that is a result of the development of European life. Everything human is European, and everything European is human . . .[99]

Christian Russia, to be sure, could not belong to Asia; but it found itself isolated from Europe and under Asiatic Mongol pressure. "And, thus, Peter acted entirely in the national spirit, bringing Russia closer to Europe and eradicating the temporary Asiatic elements introduced into it by the Mongols."[100] How bad things had become was depicted in full detail in the Kotoshikhin narrative. Belinskii spent half of the first installment of his essay quoting Kotoshikhin and even one other contemporary account, in this manner presenting in particular the ritualistic inanity as well as the judicial and penal cruelty of Muscovy. In the standard theory of the two Russias, the denigration of the first was certainly reinforced by the painstaking picture drawn by the bitter exile. Fortunately for Belinskii, Russia did not end with Muscovy or Kotoshikhin:

Having presented the way of life of Russia in the manner in which eyewitnesses paint it for us, let us now turn to that bright, blessed moment in the history of our fatherland, when Peter by his mighty "Let there be" drove away the darkness of chaos, separated light from darkness, and called forth a great country to a great existence, to a universal destiny.[101]

The second installment—and the last one to appear—began with the assertion that with Peter the Great Russia had entered the period of consciousness. The very doubts concerning the work of the reformer and criticisms of him led only to a deeper understanding and a stronger affirmation of his historical role. More recently, a new contradiction

[98] *Ibid.,* 128.
[99] *Ibid.,* 131. The break is Belinskii's.
[100] *Ibid.*
[101] *Ibid.,* 143.

emerged: many critics glorified the achievement of the first emperor and yet turned against Europeanism and even championed the historical Russian nationality, destroyed by the reformer, in their opposition to Europeanism.

The contradiction in question is extremely important: its resolution provides the true understanding of Peter the Great. This alone points to the reasonableness of that contradiction. The solution of the problem consists in this, that it be demonstrated and proved: (1) that although nationality is indeed closely linked to the historical development and the social structures of a people, the first and the second are not at all identical; (2) that both the reform of Peter the Great and the Europeanism that he introduced did not in the least change and could not change our nationality, but only revived it by the spirit of a new and much richer life and gave it a boundless sphere for expression and activity.[102]

Nothing comes out of nothing, and Peter I, like other great men, could only realize that which already existed as a potential. He had turned against the archaic Russian past, not at all against the national Russian substance. Otherwise he could never have succeeded. National substances depended on blood, on historical development, certainly on climate and geography. The Russians belonged to the melancholy north, and one found that melancholy in Pushkin's poems as much as in folk songs, for indeed Russian geography had not changed. Nor could Europeanism affect such substantive Russian qualities as energy, daring, resourcefulness, or a certain emotional sweep in both sorrow and joy. Besides, and in any case, Europeanization did not mean some sort of leveling: the English, the French, the Germans, the Dutch, and the Swiss were all equally Europeans. As for Russian willingness to renounce its historic past and to learn from the West, that constituted in fact a great virtue, for it enabled the Russians to get rid of what was bad and worthless. National vices were of two kinds: substantive, such as the egoism of the English or the religious fanaticism of the Spaniards, and historically acquired, as in the case of the political nullity of the Italians. Russian vices were, typically, acquired, in particular because of the two centuries of the Mongol yoke:

The seclusion of women, the habit of burying money in the ground and of wearing rags from the fear of revealing one's riches, extortion, Asiaticism in the way of life, a laziness of the mind, ignorance, self-contempt, in one word, everything that Peter the Great was extirpating, everything that was in Russia directly opposed to Europeanism, all that is not native in us, but has been grafted to us by the Mongols. The very intolerance of the Russians toward foreigners in general was a result of the Mongol yoke: the Mongol made anyone who was not a Russian repulsive to the Russian mind, and the word *infidel* spread from the Mongols also to others. That the most important failings of our nationality are not substantive, blood failings, but grafted ones can be best proved by the fact that

102 *Ibid.*, 183.

it is entirely possible for us to get rid of them, that we already have gotten rid of and are getting rid of many of them.[103]

Thus, modern Russian literature was waging a successful campaign against extortion and corruption, and they were bound to disappear soon together with other bad habits. "In general, all the failings and vices of our society stemmed from ignorance and a lack of enlightenment: and, therefore, the light of knowledge and education is scattering them, just as the rising of the sun scatters night mists."[104] The people responded to the reform by the battles of Poltava and Borodino. It had barely time to join Europe when it eliminated for Europe the Turkish menace. "But the people is one and the same, and Peter did not recreate it (no one, except God, could accomplish that), but merely led it from the crooked beaten paths onto the main road of world-historical life."[105] Nor was Peter the Great's timing off, or his methods and measures to blame. "Peter had no time for delay: the issue was not the greatness of Russia in the future, but its salvation in the present. Peter appeared in time: were he a quarter of a century late, well then *save us* or *save himself who can!* . . . Providence knows when to send a man on earth."[106] Spoiled Russians had forgotten how desperate the situation had been 132 years earlier or how necessary were such costly measures as the building of St. Petersburg.

Belinskii returned to the building of St. Petersburg and to a discussion of that city in general in a longish piece written in 1844 and entitled "Peterburg and Moscow."[107] One of the critic's more tolerant and nuanced essays, inspired by a certain personal sympathy and closeness to the old capital as well as to the new, and, besides, meant to be humorous in its description of life in the two cities, "Petersburg and Moscow" nevertheless left no doubt as to where its author stood. Belinskii even produced an unusual argument for the building of St. Petersburg, a reflection perhaps of the new Romantic emphasis on effort and striving:

St. Petersburg was built impromptu: what was accomplished in a month could have occupied a year. The will of a single person conquered even nature itself. It seemed that fate itself, contrary to all calculations of probability, wanted to toss the capital of the Russian empire into this region inimical and hostile to man by its nature and its climate; where the sky is pale green, where meager grass is mixed with creeping heather, dry moss, marshy verdure, and gray hillocks; where the prickly pine and the sorrowful fir reign and have their depressing monotony only occasionally broken by a stunted birch, that plant of the north; where emanations from the swamps and the dampness permeating the air penetrate both stone houses and human bones; where there is no spring, no summer, no winter, but a rotten and wet autumn raging the year around and parodying now spring, now summer, now winter. . . . It seemed that fate wanted the Russian,

103 *Ibid.*, 187. I translated *basurman* as "infidel."
104 *Ibid.*, 188.
105 *Ibid.*, 189.
106 *Ibid.*, 122. The break is Belinskii's.
107 V. G. Belinskii, "Peterburg i Moskva," *Sobranie sochinenii*, III, 763–791.

who until then had slept eternally, to work out his future by means of bloody sweat and desperate struggle because only those victories are enduring that are won by hard labor, only those conquests that are obtained by suffering and blood! Perhaps in a more favorable climate, amid less hostile nature, in the absence of insuperable obstacles, the Russian would have become proud of his easy successes, and his energy would have again gone to sleep even before it had fully awakened. And it is for that reason that he, who was sent to him from God, was not only tsar and ruler, acted not only by means of authority, but even more by means of his own example, which disarmed the obdurate ignorance and sloth nursed by the centuries.[108]

As to a comparison between the two cities, the critic met head on even the argument that Moscow represented the supreme historical treasure of Russia. St. Petersburg, he asserted, possessed in fact a greater history and greater treasures because it had the reformer: "Everywhere you see in it the living traces of its builder, and for many (ourselves included) such little buildings as, for example, the little house on the Petersburg side, the palace in the Summer Garden, the palace in Peterhof are worth not one but many Kremlins . . . There is nothing to be done—tastes differ!"[109]

Belinskii's championing of Peter the Great was unqualified and uncompromising. Not satisfied with elucidating and glorifying the emperor's general historical role, the critic was ready to defend him in every particular. To cite a single example, Belinskii justified the introduction of Western dress and the cutting of beards because "sometimes *external appearance* too is worth something. Let us say more: the external sometimes draws the internal after it."[110] Indeed, in Russia, where change spread from the top down, externalities acquired a particular significance. True, the critic believed that Peter the Great had merely begun the transformation of Russia, and he referred occasionally to the separation of the educated public from the common people resulting from the Petrine reforms: these were, however, problems of Russian historical development to be overcome in the subsequent evolution of the country, not flaws in the superhuman activity and record of the first emperor.[111]

Belinskii's was a striking and significant case of a radical Westernizer totally devoted to Peter the Great. Similar devotion permeated the thoughts and the feelings of moderate Westernizers and, if the expression be allowed, of the Westernizers of the Right, merging eventually with the sweepingly pro-Petrine attitude of the proponents of Official Nationality discussed in the preceding section of this chapter.

Timothy Granovskii, a professor of European history at the University of Moscow, has been often cited as a particularly representative "man of

108 *Ibid.*, 765–766. The break is Belinskii's.
109 *Ibid.*, 772. The break is Belinskii's.
110 *Ibid.*, 773–774, quoted from p. 773.
111 See, e.g., Belinskii, *Sobranie sochinenii*, II, 10, 135.

the forties" and as a quintessential moderate Westernizer. A highly successful lecturer, an influential teacher and friend, and in general a major
participant in the intellectual revival of the time, Granovskii left little
in writing, and this written work did not extend to Peter the Great.
Nevertheless, we know well his basic views of the reformer because of a
leading role that he played in the debate between the Westernizers and
the Slavophiles and also from his correspondence. These views were almost identical with Belinskii's, and they were held with a similar conviction and passion. Nor was the historian far behind the literary critic
in emphasizing their relevance for his own day. As Granovskii commented
on the subject of certain reactionary elements in a letter written in 1851:
"The grandfathers of these people hated Peter the Great; the grandsons
hate his work."[112] Or, to quote from a letter to a friend written in 1855,
the year of Granovskii's death: "It seems to me that since the time of
Peter the need for a fundamental and sane enlightenment has not been
as apparent in Russia as it is at the present time."[113]

As in the cases of Belinskii and of others we encountered earlier,
Granovskii's emotional commitment to Peter the Great was at least the
equal of his intellectual allegiance to the reformer. Shortly before he
died, the historian wrote as follows to Constantine Kavelin, another
prominent Westernizer:

Sunday night I was at Pogodin's, and I did not pay my visit in vain. I saw there
a portrait of Peter the Great, which he had recently purchased. This portrait had
been painted from the dead, probably immediately after death, and it had been
preserved in the Makarov family, an ancestor of which had been Peter's cabinet
secretary in the last years of his life. The artist is unknown. I am not a connois-
seur and not even a lover of painting, but it seems to me that I could have stood
repeatedly for hours in front of that painting. I would have willingly given for
it my favorite books, a part of my library. Imagine for yourself the head of the
deceased on a red pillow, which emphasizes the pallor of the face. The upper
part of the divinely handsome face carries the stamp of a majestic repose—that
repose, which can be a result of a holy, pure, boundlessly noble thought. There
is no thought anymore, but its expression remained. I had never seen such
beauty. But it is as if life had not yet frozen in the lower part of the face. The
lips are pressed in rage and sorrow. They are as if trembling. The entire evening
I looked at this image of the man, who gave us a right to history and who virtually alone proclaimed our historical destiny. The entire evening my head was
full of him. And it was only about him that Pogodin, Samarin, and I talked. It
will be your sin and shame, Kavelin, if you do not do something for a history of
the Petrine institutions. It seems to me that you alone among us can accomplish such a work with honor. For 130 years Peter has been waiting for an
appraiser. Could it be that you will not carry out the project, which you formed

[112] T. N. Granovskii, *T. N. Granovskii i ego perepiska.* Vol. II, *Perepiska T. N. Granovskogo* (Moscow, 1897), 479.
[113] *Ibid.,* 407.

at one time? What can Ustrialov do? Gather the materials: but one can not expect from him any living understanding.[114]

Nor surprisingly, when Alexander Herzen turned in exile against Peter the Great, that became one of the issues separating him from his old and close friend, Granovskii:

Why did you throw a stone at Peter, who does not in the least deserve your accusations, for you cited incorrect facts. The more we live, the more colossal the image of Peter grows in front of us. You, torn away from Russia, no longer accustomed to it, can not have it so nearby, so understandable; looking at the vices of the West, you are leaning toward the Slavs and are ready to give them your hand. Were you to live here, you too would have said a different thing.[115]

And in a letter to Kavelin, which Granovskii dictated as he lay dying, in a withering discussion of Russian public opinion, after referring to Herzen as representing one nonsensical extreme, just as Pogodin represented its opposite: "Not only would Peter the Great be useful to us now, but so would be even his cudgel, which served to teach the Russian fool reason."[116]

Belinskii's and Granovskii's convictions in regard to the reformer were common, even standard, among the Westernizers. Thus, whereas the Slavophiles strove to find pre-Petrine and anti-Petrine Russia in Turgenev's magnificent depiction of Russian peasants, the author of *Sportsman's Sketches* (*Zapiski okhotnika*) himself, a convinced and consistent Westernizer, declared that it was when looking at the peasant Khor, full of practical intelligence, originality, and eagerness to learn, that he suddenly realized that Peter the Great had been, above all, a Russian, a Russian precisely in the reforms he had undertaken.[117] To give another example, it was Michael Katkov, a conservative Westernizer in the reign of Nicholas I, later a leader of the Russian nationalist and reactionary Right, and always under the influence of German idealistic philosophy, who penned perhaps the most philosophical Westernizer formulation of Peter the Great's historical role. Katkov wrote in 1840 in *Notes of the Fatherland* (*Otechestvennye Zapiski*):

The Russian people was also for a long time outside this world historical development; it also for a long time remained untouched by the ideas that were moving humanity; for a long time it was maturing alone, enclosed on all sides, and it was only preparing—preparing quietly, barely noticeably—for its high destiny, into which it was led by the genius of great Peter. Only from the time of Peter Russia arose, a mighty, gigantic state; only from the time of Peter the

114 *Ibid.*, 453. For another description of the portrait and of Granovskii's reaction to it, see his letter to the Frolovs (*ibid.*, 436–437, esp. p. 437).
115 *Ibid.*, 448. "The Slavs" refers to the Slavophiles.
116 *Ibid.*, 455–458, quoted from p. 456.
117 See esp. V. I. Kuleshov, "Slavianofily i romantizm," *K istorii russkogo romantizma* (Moscow, 1973), 305–344, particularly p. 343.

Russian people became a nation, became one of the representatives of humanity, developing by its life one of the aspects of the spirit; only from the time of Peter the higher spiritual interests entered its organism; only from his time it began to receive into itself the content of the development of humanity. And before the Great one we had neither art, in the proper meaning of that word, nor science.[118]

Shmurlo found "perhaps the most extreme" example of the Westernizer passion for the reformer in Alexander Nikitenko's *Laudatory Oration on Peter the Great*, delivered in 1838, at a solemn gathering of the University of St. Petersburg.[119] Nikitenko (1804 or 1805–1877), a prominent conservative professor of literature and censor—better known to later generations for his memoirs—stood close to the government, but his oration had nevertheless a clear Westernizer ring in that he praised above all Peter the Great the enlightener. Indeed he stated specifically that the glory of a conqueror, of a ruler of vast domains was below that of an enlightener of his people, of a creator of a moral order. And he eulogized the reformer for giving the Russians "the honor to exist in the human manner."[120] Nikitenko asserted in effect that Peter the Great had created a new Russia out of nothing and that his work would last eternally. Moreover, he made an immense contribution to European as well as to Russian history. Europe acquired a new people, a new champion of enlightenment, fresh and enthusiastic, ready to promote everything great and beautiful, everything human. Thus, Russia defeated Napoleon and supported thrones and society against wild political passions. "Russia solemnly in front of humanity takes off itself the guilt of not having participated in its destiny; it paid all its debts to humanity in a single stroke—it gave Peter as a gift to humanity."[121] "He is a representative of his people to the highest degree. He absorbed into himself, suddenly, with a colossal force, all its life and, having reworked it in the depths of his soul, he returned it to that same people in brilliant rays of light and glory."[122] The Russian people received from the reformer "its intelligence, its moral strength, and its hands."[123] And, Nikitenko reiterated— perhaps in contradiction to his own emphasis on the intrinsic link between the first emperor and the Russian people, but in perfect accord with the view dominant from the time of Feofan Prokopovich and reaffirmed by the Westernizers—Peter accomplished everything alone. "There

118 Quoted from: V. A. Riasanovsky, *Obzor russkoi kultury*, part II, issue I (New York, 1947), 324–325.

119 A. Nikitenko, *Pokhvalnoe slovo Petru Velikomu, imperatoru i samoderzhtsu vserossiiskomu, ottsu otechestva, proiznesennoe v torzhestvennom sobranii Imperatorskogo S.-Pb. universiteta, marta 25-go dnia 1838 goda* (St. Petersburg, 1838); presented in E. Shmurlo, *Petr Velikii v russkoi literature (Opyt istoriko-bibliograficheskogo obzora)* (St. Petersburg, 1889), 48–53; my quotations will be from Shmurlo.

120 Shmurlo, *op. cit.*, 50.

121 *Ibid.*, 50–51.

122 *Ibid.*, 51.

123 *Ibid.*

had not been a single effort to aid him, not a single beginning. . . . Everything had to be created by him: the aims, the means, the people, himself. `. . . Society contributed nothing either to his purposes or to his genius. . . . Peter received everything either from heaven or from himself. . . . His mind and his will are gifts of providence; knowledge he tore by force out of the hands of a hostile fate."[124] He was indeed "a messenger of God who brought the word of truth and himself as the model to be followed to millions of people."[125] He combined this message with a boundless love for the fatherland and a perfect readiness to sacrifice himself for it. "Here I end my oration. . . . Here one can only pray."[126]

Even a quick survey of the Petrine theme among the Westernizers indicates that the usual association of them with the reformer is on the whole warranted, that most of them affirmed emphatically and consistently both Peter the Great and his work. In doing so, they continued the Russian eighteenth-century tradition, emphasizing in it, however, especially enlightenment, whereas Official Nationality stressed state power and order; and they added to the tradition new elements taken from German idealistic philosophy and Romanticism in general: history as the development of the human spirit, historic and unhistoric peoples, the historical mission of a people, heroes and leaders as incarnations of their nations, the special nature and role of a genius, and others. The resulting image of Peter the Great seemed both complete and overwhelming. Perhaps it was too much so. In any case, dissent among the Westernizers appeared, and, as one would expect, it appeared on the Left.

There was the strange case of Michael Bakunin. That "founder of nihilism and apostle of anarchy" began as an enthusiastic member of the Stankevich circle and a passionate student of German idealistic philosophy, Hegel in particular. In the late 1830s he led Belinskii in apotheosizing, in Hegelian terms, reality, in the first place the Russian autocracy. Authoritarian power remained one pole in Bakunin's thinking, and it can be argued that various specific positive judgments of the first Russian emperor survived in his mind long after his early Westernizer days.[127] But, essentially, from 1840 and 1841, Bakunin gave vent to a rebellion against authority, which was apparently demanded by his explosive and pathological character and which found expression in many remarkable offensives, from the one against God to the one against Marx. Thus, when Belinskii turned against Nicholas I and his Russia but retained the Petrine model as the desirable way for the country to advance, Bakunin

124 *Ibid.*, 52.
125 *Ibid.*
126 *Ibid.*
127 For example, in 1860, Bakunin wrote to Herzen in a letter in which he praised the Siberian governor, Count Nicholas Muraviev-Amurskii: "He loves Russia passionately and is devoted to it the way Peter the Great was devoted to it" (M. A. Bakunin, *Sobranie sochinenii i pisem, 1828–1876,* Iu. M. Steklov, ed., vol. IV, *V tiurmakh i ssylke, 1849–1861* [Moscow, 1935], 305).

swept everything out. He qualified Peter I as "a great oppressor of the Russian people"[128] and the creator of "a police state."[129] That state relied on enormous brute force, using a dehumanizing compulsion at home and threatening invasion abroad. "Russia is a state directed toward conquests."[130] In 1849 or 1850 the significance of the Petrine work was only too apparent:

The present master of Russia is a faithful successor to the political tendency created by Peter, and he is conducting that policy even more consistently than Peter. His rule is nothing other than the now mature and conscious of itself system of the man of genius, who created the Russian state; and never before was that state as threatening externally and as oppressive internally as precisely in our time.[131]

In a sense Bakunin joined the proponents of Official Nationality in emphasizing power, not enlightenment, in the image of Peter the Great, but he also marked that power with a minus, not a plus, sign. Nor was a good anarchist likely to do otherwise.

The evolution of Alexander Herzen's views on Peter the Great, as on other subjects, was more complicated and nuanced than Bakunin's. A brilliant, idiosyncratic, and precocious writer, Herzen formulated his Petrine conception in an unpublished article written in 1833, when he was only twenty or twenty-one years old. Entitled "The Twenty-Eighth of January,"[132] the day of the first emperor's death, the essay had two epigraphs: Lomonosov's statement that Peter the Great went beyond human bounds and Victor Cousin's declaration (on Napoleon) that revolution became man. Planetary orbits had been ascertained, Herzen began, but occasionally a comet seems to break the celestial order, and it takes a special effort of intellect to find its relationship to the laws of nature and its proper place in the total picture. Peter the Great was such a comet. Russians, like all Slavs, had belonged to Europe as successors to Rome

[128] *Ibid.*, 34.
[129] *Ibid.*, 40.
[130] *Ibid.*, 44.
[131] *Ibid.*, 43–44. This exposition of Bakunin's views, based on his memorandum written in a Saxon prison in defense of his revolutionary activities, does not seem to be compromised by its provenance, for the views expressed in it can be found also in the anarchist's other writings. See, e.g., the identification of Russia with force and Poland with freedom, where Peter the Great is defined as "Russian history," in Bakunin, *op. cit.*, vol. III, *Period pervogo prebyvaniia za granitsei, 1840–1849* (Moscow, 1935), 393–394. In describing the imperial Russian state as one of unrelieved oppression at home and, especially, of unlimited expansion abroad, Bakunin agreed with a pronounced European current of thought, prominent among Polish intellectuals, which had produced, for example, the fake "Testament of Peter the Great" urging world conquest. Bakunin was one of the few educated Russians of his time who were close to the Poles and championed their cause against the Russian state. For the latest scholarly discussion of the "Testament," see Hugh Ragsdale, *Détente in the Napoleonic Era: Bonaparte and the Russians* (Lawrence, 1980), esp. 13–21, 138, but also *passim.*
[132] A. I. Gertsen, "Dvadtsat osmoe ianvaria," *Sobranie sochinenii v tridtsati tomakh,* the Academy edition, vol. I, *Proizvedeniia 1829–1841 godov* (Moscow, 1954), 29–35, manuscript variants, pp. 463–465, fns. pp. 482–483.

and Byzantium and, especially, as a Christian people. But, in contrast to the general European development by means of a constant struggle, of the popes with the emperors, of the victors with the vanquished, of feudal elements with the people, of the kings with the feudal elements, the communes, and the peoples, of the propertied with the propertyless, the struggle that gave rise to the third estate, Russia remained essentially monolithic, without an opposition. Therefore, centuries behind the West, it stood as an outsider when the glorious Enlightenment began spreading in Europe. Then:

. . . Peter appeared! He formed the opposition to the people, he expressed Europe in his own person, he assigned to himself the problem of transferring Europeanism into Russia, and he dedicated his life to the solution of that problem. Germany, which had had extremely weak beginnings of a civic opposition, had obtained its Peter, equally colossal, equally mighty. The German Peter is the Reformation. It had not reached those separated from the Catholic world, and in our case the entire overturn, bloody and terrible, was replaced by the genius of a single person. Let us note, however, that Peter too, like all revolutions, was exclusively, one-sidedly devoted to one idea, and he pursued that idea by all means, including even cruelties, as it was done by the Reformation, by the French Convention. But even if we accept the necessity of Peter in Russia, and at that time more than ever, his originality, nevertheless, remains great. His appearance was necessary, but it was not forced (as the appearance of Luther). Undoubtedly, Russia would have moved forward; occasional sparks of Europeanism flew in already at the time of Godunov; they broke in with the Pretender, but would Russia have moved far with those exotic bits? What was lacking, in fact, was both a center of the movement and an accelerating push. Peter created both. The problem that he solved, although it was a necessary one for Russia, was not proposed by Russia, but by the genius of the Great one; it was not entrusted to him by the circumstance, but poured by him into the circumstances, brought by his genius into the realm of the ideas of humanity, and it was resolved also by him. Look at this pampered tsarevich, at the age of fifteen still in the arms of his nurses, surrounded by bodyguards and by the entire splendor of an Oriental court, an ignoramus who was taught nothing, whose infancy is threatened by the dagger and youth by debauchery prepared by his sister; look and bend your knees, this is Peter. Tell me, where, in what land, in what occupation there was a more original man, one for whom the circumstances had done less?[133]

Indeed, Alexander the Great, Charles the Great, and Caesar all failed by comparison; only Napoleon belonged, perhaps, with Peter I. Moreover, whereas other great historical figures usually acted by some kind of instinct, were insatiable conquerors, and did good only in passing, Peter the Great's conscious noble aim served as his steady guiding light. Herzen concluded by promising a second part—which, apparently, was never written—and by complaining how little the Russians appreciated their Peter.

Herzen's fascinating early article presented a number of themes that

[133] *Ibid.*, 32–33.

were to become popular in Westernizer literature and, even more broadly, among the intellectual Left. One was the explicit designation of Peter the Great as a revolutionary, indeed as revolution itself—perhaps largely a matter of words because what Feofan Prokopovich or Lomonosov had described had in no sense been less than a revolution, but words have their importance. The Petrine revolution led, to be sure, to the establishment of a powerful modern autocracy; but here, too, Herzen offered other possibilities. Peter I merely began the work:

> Much remained to be done; and, since progress would continue to be dialectical, there is the strong implication (though Herzen does not spell it out) that further advance would not be through the "one-sided" autocracy of Peter but by means in opposition to it. Thus Herzen was able both to admire autocracy in the past and to reject it in the present, to take pride in the accomplishments of Russia and yet to remain in the opposition—but of course the dialectic had been developed precisely to express such ambivalence.[134]

Throughout the decades of the 1830s and 1840s, Herzen kept reiterating and developing his "dialectical" understanding of Peter the Great and the Petrine historical role. In an article on "Moscow and Petersburg" written in 1842, the publicist made it clear that "Petersburg is the current coin; one can not do without it. Moscow is a rare coin, a remarkable one, let us grant it, for an enthusiastic numismatist, but it has no currency. Let us talk, then, about the city of the present, about Petersburg."[135] "From the day when Peter saw that there was only one salvation for Russia, to stop being Russian, from the day when he dared to move us into world history, the necessity of Petersburg and the uselessness of Moscow were determined. The first, inevitable step for Peter was the transfer of the capital from Moscow."[136] Petersburg, for its part, had no roots, no "heartfelt connection with the country"; indeed, it stood artificially on stakes, which were driven in at the cost of the death of hundreds of thousands of workers.[137] A year later, Herzen discussed critically in his diary European absolute rulers of the eighteenth century. Peter I and Frederick II of Prussia were the remarkable exceptions to the general sad run. "First, they are revolutionaries; second, they are geniuses; they followed their own path, they made mistakes in much that they undertook, but they had great ambitions and achieved gigantic results."[138] Herzen continued:

---

[134] Martin Malia, *Alexander Herzen and the Birth of Russian Socialism, 1812–1855* (Cambridge, Mass., 1961), 97; the entire excellent commentary on the article occupies pp. 96–98.

[135] A. I. Gertsen, "Moskva i Petersburg," *op. cit.*, vol. II, *Stati i feletony, 1841–1846. Dnevnik, 1842–1845* (Moscow, 1954), 33–42, manuscript variants pp. 426–428, fns. pp. 439–440, quoted from p. 34.

[136] *Ibid.*, 35.

[137] *Ibid.*, 36.

[138] *Ibid.*, 299. Herzen's diary for 1843 occupies pp. 256–323 of the volume, variants p. 434, fns. pp. 469–474.

Peter, a semibarbarian in appearance and spirit, but a man of genius and un-shakable in his great desire to have his country join the development of human-ity, is very strange in his savage rudeness next to the pampered and refined Augustuses and company. A man, who renounced the entire past of his country, who blushed for it, and who was establishing the new order by means of blood, contains in himself something revolutionary, even if he occupies a throne; and in fact he made no demands of feudal adoration, of ceremonies and the like, common to all at the time. He grabbed Europeanism in Holland, the best source at that time; he belonged to new Europe, he was introducing it like a barbarian, but he pushed government onto a track not at all similar to that of the Euro-pean dynasts, both worse and better, but certainly not the same. A material, positive oppression, not based on the past, revolutionary and tyrannical, ahead of the country, so it would not be able to develop freely but under a knout, Europeanism in appearance and a complete absence of humaneness inside— such is its contemporary character, which derives from Peter. Nonetheless, his figure is great in this age, and his thought is great; it has not yet quite reached realization, but probably it too will be realized. Peter, as soon as he felt his strength, got involved in a greater part of European intrigues, participated, offered his opinion, sent troops, justly and unjustly; in any case, Europe became accustomed to the name of Russia, and Russia was pushed into the family of European peoples. . . . It is strange to see how, by means of a corporal's stick and a bourgeois concept of economics in Prussia, by means of a knout and an ax in Russia, humanism is installed.[139]

And, still engaged in his "dialectical" balancing, Herzen added: "The bad means necessarily had to affect the results."[140] But perhaps the most striking and stark instance of Herzen's "dialectical" understanding of the reformer can be found a little later, in a diary entry for April 1844, where the publicist cited some particularly odious alleged examples of Peter the Great's cruelty, then declared: "To understand, to justify, not only to render justice, but to bow in front of the awesome phenomena of the Convention and of Peter is one's duty. More than that, in their very enormities one should not lose the clear sign of majesty. But not all the actors of the year 93 can be loved, and the same goes for Peter."[141]

The "dialectical" balancing could not last indefinitely. An exile from

---

139 *Ibid.*, 299–300.

140 *Ibid.*, 300.

141 *Ibid.*, 348. Herzen's diary for 1844 occupies pp. 324–400, variants p. 434, and fns. pp. 475–480 of the volume.

Cf. Herzen's other writings of the period, where parts of his concept of Peter the Great also appear, at times trenchantly, if briefly. For example, Herzen declared in 1845, in his *Letters on the Study of Nature:* "Peter the Great solemnly proved that the past, represented by an entire country, is worthless against the will of one person, act-ing in the name of the present and the future . . . from the standpoint of nature, longevity gives only one right, the right of death" (A. I. Gertsen, "Pisma ob izuchenii prirody," *op. cit.*, vol. III, *Diletantizm v nauke, Pisma ob izuchenii prirody, 1842–1846* [Moscow, 1954], 89–315, fns. pp. 319–330, quoted from p. 92). In his celebrated auto-biography, *My Past and Thoughts,* Herzen wrote that Moscow "bowed her head before Peter because in his beastly paw was the future of Russia" (A. I. Gertsen, *op. cit.*, vol. VIII, *Byloe i dumy,* Chasti I–III (Moscow, 1956), 133).

1847 until his death in 1870, Herzen proceeded to take an increasingly negative and bitter view of the Russian government and system, which he continued to consider as essentially creations of Peter the Great. Perhaps there was a shift around the year 1850. In "La Russie," an article written in 1849, the publicist explained: "Peter I did infinite good and infinite evil to Russia; but the fact for which he deserves, above all, the gratitude of the Russians, is that impulse that he gave to the entire country, that motion which he imparted to the nation, and which, from that time on, has not slowed down."[142] Still, as Herzen developed his argument, the evil seemed to dominate the good. The first emperor had no creative originality, and he merely followed the West—in which Herzen himself had just become disillusioned. The resulting amalgam was truly frightening: "Picture for yourself a union of Muscovite tsarism with the regime of German chancelleries, with the inquisitorial procedure borrowed from the Prussian military code, and you will understand how imperial authority in Russia has left the despotism of Rome and of Byzantium far behind."[143] The chapter on "Pierre Ier" in *Du développement des idées revolutionnaires en Russie,* written in 1850–1851, presented an almost unrelievedly dark picture of Peter the Great and, especially, of his successors. Moreover, though reemphasizing the thoroughly revolutionary nature of the reformer, Herzen underlined the one important connection between him and Muscovy: the policy of expansion. "There was only one single thought, which linked the Petersburg period with that of Moscow: the thought of an aggrandizement of the state. Everything was sacrificed for it, the dignity of the rulers, the blood of the subjects, justice toward neighbors, the well-being of the entire country . . ."[144] The publicist had reason to lament:

A strange thing, of all the sovereigns of the house of the Romanovs, not one has done anything for the people. The people does not remember them except by the number of its misfortunes, by the growth of serfdom, of the military draft, of the impositions of all kinds, by all the horrors of a police administration, by a war, which is as bloody as it is senseless and which has been going on in impregnable mountains for twenty-five years.[145]

The decade of the 1850s can be considered a transitional period from Herzen's original, "dialectical," but highly affirmative and forward-looking, view of Peter the Great to the negative judgment and dark pessimism of his last years. Bitterly critical assessments were prominent. Thus,

[142] A. I. Gertsen, "La Russie," *op. cit.,* vol. VI, *S togo berega, Stati, Dolg prezhde vsego, 1847–1851* (Moscow, 1955), 150–186, variants pp. 476–477, fns. 514–519, quoted from p. 170.

[143] *Ibid.,* 171–172.

[144] A. I. Gertsen, "Pierre I[er]," *op. cit.,* vol. VII, *O razvitii revoliutsionnykh idei v Rossii, Proizvedeniia 1851–1852 godov* (Moscow, 1956), 40–62, variants pp. 396–398, quoted from p. 42, break in the original.

[145] *Ibid.,* 52; the last part of the last sentence refers to the Caucasus.

Herzen wrote in 1855 in his remarkable commentary *From the Other Shore:*

The overturn by Peter I replaced the antiquated landlord rule of Russia by a European chancellery regime; everything that could be copied from Swedish and German legal codes, everything that could be transported from free municipal Holland to the land of peasant communes and autocracy was transported. But the unwritten part, which restrained authority morally, the instinctive recognition of the rights of the individual, the rights of thought, of truth could not come over and did not come over. Among us slavery increased with education; the state was growing, improving, but the individual was not gaining; on the contrary, the stronger the state became, the weaker the individual. European forms of administration and justice, of a military and a civil organization developed among us into some sort of monstrous despotism without an escape.[146]

On the other hand, some of the earlier favorable opinions of the reformer could still be found in Herzen's writings of this period, together with an emphasis on the reformer's utterly crucial role in "giving motion" to his country, in creating modern Russia. Moreover, with the death of Nicholas I in 1855 and the new reforming climate in Russia under Alexander II, Herzen began reconsidering the nature and possibilities of autocracy. He decided that the new emperor could indeed resume Peter the Great's work without having to apply the Petrine "progressive terror"; in fact, because the circumstances had changed, he could do so in security and with full popular and liberal support. "In order to continue the Petrine work, the sovereign must renounce the Petersburg period as frankly as Peter renounced the Moscow one. This entire artificial machine of imperial rule has become too old."[147] For the moment at least, the dialectic was again triumphant.

It was only after another disillusionment with the government, confirmed by the nature of the emancipation of the serfs in 1861 and the brutal suppression of the Polish rebellion in 1863, that Herzen turned unreservedly and forever against the Russian autocracy. By that time he had outlived the German idealism of his youth—although never all its traces—and disappointed by both tsarist Russia and bourgeois Europe, he found what solace he could in his hopes for the Russian peasant commune and in a tragic affirmation of his individuality and his right to protest. These ultimately humane values were all that remained from his

---

146 Gertsen, *op. cit.*, VI, 15.

147 A. I. Gertsen, *op. cit.*, vol. XIII, *Stati iz "Kolokola" i drugie proizvedeniia 1857–1858 godov* (Moscow, 1958), 29; the entire article "Revoliutsiia v Rossii" ("Revolution in Russia") occupies pp. 21–29; "progressive terror" is on p. 23. Cf. the parallel evolution *re* the Russian government and Peter the Great of another radical Westernizer, Herzen's lifelong friend and companion Nicholas Ogarev (1813–1877), in particular his unpublished article of 1856 or 1857, "What Would Peter the Great Have Done?" N. P. Ogarev, "Chto by sdelal Petr Velikii?" published by S. Pereselenkov, *Literaturnoe Nasledstvo*, 39–40 (Moscow, 1941), 317–322. "Yes! In our time, Peter the Great, with his indefatigable activity and the speed of a genius, would have abolished serfdom, reformed the bureaucracy, and raised the significance of science" (*ibid.*, 321).

originally comprehensive and optimistic Westernizer ideology. Peter the Great became a definitely negative quantity in Herzen's outlook. "I am beginning to hate Peter I with my nerves" (1860).[148] "May God spare both Eastern and Western Siberia from the calamity that Peter I was for Russia" (1861).[149] "Peter I loves passionately the navy, civilization, and I do not know what else, but he loves even more passionately denunciations, rumors, investigations, torture; and suddenly all around him become informers, the Preobrazhenskii office is flooded with cases—noble and nonnoble bones crackle on the rack . . ." (1864).[150] "We shall not say, like Plato, 'Arise, Peter!' No, let him lie in place. He did us much harm; he definitively broke respect for individual will" (1865).[151] "The people in the countryside were left outside that imposed civilization. The great pedagogue, Peter I, contented himself with riveting more strongly the chains of serfdom" (1867).[152] "It is only during these last years that we have seen all the monstrousness incubated since Peter I and the entire depth of depravity" (1868).[153]

## 5

Both the proponents of Official Nationality and the Westernizers continued, although within different, at times strikingly different, ideological frameworks and with different emphases, the Russian Enlightenment glorification of Peter the Great. The Slavophiles spoke out against the reformer. In that respect, they were the real innovators. True, the Slavophiles could claim the entire previous Russian anti-Petrine protest as their predecessor—from the generally inarticulate cries of pain and outrage of the first emperor's contemporaries to Shcherbatov's and Karamzin's elegant laments. The physical and psychological suffering brought upon the Russians by the Petrine policies, wounded national pride, grief at the collapse of moral foundations, and other themes we have already encountered, found their reflection in Slavophilism. But this, so to speak, traditional and national protest was only one of the two main elements in the Slavophile image of Peter the Great—and the less distinctive one at that; the other came from German idealistic philosophy and Romanticism in general. For the Slavophiles, like the more philosophical of the Westernizers, formulated their view of Russian history in terms of philo-

---

[148] A. I. Gertsen, *op. cit.*, XXVII, book II, *Pisma 1860–1864 godov* (Moscow, 1963), 622.

[149] *Ibid.*, XV, *Stati iz "Kolokola" i drugie proizvedeniia 1861 goda* (Moscow, 1958), 158.

[150] *Ibid.*, XVIII, *Stati iz "Kolokola" i drugie proizvedeniia 1864–1865 godov* (Moscow, 1959), 41; break in the original.

[151] *Ibid.*, 331; Herzen refers here to the 1812 Kremlin oration of Moscow Metropolitan Plato (Levshin) calling Peter the Great to help Russia in her hour of need.

[152] *Ibid.*, XX, book I, *Proizvedeniia 1867–1869 godov, Dnevnikovye zapisi* (Moscow, 1960), 35.

[153] *Ibid.*, 356.

sophical idealism and Romanticism; Peter the Great was central to that view just as that view was central to the Slavophile understanding of Peter.

In fact Slavophilism represented the fullest and most authentic expression of Romantic thought in Russia. Its central dichotomy was that of organic harmony against mechanistic division; of a unity in love, full understanding, and freedom against rationalism and compulsion; of the new ideal of Romanticism against the Age of Reason. Only the Romantic ideal became Russia, and the Age of Reason became the West. It was to the service of that ideal that Alexis Khomiakov's (1804–1860) theology, Ivan Kireevskii's (1806–1856) philosophical analysis, Constantine Aksakov's (1817–1860) historical writing, and other Slavophile works were all devoted.

Slavophilism, thus, expressed a fundamental vision of integration, peace, and harmony among men. On the religious plane it produced Khomiakov's concept of *sobornost,* an association in love, freedom, and truth of all believers, which Khomiakov considered the essence of Orthodoxy. Historically, so the Slavophiles asserted, a similar harmonious integration of individuals could be found in the social life of the Slavs, notably in the peasant commune—described as a "moral choir" by Constantine Aksakov—and in such other old Russian institutions as the *zemskii sobor.* Again, the family represented the principle of integration in love, and the same spirit could pervade other associations of people. As against love, freedom, and cooperation stood the world of rationalism, necessity, and compulsion. It, too, existed on many planes, from the religious and metaphysical to that of everyday life. Thus, it manifested itself in the Roman Catholic Church—which had chosen rationalism and authority in preference to love and harmony and had seceded from Orthodox Christendom—and, through the Catholic Church, in Protestantism and in the entire civilization of the West. Moreover, and most importantly, Peter the Great introduced the principles of rationalism, legalism, and compulsion into Russia, where they proceeded to destroy or stunt the harmonious native development and to seduce the educated public. The Russian future lay clearly in a return to native principles, in overcoming the Western disease. After being cured, Russia would take its message of harmony and salvation to the discordant and dying West.

The Slavophiles, thus, accepted Feofan Prokopovich's stark dichotomy, but reversed the value signs: the negative became the positive; and the positive, the negative. Old Russia, Khomiakov and his friends asserted, had been homogeneous, harmonious, and organic, without Western class divisions, without aristocracy and democracy, without enmity and compulsion. Russian society and Russian life had been distinguished by simplicity, by a complete absence of theatrical effects so prevalent in the West. Russian education had been based on the true learning of the Orthodox Church.

All Holy Greek Fathers, not excluding the most profound writers, were translated, read, copied, and studied in the quiet of our monasteries, these sacred embryos of the universities that were not to be . . . And these monasteries were in living, continuous contact with the people. What enlightenment in our common people are we not entitled to deduce from this single fact![154]

And yet this order of things did not last; the harmony was broken. Peter the Great appeared on the scene.

The Slavophiles could never quite understand—or explain—what enabled Peter the Great to sweep away old Russia and to institute an oppressive, mechanistic, rationalistic, Western regime in its stead. Constantine Aksakov, in particular, made of the first emperor a titan who introduced, practically single-handed, everything evil, even serfdom, into Russia. He spent much time and effort trying to prove from ancient documents that freedom, harmony, and happiness had existed in abundance in ancient Russia, but disappeared after Peter the Great. Other Slavophiles, led by Khomiakov and Ivan Kireevskii, were more willing to concede that pre-Petrine Russia had had its defects, such as a certain one-sided exclusiveness and a lack of consciousness of itself and of its mission. Also, the very excellence of the old Russian system had invited corruption:

As to my personal opinion, I think that the originality of Russia consisted in the very fullness and purity of expression, which the Christian teaching received in it—in the entire compass of her public and her private life. The purity of expression became so blended with the spirit expressed that one could easily mix the significance of the two and respect the outer form as much as the inner meaning. . . . And indeed we see that in the sixteenth century the respect for the form already exceeds in many ways the respect for the spirit.[155]

But whatever the reasons for the coming of the reformer, the Slavophiles were opposed to him and his work, to contemporary Russian government and society. Peter the Great was a despot, who interrupted the organic development of the country and who wanted to mold Russia like clay in accordance with his rationalistic and utilitarian notions and in direct imitation of the West. His reforms robbed Russia of its independent role in history and made it an appendix to the West, split educated society from the people, and led to such evils as formalism and bureaucracy.

St. Petersburg was a perfect expression of, and the natural successor to, his work. That city was the very essence of rationalism, formalism, materialism, legalism, and compulsion: it had been built out of nothing, without spiritual sanctification or historical tradition; even the ground

154 I. V. Kireevskii, *Polnoe sobranie sochinenii*, M. O. Gershenzon, ed. (2 vols., Moscow, 1911), I, 119. For a fuller treatment of Slavophilism, see my book on the subject, on which this section is based: Nicholas V. Riasanovsky, *Russia and the West in the Teaching of the Slavophiles: A Study of Romantic Ideology* (Cambridge, Mass., 1952).

155 Kireevskii, *op. cit.*, I, 219.

on which it stood was Finnish rather than Russian; yet this artificial, foreign city ruled the whole land, entire Holy Russia, by means of its compulsory decrees borrowed from the West and quite inapplicable to the Russian way of life. The dichotomy was clear as far as cities were concerned: Moscow represented the positive principle; St. Petersburg, the negative. The Slavophiles made numerous attacks on the enemy. Their approach ranged from exclamations of hate against "that city, that way of life, that activity, those people," and suggestions that St. Petersburg should drown itself to the elucidation of the fact that St. Petersburg represented a merely negative phase of Russian history and, therefore, could not contribute anything of positive value. In the words of Ivan Aksakov (1823–1886), a Slavophile like his older brother Constantine Aksakov and later a prominent Pan-Slavic journalist:

St. Petersburg as the embodiment of a negative moment of history can not create anything *positive* in the Russian sense. According to a well-known dialectical law, it is possible to return to *the positive* only through *a negation of the negation itself,* in other words through a negation of the St. Petersburg period, through a negation of St. Petersburg as a political *principle* that guided Russian life for almost two centuries. The result will be a Russian nation freed from exclusiveness and called into the arena of world history. Is that clear?[156]

No wonder that the Slavophiles kept insisting that the capital be transferred back to Moscow.

By association with the city he had created or otherwise, Peter the Great remained a continuous target of the Slavophiles. Peter Kireevskii (1808–1856), Ivan Kireevskii's younger brother and a pioneer collector of Russian folk songs, was grieved because his own first name was Peter. When Serge Soloviev and other historians demonstrated that the first emperor was not as revolutionary as he was supposed to have been and that Muscovy had been developing its connections with the West, that too became an item in the indictment:

This is perfectly correct, and everything that is true in Peter's reforms was, of course, started before him. But Peter was not merely a continuer, and precisely this forms the characteristic of his epoch. Before him only the useful had been taken from the foreigners. Foreign life had not been borrowed, our principles of life had been left intact, and Russia had remained independent. Peter, on the other hand, began to take everything from the foreigners, not only the useful and the universal, but also the particular and the national, foreign life itself with all its accidental details. . . . Therefore even the most useful, which had been accepted in Russia before Peter the Great, became of necessity not a free borrowing, but a slavish imitation. Still another circumstance was added to this: namely coercion, an inalienable attribute of Peter's actions. This coercion, in turn, changed the whole process; what had been done freely and naturally until then began to be performed through compulsion and force. Therefore, the reforms of Peter are definitively *an overturning, a revolution;* in this lies the origi-

156 I. S. Aksakov, *Sochineniia* (7 vols., Moscow, 1886–1891), V, 632.

nality and the historical significance of his work. . . . National exclusiveness (which Russia had never known before) appeared on the part of Peter. It was Peter who stood for exclusive nationality, only not for that of his own people, but for those of the West; he attempted to destroy every manifestation of Russian life, everything Russian.[157]

The Slavophile denunciation of Peter the Great came to be regarded, on the whole correctly, as the hallmark of the movement, as its particularly characteristic trait, and as its main contrast with the Westernizers. Still, the Slavophile judgment could not be entirely simple or straightforward. The ambivalence was necessitated—as in the case of Herzen and other Westernizers—by the Slavophile reliance on German idealistic thought, more specifically, on the dialectic. Khomiakov and his friends believed that every period of history had its purpose and was bound to contribute to the development and the triumph of the true principles. Even Constantine Aksakov had to admit that Peter the Great had been necessary.[158] The other Slavophiles variously developed the same idea. The reformer represented the inevitable reaction against the nationalistic exclusiveness, the ignorant respect for form, and other vices of Muscovy. This reaction was extreme, negative, and essentially wrong, but it was nevertheless bound to contribute to the higher synthesis. Even the new capital served a useful purpose:

Petersburg was and will remain exclusively the city of the government, and perhaps this split in the very center of the state will not be useless for the healthy and intelligent development of Russia. The life of the power of the state and the life of the spirit of the people became divided even as to the place of their concentration.[159]

Moscow, which was characterized by a luminous inner intelligence rather than a superficial gaiety and by depth and honesty rather than by bustle and speed was thus left free to develop the life of the Russian people, the life of the spirit. Furthermore, the fact that it was no longer the capital, but only an equal of other Russian lands, contributed to the indispensable virtue of humility. In Moscow "was now constantly developed the thought of the Russian society of tomorrow."[160]

In addition to curing certain ills of Muscovy and enabling Moscow to devote itself wholly to the life of the spirit, the St. Petersburg episode of Russian history may have conferred an even greater benefit on the country:

[157] K. S. Aksakov, *Polnoe sobranie sochinenii* (3 vols., Moscow, 1861–1880), I, 41–42; published also separately as K. S. Aksakov, *Sochineniia istoricheskie* (Moscow, 1861). This is the most important single volume in the Slavophile literature on Peter the Great, which is surprisingly sparse.

[158] This he did very sharply and in strikingly Hegelian terms, e.g., in his article "About a Contemporary Literary Argument": K. S. Aksakov, "O sovremennom literaturnom spore," *Rus,* no. 7 (1883). The article was written in 1847.

[159] A. S. Khomiakov, *Polnoe sobranie sochinenii* (8 vols., Moscow, 1900–1914), III, 27.
[160] *Ibid.,* 434.

Look at Germany. More than any other people of Europe she denied her nationality, was even partly ashamed of herself, and what happened? . . . Was this temporary renunciation really fruitless? No: Germany was rewarded by the fact that when she returned to self-consciousness and self-respect, she brought with her from the period of her humiliation the ability to understand other peoples much better than a Frenchman, an Englishman, or an Italian understands them. She practically discovered Shakespeare. We also renounced ourselves and humiliated ourselves more, a hundred times more than Germany. I hope, I am certain that when we return home (and we shall return home—and soon), we shall bring with ourselves a clear understanding of the entire world, such as the Germans did not even dream of.[161]

Unusually considerate for Khomiakov, who, together with the other Slavophiles, preferred to denounce the first emperor and his work without reservations, this passage does fit well into the Slavophile Romantic historiosophy. And it is extremely interesting in connection with the later development of the idea of Russian messiahship by Dostoevskii, Vladimir Soloviev, and others.

Whatever defects may have brought about Peter the Great's reforms and whatever ends the St. Petersburg period of Russian history may have served, the Slavophiles were convinced that that period had to end soon: Russia would then return to its organic development, to its true path in history, and it was bound to be stronger, fuller of wisdom, and more conscious of itself and of its place in the world than ever before. Slavophilism was a thoroughly optimistic doctrine: the Slavophiles believed that organic, Orthodox, Russian civilization would certainly triumph over its opponent, the materialistic and rationalistic civilization of the West and that they were destined to lead Russia to its glorious future. To the Slavophiles, Russian history was primarily a battle of civilizations: first, between Russia and outside opponents; then, still more significantly, within Russia itself, after the Western principle had entered Russia and had seized the government.

The Slavophiles were convinced that their own ideological, intellectual, and emotional lives were part of that selfsame battle. From the time of its formulation around the year 1839, Slavophilism developed in argument and debate, especially with the Westernizers. The two circles read the same books, attended the same lectures, visited the same salons, even wrote in the same periodicals. Monday evenings were usually spent at Chaadaev's, Friday at the Sverbeevs', Sunday at the Elagins', Thursday at the Pavlovs'.

The whole large literary society of the capital [Moscow] assembled there on Thursdays. There enthusiastic arguments continued late into the night: Redkin with Shevyrev, Kavelin with Aksakov, Herzen and Kriukov with Khomiakov. There the Kireevskiis used to appear, also Iurii Samarin, then still a young man. Chaadaev was a constant guest there, with his head as bald as his hand, his un-

161 *Ibid.,* 210.

exceptionable society manners, his civilized and original mind, and his eternal posing. This was the most brilliant literary time of Moscow. All questions, philosophical, historical, and political, everything that interested the most advanced contemporary minds, were discussed at these assemblies, to which the competitors came fully armed, with opposed views, but with a store of knowledge and the charm of eloquence. At that time Khomiakov led a fierce struggle against Hegel's Logic. . . . Similarly vehement disputations concerned the key problem of Russian history, the reforms of Peter the Great. Circles of listeners formed around the debaters; this was a constant tournament in the course of which knowledge, intelligence, and resourcefulness were all displayed. . . .[162]

Intellectual closeness was even more important than physical proximity or community of interests. Both the Slavophiles and the Westernizers argued within the German idealistic and generally Romantic intellectual framework, employed a kind of dialectic,[163] and utilized the same or similar concepts, such as "old Russia" or "the contemporary West," as key elements of their theoretical constructions. Only usually, notably so in the case of Peter the Great, the values of these elements were reversed: negative for one group, positive for the other, and vice versa. Thus, whereas the Slavophiles condemned the reformer as the evil genius who destroyed Orthodox and harmonious Old Russia and set the country on the vicious and disastrous Western course, the Westernizers staked the future of Russia and their own future on the success of the first emperor and his work. As Herzen, already a radical and in exile, wrote, remembering the Slavophiles and his differences with them: "The times of Peter, the great tsar, are gone; Peter, the great man, is no longer in the Winter Palace; *he is in us.*"[164] In appraising the debate, one can well maintain that the Slavophiles attributed an even more impressive power and role to Peter the Great than did the Westernizers: the latter believed essentially that the first emperor had turned Russia sharply to its logical and historically determined course, a participation in European culture and progress; the former asserted that the momentous Petrine reforms had been contrary to logic and opposed to history. In the last analysis the

[162] B. N. Chicherin, *Vospominaniia, Moskva sorokovykh godov* (Moscow, 1929), 5–6. The great Slavophile-Westernizer debate, which took the form of continuous swirling talk, went unrecorded. In trying to reconstruct it, scholars have to depend on their general knowledge of the views of the participants, on some relevant published pieces, and on the reminiscences of such figures as Herzen and Boris Chicherin (1828–1903) on the Westernizer side and Alexander Koshelev (1806–1883) on the Slavophile.

[163] The "correctness" of that dialectic is a different matter. For example, it has been argued that although Khomiakov's scheme resembled the Hegelian, his synthesis was not really a synthesis because one of the two contrasting elements was simply destroyed. D. I. Chizhevskii, *Gegel v Rossii* (Paris, 1939), 188. Cf. N. Rubinshtein, "Istoricheskaia teoriia slavianofilov i ee klassovye korni," *Trudy Instituta Krasnoi Professury. Russkaia istoricheskaia literatura v klassovom osveshchenii. Sbornik statei*, M. N. Pokrovskii, ed. (Moscow, 1927), I, 53–118, esp. p. 73.

[164] Gertsen, *op. cit.*, VII, 117. The commentary "Muscovite Pan-Slavism and Russian Europeanism" ("Panslavisme moscovite et européisme russe") occupies pp. 101–118 of the volume; it was written in 1850 or 1851 and forms part of Herzen's *Du développement des idées révolutionnaires en Russie.*

Slavophiles had little more than Peter the Great himself to explain what they considered to be his truly colossal, if disastrous, historical accomplishment. Their image of the reformer, albeit with the negative sign, must rank among the most impressive of all in the huge Petrine pantheon.

Ideological tension and certain other circumstances drove the Slavophiles and the Westernizers apart, and their close intellectual and personal association ended by about 1846. The Westernizers, who had never been thoroughly cohesive, went in different directions. In the process, as we saw, their championing of Peter the Great came to be linked to different radical, liberal, or in fact conservative outlooks; and a few of them, such as Bakunin and Herzen, even turned against their former idol. The Slavophiles, by contrast, until they died in 1856, 1860 and—a few of them—later, retained intact their views on the reformer as on everything else that mattered. The most authentic representatives of Romantic historiosophy in Russia, they also proved to be its most loyal adherents. For that reason they both remained and increasingly became isolated. Because the fundamental intellectual structure was not transmitted, there were no Slavophiles in Russia after the original ones were dead.[165] Yet in a broader, although much less precise, sense, the Slavophile contribution to subsequent Russian thought was very considerable, and that contribution certainly included the Petrine debate. The bureaucratic formalism and legalistic oppressiveness of the imperial system had never been attacked so powerfully and especially from such a strong theoretical base as they were attacked by Khomiakov and his friends. The Petrine order of things was un-Russian, artificial, indeed inhuman.[166]

[165] This is one point of my already-mentioned book on the Slavophiles.

[166] A step beyond the concept of artificiality—and not unrelated to it—is that of unreality of Peter the Great's work, in particular of St. Petersburg. Immortalized in the writings of Gogol and Dostoevskii, it emerged at the time of the Slavophile critique of the reformer and continued into the twentieth century, when it found expression most notably in Belyi's *Petersburg* (to be discussed in Chapter III, section 7). In addition to the published literature on these major writers, see Professor Orysia Karapinka's unpublished doctoral dissertation "The Idea of the City in Russian Letters from Pushkin to Tolstoy" (University of California, Berkeley, December 18, 1971).

Dostoevskii and also Tolstoi were intellectually formed in the decades during which the Slavophiles were mounting their sweeping attacks on Peter the Great and his legacy. Dostoevskii's dichotomies, e.g., between Christian humility and pride or between Russia and the West, and Tolstoi's, notably between artificial society and authentic common people, remind one strongly of the fundamental Slavophile dichotomy and of the Slavophile criticism of Peter the Great. Dostoevskii, however, began with a Belinskii-like endorsement of Peter the Great and St. Petersburg, "both head and heart of Russia," notably in his "Petersburg Chronicle" of 1847 (F. N. Dostoevskii, "Peterburgskaia letopis," *Polnoe sobranie sochinenii v tridtsati tomakh*, vol. XVIII, *Stati i zametki, 1845–1861* [Leningrad, 1978], 11–34, fns. pp. 216–229, quoted from p. 26).

Gogol, a writer whose immense creative powers operated in striking contrast to his conscious intentions, belonged to Official Nationality ideologically (as presented in my already-cited book on Official Nationality), but effectively criticized and even dissolved St. Petersburg and perhaps all of Russia in such works as "The Overcoat," "The Nose," and *Dead Souls*. He also contributed an early journalistic comparison of Moscow and

The Slavophile treatment of Peter the Great meant a decisive break in a long intellectual tradition. The tradition was that of an adoring, almost worshipful affirmation of the first emperor and his work. Drawn according to the canon of the Age of Reason into which the reformer had moved Russia, the Petrine Enlightenment image was, in a sense, an appropriate recompense to its subject for his achievement. Peter the Great and the new Russia were virtually equivalent. The image dominated the Russian intellectual and cultural scene for some 125 years. And even after the passing of the Enlightenment and a parting of ways of the government and the progressive educated public in Russia, with a concomitant split in the Petrine image, it was impossible to tell who championed and glorified Peter the Great more enthusiastically, the Westernizers or the proponents of Official Nationality. Was it Belinskii or Pogodin, Granovskii or Nicholas I himself? The Slavophiles rejected all this laudation; in fact, they turned it into its opposite, a relentless condemnation. As in the cases of many other departures in intellectual history, this stunning reversal cannot be easily or completely explained, but certain considerations help our understanding of it.

The change in the intellectual world from Enlightenment to Romanticism was of fundamental importance. Instead of necessarily subscribing to the unitary system and standard of the Age of Reason, totally dominated in Russia by the Enlightenment image of Peter the Great, one could finally try new approaches. Inarticulate protest and confused critiques—confused even in the cases of Shcherbatov or Radishchev because they could not be reconciled with the overwhelming positive aspects of the Petrine image retained by their authors—received a full theoretical foundation and support. More especially, national pride and nationalism in general no longer had to be subsumed under reason or progress; and, as the Slavophiles demonstrated, once freed of that control, they could be used as effectively against the reformer as for him.

In social terms, the Slavophile protest has been linked in the main to the landed gentry, to which all the Slavophiles belonged, and to its problems and prospects. Soviet scholars in particular have devoted close attention to establishing the exact class nature of the Slavophiles, arguing, for example, that they represented the interests of the middle gentry whereas Official Nationality spoke for the large proprietors. Though that investigation has not proved to be very rewarding, more impressive is a broader construction, which links the emergence of Slavophilism to a defense of an entire preindustrial order threatened with modernization, of gemeinschaft against gesellschaft, to borrow Tönnie's famous dichotomy, which appears to be strikingly applicable to the Slavophile teaching. In other words, it can be argued that the Petrine turn West-

St. Petersburg, written in a comic, evenhanded, and unideological manner, but containing one memorable sentence: "Russia needs Moscow; St. Petersburg needs Russia" (N. V. Gogol, *Polnoe sobranie sochinenii*, vol. VIII, *Stati* [Leningrad, 1952], 179).

ward was finally bearing full fruit, that the very nature and structure of Russian society and life were indeed changing, and that it was that change that produced the Slavophile reaction.

In spite of many utopian elements, Slavophilism was much more than mere fantasy or messianic myth; it was a serious attempt to think over from the conservative standpoint the most momentous problems of European and Russian life. The type of community advocated by the Slavophiles was by then vanishing not only in Europe but also in Russia. Precisely this fact, however, contributed most to the flowering of conservative romanticism—the owl of Minerva, as we are told by Hegel, takes flight only as the shades of dusk are falling. Indeed, the Slavophiles themselves were greatly indebted to the "process of reflection," for it was only their European culture and the feeling that their ideals were in danger that enabled them to reflect about the nature of social bonds based upon nonreflection and upon the total absorption of individual consciousness into the supraindividual consciousness of the community.[167]

[167] Andrzej Walicki, "Personality and Society in the Ideology of Russian Slavophiles: A Study in the Sociology of Knowledge," *California Slavic Studies,* vol. II (1963), 1–20, quoted from p. 20. For a full treatment, see Andrzej Walicki, *The Slavophile Controversy: History of a Conservative Utopia in Nineteenth-Century Russian Thought* (Oxford, 1975).

# III

## The Image of Peter the Great in Russia in the Age of Realism and Scholarship, 1860–1917

> Thus, a great man is a son of his time, of his people; he loses his supernatural significance, his activity loses the attribute of chance, of arbitrariness, he rises high as a representative of his people at a given time, as the carrier and expresser of popular thought; his activity acquires a great significance, because it satisfies a powerful popular need, because it leads the people onto a new road, one necessary for the continuation of its historical life.
>
> S. Soloviev[1]

### 1

Romanticism followed Enlightenment; realism replaced Romanticism. The second transformation, like the first, encompassed the entire Western civilization and cannot be understood in exclusively Russian terms. Yet Russia participated in full—some would even argue in an exaggerated manner—in the general change. The new intellectual climate fostered utilitarianism, pragmatism, positivism, materialism, an emphasis on science and scholarship, in particular on the social sciences. In Russia, as elsewhere, professors and other erudites succeeded eighteenth-century litterateurs and the philosophizing ideologues of the first half of the nineteenth century as the central spokesmen of the age. History and historical figures became above all the province of academic historians.

The image of Peter the Great, to be sure, remained immense on the Russian scene. If historical scholarship was to be emphasized, the first emperor constituted a superb and gigantic subject for it. The incessant praise of the reformer for a century and a half—which occupied the preceding chapters of this study—especially the two chief arguments, Peter the Great as the creator of the modern Russian state and power and Peter the Great as the Russian guide to progress and civilization, became main theses of modern Russian historiography. And in more limited spheres, too, such as military history or the history of education, the role of the first emperor stood out as crucial. Nor did the Petrine story lack

---

[1] S. M. Soloviev, *Publichnye chteniia o Petre Velikom* (Moscow, 1872), 2.

color, drama, or human interest! Besides, although historians came to dominate the stage, they by no means monopolized it. Statesmen referred to Peter the Great for orientation and, even, inspiration. Publicists debated the significance, assets, and liabilities of the "Petrine" course of development for Russia. Writers and artists of all sorts made their varied and disparate contributions to the Petrine theme. At the beginning of the twentieth century a cultural renaissance, referred to sometimes as the Silver Age, led to a revival and occasionally to a striking development of Petrine as well as other subjects. Only the Bolshevik victory in 1917 and the eventual Sovietization of Russian culture put an end to this period of great richness and pluralism.

Still, between 1860 and 1917 the image of Peter the Great did not maintain its intellectual and cultural hegemony in Russia to the same extent as it had earlier. The sporadic and poorly grounded attacks of the Russian Age of Reason on the first emperor and the powerful but sectarian and narrowly based Slavophile critique were succeeded by a much more widespread and detailed criticism of almost every kind. Cruelty, costs, the negative or at least dubious result of the enormous effort reappeared in a much more elaborate form, together with numerous other charges. Most important, although some of the new Petrine enthusiasts failed to see the point, the more historical, concrete, and factual the argument became, the more difficult it was for Peter the Great to retain his supreme position, which had been based on the abstract theory of the Age of Reason and on idealistic metaphysics. Also, although the image of the founder obviously profited from its association with the imperial Russian state, it also suffered in part from the increasing antagonism of Russian intellectuals to that same state, as already exemplified by some Decembrists and by Alexander Herzen, who connected his appreciation of Peter the Great's role in Russian history to what Alexander II was doing and could do for Russia. Perhaps more significant still, whereas earlier only the hopelessly Fourierist Petrashevtsy and a very few other Russian intellectuals could avoid being centrally concerned with Peter the Great, after 1860 the unconcern became more common. The first emperor remained crucially important to many educated Russians, but he was of only secondary or even peripheral significance to other members of the educated class, who were interested primarily in the common people, in impersonal sociological theories, or simply in immediately pressing matters. Altogether, on the eve of 1917 the image of Peter the Great in Russia still loomed much more than life-size, but it was no longer that of a demiurge creating being from nonbeing, writing magic words on a blank sheet of paper.

Chaadaev played a crucial role in the change of the Russian image of Peter the Great from the Age of Reason to that of Romanticism and philosophical idealism; the historian Sergei Mikhailovich Soloviev (1820–1879) had a particularly important part in its evolution from Romanticism to realism. One of the younger Westernizers, influenced especially by Granovskii, S. Soloviev paid tribute to the intellectual currents of the age. To quote from his reminiscences:

Hegel turned the heads of all, although very few read Hegel himself, obtaining him only from lectures of young professors; serious students expressed themselves exclusively in Hegelian terms. My head too worked constantly; I would snatch several facts and immediately proceed to construct on their basis an entire edifice. Of Hegel's works I read only *The Philosophy of History;* it produced a strong impression on me; I even became a Protestant for a few months, but nothing else developed; the religious feeling was rooted too deeply in my soul; and now an idea occurred to me—to study philosophy and to use the means which it offers in order to buttress religion, Christianity; but abstractions did not suit me, I had been born a historian.[2]

S. Soloviev was indeed a historian, probably the greatest Russian historian of all time. In 1845 he was invited to the chair of Russian history at the University of Moscow, and he occupied that chair for over thirty years. His most important work, his *History of Russia from Most Ancient Times (Istoriia Rossii s drevneishikh vremen),* began to come out, a volume a year, in 1851; the twenty-ninth volume, published posthumously in the year of its author's death, 1879, brought the account to 1774. S. Soloviev's early Westernism, philosophical idealism, and Romanticism in general were all the more important because, in contrast to a Bakunin or a Belinskii, the historian's thought and work developed in a remarkably continuous, cumulative manner, not by means of zigzags or reversals. Initial assumptions, therefore, retained their influence. On the other hand, decades of painstaking historical labor in a changed intellectual atmosphere produced their effect. The result was S. Soloviev's presentation of Russian history, very much including the history of Peter the Great.

The historian's most striking evaluation of the first Russian emperor was given in his already cited *Public Lectures about Peter the Great,* delivered and published in 1872 and marking the bicentenary of the emperor's birth. As quoted at the beginning of this chapter, S. Soloviev stressed that a great man belonged to his people and his time, his significance emerging from his satisfaction of a fundamental popular need, not from any supernatural attributes. Russian treatment of Peter the Great had missed that point.

For a long time our attitude to the work of Peter was unhistorical, both in the reverent respect for that work and in the condemnation of it. Poets permitted themselves to rhapsodize: "He was your god, your god, Russia!" But this view prevailed even in calmer speech, not the poetic variety; Peter bringing Russia from nonbeing into being was a commonplace. I called such a point of view unhistorical because in it the activity of a single historical individual was torn away from the historical activity of an entire people; into the life of a people

2 S. M. Soloviev, *Moi zapiski dlia detei moikh, a, esli mozhno, i dlia drugikh* (Petrograd, n. d.), 60.

there was introduced a supernatural force, acting in its own arbitrary manner, while the people was condemned to an entirely passive relationship toward it; the pre-Petrine life and activity of a people, many centuries old, were declared nonexistent; Russia, the Russian people did not exist before Peter, he created Russia, he brought it from non-being into being.[3]

In fact, the reformer's role was great, but different in nature.

One can easily distinguish two ages in the life of a people; during the first age a people lives predominantly under the influence of feeling; this is the time of its youth, the time of strong passions, of a mighty motion, which usually results in the constitution, the creation of political forms. Here are forged, thanks to a powerful fire, monuments of popular life in its different spheres, or the foundations are laid for those monuments. The second half of the life of a people arrives: the people matures, and the heretofore dominant feeling cedes little by little its domination to thought. Doubt, an urge to verify what one had formerly believed, to ask the question whether what exists is reasonable or unreasonable, to shake, to rock what had previously been considered unshakable, marks the entrance of a people into the second age or period, the period of the domination of thought.[4]

The transition, inspired by a new and strong mental activity, occurred, typically, when a people met another, more developed one. That was the story of the Romans and the Greeks or of the turning in the fifteenth and sixteenth centuries of the new Christian nations of Europe to the classical heritage.

The Russian case had its own special characteristics:

. . . in the East a state was formed in the most unfavorable conditions, with an enormous territory and a small population, needing a large army, forced to be military, although it was not at all militaristic, entirely devoid of aggressive intentions, having in mind only a constant defense of its independence and of the freedom of its population, a poor agricultural state; and as soon as the relations in it among different parts of the population began to be fixed, according to the main needs of the life of the state and the people, it presented a phenomenon well known in such states: the armed part of the population feeds directly at the expense of the unarmed, owns land, on which the unarmed man is a working serf.[5]

Poorly protected by geography, the Russian nationality held firmly in its religious boundaries, produced by its difference from other faiths to the east and the south, other Christian denominations to the west. Progress implied "grafting manufacturing and commercial activity to a poor agricultural state, giving it the sea, making it partake in the navigational enterprises of the rich states, offering it an opportunity to share in their enormous profits."[6] And, in what became perhaps S. Soloviev's most fa-

[3] S. Soloviev, *Publichnye chteniia . . .* , 3.
[4] *Ibid.*, 6.
[5] *Ibid.*, 13.
[6] *Ibid.*, 22.

mous statement on Peter the Great: "The necessity of moving onto a particular road had been understood; the attendant obligations had been determined; the people had risen and had gathered for the march; but they were waiting for someone; they were waiting for a leader; the leader appeared."[7]

In appreciating the role of the reformer, one had to realize the importance of autocracy in Russian history:

The basic conditions of the life of Russia, the significance of which has already been pointed out, the primordial hugeness of the state territory and the thinly scattered population, slowed down the development of society, of civilization, that is, the division of labor and the combination of forces, and by that very fact demanded an extraordinary activity on the part of the government in order to join and direct scattered forces to achieve general state aims; a constant danger from enemies naturally demanded a constant dictatorship, and in that manner there developed in Russia a firm autocracy.[8]

It was that autocracy that Peter the Great used to achieve the desired results. Work, which the ruler so magnificently exemplified himself, became the essence of his reign. Moreover, the reformer's activity was not arbitrary or quixotic, but, rather, linked in a most fundamental way to the course of Russian history:

A change from one age to another was taking place in the life of the Russian people, this change naturally expressed itself in a turn from the steppe to the sea, and what then does the leader of the people do? at what first occupation do we find him? he is building a ship, and when we recollect this passionate desire for the sea, for a ship, manifested in Russia in the sixteenth and the seventeenth centuries, manifested in the activity of Ivan IV and of Aleksei Mikhailovich, we shall come to understand clearly the relationship of a great man to the people, to its needs at a given time, and we shall attach a different meaning to this passion for the sea of Peter, who was bored in narrow mountainous areas, and was calm and content only at sea, while a location poor in natural attractions, but rich in water and close to the sea, was for him paradise.[9]

Logically, too, St. Petersburg appeared as the capital of the new, primarily European period of Russian history.[10]

Peter the Great had to do very much himself:

It was impossible to tell others: "Move, work, learn actively, you will see that you will manage it"; it was impossible merely to tell others and to expect success from words; it was necessary to show by example, in practice; it was necessary for a beginning people to utilize the visual method of instruction, and Peter by becoming a worker, a pupil, became because of that a great teacher of the people.[11]

7 *Ibid.,* 27.
8 *Ibid.,* 29.
9 *Ibid.,* 55.
10 *Ibid.,* 69.
11 *Ibid.,* 38. Like earlier apologists, S. Soloviev often defended point by point both

Of course, the reformer learned from Westerners and borrowed from the West. But the important thing was his Russian nature and his wager on the Russians:

No, Peter was a most authentic Russian man, who retained a firm connection to his people, his love for Russia was not a love for some abstract Russia; he lived one life with his people and he could not exist outside that life; without that he could not have believed so deeply and passionately in that people, in its greatness; only because of this faith he could entrust Russians with that which, according to the cold calculations of reason, they could not have managed successfully because of their inexperience and unpreparedness. And they settled their accounts, a great people and a great leader of the people; for his burning love, for his deep and unshakable faith in his people, that people repaid its leader with success exceeding all expectations, with unheard-of might and glory: those inexperienced Russians to whom Peter entrusted the command over his inexperienced troops, turned out to be such commanders as educated Europe could not give him; those unprepared Russian diplomats, ignorant both of the past and of the present of the states, where they were sent to represent Russia, very quickly reached the level of the most skillful European ministers.[12]

Poltava was a stunning result of it all:

. . . one of the greatest world-historical events. . . . In the thunder of the battle of Poltava there was born for Europe, for the common European life a new great people; and not only one people: in the thunder of that battle there was born an entire new race, the Slavic race, which had found for itself a worthy representative, with the aid of which it could rise to a mighty and glorious historical life. A new epoch dawned in European history.[13]

By the time S. Soloviev delivered his public lectures on Peter the Great, he had already published six volumes on the subject.[14] Amounting to a

---

the first emperor's manner of carrying out his reforms and his specific controversial measures. The historian's justification of the enforced adoption of Western dress is possibly the most remarkable in all Petrine literature:

Those who complain about the change from Russian national dress to the foreign fail to pay attention to the fact that you have here a change from ancient dress not to the dress of some particular alien people, but to the pan-European, as distinct from the pan-Asiatic, to which ancient Russian clothing belonged. What then is the main difference between pan-European and pan-Asiatic clothing? in the first tightness and brevity dominate; in the second, width and length. What is this then: chance, or does one find here an expression of the spirit of the peoples, of the spirit of their activity, their history? Long and loose clothing is an expression of a quiet life, mainly homelife, rest, sleep; short and tight clothing is an expression of wakefulness, an expression of strong activity (*ibid.,* 55).

12 *Ibid.,* 38.
13 *Ibid.,* 73.
14 These are the usually cited Volumes XIII through XVIII of S. Soloviev's *History of Russia.* More exactly, Volume XIII deals with the period immediately preceding the reign of Peter the Great whereas the last chapter of Volume XVIII covers the first part of Catherine I's reign; on the other hand, much material in other volumes, especially later eighteenth-century volumes, is relevant to the Petrine reign. I used Sergei Mikhailovich Soloviev, *Istoriia Rossii s drevneishikh vremen* (29 vols. in 6 books, St. Petersburg, n.d.).

total of almost two thousand regular-size pages, they constitute to this day one of the best histories of the reformer's reign. Complex diplomacy is presented especially well, as are the involved political developments in the Ukraine, but many other aspects of the period are also effectively treated. The historian had some striking things to say about the emperor himself and his entourage although the study was not primarily a biography. He wrote, characteristically, in a cumulative manner, relying heavily on coordinated sentences and semicolons and proceeding steadily and precisely from event to event and from year to year—over hundreds and hundreds of pages. Yet the work is by no means simply a rich collection of facts. It exhibits careful consideration of the sources, and it is animated by a general thoughtfulness, by sharp specific judgments, and by an overall intellectual structure.

That structure indicates the close links of S. Soloviev's masterpiece, usually said to mark the transition from Romanticism to realism and to mark the firm establishment of "scientific" historiography in Russia to the earlier period. For the historian's main assumptions, which we have already encountered, were the basic tenets of German idealism: organicism and teleological history, with its inexorable immanent march and its "historic" and "unhistoric" peoples. S. Soloviev has been justly credited with establishing once and for all the fundamental connection between Peter the Great and the Russian past, and indeed his intellectual outlook offered no alternative. He accomplished his purpose especially in Volume XIII, dealing with the period immediately preceding the reformer's reign, but also in the Petrine volumes proper and even in subsequent volumes. He wrote of the Russian orientation westward, both the need for it and the efforts to satisfy that need, from the reign of Ivan the Terrible and again during the Time of Troubles and in the early Romanov period. He loved to compare the reformer's views to those of Križanič or Kotoshikhin or to "louder and louder cries in Moscow from different sides about the necessity of change, about the necessity of borrowing the science, the arts, and the crafts from other, more educated peoples."[15] As S. Soloviev concluded the fourteenth volume of his *History,* the first devoted to the reign of Peter the Great itself:

In the IX century A.D. with the mouth of the Neva there began the great road from the Varangians to the Greeks; with that road, in the middle of the century, Russia began. In the course of eight and a half centuries she kept moving eastward; she came right next to the Eastern ocean, but, finally, started to pine greatly for the Western sea, by which she had been born, and again came to it to obtain the means for a renascence.

On May 16, 1703, on one of the small islands in the mouth of the Neva the ax

15 S. Soloviev, *Istoriia* . . . , XIII, column 786.

sounded; a little wooden town was being built. That little town was Piterburkh, the capital of the Russian Empire.[16]

Moreover, the organic historical evolution of Russia was essentially the same as the evolutions of other European peoples. Special handicaps, notably huge size, sparse population, and poverty, made it, and in particular the Petrine effort, more painful and more violent, but they did not change its basic nature.

The point of the evolution was to move from the age of feeling to that of the mind, from barbarism to civilization, to join fully Europe and European culture, and to participate organically in the glorious European historical life. It is in that perspective that the reformer's significance was overwhelming. One could well argue that in fundamental belief S. Soloviev remained a perfect Westernizer. Joining Europe meant many things. Yet in S. Soloviev's case, as in many others, it may be possible to emphasize two ideas or rather clusters of ideas—which we have encountered throughout this study. One had to do with Russia as a new great European power, its army and navy, its prestige, its major role in European affairs. The point had been made, of course, by Feofan Prokopovich and almost every other commentator on Peter the Great. Yet S. Soloviev had something, in fact, much, of his own to say on the subject. A superb historian, a master of diplomatic—although not military—matters, he presented a detailed, richly textured, and closely reasoned expert account of the dramatic and heroic rise of Russia in Europe. The striking pages following a description of the Treaty of Nystad[17] provide something of a summary of this aspect of S. Soloviev's *History,* very possibly its most important aspect in both content and inspiration.

Still, the other major idea, the other chief aspect of S. Soloviev's treatment of the first emperor and his reign should not be downgraded: it is the equally basic view, both in the entire Petrine cult and in the historian's own thought, of Peter the Great as the enlightener, the civilizer of Russia. Indeed, victory in the Great Northern War and the new Russian position of power and prestige could be considered primarily as a means of attaining civilization. Civilization signified to S. Soloviev education, know-how, modernity in general, but above all morality.[18] The historian was deeply concerned with the sad moral condition of the Russian people. His narrative abounded in comments on the subject and also in instances of cruelty and corruption in places high and low. Peter the Great was a dauntless champion of morality and human worth; S. Soloviev must have sympathized with Nikitenko's assertion—quoted in

16 S. Soloviev, *Istoriia* . . . , XIV, column 1270.
17 S. Soloviev, *Istoriia* . . . , XVII, columns 616–625.
18 It is this simple positive correlation between Christian morality and the progress of civilization that dates S. Soloviev's *History* even more than it is dated by its debt to German philosophical idealism.

the preceding chapter—that the reformer gave the Russians "the honor to exist in the human manner." In his own writings the historian was quick to note the emperor's order during a desperate retreat to abandon everything and "only save men as much as possible"[19] or his punishment of a murderous landlord;[20] and he dwelt at length on his heroic struggle against malfeasance in office. But he also felt that Petrine Russia, and even its ruler himself, had a very long way to go to achieve this aim of humaneness and civilization. As he remarked on one occasion: "Peter knew how to restrain himself through respect for a good human being, and countless beneficial results flowed from that; but he did not know how to restrain himself through respect for a human being as a human being."[21] Modern Russian history was a very hard struggle toward a moral and civilized society, with the reformer both leading others and engaging himself in a constant battle with his surroundings and even with himself.

If S. Soloviev used the pages following the Treaty of Nystad to summarize Peter the Great's political, even geopolitical *avant le mot,* role in European history, he devoted the conclusion to the entire reign, the section immediately after the reformer's death, primarily to the issue of barbarism and civilization.[22] After discussing briefly the literature and opinions on the first emperor and their extremist trends, he continued:

It is not the function of a historian to admire unconditionally all the phenomena of that epoch, to justify unconditionally all the means used by the Reformer to treat the ancient illnesses of Russia; but, while presenting human activity with its inevitable dark side, a historian has the right to picture the activity of Peter as the activity of a great man, who rendered a greater service than others to his people and to humanity.[23]

Times of change, of overturn, are difficult times. People complained and had good reasons to complain. There seemed to be no end to army and new naval drafts, to labor drafts, to drafts for Russian schools, or for study abroad. Money was necessary for everything, and there was not enough money. The government taxed and took all it could: the rich went broke building, as commanded, houses in St. Petersburg; the poor had their one luxury, oak coffins, monopolized by the state and sold at exorbitant prices; Old Believers paid a double tax for their belief; bearded people were taxed for their beards. Order followed upon order: look for minerals, look for dyes, provide "monsters" for museum collections, tend the sheep but not in the old manner, engage in leatherwork,

19 S. Soloviev, *Istoriia* . . . , XV, column 1415. S. Soloviev is quoting here from Golikov.

20 S. Soloviev, *Istoriia* . . . , XVI, column 231.

21 S. Soloviev, *Publichnye chteniia* . . . , 49.

22 S. Soloviev, *Istoriia* . . . , XVIII, columns 848–862.

23 *Ibid.,* column 851.

build ships in the new fashion, do not dare weave narrow cloth, and transport goods westward not northward. Confusion reigned in the new state institutions and offices. Those caught escaping service were severely punished, and gentry men were forbidden to marry as long as they were illiterate. Moreover, under new forms the old crudeness and cruelty remained. Newly emancipated pregnant women got dead drunk at disgusting parties, and high government officials quarreled with one another with utmost coarseness. Bribery ruled. ". . . the weak are subject to every violence by the strong, as before *the lord* permits himself everything in relation to *the peasant,* the noble to the ignoble people."[24] But there was the other side: the Russian people was going through a hard school, and it was learning. It learned not only arithmetic and geometry, not only school material, but also its civic obligations, a civic conduct. For the first time the government explained its orders and injunctions, its reasons for every important innovation. For the first time the attention of the Russian people was turned to state matters. The new government institutions promoted the collegial principle, initiative, action. The reformer demanded that they accomplish more rather than less, notably that the Senate become indeed the governing Senate. State institutions and beyond them the state itself rose above personal arbitrariness. Though enhancing powerfully the significance of the state, Peter the Great contributed also to the development of the individual. Education was crucial in that connection. So was the continuing decline of the old-style family, which the monarch pushed by his overwhelming emphasis on personal merit and by such measures as his prohibition of parents' arranging the marriages of their children without the children's consent. Landlords, too, were forbidden to force their serfs into marriage. Upperclass women were told to come out of their isolated quarters.

In this manner, Russians were brought up in the stern school of reform! Frightful labors and privations were not in vain. A vast program was traced for many and many years ahead, traced not on paper: it was traced on the ground, which had to open its riches to the Russian, who received, by means of science, the full right to own it; on the sea, where the Russian navy appeared; on the rivers—now linked by canals; in the state through new institutions and enactments; it was traced in the people by means of education, of an enlargement of its mental sphere, of rich supplies of mental nourishment, which were provided by the West, which it had discovered, and by the new world created within Russia itself. Most of what was accomplished was only in the beginning stage, some only crudely sketched; for much only the materials had been prepared, only the directions given; it is for that reason that we called the activity of the reform epoch a program, which Russia is carrying out to this day and which it will continue to carry out, a deviation from the program being always followed by sad consequences.[25]

24 *Ibid.,* column 852; the words italicized by the author were *muzh* and *muzhik.*
25 *Ibid.,* column 855.

The final historical verdict on Peter the Great and his reign had to be a resounding one:

No people ever accomplished such a heroic deed as the one accomplished by the Russian people in the first quarter of the eighteenth century. On the historical scene there appeared a people, little-known, poor, weak, a people that had taken no part in general European life; by superhuman efforts, by frightful sacrifices it gave a legal validity to its claims, it became a powerful people, but without aims of conquest, calmed as soon as it had obtained what was necessary for its inner life. The man, who guided that people in that deed, we have every right to call the greatest historical figure, for no one can have a greater importance in the history of civilization. Peter was not at all a conqueror seeking glory, and in that respect he was a perfect representative of his people, a tribe alien to conquest by nature and because of the conditions of its historical life. Peter's genius expressed itself in the clear comprehension of the situation of his people and of his own situation as the leader of that people: he understood that it was his obligation to lead by means of civilization that weak, poor, almost unknown people out of its sad condition.[26]

S. Soloviev completed his evaluation with an estimate of Peter the Great as a person. The reformer was a giant in moral and physical energy and strength. His powerful religious faith sustained him in defeat and saved him from arrogance in victory. "An extraordinary majesty, combined with the recognition of the insignificance of all merely human minds, a severe demand of the performance of one's obligations, a severe demand of truth, an ability to listen to the sharpest objections, an extreme simplicity, benignancy: all this strongly attached to Peter the best people, who had occasion to come close to him. . . ."[27] The historian concluded with Ivan Nepliuev's expression of grief at his sovereign's death and Andrew Nartov's claim that the first emperor, considering what he had to endure, had been wonderfully kind and forgiving—one more defense of Peter the Great against the old charge of cruelty.

In his *History,* as in his *Public Lectures,* S. Soloviev not only explained and exalted the historical role of the reformer, but also defended him on many specific matters. The apologia included the usual ascription of the emperor's defects and failings to the conditions of the time[28]—a view particularly congruent with the historian's general outlook—another explication of why the emperor had to do everything himself,[29] and even a discussion, parallel to the one in the *Lectures* but not identical with it,

26 *Ibid.,* column 856.

27 *Ibid.,* column 860.

28 ". . . let us check the information concerning the dominant vices of the society of that time, and the habits of Peter which we so much dislike in him will be explained to us" (S. Soloviev, *Istoriia* . . . , XIV, column 1061).

29 "A young, undeveloped society does not permit a division of occupations; hence the possibility and the necessity for a strong man to undertake everything, to exercise his capacities in many varied kinds of occupations; hence Peter's manifold activity; because of the same social conditions we shall see later, in a different field, the manifold activity of Lomonosov" (*Ibid.,* column 1057).

of the advantages of Western dress.[30] S. Soloviev gloried in Peter the Great's magnificent ability to rebound from defeat, whether in the first Azov campaign[31] or at Narva,[32] and he compared him favorably and in the conventional manner to Charles XII, although emphasizing more than most others the nonmilitaristic nature of his hero.[33] As so often, the treatment of the Alexis story proved to be revealing.[34] S. Soloviev began, characteristically, as a historical comparativist:

The time that we are describing was a time of heavy and bloody struggle. The firmest links are broken during such overturns; the struggle is not limited to social life, to the city square: it penetrates into the forbidden interior of the homes, introduces enmity into families. The Divine Founder of the religion of love and peace declared that He had come to bring not peace on earth but the sword, to introduce division into families, to raise son against father and daughter against mother. We find the same phenomena in secular history: everyone knows, from school recollections, the death of the sons of Brutus, sacrificed by their father to the new order of things. Not surprisingly, the frightful overturn that Russia experienced in the first quarter of the eighteenth century brought division and enmity into the family of the reformer and led to the sad fate that befell his son, Tsarevich Aleksei Petrovich.[35]

However, after this heavy, partisan, and—many would say—gauche, start, S. Soloviev proceeded as the superior historian that he was. His Alexis, in contrast to the common image, had intelligence, education, some attractive personal qualities, and deep links to the Russian society of his time. The conflict was a real tragedy, where both sides could be blamed. In fact, the father was the aggressor, and the relationship was that between "the tormentor and the victim, for there is no greater torment than to demand that one change one's nature: and that was precisely what Peter demanded from his son."[36] And yet it was clear on which side the historical right and justification lay. As the climax approached:

Everything had been said. In front of Peter there was not a son, lacking in ability and conscious of that lack, who had escaped from forced activity and had returned to bury himself in the countryside with a woman for whom he had developed a passion: in front of Peter there was the heir to the throne, firmly basing himself on his rights and on the sympathy of a majority of the Russian

[30] S. Soloviev, *Istoriia* . . . , XV, columns 1374–1375.

[31] S. Soloviev, *Istoriia* . . . , XIV, column 1148.

[32] *Ibid.*, column 1250.

[33] "Charles was born in 1682; therefore, he was exactly ten years younger than our Peter. A strong nature made itself felt early in the child; and from the very beginning that strength expressed itself in a one-sided manner; audacity, a mindless search of danger revealed a hero-conqueror exclusively, whereas in the Russian Peter one could see from his infancy the many-sidedness of a genius, the sensitivity of a genius to everything; one could see a reformer, not a soldier, not a conqueror" (*Ibid.*, column 1240).

[34] The chapter on Alexis, Chapter II, occupies columns 402–494 in the seventeenth volume of *History*.

[35] S. Soloviev, *Istoriia* . . . , XVII, column 402.

[36] *Ibid.*, column 406.

people, gladly listening to projects having the death of his father as the aim, ready to utilize an uprising, even if his father were alive, provided the rebels were strong. But that was not all; the program of activity following the occupation of the father's seat has already been outlined: people close to the father will be replaced by others; everything will move in reverse; everything that had cost the father such efforts, everything in the name of which he had suffered such misfortunes and had finally obtained power and glory for himself and for the state—all of this will be overturned, with the added proviso that, of course, the second wife and the children by her will not be spared. One must choose: either he or they; either reformed Russia in the hands of a person sympathetic to the reform, ready to continue the work, or the spectacle of that Russia in the hands of a man, who, with his Dosifeis, will be exterminating with delight the memory of the great activity. One must choose: there can be no middle ground. . . .[37]

Still, S. Soloviev's six volumes were not primarily an apology for Peter the Great, either in the large or in the small, at least not simply an apology. Rather, they constituted a huge and masterful historical work, the great bulk of which consisted of an expert narrative, with few references to the magnificent qualities of the monarch or the destiny of Russia.[38] The bad was often presented with the good. We already saw "the bad side" in the summation of the condition of Petrine Russia provided by the historian after his description of the emperor's death. No happier impression of the life of the people than that is given in such sections as the one that opens with the sentence: "The most numerous class of primary producers, the agriculturists, continued to testify to their unenviable situation by flight"[39]—or in the material contained in *History* in general. Moreover, the historian frequently retained a sober and severe note even in his praise. Like Peter the Great himself, he was glad to list Russian victories but was more concerned with Russian deficiencies and with what remained to be done. Most important, S. Soloviev made every effort to be realistic and scholarly in his treatment of the reformer and the reform. True, he came out in the end with an overwhelming affirmation of both. But presumably that affirmation could change with new evidence or, still more to the point, with a new interpretation of the already available evidence. The subject was now in the realm of historical analysis, not in those of literary eulogy or idealistic polemics.

S. Soloviev's cohesive, powerful, and influential presentation of Peter the Great and his reign profited from a number of circumstances. These included, of course, the historian's outstanding talent as well as his remarkable devotion to hard work, in the archives as well as with pub-

---

[37] *Ibid.*, column 482.

[38] The "dry," factual, narrative presentation had been characteristic of many other Petrine histories (e.g., Ustrialov's or even Voltaire's) although not of that of the more credulous Golikov, who kept marveling at the reformer and was less ready to separate fact from fiction.

[39] S. Soloviev, *Istoriia* . . . , XVIII, column 791.

lished materials. In addition to its other great merits, S. Soloviev's *History*, the six Petrine volumes included, represented a significant expansion of the source base of Russian history. S. Soloviev also gained from belonging to different traditions. A son of a priest, a deeply religious man himself, who originally reacted against the French culture of an aristocratic Russian family where he served as tutor, he came to Peter the Great and the Petrine Europeanization of Russia consciously from a more nativist orientation. Temperamentally and culturally he longed for the organic Russian history that he preached: ". . . having recognized the necessity of the Petrine period, having recognized its lawfulness, the justness with which it flowed from the preceding conditions of Russian society, I retained from my former favorite study of ancient Russian history, my former Slavophilism, the entire warm sympathy for ancient Russia, for its best people."[40] But whatever the personal factors that helped S. Soloviev attain his synthesis of Russian history, the intellectual structure and nature of that synthesis belonged, to repeat, strikingly to the ideology of the Westernizers. Peter the Great stood out as the true leader and at the same time the perfect representative of the Russian people, whom he guided to a higher level of existence. If the transition was no longer the eighteenth-century change from nonbeing into being, no longer Chaadaev's writing on a blank sheet of paper, it was described, nevertheless, as a move from the age of feeling to that of the mind, from barbarism to civilization. A close reading of S. Soloviev on Peter the Great reveals how much it is Belinskii or Granovskii writ large or rather writ in detail in spite of the intervening years, the weakening of the idealistic assumptions, and the enormous work performed by S. Soloviev himself.[41] This does not mean, however, that the historian has been falsely credited with introducing a new stage in Russian historiography, notably in Russian Petrine studies. Fundamentally of the old world, he opened by the nature and scope of his work avenues to the new. That is not an uncommon occurrence in intellectual history.

[40] S. Soloviev, *Moi zapiski* . . . , 103.

[41] Appropriately, some other former Westernizers developed thoughts on Peter the Great similar to S. Soloviev's. The most interesting and important parallel case was that of Constantine Kavelin, who has sometimes been credited with establishing, together with S. Soloviev, the continuity between pre-Petrine Russian history and the reign of Peter the Great. Kavelin, whom, it will be recalled, Granovskii implored to write a major study of the Petrine institutions and to provide a true historical evaluation of the reformer, never produced such a major study, but he did publish an eighty-page commentary on Russian history and Peter the Great, occasioned by the appearance of Ustrialov's work and of the first three Petrine volumes of S. Soloviev's History. In it Kavelin declared, after a survey of Muscovy: "In one word, everything, wherever we look, to whatever we turn, demonstrates that society and the state had already outgrown the old forms; a contradiction between these forms and the emerging content was precisely the main reason for the internal disorder and dissatisfaction" (K. Kavelin, "Mysli i zametki o russkoi istorii," *Vestnik Evropy*, Year One, Vol. II (June 1866), 325–404, quoted from p. 384).

2

S. Soloviev occupied the chair of Russian history at the University of Moscow from 1845 until his death in 1879. His student, also a son of a priest, Vasilii Osipovich Kliuchevskii (1841–1911), replaced him in 1879 and held the chair until his retirement in 1910. The two have been often described as the best and the second best historians of Russia; not infrequently the order has been reversed. S. Soloviev's first major works dealt with the earliest period of Russian history; after that, he concentrated on his mammoth general account of the development of Russia. Kliuchevskii earned the reputation of the most distinguished specialist on Muscovy, but he too came to be known best for his general course of Russian history. Differences between the two were as important as similarities: the difference between the formative intellectual impact of the 1840s and the 1860s, between a scholar interested primarily in the evolution and the manifold activities of the state and a social historian, between a master of international relations and a writer who avoided that field. Kliuchevskii's remarkable abilities included a great artistic gift or gifts. His enormously popular lectures stood out as unforgettable rhetorical and dramatic performances, and his superb use of the language made him the most quotable and the best remembered Russian academic. Add to this Kliuchevskii's special flair for presenting historical personalities, and it is not surprising that the Moscow professor's image of Peter the Great became the best-known and the most admired among educated Russians, or at least best-known and most admired after Pushkin's hero of Poltava and his "Bronze Horseman."

Kliuchevskii's lecture course of Russian history was published in five volumes—by contrast with S. Soloviev's twenty-nine volume *History*. The fourth volume was devoted largely to Peter the Great and his reign, whereas the third, covering the seventeenth century, added much to the Petrine theme.[42] Kliuchevskii also included the first emperor's reign in another course of lectures, brief and brilliant, delivered in 1886 and published under the title of *A History of the Estates in Russia*.[43] In addition, several of his special studies, usually the size of a long article or a short monograph, either centered on that reign or at least encompassed it as an important component. The former included, notably, Kliuchevskii's pre-

[42] I am using the second edition of the fourth volume: Prof. V. Kliuchevskii, *Kurs russkoi istorii*, Part IV (Moscow, 1915). In English, the Petrine part of the volume is not only available in the total *Course* but also separately in a different and better translation as V. O. Kliuchevsky, *Peter the Great* (New York, 1959). Strictly speaking, Kliuchevskii never wrote his *Course:* the work was based on the collated lecture notes of his listeners, mostly corrected and edited by the lecturer, who edited the fourth volume shortly before his death. This provenance of the *Course*, though of importance to Kliuchevskii scholars, does not materially affect a discussion of the historian's image of Peter the Great.

[43] V. O. Kliuchevskii, *Istoriia soslovii v Rossii*, 3d ed. (Petrograd, 1918).

sentation of "Peter the Great Among His Collaborators,"[44] the outstanding piece in historical literature on the entourage of the reformer, and
his "The Poll Tax and the Abolition of Slavery in Russia";[45] the latter
ranged from "The Russian Ruble of the XVI–XVIII Centuries in Its
Relationship to the Present Ruble,"[46] a tour de force, to "Eugene Onegin
and His Ancestors,"[47] whom the historian traced back to the Petrine
reform. All in all, Kliuchevskii expressed himself on Peter the Great in a
rich and varied manner, both orally[48] and in writing even if his coverage
was not quite as dense and extensive as S. Soloviev's.

Of the sixteen lectures that constitute the fourth volume of Kliuchevskii's *Course of Russian History,* the first ten are devoted to Peter the
Great and his reign and the eleventh is entitled "Russian Society at
the Moment of Peter the Great's Death." The first lecture gave vividly the
first emperor's life up to the beginning of the Great Northern War; the
second concentrated on "Peter the Great, his appearance, habits, way of
life and of thought, character." "According to his spiritual stamp, Peter
the Great was one of those simple people, who are understandable at
first glance."[49] A giant, enormously powerful physically and tremendously energetic, he was always on the go.

Peter was a guest in his own house. He grew and matured on the road and in
work under the open sky. Had he found time as he was approaching fifty to look
back on his life, he would have discovered that he was always riding some place.
In the course of his reign he wheeled across wide Russia from end to end, from
Archangel and the Neva to the Prut, Azov, Astrakhan, and Derbent. Many years
of incessant movement developed in him mobility, a need to change location
constantly, rapidly to change impressions. Haste became his habit. He hurried
always and with everything. His usual gait, especially considering the natural
length of his step, was such that a companion had difficulty keeping up with
him, going hoppity skip. It was difficult for him to sit long in one place: at
lengthy festivities he would frequently jump from his chair and run to another
room, to stretch his legs. . . . If Peter was not sleeping, riding, celebrating, or
inspecting, then he was certainly building something. His hands were always at
work, and calluses never left them. On every possible occasion he engaged in
handwork. In his youth, when he had not as yet learned many things, he would
constantly turn his own hand to the activity he was observing in a manufacturing
establishment or a factory. It was difficult for him to remain a mere observer of

44 V. O. Kliuchevskii, "Petr Velikii sredi svoikh sotrudnikov," *Ocherki i rechi, Vtoroi
sbornik statei* (Petrograd, 1918), 454–495.

45 V. Kliuchevskii, "Podushnaia podat i otmena kholopstva v Rossii," *Opyty i issledovaniia, Pervyi sbornik statei* (Moscow, n.d.), 311–416.

46 V. Kliuchevskii, "Russkii rubl XVI–XVIII vv. v. ego otnoshenii k nyneshnemu,"
*ibid.*, 123–211.

47 V. O. Kliuchevskii, "Evgenii Onegin i ego predki," *Ocherki i rechi,* 66–87.

48 The oral Kliuchevskii tradition remains strong among Russian and Soviet intellectuals. For me, it is especially linked to my father, Professor Valentin A. Riasanovsky,
who was Kliuchevskii's student.

49 Prof. V. Kliuchevskii, *Kurs russkoi istorii,* IV, 34.

someone else's work, especially of work that was new to him: his hand instinctively asked for the instrument; he wanted to make everything himself. . . . As years passed, he acquired an immense mass of technical knowledge. Already during his first foreign voyage German princesses concluded from talking to him that he knew fourteen crafts perfectly. Later, he was at home in any workshop, in any factory. After his death there remained scattered almost everywhere, where he had been, things of his own making, launches, chairs, utensils, snuffboxes, and so forth . . . he considered himself an experienced surgeon and a good dentist. On occasion people near him, who had fallen ill with some disease requiring surgery, panicked at the thought that the tsar would learn of their disease and appear, with instruments, to offer his services. It is said that after him there remained a whole sack of extracted teeth—a monument to his dental practice. But he rated the mastery of shipbuilding above everything. No state affairs could retain him when there was an opportunity to work with an ax at the docks. Up to his late years, when in Petersburg, he would not let a day pass without dropping in at the Admiralty for a couple of hours. And he attained a remarkable proficiency in that craft; contemporaries considered him the best master of shipbuilding in Russia. He was not only a penetrating observer and an experienced director in the building of a ship: he could make a ship himself, from its foundation to all the technical details of its trimming.[50]

A native of Moscow, the monarch became a real seaman, who delighted in salubrious sea air and enjoyed "a truly sailor's appetite."

The sad circumstances of his childhood and youth, which forced Peter out of the old, stiff regulated life of the Kremlin Palace; the mixed and undemanding society with which he surrounded himself later; the very nature of his favorite occupations, which made him take up in turn now an ax, now a saw or a turner's lathe, now the morals-correcting cudgel, together with a mobile, unsettled way of life, turned him into a mortal enemy of every ceremonial. Peter would not tolerate restrictions or formalities in anything.[51]

Hence the remarkable simplicity and even physical poverty of the private life of the sovereign, who had his socks darned by his family and who borrowed a stylish carriage from the Ober-Procurator of the Senate, Paul Iaguzhinskii, when he felt that a special occasion called for it. Peter the Great lived, typically, in small rooms and small buildings, with the added demand of low ceilings—indeed, artificial low ceilings had to be constructed of cloth when natural ceilings were high. Only the miser Frederick William I of Prussia could rival the Russian monarch in court frugality. Completely simple and informal in his relations with all people, the tsar played chess and drank beer with sailors, and he liked unsophisticated, gay gatherings of his usually mixed company. When he had to maintain certain boundaries, he did so in his own unique manner. Thus, when a naval lieutenant, drunk, began to cry and complain that the monarch had no one to leave them all to because Tsarevich Alexis

50 *Ibid.*, 37–39.
51 *Ibid.*, 39–40.

was stupid and would spoil everything, Peter the Great stopped him with a blow, adding: "Fool! One does not say that in public."[52]

"But, kind by nature as a man, Peter was rude as a tsar, who had not become accustomed to respect the human being either in himself or in others; the milieu, already familiar to us, in which he grew up could not teach him that respect."[53] Menshikov felt that rudeness repeatedly on his "oblong face," and others had similar experiences. Moreover, the sovereign was given to fits of rage, which only Catherine, holding and stroking his head, could check or calm. And even in his better minutes and hours, his manners and demands could be indecent and cruel. Thus, his guests, men and women, young and old, would frequently be forced to drink vodka beyond all measure and to keep celebrating, in effect under arrest, until the host would finally let them depart. The sovereign's blasphemous "drunken council" was much worse. "Peter tried to fit his dissipation with his collaborators into chancery forms to make it a permanent institution."[54] Disgusting and strange, it was not unlike the way children play, and it was not unrelated to certain widespread attitudes among the Russian people. But explanations to the effect that the sovereign tried to parody and thus condemn superstition in religion or even drunkenness and dissipation themselves were not really convincing. "It is difficult to weigh the portion of truth in that point of view; still, it is more a justification than an explanation (*skoree opravdanie, chem obiasnenie*)."[55]

Interestingly, Peter the Great had a strongly developed aesthetic sense, in particular in architecture and for landscapes, and he did much to bring Western architecture and art to Russia.

He possessed a powerful aesthetic sense; only it developed in Peter's case somewhat one-sidedly, in line with the general direction of his character and his mode of life. The habit of entering the specifics of a given matter, of working on technical details created in him a geometrical precision of vision, an astonishing judgment of eye, a feeling for form and symmetry; he grasped easily the plastic arts; he was attracted by complicated building plans; but he confessed himself that he did not like music and found it difficult at balls to tolerate an orchestra.[56]

With the passage of time and of momentous events, Peter the Great and his assistants grew in political understanding. "Through tobacco smoke and the clinking of glasses there pushes political thought, which throws a different and more attractive light on these leaders."[57] The talk turned to understanding the people, to the meaning of being the good ruler. Yet the obstacles to Petrine progress along this road were enormous—obstacles of background, character, milieu, conditions. Kliuchev-

---

[52] *Ibid.*, 43–44.
[53] *Ibid.*, 45.
[54] *Ibid.*, 49.
[55] *Ibid.*, 51.
[56] *Ibid*, 54.
[57] *Ibid.*, 54–55.

skii concluded the lecture by summarizing the issue, in his own inimitable manner, for his students:

Peter passed his life in constant and tense physical activity, always engulfed by a flow of external impressions, and, therefore, he developed in himself an external perceptiveness, an astonishing keenness of observation and a practical knack. But he was not a devotee of leisured general considerations; in every matter he grasped more readily the details of work than its general plan; he estimated better the means and the ends than the consequences; in everything he was more an entrepreneur, a master worker than a thinker. . . . Peter's misfortune resided in the fact that he remained without any political consciousness, with only an indistinct and contentless feeling that his authority had no bounds, but only dangers. For a long time this boundless emptiness of consciousness was not filled by anything. The applied character of the occupations that he had mastered since childhood, simple manual labor, interfered with reflection, diverted thought away from the subjects that constitute the necessary material of a political education; and in the person of Peter there was growing a ruler without the rules (*pravitel bez pravil*) that inspire and justify authority, without elementary political concepts and social curbs. A lack of judgment and moral instability, together with capacities of a genius and vast technical knowledge, sharply struck the eyes also of foreign observers of the twenty-five-year-old Peter; and it seemed to them that nature was preparing in him a good carpenter rather than a great sovereign.[58]

Still, the monarch learned from the West and from his own failures:

. . . he began to recognize the large gaps in his upbringing and to think deeply about concepts that he had not thought through in time, about the state, the people, about law and duty, about the sovereign and his obligations. He managed to develop his feeling of a tsar's duty into selfless service, but he could no longer renounce his habits; and, though the misfortunes of his youth helped him to tear himself away from the political affectations of the Kremlin, he failed to purify his blood from the only firm director of Muscovite politics, from the instinct of arbitrariness. To the end of his life he could not understand either historical logic or the physiology of the life of the people. . . . His entire reforming activity was guided by the thought of the necessity and the omnipotence of authoritative compulsion: he hoped by force alone to impose upon the people the blessings that it lacked, and consequently he believed in the possibility of turning popular life from its historical bed and driving it between new banks. Therefore, solicitous of the people, he pushed work to the extreme, spent human resources and lives without counting, without any economy. Peter was an honest and sincere human being, severe and demanding toward himself, just and kind to others; but, because of the course of his activity, he was more accustomed to deal with things, with working tools than with people; and, therefore, he treated people also like working tools, he knew how to use them, he guessed quickly who could do what, but he was unable and did not like to enter into their situation, to save their strength; he was not distinguished by the moral responsiveness of his father. Peter knew people, but he could not or did not always want to understand them. These peculiarities of his character found a sad reflection in his

[58] *Ibid.*, 57–59.

family relations. A great expert and organizer of his state, Peter knew poorly one little corner of it, his own house, his family, where he was a guest. He did not manage to live together with his first wife, he had reason to complain about the second, and he failed totally to get along with his son, to guard him from hostile influences, which led to the destruction of the tsarevich and endangered the very existence of the dynasty.[59]

The next seven lectures were devoted to the Petrine reforms, including a separate lecture on "Finances," one of Kliuchevskii's special interests. The nature and sequence of reforms were explained as follows:

Now we can determine for ourselves the connection between war and the reforms. At first glance, Peter's transforming activity appears to lack any plan or consistency. Gradually broadening, it encompassed all parts of the state structure, touched the most diverse aspects of popular life. But not a single part was reconstructed in one effort, at the same time and in its full extent; each reform was undertaken repeatedly, at different times in regard to different segments, as needed, as demanded at a given moment. When this or that series of reform measures is studied, it is easy to see their direction, but it is difficult to figure out why they were enacted in precisely that order. One can see the aims of the reforms, but can not always grasp the plan; to grasp it, one must study it in connection with the situation, that is, the war and its varied consequences. The war indicated the order of the reform, imparted to it the tempo and the very methods. Reforming measures followed one another in the order in which they were evoked by the needs produced by the war. The war put first on the agenda a transformation of the armed forces of the country. Military reform brought in its wake two series of measures, some of which were directed toward maintaining the regular order of battle of the reformed army and the newly created navy; and others, toward securing their support. Measures of both kinds either changed the position and the mutual relations of the estates or increased the effort and the productivity of popular labor as a source of state revenue. Military, social, and economic innovations demanded from the administration so much more and faster work, made it face such complicated and unusual problems that it could not manage them given its established structure and composition. Therefore, hand in hand with these innovations, and in part even ahead of them, went a gradual rebuilding of the administration, of the entire government machinery, as a necessary general condition for a successful carrying out of other reforms. Another such general condition was a preparation of agents and minds for reform. Executors, sufficiently prepared for their tasks, possessing the needed knowledge, were necessary for a successful functioning of the new government, as for other innovations; also necessary was a society ready to support the work of reform, understanding its meaning and its aims. Hence Peter's intense preoccupation with the dissemination of scientific knowledge, with the establishment of general and of professional, technical schools.[60]

Kliuchevskii followed his extended presentation of Peter the Great's varied reforming activity with a lecture on its significance. After a his-

[59] *Ibid.*, 59–61.
[60] *Ibid.*, 8–81.

toriographical introduction, which culminated with the views of Soloviev and emphasized the dominance of the opinion that the Petrine reform constituted a profound transformation of Russian life, the lecturer proposed a series of qualifications and questions. To begin with, there was the issue of the origin of the reform. Though indissolubly linked to the first emperor in Russian history, it came about, as already indicated, bit by bit on an ad hoc day-to-day basis under the pressure of war. Peter the Great introduced reforms almost in spite of himself, and he began to realize that he was doing something really new only in the last decade of his life, as a result, not the aim, of his activity. Moreover, the war not only produced, but also delayed reform and interfered with it, just as reform both helped and hindered the prosecution of the war. The issue of the readiness of the country for the Petrine reform was highly controversial. Antecedents were correctly detected and pointed out by historians. But "what was being prepared was a transformation in general, not Peter's reform."[61] "The reform, as it was executed by Peter, was his personal deed, a deed of unexampled violence, and yet a necessary rather than an arbitrary one. External threats to the state forged ahead of the natural growth of a people, the evolution of which came to be enveloped by stagnation."[62] Most complex was the question of the depth of the reform, crucial to the understanding of its significance. It could be profitably considered in terms of the reformer's relationship to old Russia, to the West, and to the future. Peter the Great inherited the autocracy and the social system based on the estates from Muscovy: he utilized and maintained both while giving a new emphasis to the state as such, as distinct from the person of the sovereign, and passing important additional social legislation in line with the fundamental structure of Russian society. As to the West, the first emperor was no fawning enthusiast, no uncritical admirer. Rather, he considered it a means, a way to obtain what Russia so badly needed. And he aimed to use what the West had to offer very intelligently.

Military technology and economic, financial, administrative, and technical knowledge—that is the vast realm in which Peter invited the Westerner to work and to teach Russians how to work. He wanted not to borrow from the West the ripe fruits of Western technology, but to master it, to transplant into Russia production itself, together with its main lever, technical knowledge. The thought, which had flickered vaguely in the best minds of the seventeenth century, about the necessity of raising first the productivity of the people's labor, directing it with the help of technical knowledge to the development of the untouched natural resources of the country, so that the people would be able to bear heavier state obligations—that thought was assimilated and used by Peter as never before or after: here he stands alone in our history.[63]

61 *Ibid.*, 275.
62 *Ibid.*
63 *Ibid.*, 284.

Appropriately, the reformer's foreign policy centered on the Baltic, so significant for the development of the Russian national economy. Altogether, the Petrine reign produced a great increase in the Russian forces of production. But the resulting gain went to the state and state finances, not to the individual.

The hardworking generation, whose lot it was to have Peter, worked not for itself but for the state, and after intensified and improved work was left perhaps poorer than their fathers. Peter did not leave a kopeck of state debt behind him, did not use up a single working day of his descendants; on the contrary, he bequeathed to his successors an abundant supply of means, on which they subsisted for a long time, adding nothing to the means. His advantage over us resides in the fact that he was not a debtor but a creditor of the future.[64]

Relying on the Muscovite autocracy and social system that he had inherited and borrowing broadly from the West in the interests of his country, Peter the Great was not at all a revolutionary, and his reform was not at all an overturn of everything. But the two acquired that radical meaning because of a devastating war; a desperate opposition; the enormous costs, compulsion, and violence; bitter struggle down to the last detail, with the government acting not only as a policeman, but also as a barber and a tailor—"All this would be funny, were it not so ugly."[65]

It was a revolution not according to its aims and its results, but only according to its methods and according to the impression that it produced on the minds and the nerves of contemporaries. It was more a shock than an overturn. That shock was an unforeseen consequence of the reform, but it had not been its considered aim.[66]

In sum, light and shade were mixed in the image of Peter the Great, and it was not easy to harmonize them. Indeed, even the reformer's "beneficial actions were performed with a repulsive coercion."[67] Still:

Autocratic arbitrariness as such is repugnant as a political principle. Civic conscience can never accept it. But one can be reconciled with a person in whom this unnatural power is connected to self-sacrifice when an autocrat mounts his assault straight in the name of the common good, risking to break himself against insuperable obstacles and even against his own work. Thus is one reconciled to a violent spring storm, which, while breaking age-old trees, refreshes the air and by its downpour helps the growth of a new sowing.[68]

Kliuchevskii was S. Soloviev's student. There existed a complex but fundamental connection between the work of the two historians, and it is their joint effort that gave us probably the most impressive, as well as an

[64] *Ibid.,* 285.
[65] *Ibid.,* 289.
[66] *Ibid.,* 292.
[67] *Ibid.* Elsewhere in the lectures Kliuchevskii described Peter the Great as "evoking even social initiative by compulsion" (*ibid.,* 476).
[68] *Ibid.,* 293.

immensely influential, structuring of Russian history.[69] Peter the Great was, of course, a crucial part of that historical structure. One can even write of generally idealistic, and among them specifically Hegelian, influences on Kliuchevskii by way of S. Soloviev, and perhaps even more by way of another teacher of his, also a conservative Westernizer, an outstanding legal scholar and philosopher, Boris Chicherin.[70]

But the differences were striking and far-reaching. Kliuchevskii matured intellectually in the 1860s, not the 1840s, and thus had to respond at a basic formative level to the intellectual climate of his time, that is, to positivism, utilitarianism, a certain kind of sociologizing, an emphasis on the common people, and the Russian radical and revolutionary movement itself.[71] His response was, typically, complicated and ambivalent; indeed, it has been repeatedly suggested that he buried himself in scholarship to escape his environment. However, one does not escape the environment. The result was that whereas Chicherin and S. Soloviev became famous as proponents of the "state school" of Russian historiography, Kliuchevskii developed into a great social historian although his kind of social history was intrinsically linked to the evolution of law.[72] Also, in not pledging obedience to Hegel or another peremptory guide, Kliuchevskii tended to be more eclectic than his teachers, less dogmatic, more flexible, even ironic in his approach to Russian history, an attitude that apparently suited his mental and emotional set especially well. Not surprisingly, historians argue to this day about exactly what role Kliuchevskii assigned to personality in history or what relative weights he attached to ideas and to economic factors in the evolution of a society.

Kliuchevskii's image of Peter the Great was, thus, both a continuation of the established image, from Feofan Prokopovich through S. Soloviev, and a modification of it in the new intellectual circumstances, in effect a

[69] The relationship between Kliuchevskii and S. Soloviev is an involved and inherently difficult subject. The student himself contributed several important estimates of the teacher, including "Sergei Mikhailovich Soloviev," "S. M. Soloviev, kak prepodavatel," and "Pamiati S. M. Solovieva," collected in Kliuchevskii, *Ocherki i rechi*, 5–25, 26–36, and 37–56 respectively. Of the secondary literature, I might mention A. A. Zimin's argument that Kliuchevskii came closer to S. Soloviev's historical position only later in life, when developing his *Course*, not in the 1860s (A. A. Zimin, "Formirovanie istoricheskikh vzgliadov V. O. Kliuchevskogo v 60-e gody XIX v.," *Istoricheskie Zapiski*, vol. 69 [1961], 178–196).

[70] For Chicherin's influence on Kliuchevskii, see especially S. Tkhorzhevskii, "V. O. Kliuchevskii, kak sotsiolog i politicheskii myslitel," *Dela i Dni* (1921), Book Two, 152–179, particularly pp. 162–163, 178, but also *passim*.

[71] The relationship between Kliuchevskii and the Russian radical Left of the 1860s is given full, even exaggerated, attention in a recent major work on Kliuchevskii, where it is used as the key to interpreting the historian: Akademik M. V. Nechkina, *Vasilii Osipovich Kliuchevskii. Istoriia zhizni i tvorchestva* (Moscow, 1974). The text and the notes contain valuable bibliographical information on most issues mentioned in this section of my book.

[72] No criticism is meant here. Legal history can certainly be of great relevance and importance for social history. In Kliuchevskii's particular case, which is much too big a topic to be discussed in a footnote, it may be sufficient to remark that the historian had to deal constantly with legally defined estates.

diminution of it. Where the first emperor incarnated reason for the proponents of the Russian Enlightenment and was in a sense the measure of all things and where for Westernizer philosophical idealists he expressed perfectly his people and its historic needs, Kliuchevskii had no corresponding doctrine to assert his supreme significance. The quasi-divine argument had been dispelled by S. Soloviev's criticism, if not earlier, and S. Soloviev's own affirmation of the reformer as the perfect representative of his people at a critical juncture in its history found no favor in his student's mind or eyes. To repeat Kliuchevskii's judgment of the first emperor: "To the end of his life he could not understand either historical logic or the physiology of the life of the people."[73] Nor was it clear why Peter the Great appeared at all:

So, without exaggerating or minimizing the work of Peter the Great, his significance can be expressed as follows. The reform emerged by itself from the pressing needs of the state and the people, and it was felt instinctively by a commanding human being with a sensitive intellect and a strong character, with talents harmoniously combined in one of those exceptionally happily constituted natures, who, for reasons yet unknown, appear from time to time in the midst of mankind.[74]

If Peter the Great's historical role itself was contingent and unpredictable, that applied even more strikingly to his specific activities. Not a model of enlightened despotism or an organic expression of the nature and needs of the Russian people, the reformer's rule became for Kliuchevskii—as we have already seen—a hectic jumble of desperate ad hoc measures, hurriedly enacted under the pressure of a war by an energetic monarch whose hands worked better than his head. Without any general plan, it abounded in miscalculations and mistakes. The historian's penchant for irony and paradox gave a special edge to his frequently devastating depiction of Petrine Russia. Nor would Kliuchevskii engage in apologetics. While trying to understand his subject, for example, to understand why the reformer considered it necessary to fight beards and long dress, and while fully aware of the enormous difficulties in the way of reform, he refused to rationalize mistaken or immoral actions, remaining skeptical of those who kept providing on each occasion "more a justification than an explanation."

And yet, if Kliuchevskii's Peter the Great came out diminished, he was by no means small. Part of what remained may be ascribed to the legacy of two centuries of adoration, which no single historian could entirely rework. Still, Kliuchevskii's own views also allowed much for the first emperor while his research kept reminding him of the emperor's importance. If the reform was essentially produced by the fundamental course of Russian history, by the needs of the state and the people, the ruler

---

[73] Kliuchevskii, *Kurs*, IV, 60.
[74] *Ibid.*, 290–291.

apparently strongly affected the particular character of the reform as well as its timing. And both items were significant, for Russia was threatened from the outside and had no time to lose. The first emperor engaged in remarkable activities in many fields. Interestingly, Kliuchevskii, a pioneer in Russian economic history, praised his development of the national economy very highly. Moreover, what the reformer accomplished by his ceaseless efforts proved to be very important for the future of Russia. Finally, apart from theoretical considerations, there stood Kliuchevskii's magnificent artistic image of Peter the Great himself, an image so effective that it tended to obscure its own contradictions as well as the fact that the stature of its subject was not increasing but diminishing in the changing intellectual climate of Russia.

### 3

That decline was powerfully expressed in the work of Pavel (Paul) Niko-laevich Miliukov (1859–1943), Kliuchevskii's student, a very prominent political figure and a major historian. Miliukov's fundamental contribution to Petrine studies was *The State Economy of Russia in the First Quarter of the Eighteenth Century and the Reform of Peter the Great,* an enormous book, submitted as a master's thesis at Moscow University in 1892.[75] Utilizing the extremely rich archives, the author presented in almost 700 large and compact pages of text, tables, notes, and appendixes the administrative, financial, and economic condition of Russia in its relation to the instituted changes. Following an expert discussion of the seventeenth century, he proceeded with a precise and dense, largely statistical depiction and analysis of Peter the Great's reign in three chronological stages, 1682–1709, 1710–1718, and 1719–1725, and ended with a general conclusion.

In its broad and extremely important field, Miliukov's scholarship went much beyond, in depth and precision, not only the usual pane-gyrics and publicistic comments on the reformer, but also Kliuchevskii's mellifluous lectures and even S. Soloviev's dogged tracking down of the activities of his subject. And the young historian was very much aware of his accomplishment. Still, it was Miliukov's more general conclusions that proved most resounding, and these were remarkably similar to Kliu-chevskii's views, or at least they followed one main line of the Kliuchev-skii interpretation of Peter the Great and his reign. The lack of a plan, and even of general considerations; the ad hoc, piecemeal nature of the reforms under the pressure of the Great Northern War and of other emergencies; their chaotic, patchy, partial introduction and their re-peated revamping; the stupendous costs—these and other similar asser-

[75] P. Miliukov, *Gosudarstvennoe khoziastvo Rossii v pervoi chetverti XVIII stoletiia i reforma Petra Velikogo,* 2d ed. (St. Petersburg, 1905). The first edition was published in 1892.

tions of the teacher came to be or seemed to be fully supported by the huge research of the student. After noting what had been done in the study and understanding of the cultural aspects of the Petrine reform and of the reformer's military and foreign policies, Miliukov concluded his monumental work as follows:

Then, Peter's social and state reform remained the least studied. Actually, one can talk about Peter's "social" reform only relatively speaking. With the exception of the measures undertaken in favor of the townspeople, during his last years and under the influence of mercantilism, Peter was not a social reformer. Those big changes that can be observed in his time in the condition of other estates are only indirect and least foreseen by him himself, consequences of his legislation. Introducing the poll tax, he did not expect at all to tighten, in a final manner, the knot of serfdom; and drawing the service estate into termless service and introducing inheritance by a single heir, he thought least of all that he was contributing to the creation of a corporate spirit in the noble Russian gentry and of privileged gentry property. The social process was even more linked to historical precedents than the cultural development of Russia, and it was even less dependent on the will of the legislator.

There remains that aspect of the reform that has served as the subject of our study. Its position, so it seems to us, is midway between those aspects of the process that were developing under a direct influence of the reformer and those that were developing apart from or even against his will. To change the structure of a state is more difficult than to dress a part of a population in new dress, form new regiments, and build new ships, but it is easier than to change the mores or a system of estates. The state reform was not evoked by personal plans or enthusiasms of the legislator, as were the navy or foreign dress; but it was not produced, either, by the autochthonous historical process alone. Peter's will was, of course, necessary for its realization; but this aspect of the reform went beyond his range of vision and was realized by him willy-nilly. Neither personal initiative nor historical precedents evoked this reform although both these elements joined in it; it was evoked by the current demands of the given moment, which had, in their turn, been created by both personal initiative and historical precedent.

In that sense, the reorganization of the state appears to us a secondary, derived phenomenon; and that is how it was regarded by Peter, who saw in it not an aim in itself but only a means. That means was necessary to the extent that the aims set by Peter for the state were necessary; it was timely to the extent that those aims were set by him at the right time. The necessity of those aims, which Peter's contemporaries doubted, it would be now too late and useless to doubt; as to the timeliness of setting them, there can be unfortunately two answers, depending on whether we consider them in relation to the internal or the external situation of Russia. In relation to the external situation of Russia, the timeliness of setting those aims is already proved by their successful achievement; probably this timeliness will be confirmed by a comparison of the facts of European politics, from which Russia could not absent itself. In relation to the internal situation, the answer to the question about the timeliness must be negative. New tasks of foreign policy fell upon the population of Russia at such a moment when it did not possess as yet sufficient means to carry them out. The political growth of the state had again gotten ahead of its economic development. The tripling of tax obligations (from 25 to 75 million in our money) and the simultaneous decline in population by at least 20 percent—these are the facts that by themselves prove the preceding assertion more eloquently than any details. At the price of ruining the country, Russia attained the rank of a European power.[76]

Kliuchevskii, in his capacity of an opponent during Miliukov's defense of his master's thesis, accepted the work and paid some high compliments to it, but he refused to consider it worthy of a doctoral, rather than merely master's, degree, rejecting on that point the judgment of Professor Paul Vinogradov and other colleagues (and, one surmises, of almost every academic reader of the study since).[77] It is impossible to determine to what extent Kliuchevskii objected to any shortcuts—all the more so perhaps because Miliukov had declined to work on a much more limited topic proposed by him for a master's thesis—to what extent he felt upstaged by his student and reacted against it, and to what extent he experienced the weight of his own explicit criticisms to the effect that Miliukov had failed to connect sufficiently and sufficiently clearly the nature of the state economy and the course and character of the reform and that he did not finish saying the important things he had begun to say. It might be noted that, whereas the student's views as far as they went were on the whole very close to the teacher's, Miliukov's thesis did not encompass many other aspects of Kliuchevskii's treatment of Peter the Great, including his compelling depiction of the reformer himself. But it was the other opponent, V. E. Iakushkin, who referred to the generally "negative attitude of the author both to the meaning of the reform and to its course"[78] and suggested more attention to the Petrine measures to improve the economic well-being of the people—while willingly accepting the thesis. Remarkable and controversial from the beginning, Miliukov's study has remained that to the present day, with the argument centering on the historian's very high taxation and very low population figures.[79]

[76] *Ibid.*, 545–546.

[77] The defense of the thesis is summarized on pp. 198–215 of "Istoricheskaia khronika," *Istoricheskoe Obozrenie*, vol. V (St. Petersburg, 1892), 175–248. For the author's own version, see P. N. Miliukov, "Moia dissertatsiia," *Vospominaniia (1859–1917)* (New York, 1955), I, 138–142. The text of Kliuchevskii's dissertation speech can be found in V. O. Kliuchevskii, *Sochineniia*, vol. VIII (Moscow, 1959), 177–183 ("Otzyv o issledovanii P. N. Miliukova 'gosudarstvennoe khoziastvo Rossii v pervyiu chetvert XVIII v. i reforma Petra Velikogo' "); and of Miliukov's in *Russkai Mysl*, vol. VII (July 1892), 57–66 ("Gosudarstvennoe khoziastvo Rossii v pervoi polovine XVIII veka i reforma Petra Velikogo").

[78] "Istoricheskaia khronika," 215.

[79] As a more recent example of extreme criticism of Miliukov, see S. P. Strumilin, "K voprosu ob ekonomike Petrovskoi epokhi," *Poltava. K 250-letiiu poltavskogo srazheniia. Sbornik statei* (Moscow, 1959), 179–189, especially pp. 183–188. Strumilin argues, *inter alia*, that Miliukov's alleged loss of population indicated in fact a failure to register, not death.

*The State Economy of Russia in the First Quarter of the Eighteenth Century and the Reform of Peter the Great* established Miliukov's scholarly reputation; *Outlines of Russian Culture* made him broadly popular in educated Russia. Published originally in the 1890s, reprinted, reedited, and republished later, the survey became standard reading, almost a monopoly, in its huge field. Decades later, in exile, Miliukov put out a new and much larger edition although, as he pointed out proudly, except for the prehistory and the very early period where new material was overwhelming, it remained very much the same work: time and recent scholarship had confirmed, not refuted, his views.[80] Totally inclusive chronologically and almost encyclopedic in their coverage, the *Outlines* had nevertheless to pay major attention to Peter the Great's reform.

In a long chapter entitled "Peter's Elemental Reform and the Elemental Opposition to It,"[81] Miliukov tackled the issue both broadly and incisively. Some of Peter's predecessors, much better educated than he, notably Sophia's favorite Prince Basil Golitsyn, appreciated Western culture and moved toward reform in Russia in a gradual and carefully considered manner, but they accomplished little or nothing. By contrast, Peter, ignorant and inexperienced, seized matters into his own hands and proceeded to impose immediate and violent change on Russia. That fitted the historical circumstances.

That Peter's reform was violent was as little doubted by those who were conducting it as by those who were opposing it. It was violent not only in those of its parts that were accidental and arbitrary, but also in those that were essential and necessary. More than that: the violence of the reform gave even to the essential and the necessary an accidental and arbitrary character; that is, it presented the essential in accidental forms. Therefore, to recognize the violent, personal character of the reform does not mean at all to deny its historical necessity. And, conversely, to prove the necessity of the reform does not mean at all to deny its violent character. The task of the historian in the given case consists precisely in showing why a reform, necessary in its essence, *had to be,* could not fail to be personal arbitrariness of one individual in relation to the mass, and why the application of that arbitrariness was generally *possible.*[82]

Peter the Great could impose his will because the church, and more broadly Russian religious consciousness, had been split by the schism of the Old Believers, because the ruler controlled the bureaucracy, and because Russian historical development had not provided strong and autonomous social classes to oppose him.

[80] P. Miliukov, *Ocherki po istorii russkoi kultury* (3 vols. in 4 books or parts, Paris, 1930–1937). The author's introduction to the new edition occupies pp. VII–XI of Vol. I, Part 1. In addition, Vol. I, Part 2 was finally published twenty-three years after the historian's death: P. Miliukov, *Ocherki po istorii russkoi kultury,* vol. I, part 2 (The Hague, 1964).

[81] P. Miliukov, "Stikhiinaia reforma Petra i stikhiinaia oppozitsiia ei," *Ocherki po istorii russkoi kultury.* Vol. III. *Natsionalizm i evropeizm* (Paris, 1930), 157–217.

[82] *Ibid.,* 168.

"As regards the scope and the character of Peter's personal influence on the reform, already his contemporaries differed sharply in their estimates."[83] Seeing the monarch in charge everywhere in every occupation, some were willing to believe him ubiquitous, omniscient, and omnipotent. Even the faults in his behavior, such as his almost daily drunken parties, came to be considered as higher wisdom, that is, as a way to find out the true thoughts of his besotted interlocutors. But others—and occasionally even the same people—noticed that the ruler kept neglecting state business in favor of arts and crafts or of a personal selection of army recruits and that he kept making fantastic mistakes, even in naval affairs. "Was Peter himself his own Providence, or did Providence accomplish its task while bypassing him and even in spite of his acts?"[84] Originally interested in military glory, as prompted by Lefort and other foreigners, although also displaying his own rather utilitarian and prosaic approach, the monarch spoke later of his aim being that of turning cattle into human beings or, more politely, children into adults. He was sadly miscast: "Uneducated himself, he cannot be an educator or a pedagogue of his people already for the simple reason that he has no idea of the aims or the methods of pedagogy."[85] Obviously, only the externals could be introduced in the Petrine manner, while the barbarian inside remained unreformed. These externals had their value, to be sure: new forms, even without content, at least deny the old, and their significance was properly appreciated by the Slavophiles or again demonstrated by Miliukov's educated contemporaries in their battle over the short hair of the new emancipated woman. "In any case, it is impossible to find either in the reformer or in the reform a fully conscious attitude toward the culture that is being borrowed, a full understanding of what constitutes its content."[86]

But was Peter the Great at least in control of his own narrowly conceived reform?

Even that can not be said. To grasp the reform in its entirety, to think it through in advance, to plan it, and then to translate it into practice sequentially and systematically, for all that Peter had too little knowledge and time, and, above all, his nature was not suited for it. The same directness of nature that precluded understanding deeper and finer aspects of European culture made systematically thoughtful activity impossible. The restraining centers are working as yet too feebly in that mental apparatus.[87]

Utterly impatient and impulsive, the monarch applied himself entirely to the occupation of the moment:

With that kind of temperament, Peter always devoted himself passionately to the matter that interested him that particular minute and forgot everything else.

83 *Ibid.*, 180.
84 *Ibid.*, 182.
85 *Ibid.*, 183.
86 *Ibid.*, 186.
87 *Ibid.*

His work dissolved into details, in which Peter immersed himself fully: in them he felt his own strength; with them he filled his entire time; through them he satisfied his need to labor. But, by this very fact, the general plan was moved to a secondary position; no time was left for concentrated thinking about it, and in any case that was not his habit. That is why it was necessary for Peter to look for resources, for impulses for his detailed work, on the outside. That is why he caught so avidly all kinds of direction and advice from elsewhere and put them so quickly into practice without coordinating them and thinking them through provided only they suited at all the general direction of his interest at the given moment.[88]

In the first half of the reign, that general direction was simply to win the war. In the second, the monarch became interested increasingly in a good system of government and in justice at home. As usual, he lacked a general plan; rationalized after, rather than thought before, the event; and apparently regarded good government as a clever new bit of military tactics or an improved gun that could be borrowed from abroad. He did have one asset, however.

In the absence of ideas, there remains only a feeling that constantly raises Peter above all the trifles and the details with which he is choking himself every minute. This feeling is very strongly developed in Peter, and it is the only one that disciplines him, that replaces for him all the restraints not provided by his upbringing. This is the feeling of his responsibility, the feeling of duty, of obligation imposed from the outside. It is curious that this feeling of duty to the motherland, too, assumes in Peter's case the form best understood by him and his entourage, the form borrowed from military service, that of military discipline. He *serves* the fatherland, not only as the tsar, as "the first servant," like Friedrich the Great; no, he serves it, first of all, as a drummer, as a bombardier, as a rear admiral, as a vice admiral.[89]

Without a plan or a system, Peter the Great could not control the reform, but he came to be linked, strikingly and personally, to its countless colorful details. If this was Providence, it was that of the fetishists, not the deists! Also:

If this primitive nature had no firm skeleton of thought, it had, on the other hand, no stubbornness of a systematizer either. There was no doctrine, but also no addiction to doctrine. Peter admitted his mistakes with an astonishing ease and quickness, and he was never too tired to begin anew. Thus, if his reform were not the straight road to the goal, it did not draw circles around it or, even less so, mark time in one place either. Usually (although not always, as we shall see) a mistake served as a lesson; a new experiment introduced a correction: that was, as Peter himself loved to put it, his school. Of course, with such an imperfect method, studying could continue endlessly. Peter was mistaken when, in connection with the Treaty of Nystad, he defined the period of his training as that in the guilds (seven years) multipled by three. He died without finishing

88 *Ibid.*, 187.
89 *Ibid.*, 189–190.

the course and without passing the examination in many very essential subjects of the reform program.[90]

A review of the main parts of the Petrine reform confirmed, Miliukov was certain, that unflattering estimate:

The establishment of a permanent army and the securing of its support is, of course, one of the most important results of the reform, and one that attracted the greatest part of Peter's care and efforts. But it should be known what sacrifices had to be made in human beings and money to achieve that result. Only then shall we be convinced that the result bore no correlation to the efforts, that an enormous part of them was spent inexpediently and fruitlessly. And if we turn from the army to military science, we shall see that there Peter remained to the end of his life a most slow-witted student. We are not even speaking about the defeat at Narva; Peter himself recognized that that was a case of "infantile playing" and that "we began the war as if blind, not knowing the strength of the enemy or our own condition." But when the same mistake, again because of Peter's personal fault, was repeated at the Prut, when in the penultimate year of his life the campaign to capture Derbent brought back the memory of Golitsyn's Crimean campaigns, then no doubt is left concerning the character of Peter's personal influence on the course of military operations. The defeat of the army of Charles XII, like the defeat of the great army of Napoleon, is mainly their own work and the work of natural conditions in Russia.[91]

The monarch's personal participation was much more striking in the creation of the navy; but that too became a story of tremendous expenditures, incompetence, and waste. "The meagerness of results, compared to the grandiose means spent, comes out here especially clearly."[92] Hurry, fragmentariness, lack of coordination, mistakes, and costs recurred in such other areas as government institutions and finance or schooling for that matter, all already discussed in other parts of the *Outlines*. St. Petersburg, constantly and disastrously built and rebuilt, stood as the epitome of Peter the Great's reforming style; the monarch died as he was in the process of converting the capital into a city of canals entirely.

Peter's personality is seen everywhere in his reform: its stamp lies on every particular. And it is precisely this that imparts, to a large extent, to the reform an elemental character. This endless repetition and accumulation of experiments, this ceaseless cycle of destruction and creation, and in the midst of it all some kind of an inexhaustible living force, which can not be broken, or even stopped, by any sacrifices, any losses, any failures—these are all traits that remind us of the wastefulness of nature in its blind elemental creativity, not of the political arts of a statesman. Coming to this conclusion, we must not forget yet another trait that kept appearing in the foregoing exposition. It is exactly in *this* form that the reform appears no longer as a miracle and descends to the level of the surrounding reality. It had to be like that to correspond to that reality. Its fortuity, arbitrariness, individuality, violence are its necessary traits. And, in

90 *Ibid.,* 191.
91 *Ibid.,* 191–192.
92 *Ibid.,* 192.

spite of its strikingly antinational exterior, it is fully rooted in the circumstances of national life. The country received the only kind of reform of which it was capable.[93]

Like Miliukov's M.A. thesis, the *Outlines* could well be described as critical of Peter the Great and his reform. And they evoked the ire of the admirers of the first emperor.[94] Still, it is interesting to observe what a central position Peter the Great occupied in the historian's account of Russian history and culture and how he was credited—as the preceding passage indicates and in spite of the fact that all idealistic scaffolding had supposedly long been gone—even with bringing to Russia the only reform that was appropriate for its time and its place. Also, ironically—the kind of irony better appreciated by Kliuchevskii than by Miliukov—*Outlines of Russian Culture* was written from a narrowly Westernizer (i.e., in a sense, Petrine), point of view.[95] The author accepted the Petrine reform, but he demanded more of it, more deeply, more thoroughly. Peter the Great would have certainly agreed with that.

In another work, Miliukov allowed apparently even more for the first emperor's historical role, moving closer to S. Soloviev's position:

We shall see what exactly Peter's personal role consisted of. In a general way, it can be stated that his epoch marked the passage of Russia from an unconscious evolution, spontaneous so to speak, due to the genius of the nation, to a more conscious evolution, more directed toward a goal, more willed. To be sure, Peter's first reforms, by contrast with the general character of his work, seemed more the result of caprice and interrupted the organic evolution. It is in this sense that one can call Peter the Great "the first Russian revolutionary." In fact, his first attempts at reform had more of a destructive character; it is only later that he undertook the work of reconstruction. This passing from the unconscious and the impulsive to the conscious and the systematic is the distinguishing trait of the great reform undertaken by Peter and marking a period of transition.[96]

The account of the reign that followed restated many of Miliukov's views, but it allowed more for the second, positive period of reform. Certain particular assertions, including some important ones, read more like the standard praise of Peter the Great than the historian's celebrated critique of him: "Peter did not limit himself to Europeanizing the exterior of his subjects. He is also the founder of the Russian intellectual class."[97]

[93] *Ibid.*, 195.
[94] See, e.g., Akademik S. F. Platonov, *Petr Velikii, lichnost i deiatelnost* (Leningrad, 1926), 27–32. In addition to his own criticism of Miliukov, Platonov cites N. P. Pavlov-Silvanskii's.
[95] This is my considered judgment, which I might develop and argue on a more appropriate occasion. When making the comparison, one should, of course, be aware of the passage of some two centuries and of personal contrasts, e.g., that Peter the Great was a religious man whereas Miliukov took a negative view of religion.
[96] Paul Milioukov, Ch. Seignobos, and L. Eisenmann (and seven others), *Histoire de Russie*, (3 vols., Paris, 1932); the parts written by Miliukov included the chapters on Peter the Great's reign, I, 267–427; quoted from p. 268.
[97] *Ibid.*, 397. Miliukov treated Peter the Great most favorably in a commemorative article published in 1925, where he proclaimed the Petrine reform a success, fully jus-

Still, Miliukov did earn, on the whole, his reputation as a leading critic, even a denigrator, of Peter the Great. As I tried to indicate, his criticism was one logical development in the evolution of the Russian image of the first emperor. With the simple ideology of the Age of Reason far behind and even the Hegelian and other idealistic assumptions no longer tenable, the reformer was bound to descend from his ethereal heights. S. Soloviev's insistence on empirical scholarly research and precision could well result in Miliukov's picture of human weakness, error, and confusion. But at least one other factor must be added, the political. Opposition to compulsion and tyranny had always interfered in one way or another with the image of Peter the Great. The issue accounted both for the bulk of apologetic writing and, largely, for the violent Slavophile protest; for Catherine the Great's claim to have given a human face, so to speak, to the Petrine reform; and for Belinskii's all-out defense of that reform, even where inhuman, precisely because it led to humaneness. S. Soloviev essentially agreed with Belinskii, as we have seen, on that crucial point. Kliuchevskii was much less certain. He clearly stigmatized compulsion, the fact that everything had to be forced by the autocratic government as the least desirable and the most vulnerable aspect of the Petrine reform. It was Kliuchevskii who declared: "Joint action of despotism and freedom, enlightenment and slavery—this is a political squaring of the circle, a riddle that we have been solving in the course of two centuries since the time of Peter and have not solved as yet."[98] But Kliuchevskii, fundamentally a conservative, remained highly ambivalent both about the historical role of the Russian autocracy and about its contemporary potential. Miliukov, a doctrinaire liberal, a leader of the Constitutional Democratic Party, exhibited no such ambivalence. Indeed, his image of Peter the Great incorporated some of the bitterness and the venom that were characteristic of the attitude of the more radical intelligentsia of the time toward the tsarist system and that were to become a main motif in the Soviet treatment of the Russian autocracy in general and of Peter the Great in particular.

# 4

Like S. Soloviev, Kliuchevskii, and Miliukov, Professor Mikhail Mikhailovich Bogoslovskii (1867–1929) both studied and taught Russian history at Moscow University. Kliuchevskii's devoted student and Miliukov's younger contemporary, Bogoslovskii became a leader in Petrine scholar-

---

tified by the subsequent course of Russian history while still presenting a devastating picture of that reform as well as of the reformer himself (P. Miliukov, "Petr Velikii i ego reforma (K dvukhsotletnei godovshchine)," *Na Chuzhoi Storone,* Vol. X [Prague, 1925], 11–28). The article appeared also in French: P. Milioukov, "Pierre le Grand et sa réforme (Pour le deuxième centenaire de la mort de Pierre)," *Le Monde slave* (February 1925), 157–185.

[98] Kliuchevskii, *Kurs,* IV, 293.

ship a decade later than Miliukov: his *The Oblast Reform of Peter the Great. The Province. 1719–27*, also an M.A. thesis, came out in 1902, exactly ten years after Miliukov's pathbreaking *State Economy* to which it paid tribute in the introduction and in the text itself.[99] Moreover, Bogoslovskii remained dedicated to the Petrine theme throughout his work as a historian. His only major non-Petrine scholarly contributions, including his two-volume doctoral dissertation, dealt with the seventeenth century, that is, the period immediately preceding Peter the Great (one is reminded of the fact that Miliukov and, of course, Kliuchevskii were also distinguished specialists in that period). Bogoslovskii spent the last fifteen years or so of his life writing an enormously precise and detailed study of the exact facts of Peter I's life and reign, which he called "materials for a biography." Five volumes, published posthumously, brought the story to 1701.[100]

A massive book devoted to a single major Petrine reform, one that was unsuccessful and of a short duration as it turned out, *The Oblast Reform* set the stage for its central topic by a lengthy discussion of the nature of Peter the Great's activity in general. Bogoslovskii stressed its rationalistic character and the all-pervasiveness of the new role of the government as it tried to replace custom by a reasoned system. "There was nothing exceptional in the absolutism and the rationalism of the Petrine state: they were general European phenomena of the seventeenth century. That was the time of Louis XIV; of the Stuarts; of the Brandenburg princes, unlimited masters and organizers of their land; of Charles XI in Sweden."[101] Peter the Great, in his turn, tried to establish, particularly in the second half of his reign, a well-ordered, "regulated," state; and, in a new departure for Russia, he invariably explained his legislation to his subjects and asked for their conscious adherence.

Thus, the transformation of Russia into a European state, common good as the aim of the state; absolute power as the director in achieving that aim; reason as the guiding principle in its activity; an all-encompassing, down to trifles, fine net of supervision of the subjects as the best method to attain that aim—these were the ideas and opinions around which the reforming thought turned, these were the tasks that the reform set for itself. Peter's legislation is permeated with these ideas. It constitutes the means of state supervision of the subjects, calculated for a different psychology from the former; it appeals not only to the feeling of fear, with severe threats, but also to the mind, teaching and trying to convince. Peter saw himself as a pedagogue teaching children, as a master surrounded by lazy pupils: "our people are like children, who will never study the alphabet unless a master forces them to, who are vexed by it, but who, when they learn, thank you later, something that is clear from all present happen-

99 M. Bogoslovskii, *Oblastnaia reforma Petra Velikogo. Provintsiia 1719–27 gg.* (Moscow, 1902). An *oblast* was an administrative territorial subdivision.

100 Akad. M. M. Bogoslovskii, *Petr I. Materialy dlia biografii* (5 vols., n.p., 1940–1948).

101 Bogoslovskii, *Oblastnaia reforma*, 14.

ings—has not everything been done by compulsion, and already one hears thanks for much of it."[102]

Institutions played a crucial role in the transformation of a society. Peter the Great gradually decided to borrow them from the West:

Thus his reform went through its full cycle: beginning with the borrowing of foreign dress, it ended with the borrowing of a state system.

It would be risky, however, to draw a parallel between these two poles of borrowing. European dress was borrowed without any particular selection and entirely, as it was worn by Europeans. Institutions were not copied without selection and slavishly. A certain selection was made among Western models, and the selected ones were subjected to a reshaping in accordance with the conditions of the country, where they were to be introduced.[103]

Sweden was chosen as the exemplar for the Russian administrative reform because of similar natural and living conditions in the two countries, because of the recognized excellence of the Swedish administration, and because Russians had already become acquainted with the Swedish system, having occupied, in the course of campaigns, territories ruled by Sweden and having engaged Swedish prisoners of war in Russian civil service. But Swedish institutions were appropriately modified and combined with native Russian elements or with borrowings from elsewhere. "Least of all can Peter be accused of an intention to copy foreign institutions slavishly."[104] Miliukov was correct, to be sure, to emphasize the absence of a clear plan or demarcation of the administrative reform, as well as of a correlation between it and other reforms.

And yet, in spite of all that chaos in the midst of which the new state institutions were being worked out, one can not fail to discern in them, in their external structure as well as in the aims which their activity was meant to attain, the presence of certain general basic principles . . .

Two main traits mark the organization of the new institutions. They were: first, a logically correct division of administration into its parts, and, second, the unity of the entire system. A correct division and a streamlined synthesis were, of course, the demands of reason, which introduces them wherever it acts, because they are necessary conditions of its work. And it was in these traits of the institutions that there was reflected the stamp of that rationalistic epoch of enlightened absolutism during which the reform was enacted.[105]

The rational structuring of administration into logical parts and its standardization throughout the country were a step forward, indeed, from incoherent old Russia. "In the borrowing of institutions one can see a

102 *Ibid.*, 24.
103 *Ibid.*, 29.
104 *Ibid.*, 31.
105 *Ibid.*, 37–38.

yearning toward a rational, and, therefore, panhuman, order, and not at all simply a desire to imitate a foreign model."[106] The new system was a strikingly bureaucratic one, as befitted the age. Full of optimism and idealism, Peter the Great even extended the administrative reform beyond the Swedish model to encompass not only the physical well-being, but also the mental and moral development of his subjects.

The *oblast* reform failed, to be sure, and it was repealed as early as 1727. Its requirements exceeded the Russian capacities of the time. Bogoslovskii's careful treatment of his topic included such issues as "the absence of resources to satisfy local needs" and "the absence of initiative, as a result of working exclusively for central authorities" or, in the case of the judicial part of the reform, "reasons for the lack of success of the judicial reform," "the slowness of the courts," "their powerlessness," "the want of respect for them in society"; larger sections dealt with "the insufficiency of financial means," "the insufficiency of personnel," and "the insufficiency of preparation of the personnel in the service."[107] Still, the historian was convinced that the abortive reform was not entirely a loss:

Both in the external structure of the *oblast* institutions of the year 1719 and in their aims, there were new traits that reflected the demands and the views of enlightened absolutism. In the external structure these were a standardization of the organizational form and of activity, a regular division into parts. These characteristics exercised their influence on the subsequent order of things, and they came to be, more or less, part of it. An essential difference of the new *voevoda* administration, established in 1727, from the *voevoda* administration in the seventeenth century consists in its standardization, which put an end to the chaos and the mixture of calibers embodied in the prereform local administration with its medieval, historical character. The local government that began to function in 1727 represents in itself a symmetrical hierarchical system, a perfect bureaucratic pyramid, both in terms of the territorial subdivisions of the *oblast* and in terms of the *oblast* administration.[108]

As to the first emperor's noble aims in regard to enlightenment, philanthropy, and moral perfectioning—all of which were to be promoted by the *oblast* reform of 1719—they proved to be impractical, surging ahead of their time, a time when Russia still had to concentrate on the prior task of attaining its natural boundaries.

Although Bogoslovskii never wrote another Petrine study of the nature and scholarly weight of his *Oblast Reform,* he continued to deal with Peter the Great and his reign in many briefer specialized pieces as well as in a few more general accounts. For example, in 1912 he contributed to a joint volume on the first emperor an interesting and revealing piece

106 *Ibid.,* 58.
107 *Ibid.,* pp. XI, XIII. The quoted subheadings, taken from the table of contents, are not reproduced in the text itself, but they indicate well the substance of the corresponding pages.
108 *Ibid.,* 519–520.

entitled "Peter the Great (An Attempt at a Characterization)."[109] After a striking depiction of the reformer's physical appearance and prowess, the historian continued:

There are the same large traits in his moral build. His moral nature was capable of swinging widely both in this direction and in that, both in the positive direction and in the negative. Peter was capable of a noble deed, of self-sacrifice. In fact, he perished from such a deed. In late autumn of 1724 he threw himself, without hesitation, into icy waters in order to save a boat of drowning sailors, with the result that he caught a violent cold and paid with his life for the saving of the sailors. He could not bear an experiment on a swallow put under the bell of an air pump, an experiment performed by court doctor Areskin. When the air under the bell was drawn off to the extent that the bird began to sway and her wings to flutter, the tsar told Areskin: "Enough, do not take its life from a harmless creature; it is not a highwayman," and he let out the bird. At the same time he could look with perfect calm at the most cruel tortures and executions, to which those whom he considered enemies of his cause were subjected. Settling accounts with the rebellious streltsy, he cut off with his own hands the heads of several of them. He was capable of tireless work, but also of making merry without any restraint. He was capable of giving himself to dissipation, the description of which exceeds any measure of imagination, as during the celebrations on the occasions of launching a new ship, when guests got so drunk that they were carried out as if dead, and some did render in fact their souls to God, or at the meetings of the all-drunk and all-clowning council, assembled under the chairmanship of the prince-pope his senior teacher, N. M. Zotov, while Peter himself, performing the role of the senior deacon, proved inexhaustible in his inventiveness, devising various processions and celebrations for the council.[110]

Peter the Great remained simple and parsimonious even after he became one of the mightiest monarchs of Europe. In fact, nothing upset him so much as elaborate court etiquette, for instance, on the occasion when he, splendidly garbed, had to receive a Persian ambassador, who delivered a long, flowery oration and then, following Persian custom, crawled up the steps of the throne to kiss the Russian sovereign's hand. By contrast, the first emperor was perfectly in his element as a common worker, and he took every opportunity to work, even breaking open nailed-down windows when it turned out to be too hot at a high society wedding reception. "It was the fate of this tsar-worker to rework Russia."

The tsar reworked Russia not without some general political thinking. True, he, an entrepreneur and a practitioner in the main, was alien to abstract theories. But that which was practical in the opinions of the time he assimilated well. A changeability of intentions and plans in his reforming activity, expressed in fragmentary and often contradictory ukases, which followed one another from his pen, does not demonstrate as yet the absence of a political ideal: it consti-

[109] M. Bogoslovskii, "Petr Velikii (Opyt kharakteristiki)," ed. V. V. Kallash, *Tri veka. Rossiia ot Smuty do nashego vremeni.* Vol. III. *XVIII vek. Pervaia polovina,* 15–33.
[110] *Ibid.,* 20–22.

tutes merely a sign of passionate bursts in the pursuit of that ideal. Inspired by the ideal, Peter grabs now one, now another means, which seems to him to lead to the attainment of the ideal; disappointed in the results, he abandons what he began, changes it for another means, which carries him away, with all the fervor of his ardent nature. But in all this intense activity, in all this rapid change of intentions and undertakings, one yearning, one political ideal can be seen clearly. It becomes clearer all the time in the measure that Peter himself develops, in the measure that he becomes more broadly acquainted with the Western European world, an acquaintance that began with rides to the German suburb and ended with visits to the most important European states, which began with an invitation to the German carpenter Timmermann and ended with contacts with one of the greatest thinkers of that age, Leibniz, which began with questions about how to work with an astrolabe and how to sail a toy skiff and led to a study of European state institutions. That sacred aim, that ideal of Peter was Russia as a European state.[111]

That meant at the time the triumph of enlightened absolutism. Besides: "That was an age of a brilliant flowering of political thought, when there shone on the philosophical horizon stars of the first rank: Grotius, Pufendorf, Hobbes, Locke, and other stars, minor ones, now already forgotten. That was the time of the domination of rationalism in political philosophy, which reduced everything to reason and tried to explain everything from the principles of reason."[112] State supervision and activity, the embodiment of practical reason, spread to everything. Peter the Great's legislation acquired characteristically an all-encompassing character, always based on the rational approach, persuading as well as ordering and threatening, never flagging in its effort.

Bogoslovskii added to his image of the first emperor in some of his specialized studies, such as an intriguing piece on "Peter the Great According to His Letters."[113] A good and prolific letter writer—although most of his letters were quite brief—the monarch revealed in his letters not only his attitude toward his correspondents and his own interests, but also some remarkable personality traits.

Peter the Great's mind was distinguished not only by the ability to master at the same time a multitude of different subjects and not to get lost amid that multitude; its distinguishing characteristic was also the ability to encompass simultaneously and with equal interest subjects of entirely different calibers. His thought could be working on the most important problems of foreign relations, on a plan of a military campaign, on major administrative issues and so on, and at the same time it could, with an equal clarity, reach down to the very last trifles. . . . A combination of Peter's correspondence of major subjects with trifles constitutes one of the most astonishing traits of that correspondence.[114]

111 *Ibid.*, 25–26.
112 *Ibid.*
113 M. Bogoslovskii, "Petr Velikii po ego pismam," *Sbornik statei v chest Matveia Kuzmicha Liubavskogo* (Petrograd, 1917), 216–250. Slavica–Reprint Nr. 57 (Düsseldorf and Vaduz, 1970).
114 *Ibid.*, 237.

It was also in the first emperor's letters that Bogoslovskii found proof of his invariable devotion to duty, his steadfast determination, his modesty.

Dissatisfied with a merely fragmentary search for truth, the historian devoted the last part of his life to an attempt at as complete a reconstruction as possible of the Petrine past. He explained his project, "materials for a biography," as follows:

The purpose of the present work was to give, to the extent possible, a more detailed description of the life and activity of Peter the Great. For that purpose I tried to gather all the information that has been preserved about him in different kinds of sources. I arranged my narrative, as much as possible, in the simplest chronological manner. I strove, as far as the sources allowed, to reconstruct Peter's life day by day, to depict it as it had taken its course in reality, to observe the actions he had performed, to puzzle out the feelings that had inspired and excited him, to imagine the daily impressions that he had imbibed, and to follow the ideas that had arisen in him . . .

Very much, of course, has been written about Peter the Great. In that enormous literature, two defects have always struck my eyes: in the realm of facts, their not always critically and firmly established authenticity; in the realm of general judgments, their not always sufficient foundation. Developing under the influence of general philosophic systems, our historiography made at times too hasty generalizations, not based on facts and running ahead of the uncovering and the critique of factual material. I wanted to gather facts, reliable facts, which, having been gathered in a sufficient quantity, lead by their multiple repetition to sound general judgments. Perhaps, what I have gathered will prove not to be superfluous and will at some future time be taken into consideration in the formation of such general judgments.

Large and complex historical events can be decomposed into simple and simplest facts down to separate daily actions, feelings, and thoughts of the particular individuals who took part in them. To know exactly any mechanism, one must disassemble it into those simplest facts that composed it and to study those facts exactly. And it was with the decomposition of a complex fact into its simplest composing elements and with the exact depiction of those elements that I was in the main occupied. That seemed to me to be the best method to reach my set goal: to give a critically verified presentation of so complex a historical fact as was the life of Peter the Great.

I encountered not a few obstacles on my path, the chief of which was the presentation of facts itself. It is incomparably easier to construct broad generalizations than to present even a simple, but critically verified, fact, so that one could fully guarantee the authenticity of the presentation. The broader the generalization, the easier it is to construct it. But there is nothing more difficult than to communicate a simple historical fact with full precision, that is, completely as it happened in actuality, in the real world.[115]

[115] Bogoslovskii, *Petr I. Materialy*, Vol. I, 10–11. When the first volume finally came out in 1940, V. Lebedev declared emphatically in the Preface: "All preceding works on Peter I are far inferior in their wealth of facts to the work of Academician Bogoslovskii . . . Any reader interested in the history of his motherland will find in this book abundant material to become acquainted with some of the greatest events." He added, less enthusiastically: "May the reader not seek in this book the life of the popular

To repeat, the historian's five posthumously published volumes carried his effort into the year of 1701.

Like Miliukov a student of Kliuchevskii, Bogoslovskii started from his distinguished teacher's searching and critical approach to Peter the Great and his reign. However, whereas Miliukov carried the criticism, in a sense, to its extreme, virtually dissolving the reign in frantic ad hoc measures, errors, contradictions, and confusion, Bogoslovskii, whether because of his character, intellectual preferences, or conservative political views, tried to save what could be saved by a responsible historian from the Petrine activity. Thus, the *oblast* reform, a recognized, even classical, failure, demonstrated to him, nevertheless, the logic, breadth, and idealism of the Petrine effort, and he found much that was positive in its aftermath. As in Miliukov's case, Bogoslovskii's approach led to dangers, small and large, only in the opposite direction. Bogoslovskii, perhaps, lacked the information to doubt that Peter the Great died because of rescuing sailors (his "materials" too never reached 1725, only 1701), but he could have calculated that the monarch personally killed, or executed, more than "several" *streltsy*. More seriously, it would have been better to argue that "the attainment of natural boundaries" had to precede improvement at home rather than to assume it. Interestingly, Bogoslovskii eschewed any explicit general historical theories to support his views, almost as if he wanted to confirm the Marxist vision of "bourgeois historians" afraid of historical laws and broad constructs once the bourgeoisie had passed its prime. Indeed, he devoted himself to his "materials," that acme of nominalism, just when his Marxist colleagues were engaging in their broadest, and wildest, generalizations, some of which will be discussed in the next chapter.

5

If late Russian imperial historiography could be accused of the lack of a unifying and guiding ideology, it certainly possessed richness and variety. And some of that richness and variety was reflected in its treatment of Peter the Great and his reign. In addition to the remarkable Moscow University "school" of S. Soloviev, Kliuchevskii, Miliukov, and Bogoslovskii—of course, in itself rich and varied—historians elsewhere in the empire—and other historians in Moscow for that matter—were also concerned with the first emperor and his work. Only a few paralleled Bogoslovskii in making the reformer and his activities the abiding center of their lifework. Many, however, dealt with the first emperor in a significant and diverse manner as they studied the institutions, social history,

---

masses and of oppressed peoples groaning under the yoke of feudal lords-serfowners. A social characterization of the movement of the *streltsy* of 1682 is not given or the struggle of feudal groups whereas many facts are treated from the point of view of psychologism." The Preface occupies pp. 5–9 of the volume; I quoted from p. 9.

or economy of modern Russia. Whole branches of historiography, such as the history of education and even of culture in general, in modern Russia or modern Russian military history had to be anchored, so to speak—the verb is appropriate—in the reign of Peter the Great. Through it all the image of the sovereign, although, as we know, already firmly set and developed over a century and a half, received further contributions and experienced additional shifts of emphasis.

Professor Alexander Brückner (Aleksandr Gustavovich Brikner in transliteration from the Russian, 1834–1896) was one of the historians for whom Peter the Great remained central throughout his life and work. Born in St. Petersburg, where he obtained his primary and secondary education, bilingual in Russian and his ancestral German, as well as fluent in several other European languages including Swedish, Brückner studied at the universities of Heidelberg, Jena, Berlin, St. Petersburg, and Dorpat, and taught in the Law School (*Uchilishche pravovedeniia*) and the university in St. Petersburg and in the universities of New Russia (*Novo-rossiiskii,* in Odessa), Dorpat, and, nominally, Kazan. The Russian-German historian's main interest was the Westernization of Russia, and his chief protagonists were Peter the Great and Catherine the Great, to whom he devoted his two major works. Brückner also wrote on such topics of the Petrine period as Ivan Pososhkov, Patrick Gordon and his famous diary, and Peter the Great's journeys abroad. One of his late works, *Die Europäisierung Russlands,* has been described as a result and summary of all his research.

Profusely illustrated and meant to be popular as well as up-to-date in its scholarship, the Russian version of Brückner's *History of Peter the Great* occupied well over 700 pages; but its point of view was made strikingly clear in the very first paragraph of the Introduction: "The historical development of Russia in the course of the last centuries has consisted mainly in its transformation from an Asiatic state into a European one. The most remarkable epoch in this process of the Europeanization of Russia was the reign of Peter the Great." Always aware also of the Western side of the Russian-European relationship, Brückner ended the Introduction by discussing the increasing Western interest in Russia and citing Leibniz's observation to the effect that important changes were then in the process of being enacted by such non-European rulers as the emperor of China, the "king" of Abyssinia, and the tsar of Muscovy.[116]

What followed was an intelligent, comprehensive, learned but, on the whole, quite conventional retelling of the Petrine reign, distinguished possibly only by a greater-than-usual attention to the Western connec-

---

[116] A. G. Brikner, *Istoriia Petra Velikogo* (St. Petersburg, 1882), quoted from p. V. The original German version was published three years earlier: A. Brückner, *Peter der Grosse* (Berlin, 1879). The translation was done by Brückner himself. On Peter the Great and Leibniz, see Vladimir Gere, *Otnosheniia Leibnitsa k Rossii i Petru Velikomu po neizdannym bumagam Leibnitsa v Gannoverskoi biblioteke* St. Petersburg, 1871). The author (1837–1919) taught European history at Moscow University from 1865.

tions of the emperor and to Western sources for that period. The historian did not forget the dark side, such as the cruel repression of the *streltsy* or the tragedy of Tsarevich Alexis, probably dead as a result of torture although possibly executed outright, but there was no mistaking his fundamental, if qualified, appreciation of the Petrine reform. Thus, the chapter on the state institutions began:

Concern with the well-being of the people lay at the foundation of Peter's administrative and legislative activity. Contrary to the principles of Machiavellism, which aimed mainly at increasing the political authority, power, and means of the state, Peter was a true representative of enlightened absolutism who regarded successes in the field of foreign policy and unlimited monarchical authority merely as the means for the achievement of the main aim: the development of the riches and the education of the people. Therefore, Peter, though most intensely engaged in problems of foreign policy, never let out of sight questions of administration, legislation, justice, police. Not in vain did Leibniz rejoice over the battle of Poltava, especially because that success of the tsar could give him the opportunity to occupy himself more successfully than before with the internal transformation of the state. Until an appropriate Russian position among the European powers could be secured, one could not undertake a systematic reform of the state and the social organism. The danger that threatened Russia on the part of external foes interfered with calm and comprehensive activity in the management of internal affairs. Not for nothing did Peter's numerous ukases and orders carry the stamp of a daring experiment of an idea that has not quite matured, of an excessively rapid execution of insufficiently developed projects. In the many prescriptions, laws, instructions, having as their aim the good of the people, the securing of order and of the principles of political morality, there resided compulsion, an insufficient acquaintance with the situation, a violation of many interests and rights.[117]

The tsar lacked competent Russian assistants, and his foreign advisers tended to be doctrinaire and insufficiently aware of Russian needs. Only gradually were the old institutions subjected to reform. Yet matters improved with time. "Peter himself was becoming, always more and more, the soul also of the internal government."[118] In economic affairs, too, as in politics and in administration, the reformer was striving for the well-being of the people although he was also enormously hard-pressed just to make ends meet.

Brückner's explicit image of the first emperor, "Peter's Personality,"[119] broke no new ground. The historian stressed the contrast between the remarkable ruler and his predecessors on the Russian throne: his simplicity, sociability, heavy schedule beginning at four o'clock in the morning, delight in work, modesty in personal habits and style of life. On the other hand, the monarch was given to staging wild, at times elaborate, parties and festivals and even to caricaturing religious rites and cere-

---

117 Brikner, *Istoriia Petra Velikogo*, 589–590.
118 *Ibid.*, 591.
119 The section "Lichnost Petra" is in *ibid.*, 670–682.

monies. The new Russian court, which had abandoned the stiff Muscovite etiquette but had not yet acquired Western refinement, was a wild place. Continuing, Brückner praised Peter the Great's abilities as a letter writer and then turned to the remarkable scope of his knowledge and interests:

One can not help being astonished by the broad scope of Peter's encyclopedic education. We already spoke about his study of the natural sciences when pointing out the significance of the tsar's first journey abroad. The arts, painting and architecture, attracted his attention much later. He ordered the copying of the plans and drawings of the famous castle of Ildefonso in Spain; when erecting various palaces in Russia, he used as his models beautiful buildings of that kind in Western Europe; he looked after the gathering of collections of paintings, engravings, sculptured objects. The creation of magnificent parks under Peter's direct personal supervision, for example, in Peterhof, in Katharinenthal, and so on, reveal in him love of nature, a penchant for elegant gardening.[120]

Peter the Great was also a notable geographer, drawing pioneering maps himself; gathering all the possible geographic information, with a special interest in waterways; organizing and sending geographic expeditions: such momentous later developments as Vitus Bering's discovery of the Bering Strait were primarily a result and continuation of the first emperor's personal initiative. Brückner ended the section with a summary reference to the monarch's health and illnesses and with a brief, but dramatic, account of his death.

As to the general conclusion to the entire study, the historian wrote as follows:

Historical development takes place essentially independent of particular individuals. Without Peter, too, Russia would have become a European state; he did not create a new direction in the historical development of Russia. But, because of the genius and the power of will of Peter the patriot, Russia moved ahead especially quickly and successfully in the direction that had already been indicated to it. The people, which created Peter, can be proud of that hero, who was a product, so to speak, of the contact between the spirit of the Russian people and panhuman culture. A deep understanding of the necessity of such a joining of the two principles, the national and the cosmopolitan, gave Peter, for eternal time, one of the first places in the history of humanity.[121]

In the conclusion to his later work, *Die Europäisierung Russlands,* Brückner was to write of Russia's joining Europe successfully and indissolubly in the eighteenth century and of its "high and beautiful task" of spreading European culture in Asia.[122] Though he meant to keep Peter the

120 *Ibid.,* 676.
121 *Ibid.,* 686.
122 The last statement may be more correctly attributed to C. Mettig, a Dorpat student of Brückner who finished and prepared for publication the volume after the death of the historian, rather than to Brückner himself. In either case, it represents an interesting extension of the Petrine image whereas Brückner's extremely high opinion of the reformer remains intact without it (A. Brückner, *Geschichte Russlands biz zum des 18. Jahrhunderts,* Vol. II, C. Mettig, *Die Europäisierung Russlands in 18. Jahrhun-*

Great's historical role within human limits, a mere mortal could hardly ask for a more glorious destiny or accomplishment. Or, to put it differently, the Russian-German historian, noted for his optimism, lacked the sharp critical edge of the Moscow "school."

Brückner had very important links with the northern capital, but his own university education was peripatetic, and his teaching was done in the main in Dorpat University. The St. Petersburg historical "school" proper is usually associated with Professor Konstantin Nikolaevich Bestuzhev-Riumin (1829–1897) and his disciples. A prominent historian, organizer, publicist, and public figure, Bestuzhev-Riumin studied at Moscow University, counting Granovskii, Kavelin, Pogodin, and S. Soloviev among his teachers, and he taught Russian history in St. Petersburg University from 1865 to 1884. A specialist in the early period—his most important work, the two-volume *Russian History,* never went beyond 1584—and particularly in its sources, the St. Petersburg professor made no major contribution to the Petrine studies. Still, he had to deal repeatedly with Peter the Great in occasional lectures, reviews, in his examination of the teaching of the Slavophiles and its influence in Russia, and in his historiographical essays, a field in which he was a pioneer.[123]

Bestuzhev-Riumin perhaps summarized his views on the reformer best in an address to a solemn gathering of St. Petersburg University delivered on May 31, 1872, and marking the bicentennial of the monarch's birth. The address was entitled "Reasons for the Different Opinions on Peter the Great in Russian Scholarship and in Russian Society."[124]

Two hundred years have passed since the birth of Peter the Great, almost one hundred and fifty since his death; his name is on everyone's lips, monuments to him stand in Russian cities; and yet both scholarship and society still stop in perplexity in front of the colossal image of Peter, the gigantic deed he accomplished. Up to now, as at the time of his activity, that activity is discussed from different sides: at times there resound the most irresponsible panegyrics, not infrequently the most groundless blame.[125]

To be sure, progress had been made. Informed opinion could no longer follow Sumarokov or even Lomonosov and Karamzin. S. Soloviev had led the investigations establishing that "Peter's activity was the most ener-

---

derte (Gotha, 1913), 471–472). The first volume, entitled *Die Europäisierung Russlands. Land und Volk,* was published in Gotha in 1888.

123 For the latest study of Bestuzhev-Riumin, see Hartmut Klinger, *Konstantin Nikolaevič Bestuzev-Rjumins Stellung in der russischen Historiographie und seine gesellschaftliche Tätigkeit. Ein Beitrag zur russischen Geistesgeschichte des 19. Jahrhunderts* (Frankfurt am Main, 1980), with a bibliography of the historian's works on pp. 230–232. Historiographical essays, including those dealing with Tatishchev, Karamzin, Pogodin, and S. Soloviev, can be found in: K. Bestuzhev-Riumin, *Biografii i kharakteristiki* (St. Petersburg, 1882).

124 K. Bestuzhev-Riumin, "Prichiny razlichnykh vzgliadov na Petra Velikogo v russkoi nauke i russkom obshchestve," *Zhurnal Ministerstva Narodnogo Prosveshcheniia,* Part CLXI (St. Petersburg, 1872), (5–6), 149–156.

125 *Ibid.,* 149.

getic expression of that which had constituted the aim and the ardent wishes of his predecessors, that Peter's genius revealed itself mainly in the ability to find the means needed for his aim, and to move steadfastly toward that aim, and especially in the final clarification of what that aim was."[126] Peter the Great saw clearly what had been hazy to his predecessors, but there was no break between the two periods. Yet the general opinion in Russia judged matters differently. Why?

Novelty always brings division until it is accepted by all the people, and it also brought new demands. The Muscovite government and society were becoming increasingly conscious of their deficiencies, but they were doing relatively little about it, and they were doing it slowly. Shcherbatov might well have been correct when he estimated that, without the great reformer, the development of Russia would have been retarded by a whole century. And, in addition, Sweden and other neighbors threatened. "But Peter appeared, and he appeared—great historical luck—precisely in that minute, when everything was ready, and when his appearance was most needed."[127] An autodidact, the monarch retained the habit of learning all his life. He also developed his innate capacity to recognize ability and to fit people to the jobs where they could serve best. But he demanded hard, continuous service, ordering his assistants to study new things at home or abroad.

The unfortunate Tsarevich Alexis fell victim to his inability to understand the legitimacy of his father's demands, victim to his contemplative nature, which found a ceaseless activity revolting. And it is only from this point of view that the tragic collision between father and son can be explained. From this point of view, too, can be explained Peter's measures against the monks and his general attitude toward the clergy: he saw no support in it for himself, but rather adherents of Alexis who "were not in an advantageous position" and who were seeking such a position.[128]

For Peter the Great, at whatever price, the needs of the state came first and always:

Concern with the power of the state, with its political significance, was Peter's first concern; everything else was the means for the attainment of that highest goal. The state needs technicians, and institutions are created fit to educate these technicians, seafarers, artillerymen, engineers, medics; without manufactures and trade of one's own there can be no well-being of the state, no flourishing of its finances—to achieve the desired aim self-government is given to the townspeople, advantages to those who want to establish factories and plants, to Russian merchants who are trading abroad, and so on; whenever this or that kind of manufacturing is being established, rules are issued how to prepare Russian leather, and the like; severe punishments are set for not observing the

126 *Ibid.*, 150.
127 *Ibid.*, 152. Actually, as indicated in Chapter 1, Shcherbatov calculated the likely retardation as 130 years.
128 *Ibid.*, 153–154.

rules; the state takes manufacturing fully into its jurisdiction, in line with the theory then dominant in Europe and represented by the famous Colbert.[129]

It was, thus, the enormous Petrine effort that originally created the opposition. Moreover, in the century after the reformer's death many Russians were provoked by the blind admiration of the West in their country, by the preference for the French language in educated society, and so on. Naturally, a reaction, even an idealization of old Russia, followed:

In the teaching of the Slavophiles (in its original version), this idealization received its final form. There are justified aspects in their objections, but these refer mainly to the consequences of Peter's activity, which did not depend on him and which he had not foreseen: not a few extraneous elements became mixed with Peter's great deed as soon as the continuation of his cause became a possession of others, often people much inferior to him. And, in part, these objections refer to Peter's methods and means. His means and methods were borrowed from the past of the Muscovite state or even from examples in contemporary Europe, which was living through the age of Louis XIV. Peter's critics, therefore, are wrong in that they do not distinguish sufficiently clearly all these manifold elements in his work and do not stop to consider the issue as to what belonged to him himself, what to his time, and what, finally to his successors.[130]

Thus, the panegyrists, especially prominent among intellectuals dazzled by Western culture, and the undifferentiating critics continued arguing at cross-purposes as Russian history continued its course. Yet there was reason to hope that that course was finally bringing the resolution to the argument:

. . . now, however, we are beginning to come out onto a different road, and, possibly, Peter's ardent thought will be realized—to see us also in the field of science and scholarship equal members with other great peoples of the world, and, possibly, in the future lawgivers, military commanders, and poets will represent the Russian land in the great pantheon of world history. Then Peter's deeds will receive their consummation, and, possibly, only then contradictory talk about them will cease, and the whole of thinking Russia will recognize, with one voice, the importance of the reform, and not only in the political sense, although its main goal was indeed, as I already said, the external might of Russia. That time, let us hope, is near; the dawn already looms on our horizon. Then also we shall obtain a full history of Peter because of the lack of which we are still in debt to his great memory.[131]

In its powerful, although qualified and "scholarly," endorsement of Peter the Great and his work, its emphasis on the continuity of the Russian past and its optimism for the Russian future, the St. Petersburg University bicentennial speech was very close to the Moscow University one, and

129 *Ibid.*, 154.
130 *Ibid.*, 155.
131 *Ibid.*, 155–156.

indeed Bestuzhev-Riumin was proud to consider himself S. Soloviev's student.

There were other commemorations besides. At a solemn gathering of the Imperial Academy of Sciences, again on May 31, 1872, the general address was delivered by Academician Iakov (Jacob) Karlovich Grot (1812–1893), a leading specialist in Russian language and literature, who had previously taught at Helsingfors University and at his alma mater, the celebrated lycée in Tsarskoe Selo. It was entitled "Peter the Great as Enlightener of Russia."[132]

At present the Russian people is experiencing important moments: resurrecting the most glorious epoch of its past, they bring together again Russia and the greatest protagonist of its history, they serve as a persistent reminder of his great, by no means entirely attained as yet, goals of enlightenment. The eighty million population of a colossal state is celebrating a memorable day, the day when in the Russian land there appeared for the first time that mighty spiritual force, that was to leave an indelible imprint on the fate of entire Europe. And in those moments not Russia alone but the entire Slavic world proudly calls Peter *its own*. The Academy of Sciences joins the general celebration of the land, not only because Peter is its creator, because his thought is reflected to this day in every pulse of its existence, but mainly because he was a tireless champion of the highest interests of humanity, because he laid the foundation for the enlightenment of his mighty nation and led it into the circle of the active members of the educated world. His whole life was work, care, a ceaseless struggle, but struggle that almost always ended in victory: a life-and-death struggle with his own family, his sister, his wife, his son; a bloody struggle with enemies, internal and external; finally, a determined struggle with ignorance, prejudices, superstition, a struggle under the banner of thought and truth. That last one was the most honorable and the most fruitful struggle that it was Peter's lot to wage. The fruits of education were the most substantial result of all the deeds of the Great one, and it is to that ever-to-be-remembered achievement of his that my address will be chiefly dedicated.[133]

After a brief discussion of Peter the Great's upbringing, which stressed both the extent of his interests and knowledge and his regret that he had

---

[132] Ia. Grot, *Petr Velikii, kak prosvetitel Rossii* (St. Petersburg, 1872). On the same day the Academy listened to more specialized reports on Peter the Great by its members: by the secretary of the Academy, the statistician and economist Constantine Veselovskii, on Peter the Great as the founder of the Academy; by the astronomer Otto Struve on Peter the Great's services to the development of mathematical geography in Russia (K. S. Veselovskii, *Petr Velikii kak uchreditel Akademii nauk* [St. Petersburg, 1872], O. V. Struve, *Ob uslugakh, okazannykh Petrom Velikim matematicheskoi geografii Rossii* [St. Petersburg, 1872]). Struve's, Veselovskii's, and Grot's Petrine addresses were published together in the twenty-first volume of the *Proceedings* of the Academy: *Zapiski Imperatorskoi Akademii Nauk*, Vol. XXI (St. Petersburg, 1872), 1–19, 20–30, 31–86, respectively. Also in 1872 the Academy published a study of Peter the Great's contribution to geographical knowledge in general, written by another academician, one of the outstanding natural scientists of the time: K. E. v. Baer (Karl Maksimovich Ber), *Peter's des Grossen Verdienste um die Erweiterung der geographischen Kenntnisse* (St. Petersburg, 1872).

[133] Grot, *Petr Velikii*, 1–2.

not received a more thorough education, the speaker turned to the reformer's character and behavior. The ruler's incessant labor, often heavy and menial—and his simplicity and parsimony too, for that matter—carried a lesson: "To instill in the Russian people respect for labor, he becomes the first laborer among his people, the tireless 'eternal worker.' Here lie the root enlightenment idea and aim of Peter."[134] As to character: "The most outstanding trait of Peter's spiritual nature was his love of truth, his hatred of every falsehood."[135]

The necessity, the inevitability of a fundamental reform of the Russian way of life followed from its very conditions; the state could not remain in its former situation; it had either to become a victim of powerful neighbors or to enter a new road of development. It was then that the mysterious spirit of life brought forth in the person of Peter an unexpected means of a renovation of Russia.[136]

Grot proceeded to defend Peter the Great, generally in the standard manner, against charges of preferring foreign things and foreigners to Russians and against those of relying on violence and compulsion. In the process, he maintained: "Not foreigners as such were needed by Peter. Foreigners served him merely as means for his plans, as teachers of Russians."[137] And he presented an extremely negative view of the Muscovite society and way of life. The defense of the building of St. Petersburg was rather drastic:

Finally, let us observe that, in the eyes of Peter, the great state aim, which he pursued in the matter, could serve as the justification of the forced perishing of whole masses of people in the building of Petersburg. As a skilled commander who sometimes prefers a bloody but decisive battle to a long wearing out of the army, so to Peter it could seem permissible to sacrifice many people at a single stroke in order to eliminate finally one of the age-old obstacles that Russia had met on its way of development.[138]

As to the results of the Petrine reform, it has become common to label the change rather superficial, indeed purely external. That, the orator asserted, failed to recognize the limitations of one short life and confused the roles of the initiator and his successors. After him: "Not all of Peter's plans were carried out; not infrequently just the opposite was done."[139]

Grot proceeded with an extended laudatory discussion of *The Spiritual Regulation* and of Feofan Prokopovich, the most valuable assistant, almost an avatar of the monarch in the sphere of enlightenment—perhaps, under the circumstances, a not unbecoming eulogy of that remarkable cleric, who could lay the best claim to being the father of all Petrine eulogies. Then he moved from religion and morality to Peter the Great's

134 *Ibid.*, 10.
135 *Ibid.*
136 *Ibid.*, 11.
137 *Ibid.*, 17.
138 *Ibid.*, 23.
139 *Ibid.*

own writings and to his fundamental pioneering efforts in establishing modern book publishing, translating—presented by Grot at length—mapmaking, and the like in Russia. The orator concluded with references to the appreciation of the first emperor in folk literature and with the assertion of his special relevance to postemancipation Russia although the circumstances and the means necessary for development had changed.

Russia will only then be a truly great country, when it joins a corresponding internal development to its powerful material growth. That was what Peter wanted, for which he exercised his efforts. And only on condition of recognizing that truth and intending to realize it will it be justified to call the celebration commemorating the birth of the great Enlightener a celebration of the Russian people.[140]

Although he spoke as a veteran scholar and although he referred respectfully to S. Soloviev, Grot himself belonged to an even older generation, and much of his Petrine address had an unabashed, essentially eighteenth-century, eulogistic, and rationalist ring.

The address also had, to be sure, contemporary implications. But whereas Grot brought them out mainly in the peroration, one learned Petrine item published in that bountiful year distinguished itself by its explicit topicality. An unsigned article in *The Messenger of Europe* entitled "State Ideas of Peter the Great and Their Fate" proposed to make a contribution by dealing not with the reformer's reign as such, nor with its antecedents, but "with the period that followed it, that period that in time continued the work of reform, but that, in the process, more especially in the development of state institutions, made not unimportant deviations from the original ideas of the reformer."[141] Peter the Great was a true Russian in every way, the author maintained, in contrast to his successors, at least the more immediate ones; he was fully aware of popular needs and completely devoted to his people, sacrificing the dynastic principle itself for its sake.

---

[140] *Ibid.*, 45.

[141] "Gosudarstvennye idei Petra Velikogo i ikh sudba," *Vestnik Evropy* (1872), no. 6, 770–796, quoted from p. 772. The author was apparently A. N. Pypin, for whom also see below. Commemorative pieces that year ranged from numerous general books and essays to a study of the reformer's portraits, such special topics as his activity in the far north, and bibliographical contributions. See, e.g., P. N. Petrov, *Petr Velikii, poslednii tsar moskovskii i pervyi imperator vserossiiskii* (St. Petersburg, 1872); C. Sadler, *Peter der Grosse als Mensch und Regent* (St. Petersburg, 1872); I. V. Sokolovskii, *Petr Velikii, kak vospitatel i uchitel naroda* (Kazan, 1873); A. A. Vasilchikov, *O portretakh Petra* (Moscow, 1872); *Kartiny iz deianii Petra Velikogo na severe* (St. Petersburg, 1872); N. Tikhomirov, *Sbornik literaturnykh proizvedenii, otnosiashchikhsia k Petru Velikomu* (St. Petersburg, 1872). One item linked to the commemoration deserves special attention: V. I. Mezhov, *Iubilei Petra Velikogo. Bibliograficheskii ukazatel literatury Petrovskogo iubileia 1872 g., s pribavleniem knig i statei o Petre i voobshche, iavivshikhsia v svet s 1865 do 1876 g. vkliuchitelno* (St. Petersburg, 1881). Mezhov's bibliography has 1049 entries.

Peter did violence to the habits of his people, that is true; but all the great moments of our history before Peter led precisely to the appearance, finally, of such a protagonist as he, and, therefore, it can be said that it was not he who did violence to the will of the Russian people, but the Russian people itself, in the person of Peter, who made a great effort with itself as object, arose from sleep and ignorance, caused by secondary factors, and went after him thither, whither it had been called by its own greatest achievements of the past: the reception of Christianity; the destruction of the scourge of Europe, the Mongols; the founding of Kiev, Novgorod, Iuriev; the deeds of Vladimir, of Ivan III, of Riurik, and of his first descendants in eastern and western Rus.[142]

Peter the Great, of course, maintained autocracy, but he also believed in popular participation, in a more active role for society.

The introduction of a system of centralization and the swallowing of the *zemstvo* element by the bureaucracy did not result from Petrine institutions, but, to the contrary, from deviations from them; and one can consider the establishment of these principles among us to be a result of the Petrine reform, if at all, only according to the rule: *post hoc, ergo propter hoc.* That deviation occurred later, at the time of Peter's successors, and it manifested itself as an imitation of French *forms,* whereas the spirit that those forms contained was quite different in France and in our case.[143]

Additionally, Peter III, not Peter I, modeled everything on the Prussian barracks, and it was his system that led logically to Arakcheev. Despotic in his methods and especially in his temporary and ad hoc ukases, the reformer, nevertheless, had believed in the fundamental rule of law, and he had given to the Senate an impressive legal position and power, which his successors failed to perpetuate or honor. More than that: "Peter wanted to hand over to the estates the administration of both country and town: the well-being of provinces into the hands of the gentry, the well-being of towns into the hands of the urban estate, leaving it to that estate itself to establish town police and to control it completely."[144] Both the greatness of the reformer and the implications of his work left little doubt:

it is outside the limits of this cursory sketch that there lies the majestic picture of the sudden elevation of Russia into the ranks of first-class European states, of the sudden creation in a country that had not known either manufacturing or schools of all the elements necessary for the performance of its new calling. Until Peter, Russia had almost nothing in common with Europe; at the time of Peter's death, true, still only on the surface, but already quite effectively, life linking it to Europe swirls: the navy, the regular army, European institutions, the financial resources increased fivefold and giving it power equal to that of the mightiest neighbors while provincial and diocesan schools and 230 plants and manufactories, created as if by magic, work toward the development of the internal

142 "Gosudarstvennye idei," 772.
143 *Ibid.,* 773.
144 *Ibid.,* 780.

potential. Russia already has an Academy of Sciences; Russia soon after Peter's death is already outfitting a scientific expedition. Now that we are returning, in part also in the matter of institutions, to the road first shown by Peter, now that we are renouncing the swallowing of both the *zemstvo* and the judiciary by bureaucracy alone, now that we witness the awakening of the elective *zemstvo* element, now that we see in the state the independent power of the judiciary, let us pay proper tribute to Peter the Great, the founder and initiator of our entire development, and let us remember what he considered Russia to be capable of already one hundred and fifty years ago.[145]

But to move beyond 1872 and to return to the St. Petersburg historical "school," it is worth noting that at least one of Bestuzhev-Riumin's important and close students, Professor Evgenii Frantsevich Shmurlo (1853–1935), did devote, in contrast to his mentor, a lifetime of research and writing to Peter the Great. Shmurlo's main preoccupation was the historiography of Peter the Great or, more broadly, the first emperor's image. His published contributions to that theme included such studies as *Peter the Great in Russian Literature (An Attempt at a Historical-Bibliographical Survey)* and *Peter the Great in the Judgment of Contemporaries and of Succeeding Generations*[146]—frequently cited in my present work—and a considerable number of more specialized pieces, their subjects ranging from the fall of Sophia and the beginning of the Russian navy to Voltaire's book on Peter the Great. Shmurlo, who spent a number of years in Rome, paid special attention to Russian contacts with southern and Romance Europe in both the Petrine and the pre-Petrine periods. The volume of Petrine documents that he published in 1903 contained primarily Roman and Venetian sources.[147] In 1900 the historian started to put out his "Critical Notes on the History of Peter the Great," beginning with the ruler's celebrated first journey abroad, an attempt to reconstruct the exact events on the basis of contemporary sources, not unlike Bogoslovskii's later, and still more heroic, effort. The "notes" never reached the year 1700.[148]

Shmurlo's treatment of Petrine historiography and imagery was pioneering, erudite, expert, and intelligent. Although a strong proponent of Peter the Great, the historian belonged to a post-S. Soloviev generation and recognized "the two sides" to the Petrine question. Moreover, he

145 *Ibid.,* 792–793.

146 E. Shmurlo, *Petr Velikii v russkoi literature (Opyt istoriko-bibliograficheskogo obzora)* (St. Petersburg, 1889); E. Shmurlo, *Petr Velikii v otsenke sovremennikov i potomstva* (St. Petersburg, 1912).

147 E. Shmurlo, ed., *Sbornik dokumentov, otnosiashchikhsia k istorii tsarstvovaniia imperator Petra Velikogo.* Vol. I. *1693–1700* (Iuriev, 1903).

148 E. Shmurlo, "Kriticheskie zametki po istorii Petra Velikogo," *Zhurnal Ministerstva Narodnogo Prosveshcheniia* (St. Petersburg), *Volume 239* (May–June 1900), 54–95; *Volume 330* (July–August 1900), 193–234; *Volume 331* (September–October 1900), 335–366; *Volume 338* (November–December 1901), 237–249; *Volume 340* (March–April 1902), 421–439; *Volume 341* (May–June 1902), 233–256. In spite of the promise of continuation, I was unable to find any subsequent installments of the "critical notes" either in later issues of the *Zhurnal Ministerstva Narodnogo Prosveshcheniia* or elsewhere.

apparently developed something of a collector's passion for gathering, rather than avoiding, evidence, whichever way that evidence might lead. Also, Shmurlo's discussion of his particular subject was greatly enhanced by his superb general knowledge of the Petrine and post-Petrine periods of Russian history. Unfortunately, Shmurlo's work on the Petrine image was not only pioneering, but also sketchy, fragmentary, and remarkably unfinished—qualities, incidentally, that the author himself fully recognized. The first version, that of 1889, tried to deal with the subject more or less up to Shmurlo's own time, but it was so brief, general, selective, and sketchy as to be of relatively little scholarly value. The much expanded 1912 variant, which was meant to be continued by another book or books, limited itself to the eighteenth century to make an important and solid, if by no means exhaustive or definitive, contribution in that area. Yet the 1912 volume was also unfinished. Not only did the subsequent volumes fail to appear, but the work itself remained incomplete chronologically, thematically, and in terms of its own organization. And so it went, as already suggested in part, with Shmurlo's other Petrine projects, less relevant to the purposes of the present study. Still, as far as the Petrine historiography and imagery are concerned, Shmurlo stands as a valuable pioneer in a field in which very much remains to be done.

Professor Sergei Fedorovich Platonov (1860–1933) was Bestuzhev-Riumin's best-known student and the most famous representative of the St. Petersburg "school." The greatest specialist on the Time of Troubles, 1598–1613, and in general one of the most brilliant historians of his country, Platonov concentrated on the pre-Petrine period. Yet professor of Russian history at St. Petersburg University from 1888, he had to deal with the reforming tsar in a major way in his course of lectures, a course that in the decades preceding the revolution was second in popularity and authoritativeness only to Kliuchevskii's.[149] Also, in 1926, in changed circumstances, Platonov published a short book, *Peter the Great, Personality and Activity,* which treated the historiography of the reformer's reign as well as the reign itself.[150]

In his celebrated lectures in Russian history, Platonov approached the reign of Peter the Great through an extended historiographical discussion, which stressed S. Soloviev's importance in introducing the proper scholarly treatment of the first emperor, followed by a survey of Muscovite politics and life at the end of the seventeenth century—"We must now establish for ourselves, what it was that Peter the Great found and from which point he had to begin."[151] A fine teaching device, the approach had also a more basic meaning: Platonov was to argue that autoc-

[149] Professor S. F. Platonov, *Lektsii po russkoi istorii* (St. Petersburg, 1904). The section on Peter the Great occupies a little over 100 pages, pp. 352–460, of this large volume of some 600 pages.

[150] *Petr Velikii, lichnost i deiatelnost,* already cited earlier in note 94, with regard to Platonov's criticism of Miliukov's views.

[151] Platonov, *Lektsii,* 367.

racy became the fully dominant and decisive state form in Russia, at the expense of more personal relations, precisely in the crucial seventeenth century; the first emperor inherited it, adopted it, perhaps adapted it, but he changed that fundamental political system very little; in a sense, in politics he ended at the same point from which he had started. In the great debate concerning the meaning of the new Petrine political and administrative institutions and of their relationship to the Russian past, Platonov championed an extreme emphasis on continuity as against change.

Following an on the whole conventional presentation of Peter the Great's childhood and youth, of the first years of the reign, and of diplomatic and military matters, the St. Petersburg professor turned to the issue of reform. In a way, he agreed with Kliuchevskii and other newer historians, who had focused on the frantic, disorganized, ad hoc aspects of the reformer's activity.

Thus, Peter engaged in his reforms without a preconceived plan, and his activity took military needs into account. The idea of the general good of the people conditioned the entire work of the reformer. With a profound understanding of the national interest, he undertook the war against Sweden, and in victories he sought not personal glory but better conditions for a cultural and economic thriving of Russia; his internal activity, too, Peter directed toward the attainment of the good of the people. But when the Swedish war became Peter's main task, demanding enormous efforts, then Peter of necessity devoted himself fully to it, and his internal activity fell into a dependence on military requirements. The war demanded troops; Peter sought means for a better organization of the armed forces, and this led to the military reform and to the reform of the gentry service. The war demanded financial means: Peter sought ways to raise the taxable resources (in other words, the economic condition) of the state, and that led to the reform of taxation, to the encouragement of manufacturing and of trade, which Peter always regarded as a mighty source of popular well-being. Thus, under the influence of military needs Peter made a number of innovations: certain innovations necessarily led to others, and, when the war already became less burdensome, Peter could bring everything he had accomplished inside the state together into a single system, complete the new administrative organization, and give his work a symmetrical appearance. Such was the course of Peter's internal activity.[152]

The preceding passage illustrates agreement among leading historians, but also perhaps a more fundamental disagreement. Where Kliuchevskii saw irony and paradox and Miliukov saw confusion worse confounded, Platonov, with his remarkable systematizing mind, recognized the obstacles but sought nevertheless in the end logic and meaning. He proceeded to provide logic and meaning to the Petrine reforms, grouping them heuristically into measures concerning the estates, administrative

[152] *Ibid.,* 423.

measures, military organization, measures for the development of the national economy, and measures affecting the church while readily admitting that the clearly presented system was his own pedagogical device and that a chronological account would give his listeners only disjointed ukases and an incoherent retelling of separate enactments.

However, as Platonov insisted, Peter the Great's work, although important, was not at all revolutionary:

To what conclusion does our study of Peter lead us? Was his activity a traditional activity, or was it a sharp unexpected and unprepared overturn in the state life of Muscovite Russia?

The answer is pretty clear! Peter's reforms were not an overturn in their essence and in their results; Peter was not a "tsar-revolutionary," as he is sometimes called.

First of all, Peter's activity was not a political overturn: in foreign policy, Peter followed strictly the old paths, struggled against the old enemies, achieved unheard-of success in the West, but did not eliminate through his successes the old political problems with regard to Poland and Turkey. He did much to reach the dearest aims of Muscovite Russia, but he did not finish everything . . .

Peter's activity was not a social overturn either. The position of the estates within the state and their mutual relations experienced no essential changes. The attachment of the estates to state obligations remained in full force; only the order of the performance of those obligations changed . . .

In Peter's economic policy, in its aims, again, one can not see a sharp turning. Peter defined clearly the problem, toward the solution of which others had moved with unsteady steps before him: the problem of raising the productive forces of the country. His program of developing national manufacturing and trade had been known in the seventeenth century, theoretically to Križanič, practically to Ordyn-Nashchokin. The results, obtained by Peter, did not place the popular economy on a new foundation. Under Peter, too, agircultural labor remained the main source of popular wealth, and Russia, which possessed after Peter more than 200 manufactories and plants, remained nevertheless an agricultural country, with commerce and manufacturing very poorly developed.

In regard to culture, also, Peter did not introduce any new revelations into Russian life. Old cultural ideals had been shaken before him; in the seventeenth century, the issue of new principles in cultural life had become a strikingly present issue. Tsar Alexis in part and Tsar Theodore entirely were already representatives of the new direction. In this respect, Tsar Peter was their direct successor. But his predecessors were students of Kievan theologians and scholastics whereas Peter was a student of Western Europeans, bearers of a Protestant culture. Peter's predecessors cared little about the dissemination of their knowledge among the people whereas Peter considered it to be one of his main tasks. By this fact, he differed substantially from the seventeenth-century sovereigns. So Peter was not the creator of the cultural issue, but he was the first person who decided to realize a cultural reform. The results of his activity were great: he gave to his people a full opportunity for a material and spiritual contact with the entire civilized world. Still, these results should not be exaggerated. Under Peter, education reached only the highest layers of society, and then weakly; the popular masses retained their old world view.[153]

Whereas the Petrine reform was, thus, not at all a radical overturn—Platonov argued—it did, all the same, produce the impression of such an overturn, and for two reasons: the reformer's nearsighted contemporaries failed to observe the connection between what Peter the Great was doing and the Russian past and saw only what appeared to them to be a willful destruction of everything around them; the reformer himself hated the old order against which he had to struggle originally for his very survival, and he brought that "militant quality of his activity, unnecessary cruelties, compulsion, and severity of measures"[154] into all his later undertakings.

Platonov's last extended excursus into Petrine history, *Peter the Great, Personality and Activity,* published in 1926, produces a sad impression. The famous historian wrote his short book in bitterness, even rage, at the new, extreme, and vulgar denigration of Peter I. In the process he failed to do justice to his antagonists or to himself. Platonov's immediate targets were the writers Alexis (Aleksei Nikolaevich) Tolstoi and Boris Pilniak, but he also criticized in retrospect such historians as Kostomarov and, especially, Miliukov.[155] *Peter the Great* had, in effect, two distinct parts: a historiographical critique and a brief account of the first emperor himself, which, contrary to the *Lectures,* emphasized the man more than the reign. In that last part, Platonov tried once more to take the measure of the difficult, even paradoxical, monarch.

Through a maze of biographical detail and trivia, the historian re-created the already well-known image of the first emperor. Like most other scholars of his generation, he used shade as well as light, dwelling at length on the ruler's dissolute and strange pastimes and not shirking the issue of cruelty. In fact, Platonov wrote: "In the person of Stephen the Bear there were joined the functions of a jester and of an executioner, just as in the person of Peter himself tendencies toward joyful humor coexisted with those toward somber cruelty. Evidence remains that Peter could at one and the same time engage in bloody investigations, with torture and executions, and abandon himself to carefree

---

153 *Ibid.,* 457–458.

154 *Ibid.,* 459.

155 Soviet contributors to the image of Peter the Great, including Pilniak and Tolstoi, will be discussed in the next chapter. For Miliukov, see the earlier section 3. Nicholas Kostomarov (1817–1885) was an important historian of ancient Russia and the Ukraine, professor of Russian history at St. Petersburg University from 1859 to 1862, who published in 1876 a rather uninspired and traditional factual account of Peter the Great, in a series devoted to leading protagonists of Russian history: N. Kostomarov, "Petr Velikii," *Russkaia istoriia v zhizneopisaniiakh ee glavneishikh deiatelei,* Vol. II, Section II (St. Petersburg, 1876), chap. XV, 537–785. Kostomarov did make some interesting observations, for instance, in depicting the Russian ruler as the very opposite of Hamlet (p. 780).

gaiety."[156] Yet that was an age "before Becarria," when cruelty was very common.

Putting aside what pertains to an unhappy childhood and a bad upbringing, to the general influence of a rude epoch and a savage milieu, to the embittering circumstances of a familial and a political struggle, what is there left to judge Peter's personal qualities?

First of all, it is the extraordinary richness of Peter's native endowments that immediately evokes an involuntary astonishment of everyone who becomes acquainted with him. His hands can do absolutely everything. . . . His eye is quick and sure; he observes quickly and precisely. His mind is all-encompassing, although not inclined toward abstractions; its distinguishing quality is the ability to work simultaneously on many disparate subjects and, be it added, with equal attention and success . . . Persevering in serious work, he, whenever possible, readily introduces a joke into it. This penchant for alternating absorbing work with play and laughter appeared in Peter's youth from an overabundance of forces, which were sufficient for everything, from "the joy of life," with which his strong and nervous nature was richly endowed.

Next, from Peter's earliest youth there was manifested in him an active, one may say a passionate, love of learning, a deep attraction to and interest in all branches of science. . . .

Linked to that quality was another one: the habit and the love of work, more exactly, of activity. Peter, by his very nature, knew no inactivity and no boredom connected with it. He considered work to be a necessary condition of social and personal well-being; he demanded work from others, and himself set the example. . . .

Peter's life of work and his close acquaintance with the task of governing developed in him one most valuable quality that can not be called anything else but strict honesty. He loved truth and hated falsehood, deceit, and extortion. The task of governing the state he considered to be his sacred duty, and he carried out his obligations with the utmost conscientiousness. He regarded himself as a servant of the state, and he wrote about himself, sincerely: "I have not spared my life for my fatherland and my people, and I am not sparing it."[157]

Subject to violent rages, the emperor sadly recognized the limitations of his own self-control, his own will. As he expressed it to those surrounding him before his death: "Learn from my example what a poor creature man is."[158]

Like Platonov, two other outstanding historians of the St. Petersburg University "school," Aleksandr Sergeevich Lappo-Danilevskii (1863–1919) and Nikolai Pavlovich Pavlov-Silvanskii (1869–1908), specialized in earlier periods of Russian history, but made contributions to the Petrine theme. Lappo-Danilevskii wrote on Russian manufacturing and trade in the first half of the eighteenth century and included the first emperor,

156 Platonov, *Petr Velikii*, 107.
157 *Ibid.*, 111–113.
158 *Ibid.*, 114. A more literal translation of *zhivotnoe* would be "animal" rather than "creature."

for example, in his interpretive survey of the evolution of the idea of the state in postmedieval Russia.[159] It was also Lappo-Danilevskii who addressed the Imperial Academy on the time-honored subject of Peter the Great as the founder of the Academy, on the occasion of the tercentenary of the House of the Romanovs.[160]

Pavlov-Silvanskii, known best for his brilliant, if more than controversial, interpretation of medieval Russia as feudal, worked very extensively in the archives where he was employed, including the archives of the first decades of the eighteenth century. He produced a number of commentaries and brief studies, which emphasized the personal role of Peter the Great in the legislative and general reforming activity of the period, as well as the loss of the progressive momentum once he died.[161] At the same time the historian agreed with Platonov and even went beyond Platonov in emphasizing the continuity of the Petrine effort with the past and its wholly nonrevolutionary nature.

In our country, the greatest exertion of the reforming power of a modern state in the age of Peter I did not alter the main foundations of the social and the state system. The Petrine reform, as it is proved by the new historians in a series of monographs, did not in the least imply a fundamental break in our history. The estate structure of the state came out of the age of reform without substantial changes whereas serfdom, which formed the foundation of that structure, only gained strength after Peter.[162]

The Petrine reform did not rebuild anew the old building, but only gave it a new facade. Our history must under no circumstances be divided into two epochs: the pre-Petrine and the Petrine, as was done formerly. The time of Peter the Great is only one of the stages in the development of the modern state, which, in our case, was formed in its main elements in the sixteenth century and existed until the middle of the nineteenth. The seventeenth and the eighteenth centuries and, in part, the nineteenth are closely tied together into a single period. They are tied together into a single whole, as an absolute monarchy based on estates, by the estate structure, which lies at the foundation of the state system. They are united by serfdom, which was formed at the beginning of the Muscovite state, only gained ground after Peter, and lasted from 1600 (approximately) until 1861. This is a single period of a state, based on estates, with a monarchical

[159] A. S. Lappo-Danilevskii, *Russkie promyshlennye i torgovye kompanii v pervoi polovine XVIII veka* (St. Petersburg, 1898–1899); A. S. Lappo-Danilevskii, "Ideia gosudarstva i glavneishie momenty ee razvitiia v Rossii so vremeni smuty i do epokhi preobrazovanii," *Golos Minuvshego*, no. 12 (December 1914), 5–38.

[160] A. S. Lappo-Danilevskii, "Petr Velikii, osnovatel Imperatorskoi Akademii Nauk v S. Peterburge," *Rechi, proiznesennye na torzhestvennom sobranii Imperatorskoi Akademii Nauk po sluchaiu trekhsotletiia tsarstvovaniia doma Romanovykh* (Petrograd, 1915), 33–88. Early in the address, the speaker skillfully discussed the broad range and high level of the reformer's interests.

[161] In this connection, Platonov cited an article written by Pavlov-Silvanskii, under a pseudonym, in criticism of Miliukov (note 94 earlier). See also especially N. P. Pavlov-Silvanskii, "Mneniia verkhovnikov o reformakh Petra Velikogo," *Ocherki po russkoi istorii XVIII-XIX vv.* (St. Petersburg, 1910), 373–401.

[162] N. Pavlov-Silvanskii, *Feodalizm v drevnei Rusi* (Petrograd, 1924), 153. The work was originally published in 1907.

authority, which gradually becomes absolute as it increases in strength at the expense of the power of the estates, which had formerly restricted it.

In the general course of our social and state development there stand out, as basic transitional epochs, not the time of the Petrine reform, but the sixteenth century, the century of the formation of the Muscovite state, and, earlier, the epoch of the transition to the appanage system, the twelfth to thirteenth centuries.[163]

Pavlov-Silvanskii went a long way from Feofan Prokopovich or even S. Soloviev.

Vasilii Ivanovich Semevskii (1848–1916), still another major historian, also had close connections with St. Petersburg University, but in his case they were negative and destructive as well as positive. Bestuzhev-Riumin refused to accept Semevskii's *Peasantry in the Reign of the Empress Catherine II* (*Krestiane v tsarstvovanie Imperatritsy Ekateriny II*) as a master's thesis, reversing himself apparently because of the assassination of Alexander II and the criticism of the emancipation reform in the preface to the thesis. Semevskii obtained both his master's and his doctor's degrees at Moscow University, working with Kliuchevskii, among others. He returned to teach at St. Petersburg University, but, because of Bestuzhev-Riumin's violent hostility and recurrent political considerations, his position there was a very restricted one, and it proved untenable eventually, the dismissal coming in January 1886.[164] The historian of serfdom and of the attitude of the Russian society toward serfdom for his and subsequent generations. Semevskii also wrote on other subjects in intellectual history and politics. Yet he had little to say about the first emperor. Thus, in his doctoral dissertation and *magnum opus, The Peasant Question in Russia in the Eighteenth and the First Half of the Nineteenth Century*,[165] Semevskii began with Peter the Great (with V. V. Golitsyn just before Peter the Great, to be more exact) but did not pay much attention to him. It was a sign of the new intellectual climate in Russia as well as of the development of Russian historiography that to historians such as Pavlov-Silvanskii, interested in the fundamental periodization of Russian history, or Semevskii, interested in serfdom, Peter the Great did not loom very large.[166]

163 *Ibid.,* 156.
164 See especially Michael B. Petrovich, "V. I. Semevskii (1848–1916): Russian Social Historian," John Shelton Curtis, ed., *Essays in Russian and Soviet History in Honor of Gerold Tanquary Robinson* (Leiden, 1963), 63–84.
165 V. I. Semevskii, *Krestianskii vopros v Rossii v XVIII i pervoi polovine XIX veka* (2 vols., St. Petersburg, 1888).
166 V. I. Semevskii's brother, Mikhail Ivanovich Semevskii (1837–1892), writer and publicist, was fascinated by Peter the Great and his times. He produced such books, based on primary sources, as his account of Anne and William Mons and a volume of political police cases from the reign, supplemented by a few additional pieces on topics ranging from the first emperor's dreams to his humor. As the subjects of the books might suggest, M. Semevskii's view of the first emperor was a hostile one, emphasizing in particular cruelty and crudity although he was no kinder to the Mons, the Russian governing group as a whole, or the European mores of the time. M. I. Semev-

The first emperor remained crucially important and glorious, however, to many other specialists, for instance, in the field of culture. Characteristically, the distinguished St. Petersburg literary historian, Aleksandr Nikolaevich Pypin (1833–1904), wrote in 1864 in his survey of the development of Russian science and scholarship in the eighteenth century:

It is well known by what a tremoudous variety the theoretical and practical interests of Peter himself were distinguished, how much personal care and labor he put into the original introduction of elementary knowledge and into the establishment of higher learning on Russian soil. The history of the whole of Russian science and scholarship goes back to his time and very often to his own personal initiative.[167]

Not surprisingly, Pypin complained in a review article that Kostomarov's previously mentioned study of the first emperor, as well as Victor Goltsev's *Legislation and Mores in Eighteenth-Century Russia*,[168] were biased against Peter the Great. Kostomarov should have linked the reformer's defects more closely to the conditions and standards of the time and to the enormous personal obstacles that he had to overcome, should have appreciated better that he was interested not only in technology but also in the establishment of enlightenment in Russia, should have valued properly his love of and devotion to the Russian people, and not merely the interests of the state. Goltsev, too, failed to judge correctly either the nature or the beneficial results of the Petrine state.[169]

And, in general, in spite of a few exceptions such as Miliukov, cultural historians—and especially historians of education and enlightenment in modern Russia—treated Peter the Great very favorably. The approach was largely set by the first major figure in the field, Academician Petr Petrovich Pekarskii (1828–1872), who studied extensively the sources and

---

skii, *Ocherki i rasskazy iz russkoi istorii XVIII v. Tsaritsa Ekaterina Alekseevna, Anna i Villim Mons, 1692–1724*, 2d rev. and enlarged ed. (St. Petersburg, 1884). M. I. Semevskii, *Ocherki i rasskazy iz russkoi istorii XVIII v. Slovo i delo! 1700–1725*, 2d rev. ed. (St. Petersburg, 1884).

[167] A. Pypin, "Russkaia nauka i natsionalnyi vopros v XVIII-m veke," *Vestnik Evropy*, Vol. (year) XIX (1884), no. 5 (May, 212–256, no. 6 (June), 548–600, no. 7 (July), 72–117; quoted from p. 224; I translated *nauka* as "science and scholarship."

[168] V. Goltsev, *Zakonodatelstvo i nravy Rossii XVIII veka* (Moscow, 1885).

[169] A. Pypin, "Novyi vopros o Petre Velikom," *Vestnik Evropy*, vol. (year) XXI (1886), no. 5 (May), 317–350. Goltsev (Viktor Aleksandrovich, 1850–1906, a legal scholar and publicist) responded:

I belong to that group of historians that considers that in the Petrine reform and the post-Petrine regime there was much crude and noxious breaking, too much cruelty, too little care for man and citizen. In order to increase the power of the state, not always, it might be added, correctly understood, in order to satisfy the egoistic desires of particular individuals and of certain social groups, the essential interests of the popular masses were not infrequently sacrificed.

V. Goltsev, "K voprosu o petrovskoi reforme," *Russkaia Mysl*, Vol. (year) VII (August 1886), 170–175, quoted from p. 173.

wrote factually rich books on *Scholarship and Literature in Russia under Peter the Great;* the first volume was devoted to *An Introduction to the History of Enlightenment in Russia in the Eighteenth Century;* the second, to *A Description of Slavonic-Russian Books and Printing Presses in the Years 1698–1725.*[170] Although given more to gathering the facts than to their analysis or interpretation, Pekarskii left no doubt as to the importance of Peter the Great for Russian culture. In the words of Grot in his bicentennial address, describing Pekarskii's work: "In that picture, the most active figure, the soul of the entire enterprise, is Peter himself, not only as the mover but also as the creator of our original book literature who by his efforts opened the way to its most glorious protagonist, Lomonosov, and to all who followed him."[171] Pekarskii's two-volume study came out in 1862, but many of its points were repeated by leading historians of later generations: in 1874, by the Kievan professor Mikhail Flegontovich Vladimirskii-Budanov (1838–1916) in *The State and Popular Education in Eighteenth-Century Russia;*[172] in 1912 by the St. Petersburg University professor Sergei Vasilievich Rozhdestvenskii (1868–1934) in *A Survey of the History of the Systems of Popular Education in Russia in the Eighteenth-Nineteenth Centuries.*[173] Rozhdestvenskii, in particular, emphasized not only the first emperor's contribution to professional education, with which the historian was much concerned, but also the value of his pioneering practical schools for the general cultural advancement of the country.

Legal scholars were also interested in the reign of Peter the Great and its impact on Russian history, adding copiously to the contributions of "straight" historians. In fact, Vladimirskii-Budanov was a distinguished specialist in the evolution of Russian law, and he conceived of his book on the state and popular education as part of a larger project of a legal history of education in Russia.[174] (Pekarskii, too, was trained in law, but he switched fields.) A few scholars produced works on legal matters in the Petrine reign itself. Thus, Professor Aleksandr Nikitich Filippov (1853–1927), who was educated at the Moscow, Heidelberg, Berlin, and Prague universities and taught at those in Moscow and Dorpat, published in 1891 a study *On Punishment According to Peter the Great's Legislation, in Connection with the Reform,* which contained a long part entitled "A General Survey of the Basic Principles of the Petrine Legisla-

170 P. Pekarskii, *Nauka i literatura v Rossii pri Petre Velikom.* Vol. I. *Vvedenie v istoriiu prosveshcheniia v Rossii XVIII stoletiia.* Vol. II. *Opisanie slaviano-russkikh knig i tipografii 1698–1725 godov* (St. Petersburg, 1862).

171 Grot, *op. cit.*, 35.

172 M. Vladimirskii-Budanov, *Gosudarstvo i narodnoe obrazovanie v Rossii XVIII-go veka.* Part I. *Sistema professionalnogo obrazovaniia (ot Petra I do Ekateriny II)* (Iaroslavl, 1874).

173 S. V. Rozhdestvenskii, *Ocherki po istorii sistem narodnogo prosveshcheniia v Rossi v XVIII-XIX vekakh,* Vol. I (St. Petersburg, 1912).

174 Vladimirskii-Budanov, *op. cit.*, p. I.

tion.”[175] Filippov also became a leading authority on the Supreme Secret Council, that is, on the period immediately following the first emperor's reign. Other legal historians dealt with institutions, such as the procuracy or the Senate, created by Peter the Great and bequeathed by him to his successors. The St. Petersburg University professor Aleksandr Dmitrievich Gradovskii (1841–1899) wrote on *The Higher Administration in Russia in the Eighteenth Century and the Procurators-General,*[176] a subject reconsidered several decades later by Vasilii Ivanovich Veretennikov (1880–1942) in his *Survey of the History of the Procurator-General in Russia in the pre-Catherinian Period,*[177] based not only on published legislation, utilized by Gradovskii, but on rich use of the archives. Still other legal scholars included the Petrine impact within a broader major topic, as when the Kievan professor Aleksandr Vasilievich Romanovich-Slavatinskii (1832–1910) produced his still fundamental study of *The Gentry in Russia from the Beginning of the Eighteenth Century to the Abolition of Serfdom*[178] or the Kharkov and Dorpat professor Ivan Ivanovich Ditiatin (1847–1892) presented his *Organization and Governance of the Towns of Russia* in the eighteenth century.[179] Not surprisingly, legal scholars were more likely to see continuity with the past in the Petrine activity and age than cultural historians, and they were also more inclined to treat the reformer in a minor key.

Pavel Vladimirovich Verkhovskoi's *The Establishment of the Spiritual College and the Spiritual Reglament: A Contribution to the Question of the Relationship of Church and State in Russia* deserves special notice.[180] A canonist and Warsaw University professor, Verkhovskoi (1879–    ) was sympathetic to the reformer's person and to many of his efforts—the book contains some of the most judicious pages on such difficult issues as the monarch's own religious views—but he both gave the outstanding analysis of the ecclesiastical reform and, in effect, condemned it as an unbecoming subordination of church to state.

[175] Aleksandr Filippov, *O nakazanii po zakonodatelstvu Petra Velikogo, v sviazi s reformoiu* (Moscow, 1891). “Obshchii ocherk osnovnykh nachal petrovskogo zakonodatelstva” occupies pp. 1–128.
[176] A. D. Gradovskii, “Vysshaia administratsiia Rossii XVIII st. i general-prokurory,” *Sobranie sochinenii*, Vol. I (St. Petersburg, 1899), 37–297. The work was first published in 1866.
[177] V. I. Veretennikov, *Ocherki istorii general-prokuratury v Rossii do-ekaterininskogo vremeni* (Kharkov, 1915). Veretennikov was also the author of a study of the Petrine Secret Chancellery: V. I. Veretennikov, *Istoriia Tainoi kantseliarii petrovskogo vremeni* (Kharkov, 1910).
[178] A. Romanovich-Slavatinskii, *Dvorianstvo v Rossii ot nachala XVIII veka do otmeny krepostnogo prava* (St. Petersburg, 1870).
[179] I. Ditiatin, *Ustroistvo i upravlenie gorodov Rossii.* Vol. I. *Vvedenie. Goroda Rossii v XVIII stoletii* (St. Petersburg, 1875).
[180] P. V. Verkhovskoi, *Uchrezhdenie Dukhovnoi kollegii i Dukhovnyi Reglament, K voprosu ob otnoshenii Tserkvi i gosudarstva v Rossii. Issledovanie v oblasti istorii russkogo tserkovnogo prava.* Vol. I. *Issledovanie* (Rostov-on-Don, 1916).

Canon law and even law *tout court* aside, however, Peter the Great and his reign became a direct, or at least an indirect, concern of a bewildering variety of modern Russian historians. Some inkling of their range can be obtained by comparing such significant works as Aleksandr Aleksandrovich Kisewetter's (1866–1933) study of townspeople and their organization in Russia in the eighteenth century;[181] Iurii Vladimirovich Gauthier's (1873–1943) History of the *Oblast Administration in Russia from Peter I to Catherine II,*[182] where Gauthier continued Bogoslovskii's work; Mikhail Aleksandrovich Polievktov's (1872–1946) monograph on the Baltic question in 1721–1725;[183] and Mikhail Vasilievich Klochkov's *The Population of Russia under Peter the Great According to the Censuses of That Time.*[184]

Modern Russian military history has been linked to Peter the Great from its very inception. Indeed, the official Petrine "History of the Swedish War" (*Gistoriia Sveiskoi voiny*), although unfinished and unpublished, can be cited as the beginning of all modern Russian historiography. And, of course, the attributes of the hero and victor of Poltava, the creator of the Russian navy, and in general of a supremely brave and successful military and naval commander were central to the Petrine image from its origin and to the glorification of that image throughout the eighteenth century and well into the nineteenth. Yet major Russian historians of the postemancipation period failed on the whole to emphasize that crucial Petrine aspect. S. Soloviev devoted relatively little time or space to military history proper whereas he paid minute attention to diplomacy and certain other matters. Kliuchevskii treated the first emperor's military prowess lightly and even ironically; Miliukov went to the extent of charging him with total incompetence in war. Although Platonov and some other important figures can be mentioned on the other side of the issue, in general, Russian historians of the period showed little interest in military history and but a weak desire to glorify success in war—no doubt, a reflection of the general intellectual climate of the time. Fortunately for the luster of the Petrine image, the military specialists were different. In sum, imperial Russian military historiography, which grew with the general growth of Russian historiography, treated Peter the Great enthusiastically and at all levels, from more popular

181 A. A. Kizevetter, *Posadskaia obshchina v Rossii XVIII st.* (Moscow, 1903).

182 Iu. Gote, *Istoriia Oblastnogo upravleniia v Rossii ot Petra I do Ekateriny II.* Vol. I (Moscow, 1913). The second volume was published twenty-eight years later: Akad. Iu. V. Gote, *Istoriia Oblastnogo upravleniia v Rossi ot Petra I do Ekateriny II,* Vol. II (Moscow and Leningrad, 1941). Gauthier represented one of the most important links between pre- and post-Revolutionary historiography.

183 M. Polievktov, *Baltiiskii vopros v russkoi politika posle Nishtadtskogo mira (1721–1725)* (St. Petersburg, 1907).

184 M. Klochkov, *Naselenie Rossii pri Petre Velikom po perepisiam togo vremeni.* Vol. I. *Perepisi dvorov i naseleniia (1678–1721)* (St. Petersburg, 1911). Klochkov took a much more restrained view of the Petrine "depopulation" of Russia than Miliukov.

works to textbooks and more specialized studies, readily granting him genius as well as heroism.[185] It built up a legacy to be further expanded and developed by Soviet specialists.

The Petrine image in the narrow sense, Peter the Great as a human being, also attracted the attention of historians and other scholars in the last decades of imperial Russia. In addition to Kliuchevskii's memorable image and many other images by many other lecturers, there were some more unusual approaches, such as an analysis of the first emperor's genius[186] or a discussion of the psychological parallels between him and Ivan the Terrible.[187] On the whole, Peter the Great remained a remarkably durable figure, as originally depicted by Feofan Prokopovich and other contemporaries. True, fantastic eulogies of him were no longer common, and the negative characteristics of the reformer were no longer brought forth only to be justified or explained away. They stood instead in their own right and, in fact, not infrequently occupied—that is a matter of taste—too much of the picture. But they were invariably accompanied by striking positive traits; and the total mighty, tortured, paradoxical image was not difficult to recognize.

A booklet published on the eve of the February Revolution entitled *Peter I the Great (Tsar of Muscovy and Emperor of All-Russia)*,[188] presented well, if rather starkly, the current emphases in the Petrine image. The reformer had been a complex figure, with more maternal than paternal traits, including "the Naryshkins' thoughtlessness." Alcohol and cruelty, alcohol and blood, affecting each other, ran as a leitmotiv throughout his reign, once he had learned terror and evil from Sophia, the *streltsy*, and others around him. The monarch died in despair after even Menshikov and Catherine had betrayed him, frantically seeking religious consolation while failing to appoint a successor to the throne. But Peter the Great was also a genius, in particular because of his most rare ability to turn to new thoughts and new things, to understand them immediately, to appreciate them independently and critically. And he combined this understanding with stunningly energetic action. The reformer did everything for the fatherland, in which he believed and

[185] A. K. Baiov, *Istoriia russkoi armii: kurs voennykh uchilishch* (St. Petersburg, 1886); N. L. Iunakov, *Severnaia voina* (2 vols., St. Petersburg, 1909); G. A. Leer, *Obzor voin Rossii ot Petra Velikogo do nashikh dnei: Posobie dlia izucheniia voennoi istorii v voennykh uchilishchakh*, 2d ed. (St. Petersburg, 1893). (The part on the Great Northern War, pp. 1–67, was written by P. K. Gudim-Levkovich.) G. A. Leer, "Petr Velikii kak voennyi genii," *Voenno-istoricheskii sbornik* (1865), nos. 3, 4. A. Z. Myshlaevskii, *Petr Velikii. Voina v Finliandii v 1712–1714 g. Sovmestnaia operatsiia armii, galernogo i korabelnogo flotov* (St. Petersburg, 1896); A. K. Puzyrevskii, *Razvitie postoiannykh reguliarnykh armii i sostoianie voennogo iskusstva v veke Liudovika XIV i Petra Velikogo* (St. Petersburg, 1889).

[186] P. I. Kovalevskii, *Petr Velikii i ego genii* (St. Petersburg, 1900).

[187] K. Iarosh, *Psikhologicheskaia parallel. Ioann Groznyi i Petr Velikii* (Kharkov, 1898).

[188] N. N. Firsov, *Petr I Velikii, Moskovskii tsar i imperator vserossiiskii* (Moscow, 1916).

through which he justified his life; the people recognized that and accepted him. Indeed, the author concluded, in a sense, the first emperor had been unselfish and modest.

6

Although historians and allied scholars played the major role in maintaining and developing the Petrine image in late imperial Russia, they were by no means the only Russians concerned with it. Rather, Peter the Great's memory and influence extended from the highest spheres of the government to its radical opponents, and from Modest Musorgskii's great opera *Khovanshchina* to literary potboilers. Perhaps the Bronze Horseman was not riding quite as hard in pursuit as when Pushkin had recorded the phenomenon, but the hoofbeat of his horse still resounded in Russian government, society, and culture.

Nicholas I was the last Russian sovereign for whom Peter the Great constituted a living presence, to be considered in state and even personal, matters. Later monarchs, as well as their ministers and other high officials, took a more detached, "historical" view of the first emperor, and they were much less personally, emotionally involved with him. Not that they lost interest altogether. For one thing, they had to deal all the time with Petrine institutions, Petrine legislation, Petrine traditions. For another, the established state doctrine of Official Nationality was not repudiated until 1917, and, as we know, it assigned an extremely high place to Peter the Great. Nor were his attractions and his uses necessarily limited for Russian officials, as for other Russians, to that place.

Peter the Great and his image, therefore, recur in studies dealing with government and politics in nineteenth- and early twentieth-century Russia. Thus, Professor Daniel T. Orlovsky, writing on the Russian Ministry of Internal Affairs, 1802–1881, notes that the proponents of the ministries "chose as their historical model the regulated, or well-ordered, police state of Peter the Great" and that the founding "1802 Manifesto portrayed the ministries as the heirs of Petrine tradition and philosophy of government."[189] The historian discusses, later in the book, the impact of the reformer on possibly Alexander II's ablest and most important minister of internal affairs, Petr Aleksandrovich Valuev (1814–1890), who occupied that crucial position from 1861 to 1868:

Valuev advocated that the government energetically take the initiative in social, economic, and political questions, in contrast to Nicholas' system of immobility. Valuev's writings show a preoccupation with change, movement, and development—ideas common to certain early and mid-nineteenth-century European conservative and liberal thinkers. But here his model was also Peter the Great. Valuev wished to re-create the Petrine police state, bring institutions to the fore

189 Daniel T. Orlovsky, *The Limits of Reform: The Ministry of Internal Affairs in Imperial Russia, 1802–1881* (Cambridge, Mass., 1981), 5.

within the old ministerial framework, and institutionalize the idea of creative, but selective, borrowing from the West. He admired Peter for comprehending the benefits of Western enlightenment for Russia. Peter's reign was dominated by two great ideas: "the enlightenment and enrichment of the state, and the strengthening and security of autocracy."[190]

Or, to take a different example, a study dealing with a somewhat later period and a reactionary figure, Professor Robert F. Byrnes in his book on Konstantin Petrovich Pobedonostsev (1827–1907), the Ober-Procurator of the Holy Synod from 1880 to 1905 and the chief theoretician and protagonist of reaction in Russia during that quarter of a century, has seventeen references to Peter the Great: six of these, citing eight pages, are to Pobedonostsev's view of the first emperor, and two more to the view held by his father, a Moscow University professor of Russian literature, Petr Vasilievich Pobedonostsev (1771–1843).[191] The older Pobedonostsev was in perfect accord with Official Nationality and its glorification of Russian monarchs, especially select monarchs, and in particular Peter the Great. Constantine Pobedonostsev, apparently, naturally followed his father's orientation, but as a Moscow University professor of civil law and a proponent of legal reform, he also cited and quoted the first emperor in the reforming sense. More interestingly, even after he had become a full-fledged paladin of reaction, he still interpreted Peter the Great and his historical role positively, if narrowly.

He wrote favorably of Peter because Peter had placed the interest of the state first, "collected all the power around one center and directed it toward one goal," and made Russia a larger, stronger, and more industrial power. His appraisal was sharply critical of those who believed that Russia had enjoyed a golden age before Peter. He was particularly critical of the Slavophiles (although he never mentioned them as a group) because in their attacks on Peter the Great they were "carried away by their historical ideal, the features of which they find in the ancient history of Russia before Peter." He was also critical of the Westerners, whom he denounced for interpreting Peter's age and actions according to their own preconceived ideas and for asserting that Peter wanted to make Russia a Western state.

According to Pobedonostsev, Peter did not wish to give Russia new institutions and was not opposed to the old ones. He strengthened the power of the *pomestchik* only when it was to the interest of the state. He was personally opposed to serfdom, but recognized that he could not eliminate it or even reduce its significance. On the one hand, he made more severe the decrees concerning runaway serfs and tightened internal passport regulations. On the other hand, he eliminated abuses when he could. He was a great man because he saw the needs of his age clearly and undertook nothing that was in sharp contradiction with the concepts then generally held. He was unaffected by moral or philosophical principles. He simply acted in the interests of the state, using the established institu-

---

190 *Ibid.*, 70–71.
191 Robert F. Byrnes, *Pobedonostsev, His Life and Thought* (Bloomington and London, 1968). My count is based on the explicit references in the index.

tions when possible to increase the state's power and authority and revising the established institutions when necessary.[192]

Many more examples could be cited to indicate that Peter the Great remained a powerful memory and even a magnet to numerous Russians in and out of the government, who thought in terms of Westernization, modernization, reform, progress—like Chekhov who erected a statue to the first emperor in Taganrog—or simply in terms of the stability and the strength of the Russian state and of its role in the world. Direct links seemed to connect the first emperor with later reformers, with liberals and conservatives of different kinds,[193] and even with figures farther to the Right. Indeed, not only Pobedonostsev, but also Nikolai Iakovlevich Danilevskii (1822–1885), the author of a pseudoscientific racist tome, *Russia and Europe* (*Rossiia i Evropa*), published in 1869, and Konstantin Nikolaevich Leontiev (1831–1891), an extreme and paradoxical ideologist of the Right, credited Peter the Great with important achievements. Danilevskii, whose own doctrine of pseudobiological racial organisms denied the very idea of Westernization, appreciated nevertheless the first emperor's political and military successes. Leontiev, who propounded a theory of three cultural stages, those of primitive homogeneity, of differentiation, vitality, and creative achievement, and of the subsequent leveling and death, believed that Peter the Great introduced into Russia the second, that is, the only desirable, phase of existence. It took Lev Nikolaevich Tolstoi (1828–1910), when he turned against modern civilization, to denounce uncompromisingly, somewhat like the Slavophiles earlier, the first emperor and his works. It is worth noting that both the Slavophiles and Tolstoi were so free to criticize because they were willing to write off, at least in theory, modern Russian culture and the class that carried it.[194]

The situation was different on the Left, however. Protest against Peter the Great as a tyrant and against his reforms as based on compulsion, which had split the Decembrists on the Petrine issue and had brought Herzen into the antiPetrine camp, continued. Moreover, the radical

192 *Ibid.*, 323–324. *Pomestchik,* or *pomeshchik,* means "landlord."

193 To mention one more such conservative liberal, or liberal conservative, Professor Richard Pipes writes near the end of his magisterial study of Petr Berngardovich Struve (1870–1944), economist, political figure, and political thinker: "National Russia for him was always the Russia of St. Petersburg, personified by Peter the Great and Pushkin: cosmopolitan, European, self-critical" (Richard Pipes, *Struve: Liberal on the Right, 1905–1944* [Cambridge, Mass. and London, 1980], quoted from p. 448). See also the first volume: Richard Pipes, *Struve: Liberal on the Left, 1870–1905* (Cambridge, Mass., 1970).

194 Students of the image of Peter the Great will forever regret that Tolstoi abandoned his plan to write a novel from the Petrine epoch—leaving us only some fragments and notes—and occupied himself instead with more proximate topics. For the latest treatment of the issue and in particular for an explanation of why Tolstoi abandoned his Petrine project, see Walter Smirnyv, "Lev Tolstoi's Unfinished Novel on the Epoch of Peter I: the Enigma of Russia in an Enchanted Circle," *Russian Literature Triquarterly,* no. 18 (1982), 102–116.

intellectual climate of the 1860s and subsequent decades in Russia was adverse to the glorification of any ruler. Eventually vaguely described as populist, it nurtured emphasis on the peasant masses, not the monarchs or the court circles, and, in terms of history, on social and economic history, not the dynastic or the diplomatic. We have already encountered it in such historians as V. Semevskii and even, to an extent, Kliuchevskii, and it was more pronounced in doctrinaire thinkers. Leo Tolstoi's views in his last period can be considered as one idiosyncratic extreme of populism. A little later in the century, in Russia, another and much better structured ideology of the Left, Marxism—to be discussed in the next chapter—again sharply reduced the role of personality in history and shifted attention to other matters. Yet the Petrine picture on the Left was by no means simple. The reformer frequently remained linked to such desirable concepts as "Westernization," "secularization" or "progress." Though, on the one hand, he could be denounced as the creator and the epitome of the oppressive tsarist system,[195] it could still be argued, on the other, that it was the later rulers, whether Nicholas I or Alexander III, and their governments, who were responsible for the stagnation and the reaction in Russia by abandoning, rather than pursuing, the reformer's progressive policies.

Nikolai Gavriilovich Chernyshevskii (1828–1889) made fundamental contributions to the radical climate of "the sixties" in Russia, and his influence extended later to populism, to the Russian Left in general, even to Lenin and Russian Marxism. Chernyshevskii's attitude toward Peter the Great closely resembled Herzen's in substance and sequence, although it was much less nuanced and ambivalent. Also, the younger man was much less concerned with the first emperor than the publisher of *The Bell* with his background of the idealistic forties.

Chernyshevskii began by endorsing Peter the Great and his work. Thus, he wrote in his well-known *Essays on the Gogol Period of Russian Literature,* first published serially in 1855–1856:

195 In his celebrated *Memoirs of a Revolutionist,* first published in 1899, Peter Kropotkin mentions Peter I only three times. There is a reference to old Muscovite families (including Prince Kropotkin's own) "whose names were so frequently mentioned in the pages of Russian history before the times of Peter I, but who subsequently disappeared to make room for the newcomers," and the following two passages: "From my house I was taken to the Third Section, that omnipotent institution which has ruled in Russia from the beginning of the reign of Nicholas I. down to the present time, a true 'state in the state.' It began under Peter I. in the Secret Department, where the adversaries of the founder of the Russian military empire were subject to the most abominable tortures, under which they expired. . . ." And, after being taken to Peter-and-Paul Fortress: "Here Peter I. tortured his son Alexis and killed him with his own hand. . . . And from the times of Peter I. for a hundred and seventy years, the annals of this mass of stone which rises from the Neva in front of the Winter Palace were annals of murder and torture, of men buried alive, condemned to a slow death, or driven to insanity in the loneliness of the dark and damp dungeons" (Peter Kropotkin, *Memoirs of a Revolutionist* (New York, 1962), 2, 225, 231 respectively. As an anarchist, Kropotkin was particularly distant from and hostile to Peter the Great.

In time we shall also acquire, like other peoples, thinkers and artists who act in the name of science or of art alone, but, until we reach in education the level of the most advanced nations, each one of us has another task, closer to the heart—to help, to the best of one's abilities, the further development of that which Peter the Great began. That task still demands, and probably will continue to demand for a long time, all the intellectual and moral resources, which the most gifted sons of our motherland possess. A Russian who has a sound mind and a sensitive heart could not be until now and cannot be at present anything but a patriot in the sense of Peter the Great—a worker in the great cause of the enlightenment of the Russian land.[196]

Other Petrine references in Chernyshevskii's writings of the 1850s similarly leave no doubt that the critic, at that time, fully supported the first emperor and his guiding role in Russian history, much as Belinskii and other Westernizers had done before him.[197]

But Chernyshevskii's enthusiasm did not last. Parallel to his total disillusionment with Alexander II and the emancipation reform, the critic changed his opinion on Peter the Great and his attitude toward him. He expressed his new views in an article dealing with Chaadaev's "Apology of a Madman," which was meant to be published as early as January 1861, but failed to pass the censor.[198]

It seemed to him that Peter the Great found his country to be a blank sheet of paper, on which he could write whatever he wanted. Unfortunately, not so. Words had already been written on that sheet, and the same words had been written in the mind of Peter the Great himself, and he merely once more repeated them in a larger type on the written-over sheet. These words are not "the West" and not "Europe," as Chaadaev thought; their sounds are not at all of that kind: European languages have no such sounds. How can a Frenchman or an Englishman and, in general, any kind of German pronounce our *Shch* and *Y!* These are sounds of Oriental peoples, living in the midst of wide steppes and boundless tundras. . . . Until the sources were analyzed—and that took place already after Chaadaev's youth—one could not even distinguish the fact that the purpose of Peter's activity was the creation of a strong military state. That simple and natural urge of the great reformer was concealed from our eyes by the fog of all kinds of pompous sentences. Lomonosov took Pliny's panegyric to Trajan and, while translating it into Russian, put, instead of the names "Trajan" and "Rome," "Peter" and "Russia." These views stayed until lately. To Peter were ascribed all those qualities and inclinations that had been ascribed in no matter which panegyric to no matter what famous ruler. From Titus we took mercy, from Brutus relentless justice, from Louis XIV splendor, from Cincinnatus

196 N. G. Chernyshevskii, *Ocherki gogolevskogo perioda russkoi literatury* (Moscow, 1953), 169.
197 Cf. "The brilliant deeds of the time of Peter the Great and the colossal personality of Peter himself conquer our imagination; indubitably enormous is also the substantive greatness of the task which he accomplished" N. G. Chernyshevskii, *Polnoe sobranie sochinenii v piatnadtsati tomakh.* Vol. V. *Stati 1858–1859* (Moscow, 1950), 70.
198 N. G. Chernyshevskii, "Apologiia sumasshedshego," *Polnoe sobranie sochinenii v piatnadtsati tomakh.* Vol. VII. *Stati i retsenzii 1860–1861* (Moscow, 1950), 592–618, notes pp. 1033–1034.

simplicity, from Aristides love of truth, from Richelieu the art of diplomacy, and, when we put all this together, we proclaimed: "Here is Peter the Great!" Chaadaev was so intelligent that he did not believe this nonsense; still, he was a man of his time, and its mark was left on him. He could reject the panegyric mode, but he became enthusiastic at the name of Peter the Great. He also accepted from the books of his youth the idea that Peter's deep purpose was the transformation of Russia into a European country, understanding by European country a land where the high European civilization dominates. Now it is believed that to ascribe such an intention to Peter the Great means to present him as a weak dreamer, an impractical idealist, defects that were not in his character; it is believed that Peter's aim was much simpler, more practical, more in accord with his situation and views. He needed a strong regular army that would know how to fight no worse than Swedish and German armies; he needed to have good foundries, powder factories; he understood that the items of military power were unreliable unless his subjects learned to manage military affairs themselves, as Germans manage them, unreliable as long as we remained in military matters dependent on foreign officers and technicians; therefore, he found it necessary to teach Russians to be good officers, engineers, founders. Once started on that road, preoccupied with the thought of establishing an independent Russian army in the form in which armies existed among the Germans and the Swedes, he, because of his energetic nature, went very far in that direction, and, borrowing from the Germans and the Swedes military institutions, borrowed also opportunely, in passing, everything in general that caught his eye. But these additions were only a secondary matter, unimportant; the military institutions constituted the main thing.[199]

When some Russians objected, Peter the Great characteristically took repressive and punitive measures: he cut off their beards and let their wives out of seclusion. He fought old Russia because of its hostility to him, not because of any broad appreciation of the West. He introduced a German-style administration, not necessarily better than what it replaced, to help him with his one aim of military reform. Nor was Chernyshevskii willing to accept the argument that the only important fact was Westernization itself, not how it came about: the purpose determined the spirit and the results of change.

The result of Peter the Great's activity was that, having acquired a good regular army, we became a powerful military state, not that we changed in any other respect.

Peter the Great is blamed by some people for introducing among us Western institutions, which changed our life. Not at all, our life changed in no way except the military aspect because of him, and no institutions that he introduced, except the military ones, exercised any influence on us. The names of the positions changed, but the positions retained their former attributes and were held in the old manner. The governor was the same *voevoda;* the colleges, the same *prikazy*. Beards were cut off, German clothing put on; but the understanding remained the same as with the beards and ancient dress. The *assemblées* were attended, but family life with all its customs retained its old form. The husband

199 *Ibid.*, 610–611.

did not cease beating his wife and marrying his son according to his own, not the son's, choice. It is a vain thought that Peter the Great's reform changed anything in the condition of the Russian nation. It changed only the situation of the Russian tsar in the circle of European sovereigns. Formerly he had no strong voice in their counsels; now he acquired that voice because of the good army created by Peter.[200]

And to explain further and support the argument:

In Peter the Great's own case, all concepts important for social life and all principles of action were entirely Russian concepts and principles of the times of Aleksei Mikhailovich and Fedor Alekseevich. He differed from his opponents not by the character of his ideas, but only by the fact that he understood, and they did not understand, the need to organize the army according to the German model. They thought that the former army was good—he found it to be bad. But why one needs an army, how a state should be organized, by what means it should be governed, what the relationship should be between the authorities and the nation: he thought about all that in exactly the same manner as his opponents. He was a true Russian, who did not forsake a single concept or habit important in social life and dominant among us at the time of his childhood and youth. To be convinced of this, one simply has to pay attention to how he acts. His manner of acting is purely national, without the slightest admixture that is Western in character. Because of the special circumstances of our history, in the seventeenth century the essence of Russian character in social life was defined by a double relationship of authority to form. In the first place, authority stood above any forms, and there were no forms that could restrict its activity. Louis XIV could dream that his will alone rules France; it was indeed strong, but there were forms without which it could not manage and that frequently interfered with it: there existed *parlements;* there existed provincial estate assemblies. We had no such obstacles.[201]

Chernyshevskii concluded:

We have dwelt so long on Peter the Great's reform because the character of all subsequent state activity corresponded perfectly to its character. All our emperors and empresses continued the work of Peter; no one doubts that. The opinion on the reform, enacted in the beginning of the eighteenth century, determines the opinion on the continuation of that reform up to most recent times.[202]

The fact that the Russians were never Westernized, but were merely given a Western military establishment, Chernyshevskii added, held a certain promise: it meant that Westernization had never been tried in his native land, not that it had failed. But it was preposterous to claim Russian superiority over the West or the likelihood of Russia's replacing the West in world leadership, a tendency that could be discerned among the Westernizers as well as among the Slavophiles.

200 *Ibid.,* 612.
201 *Ibid.,* 613–614.
202 *Ibid.,* 614.

Apparently, Chernyshevskii retained his highly critical view of Peter the Great for the rest of his life. Indeed, writing in 1879 on the subject of his early relations with the poet Nicholas Nekrasov, he forgot, it would seem, that he had once admired the first emperor and presented himself as the monarch's principled opponent even in the 1850s. The critic added on that later occasion: "Now too I believe that Mohammed Ali was not beneficial for Egypt. I do not judge Mohammed II's activity as beneficial for Turkey."[203]

Literary and social critic Nikolai Aleksandrovich Dobroliubov (1836–1861) was Chernyshevskii's closest and most important associate. Dobroliubov expressed himself at length on the subject of Peter the Great on one occasion: in his three-part review in *The Contemporary (Sovremennik)* in 1858 of the first three volumes of Ustrialov's Petrine history, the review totaling 120 pages.[204] The critic censured the historian for preferring the biographic approach to a more fundamental general presentation, a trend only too common in Russian historiography: "Unfortunately, historians almost never avoid the strange attraction to personalities, at the expense of historical necessity. At the same time all histories strongly display a disregard for the life of the people, in favor of some special interests."[205] Also, Ustrialov made the first emperor's activities too logical, meaningful, coordinated, even prescient. Yet on the whole Dobroliubov firmly endorsed Ustrialov's work of erudition and scholarly discrimination and precision, and he tried to retell its rich content to his readers. Moreover, he also endorsed Peter the Great. Writing under the epigraph from Belinskii to the effect that the reformer had acted entirely in the spirit of the people when he had proceeded to bring his fatherland closer to Europe and to root out the Asiatic elements temporarily introduced into it by the Mongols, the younger critic largely repeated the basic judgment of the older one, although in the more somber and stark tones of a later generation.

Yes, Peter solved problems that had been assigned to the government already long ago by the very life of the people—this is his meaning; these are his achievements. The partisans of old Russia assert in vain that what Peter introduced into our life was wholly incongruous with the historical course of development of the Russian people and antagonistic to the interests of the people. Vast reforms, opposed to the character of a people and to the natural course of history, even if they succeed at first, are not durable. But Peter's reforms have long ago become among us a possession of the life of the people, and this alone must

203 N. G. Chernyshevskii, "(Zametki o Nekrasove) Zametki pri chtenii 'Biograficheskikh svedenii' o Nekrasove, pomeshchennykh v I tome 'Posmertnogo izdaniia' ego 'stikhotvorenii'. SPb. 1879," *Polnoe sobranie sochinenii v piatnadtsati tomakh,* Vol. I (Moscow, 1939), 742–754, fns. pp. 814–816, especially pp. 746–747 and note 6 on pp. 815–816.
204 N. A. Dobroliubov, "Pervye gody tsarstvovaniia Petra Velikogo (Istoriia tsarstvovaniia Petra Velikogo. N. Ustrialova. Spb. 1858, tri toma)," *Sochineniia,* Vol. II, 6th ed. (St. Petersburg, n. d.), 60–180.
205 *Ibid.,* 68.

make us consider Peter a great historical figure, who understood and met the
real needs of his time and his people, not some sort of a sudden jump in our
history in no way connected with the previous development of the people. That
last view, shared by many, stems, of course, from the fact that in our midst attention is frequently paid primarily to the external forms of life and government,
in which Peter did in fact introduce sharp change. But if we look into the substance of what is hidden under the forms, it will turn out that the transition
was not at all so sharp, and on both sides, that is, that in the time prior to Peter
we did not feel such a frightful repulsion from everything European while at
present there is no such absolute renunciation of everything Asiatic, as is usually
ascribed to us. In one word, a careful consideration of the historical events and
of the internal condition of Russian in the seventeenth century can prove that
Peter, by means of a series of energetic government reforms, saved Russia from
a violent overturn, the beginning of which already had manifested itself in the
popular disturbances under Aleksei Mikhailovich and in the rebellions of the
*streltsy.*[206]

Dobroliubov died in November 1861, closing the issue of the further
evolution of his views on Peter the Great or on anything else.

Other intellectuals of the Left joined Chernyshevskii in the early 1860s
in commenting on the Petrine theme. Characteristically, they exercised
their sarcasm at the expense of the existing historiography, especially of
the apologists of the first emperor, and made hash of the items they discussed. Characteristically too, they emphasized the horrible cruelty and
backwardness of Russian life when Peter I appeared on the scene. Yet
they were much more circumspect in dealing with the reformer and even
sometimes firmly supported him and his work. In 1861 an unsigned
article in *The Contemporary,* which belonged apparently to Maksim
Alekseevich Antonovich (1835–1918), critic and geologist, denounced concentration in Petrine studies on such topics as the tragedy of the Lady-in-
Waiting Mary Hamilton, too trivial a subject to be of any scholarly or
educational use; the story of Alexis, the critic admitted, could be of use,
but not as handled by C. Sadler or by Pogodin, against whom Sadler had
directed his work.[207] I. Shishkin's review article of the same book by
Sadler in 1861 in *The Russian Word* became a list of examples of torture
typical of the Petrine age. Yet its author came to the following conclusion:

---

[206] *Ibid.,* 79.

[207] Antonovich wrote his article as a review of C. Sadler's "historical justification of
Peter I." Sadler was provoked especially by M. P. Pogodin's "The Trial of Tsarevich
Aleksei Petrovich" (M. Pogodin, "Sud nad tsarevichem Alekseem Petrovichem," *Russkaia
Beseda* [1860], 1–84), where the historian and ideological pillar of Official Nationality
(see Chapter II, section 3, earlier), who had been glorifying Peter the Great for decades,
passed severe moral judgment against him. *Re* Pogodin, it is tempting to suggest that
even he was affected by the more critical spirit in the new reign; it is more likely,
however, that he was adversely influenced by his study of the sources, something that
similarly affected Pushkin and others (M. A. Antonovich, "Opyt istoricheskogo opravdaniia Petra I-go, protiv obvineniia nekotorykh sovremennykh pisatelei. Karla Zadlera.
St.-Peterburg. 1861 g.," *Sovremennik. Literaturnyi zhurnal,* Vol. 87, 161–172).

And there could be no other reform, taking into account those qualities of the people, those beliefs and customs, those views and tendencies, an idea of which we tried to give to our readers by means of all the preceding extracts, references, and stories. We could cite many more most piquant facts to support the opinion that it was positively necessary to refresh the stuffy and stale air of pre-Petrine Russia by means of ventilators not of Russian construction. We could group together many more most eloquent arguments that would prove in the most irrefutable manner the necessity of the Petrine reform: but, first, we think that what we have said is already sufficient to disappoint the reader somewhat in the unimaginable charm of our ancient way of life; second, we want to speak here not at all about the necessity of the Petrine reform (we can only pity people who still doubt that necessity and advise them to turn to a good doctor-psychiatrist if it is not too late for a doctor-psychiatrist to do something for them), but about the fact that that reform could hardly have been executed in any manner other than the manner in which it was executed by Peter the Great.[208]

In the populist decades that followed the 1860s, interest in Peter the Great declined. It can even be said that, to the extent that populism permeated Russian intellectual life, other themes replaced the Petrine theme. In contrast to the Slavophile views, the first emperor was not prominent as an opponent either, although sometimes, as in the case of Kropotkin's autobiography quoted earlier, he was linked to the general tsarist system of oppression. Yet sporadic efforts to affirm, indeed appropriate, the reformer, as against his successors and other claimants to his heritage, continued. The leading populist political thinker and literary critic Nikolai Konstantinovich Mikhailovskii (1842–1901) wrote in his survey of Russian literature in the Petrine bicentennial year of 1872:

And, in general, Peter was too much permeated by the idea of the state—which, by the way, was not in his case either a dynastic or a police idea—to force upon the individual tight estate limits. His task consisted in bringing on the arena of history not the *individual,* narrow and limited by one-sided estate interests, but the fully developed *human being.* Peter himself served the interests not of a dynasty, but of the Russian people. Therefore, it was perfectly natural for him to demand from others service to the same Russian people and not to this or that estate. Of course, he could, as a temporary measure, demand at least a certain broadening of individual interest, for instance, within the confines of an estate or a home territory. But, certainly, Peter understood deeply that that was only a temporary measure; and he would have been very much surprised had he learned that by the day of his two-hundred-year jubilee that stage, that station had become the aim of the journey . . .

Serve the Russian people, drown all personal interests in the interests of the people—and you will be following in his footsteps. But you will not be following

208 I. Shishkin, "Panegiristy i poritsateli Petra Velikogo. (Opyt istoricheskogo opravdaniia Petra I-go protiv obvinenii nekotorykh sovremennykh pisatelei. Karla Zadlera. S. Peterburg. 1861)," *Russkoe Slovo. Literaturno-uchenyi zhurnal* (1861), no. 8., quoted from Section II, p. 17.

in Peter's footsteps if you expand the boundaries of the fatherland or demand that we march, without fail, after Western civilization. Although in his time Peter did expand the boundaries of Russia and did march after Western civilization, doing that solely in the interests of the people, since then the concepts of Western civilization and of the people have become much more complicated, and a new reconsideration is necessary.[209]

Peter the Great nourished not only scholarship and ideology, but also literary entertainment. In the second half of the nineteenth century, as earlier, stories and novels on the Petrine theme—or at least set in the Petrine epoch and with some mention of the reformer and his work— continued to appear. Anecdote and adventure were their stock in trade. Thus, E. A. Salias de Turnemir's Petrine novel dealt with the Astrakhan rebellion and more specifically with the rumor associated with it to the effect that all Astrakhan girls were to be married to foreigners, and G. P. Danilevskii's contribution depicted Prince A. Bekovich-Cherkasskii's tragic expedition to Central Asia. Daniil Lukich Mordovtsev (1830–1905) published at least five such books, distinguished, as Professor Xenia Gasiorowska pointed out, by the fact that one and only one of them, *Idealists and Realists (Idealisty i realisty)*, which came out in 1878, belonged to the anti-Petrine tradition (in this case, pro-Alexis and his party) whereas the others followed the usual eulogistic line. More conventional was Aleksandr Vasilievich Arsenev (1854–1896), a writer for children as well as a historical novelist, whose two Petrine contributions Professor Gasiorowska summarized as follows:

*Arisha the Ducky.* 1889. Arisha, nicknamed "the Ducky," is Peter's fictional goddaughter, born in 1722, during the Tsar's visit to her father's smithy. She is taken to see Peter on his bier three years later. Orphaned, she is apprenticed to a Dutch seamstress and eventually marries her son. Numerous Petrine anecdotes are woven into the plot.

*The Tsar's Verdict.* 1889. The fictional plot illustrates Peter's love of justice, his respect for his own laws, and the awe he inspires. The hero, Gur, is unfairly deprived by the Senate of his land. In despair he dares to request Peter's intervention, which is forbidden. Luckily, Peter becomes interested in the case, looks into it, and fines the senators, returning the land to Gur. He is also present at Gur's marriage to the heroine, Anna.[210]

## 7

The end of the nineteenth century and the first decades of the twentieth witnessed a striking enrichment of Russian thought and culture. Whereas

[209] N. K. Mikhailovskii, "Iz literaturnykh i zhurnalnykh zametok 1872 goda," *Sochineniia*, Vol. I (St. Petersburg, 1896), columns 634–810, quoted from columns 650–651. Cf. A. N. Pypin's article in *Vestnik Evropy* presented in section 5 above, and an 1872 jubilee contribution from the Left: [S. S. Shashkov], "Vsenarodnoi pamiati tsaria-rabotnika," *Delo* (1872), no. 7, Section I, 291–324.

[210] Xenia Gasiorowska, *The Image of Peter the Great in Russian Fiction* (Madison, Wis., 1979), especially pp. 186–190, quoted from p. 186.

the views of Official Nationality and diverse ideas associated with such figures as Miliukov, Chernyshevskii, Mikhailovskii or Plekhanov continued their sway and sometimes, as in the case of Marxism, even gained strength, there occurred in Russia a remarkable aesthetic-metaphysical-religious eruption giving rise to the splendid artistic, literary, and intellectual culture of what has sometimes been called the Silver Age. The Petrine theme was not central to the Silver Age, concerned as it was with the fundamental issues of artistic expression, religion, and thought. Yet it was not far removed from the center, once the protagonists of the new approach turned to Russian history and Russian life. And it could be treated in a novel manner, often different from the more prosaic ways characteristic of the preceding decades.

Vladimir Sergeevich Soloviev (1853–1900) was the greatest forerunner of the Silver Age and the most important influence on it, with the possible exception of Dostoevskii. Generally considered the outstanding Russian philosopher of all time as well as a leading publicist and intellectual-at-large of his epoch, he was a son of Sergei Mikhailovich Soloviev, the historian.[211] In V. Soloviev's case it is especially difficult to separate the Petrine theme from the total outlook, for it was frequently intertwined, at least implicitly, with such main preoccupations of the philosopher as religious ecumenism and the Russian mission. Also, V. Soloviev changed his views, perhaps catastrophically, at the end of his life. Still it was he who provided a rather clear and explicit quasi-religious justification of Peter the Great, in particular in an article, "Several Words in Defense of Peter the Great," dating from 1888 and repeatedly republished.[212]

"The epoch of reform," indissolubly linked to the name of Peter the Great, constitutes for us the focal point of Russian history. I mean not the person of the reformer, but his *cause*. For him who takes a negative attitude toward that cause, Russian history, which, presumably, could be turned onto a completely false and destructive path by the arbitrary action of a single person, is obvious and hopeless nonsense. Defending the cause of Peter the Great against the recently renewed attacks, we champion the meaning of Russian history, the true significance of the Russian state . . .

In terms of its general meaning and direction, Peter the Great's reform was not something entirely new for the Russian people: it renewed and continued the traditions of Kievan Russia, interrupted by the Mongol invasion and by the all-encompassing work of the unification of the state. Whatever Peter the Great's personal qualities and actions were, he, by his historic deed, brought Russia back to that Christian way, which she had first entered at the time of St. Vladimir.

211 Vladimir Soloviev dedicated his most accomplished work, *A Justification of the Good,* "to my father the historian Sergei Mikhailovich Soloviev and my grandfather the priest Mikhail Vasilievich Soloviev, with the feeling of a living recognition of an eternal link."

212 V. S. Soloviev, "Neskolko slov v zashchitu Petra Velikogo," *Sobranie sochinenii* (n.p., n.d.), Vol. V, 161–180; also published as Vladimir Soloviev, "Ocherki iz istorii russkogo soznaniia," *Vestnik Evropy. Zhurnal istorii, politiki, literatury,* Year 24, Book 5 (May 1889), 290–303.

Exchanging her national idolatry for a panhuman faith that recognizes "neither Hellene nor Jew," Russia by that very fact renounced her pagan isolation and aloofness, recognized herself as a component part of the single human entity, assimilated its true interests, joined its world-historical fate. The adoption of Christianity, if it were sincere, could not stop with the verbal confession of certain dogmas and with the performance of pious rites; it imposed upon the converted people a practical task: to transform its life according to the principles of the true religion, to organize in the spirit and meaning of that religion all its affairs and relations.[213]

Kievan Russia,-indeed, undertook to do so although hesitantly and hindered by many obstacles. St. Vladimir's kindness and care for the poor were fully Christian, and these sentiments were repeated a hundred years later by Vladimir Monomakh. Moreover: "This mood could not be considered something exceptional and fortuitous. Although few lived as nobly as Monomakh, all thought the way he thought."[214] In fact, located between Byzantium and Western Europe and unencumbered by such one-sided phenomena as Western feudalism and Byzantine despotism, Kievan Russia offered the best opportunity for the development of a Christian society. But this goal was not reached because of the steppe invaders. The weak Kievan state crumbled. And it was the great effort and the special merit of Muscovite Russia to create finally an effective strong state. "But, devoting itself wholly to that national-political task, the Russian people easily accepted in the Muscovite period the necessary means (the strong state element) as the goal itself of its historical life, and that was followed inevitably by a darkening and a disfiguration of the religious-moral ideal, by a deviation from the Christian way."[215] Isolated and feeling superior tu the Mongols, the Russians developed an overweening pride, especially after they defeated their conquerors. The Greeks, too, after the fall of Constantinople, turned from teachers to mendicants, buttressing the Russian conviction that Russia was the only truly Christian land in the world. The Muscovite order and way of life were, thus, by no means truly Christian. "That system had a religious foundation, but its religion was reduced exclusively to right belief and ritual piety, which imposed no moral obligations on anyone."[216] Religion and morality, therefore, remained completely unrelated to political and social matters.

The church, by contrast, became most closely linked to the state. "Just as in the understanding of the Russian people, beginning with the Muscovite epoch, Christianity lost its intrinsic universal meaning and was transformed into a religious attribute of Russian nationality, so too the church naturally ceased being an independent social group and blended into one indivisible whole with the national state, assimilating completely

213 V. Soloviev, "Neskolko slov," 161–162.
214 *Ibid.*, 162.
215 *Ibid.*, 162–163.
216 *Ibid.*, 164.

its political task and its historical purpose."[217] The church made an enormous contribution, or rather contributions, to the Russian state—"the highest spiritual forces of the Russian people, represented by the church, were entirely devoted to a single historical task: the creation and strengthening of the state autocracy. We know how necessary was that task."[218] But the devastating one-sidedness of the Russian development was bound to tell. The crisis struck with the *raskol,* the split of the Old Believers. Although correct in some of their criticism of the established church, they represented "in essence merely the extreme expression of that pagan savagery into which Russia had fallen in the Muscovite epoch."[219] But the ruling church, too, proved its un-Christian parochialism and its inability to handle the crisis. Therefore:

An unprejudiced and careful look at the historical circumstances that preceded and accompanied the establishment of the Synod will not only restrain us from unjustly reproaching the great shadow of the Reformer, but will also force us to recognize in the above-mentioned institution one of the proofs of that providential wisdom, which never betrayed Peter the Great on important occasions. The abolition of the patriarchate and the establishment of the Synod was not only a necessary measure at that given moment, but also a positively useful one for the future of Russia.[220]

The change in the religious leadership was thus entirely warranted; the real question was, however, who would guide Russia next and how.

Neither the spiritual authorities in the person of Patriarch Nikon nor the church people in the person of Archpriest Avvakum told or could tell the united and exalted Russian state what its further historical task was to be. The bearer of the state power himself told that to Russia; he told it and he put it into practice. I even hesitate to call him a great human being, not because he was not sufficiently great, but because he was not sufficiently a human being. Our historical giant resembled mythical giants: like them, he was an enormous elemental force, embodied in a human form, a force directed entirely outward, not entering inside itself. Peter the Great had no clear comprehension of the *ultimate* aim of his activity, of the highest purpose of a Christian state in general and of Russia in particular. But he felt with his entire being what at the given historical moment had to be done for Russia in order to direct it to the true path, to bring her closer to that highest task—and he put all of himself, brought his entire elemental might into that undertaking. The question of personal qualities and vices is of no interest at all here. The important thing is that the deed, accomplished by Peter the Great, was the most useful and necessary one and that he accomplished it firmly . . .

The entire point was, for the time being, to break the wall separating Russia from humanity, to break the intellectual order and the order of daily life based on pagan isolation. That task Peter the Great accomplished durably, irreversibly.

217 *Ibid.,* 165–166.
218 *Ibid.,* 167.
219 *Ibid.,* 175.
220 *Ibid.,* 174.

Whatever reactionary trends may arise in later times, it is not in their power to make Russia retrace the road opened to her by Peter. Whatever blinded or evil-intentioned persons may say or devise, Muscovite Russia is buried, and she will not rise . . .

For every people there are only two historical paths: the pagan path of self-satisfaction, stagnation, and death, and the Christian path of self-consciousness, perfectioning, and life. Only for an absolute being, for God, self-consciousness is self-satisfaction, and immutability is life. But for every limited being, therefore also for a people, self-consciousness is necessarily *self-condemnation,* and life is change. Therefore, true religion begins with the preaching of *repentance* and of internal *change.* Christianity so entered world history; so, too, begins the Christian path of self-consciousnness of every human being and people. In spite of all appearances, Peter the Great's reform had essentially a deeply Christian character because it was based on the moral-religious act of a national self-condemnation.[221]

To be effective, self-condemnation had to be repeated, nay, continuous: hence the significance of Kantemir's satires, Novikov's critique, Fonvizin's comedies, Griboedov's depiction of the Russia of Alexander I, Gogol's of that of Nicholas I, Saltykov's of the epoch of Alexander II. And as Russia took a negative view of herself, she began advancing on the road of Christian politics. "The first most important and difficult step consisted in changing the attitude to other peoples, in recognizing them as equal members of humanity and, in addition, as members ahead of us in enlightenment."[222] Slow at first, progress gained with time:

The repeal of capital punishment under Elizabeth, the abrogation of torture under Catherine II, the abolition of serfdom under Alexander II—these are the major fruits of that Christian direction, which "the Antichrist" Peter gave to Russian internal policy.

There is no need to prove that it is also to the Petrine reform that Russia owes all its present education and all the treasures of its literature. If any question could arise here, it has already been answered by the two greatest representatives of Russian education and literature in this century and the last, Lomonosov and Pushkin, who linked their names indissolubly to that of Peter.

An always deeper penetration with the principles of panhuman Christian culture, accompanied by a constantly critical attitude toward one's own social condition—here lies the only way to develop all the positive forces of the Russian nation, to demonstrate true originality, to take an independent and active part in the world course of history. The correctness of that way is proved not only by its positive results—for everything good that we have had in no matter what domain in the course of the last two centuries was achieved precisely following that way—it is also proved, on the other hand, by the total failure of the Russian spirit on those occasions when it deviated from the Christian direction and returned in one form or another to the pre-Petrine paganism.[223]

[221] *Ibid.,* 177–178.
[222] *Ibid.,* 179.
[223] *Ibid.,* 180.

With the coming of the Silver Age and in line with the rich variety of its intellectual and artistic products, treatments of the Petrine theme and even mere references to Peter the Great frequently differed sharply from one another in point of view and approach, and they contrasted as a rule, separately and together, from the contributions of the preceding decades.

Dmitrii Sergeevich Merezhkovskii (1865–1941), a central figure in the ideological and cultural renaissance, provided a large-scale treatment of the first emperor in his famous and popular two-volume novel, *Peter and Alexis,* which came out in 1905 and concluded a trilogy, the first two parts of which had dealt with Julian the Apostate and Leonardo da Vinci.[224] Like so many others of his generation, Merezhkovskii wrote under the sign of Dostoevskii—although without Dostoevskii's genius—and engaged in a hard-hitting, at times gripping, psychological depiction and analysis, for which the tragedy of Tsarevich Alexis offered an ideal subject. Love, hatred, pity, terror, intuitive penetration, and emotional blindness, in their rapid alteration and extreme form, constituted the very stuff of the novel. The well-known figures, facts, and anecdotes of the Petrine age provided the setting. The author treated his two protagonists with a great sensitivity and understanding: Alexis, profoundly Christian and desperately loving his father, emerged as a hero and really a saint, in spite of—perhaps because of—his ineffectiveness and many other defects. But Peter, too, stood out for his sterling qualities: an absolute devotion to duty, heroic labor, a simple belief in God, suffering. The intellectual world of the novel, to be sure, at times resembled the Silver Age much more than the first quarter of the eighteenth century, for example, when Alexis grounded his faith in Russia on the conviction that it had retained, in spite of its backwardness and vices and in contrast to the West, faith in Christ. But the story was quite effective in its own terms.

However, *Peter and Alexis* was not simply a contribution to psychological realism. Characteristically for Merezhkovskii, it abounded in sensationalism, sex, and violence, and, even more characteristically, it was full of religious and philosophical—or pseudoreligious and pseudophilosophical—matters and implications. Old Believers and sectarians, depicted at great length and in a striking variety of episodes, including a mass suicide by burning and the staging of a ritual murder, provided particularly rich material for these purposes. More important for the student of the Petrine image, the first emperor, too, served a quasi-religious-metaphysical aim. The full title of the novel was *The Antichrist. Peter and Alexis.* Peter, to repeat, was skillfully presented as an impressive and tortured human being, indeed a mortal with a firm belief in God, and the presentation was a consistent one throughout the two volumes. Yet he struck some others, Alexis in particular, as the Antichrist. More exactly, the tsarevich saw two beings in the body of the tsar: a loving father, whom,

[224] I used D. S. Merzhkovskii, *Antikhrist. Petr i Alexsei* (2 vols., Berlin, 1922).

in turn, he loved beyond all measure, and that other one, the werewolf, *oboroten,* the Antichrist. In his nightmares Peter turned into an enormous whiskered and clawing cat; in fact, when the tsar lost all self-control and attacked the tsarevich, others "became pale and crossed themselves as they approached the doors and listened to the frightening sounds, which reached them from there; it seemed that there a beast was tearing a human being with his teeth."[225] Merezhkovskii's transition from his earlier "Hellenic" views to an affirmation of spiritual Christianity as against the rationalist and godless West provided some of the ideological scaffolding for the strange novel.

In 1910–1911, Andrei Belyi (Boris Nikolaevich Bugaev, 1880–1934), one of the great Russian poets and prose writers of the Silver Age and in general, published a much more remarkable and a stranger novel on a Petrine theme. True, *St. Petersburg*—often compared to James Joyce's *Ulysses* and preceding it by a decade—dealt with the capital city in the tumultuous year of 1905, not with the first emperor when alive or with his time. But the enthralling, nightmarish, symbolist narrative raised more brilliantly than ever—or at least since Pushkin—the issue of the Petrine work and legacy, represented by the city and by the Russian imperial government when challenged by the forces of anarchy and dissolution. The novel, compressed in time, centered on the conflict between the two Ableukhovs, father and son, a leading official and a reluctant revolutionary terrorist, whose bomb kept ticking through most of the tale before exploding. The larger confrontation, however, was that between the city of Peter, a symbol of order, organization, rationality, and Westernization in Russia, and the seething, revolutionary, "Asiatic" masses. A mysterious Persian, a figure of delirium, materialized or seemed to materialize at one point; a Mongol face glared from a wall; the horsemen of Genghis Khan again rode in the steppe whereas, on the other hand, the Bronze Horseman himself joined the protagonists. Merezhkovskii's apocalyptic visions seemed tame compared to Belyi's intensity.

Catastrophe fitted the literary style and the circumstances of the Silver Age, marked by the revolution of 1905, and, after that, by the revolutions of 1917. Catastrophe was basic to the creativity of the greatest poet of the age, Alexander Blok. The old world was disappearing. In terms of the Petrine theme, the distinguished symbolist poet Innocent Annenskii (Innokentii Fedorovich Annenskii, 1856–1909) was willing to write it off even before the First World War in his poem "Petersburg," which used, once again, the Bronze Horseman as a main element:

> The yellow vapor of a Petersburg winter,
> The yellow snow sticking to the pavement.

[225] Merezhkovskii, *op. cit.,* Vol. II, 274. The author also occasionally described Petrine activities in a manner suggesting the presence of the forces of evil. Cf. the depiction of shipbuilding at the Admiralty, which ends with the sentence: "The Admiralty resembled the smithy of hell." (*Ibid.,* 96.)

> I do not know, where you are and where we are,
> I know only that we are fused firmly together . . .
>
> The magician gave us only stones,
> And the Neva of a brown-yellow color,
> And the deserts of empty squares,
> Where people were executed before dawn . . .
>
> And how mighty and daring he was,
> But his furious steed betrayed him,
> The tsar did not manage to crush the snake,
> And the pressed down creature became our idol.
>
> No kremlins, no miracles, nothing sacred,
> No mirages, no tears, no smile.
> Only stones from frozen deserts,
> And the consciousness of a fatal mistake.[226]

Still, criticism—to the point of returning to the legend of the Anti-christ—rebellion, and despair, richly varied though they were in the works of such writers as Merezhkovskii, Belyi, and Annenskii, by no means exhausted the treatment of the Petrine theme in the Silver Age. There was also the equally important positive side. It found its main nourishment in the glory of the cultural renaissance itself and in the intrinsic links of that renaissance to the city of Peter. Thus St. Petersburg became a leitmotiv in the poetry of Anna Akhmatova and a leitmotiv of stunning beauty and affirmation. It found expression in such poems as Blok's "Peter," where the Bronze Horseman guards his city,[227] or Osip Mandelstam's (Osip Emilevich Mandelshtam, 1891–1938) *"Hier stehe ich—ich kann nicht anders,"* where Peter the Great is juxtaposed with Luther and "The Admiralty":

> The northern capital, a poplar tree droops, dusty
> a transparent clock-dial tangled in leaves,
> and through dark foliage a frigate, an acropolis
> shines in the distance, brother to water, brother to sky.
>
> An air-boat, a mast no one can touch,
> a measure for Peter's heirs,
> and his lesson: a demigod's whim is not beauty,
> but the predatory eye of a carpenter, is.
>
> Four elements united, rule us, are friendly,
> but free man made the fifth.
> This chaste-constructed ark: isn't the
> superiority of space denied?

---

[226] Innokentii Annenskii, *Posmertnye strikhi* (Petersburg, 1923), 46–47. I translated and quoted four of the seven stanzas. Annenskii's poem was written in response to Blok's poem mentioned in my next paragraph.

[227] A. Blok, "Petr," *Gorod moi . . . Stikhi o Peterburge-Petrograde* (Leningrad, 1957), 72–75. The poem dates from 1904. The entire book is directly relevant to my subject.

Capricious jellyfish cling, angry;
anchors rot, abandoned like ploughs—
and there, the three dimensions burst their bonds
and universal oceans open.[228]

The painters sang of the city with the poets. The remarkable revival of the graphic arts in Russia, which formed a major part of the cultural renaissance, enriched greatly the Petrine theme. Although my study does not deal with the fine arts, it is at least necessary to bear in mind the contribution of such figures as Alexandre Benois (Aleksandr Nikolaevich Benua, 1870–1960), artist and decorative artist, art historian, editor and publicist, director of the Hermitage museum, and a true painter of St. Petersburg. Incidentally, it was Benois who drew the best illustrations for *The Bronze Horseman.*

Nor can this magnificent affirmation and poeticization in the Silver Age of St. Petersburg be considered as irrelevant or merely peripheral to the image of Peter the Great proper. As indicated repeatedly earlier, the two could not be separated. Belyi penetrated very well indeed the connection between the regular streets and squares of the capital, the first emperor, and the imperial order in Russia. If the city were constructed by the effort, will, and legacy of one man, if modern Russian government, culture, and genius came with that city, was not then modern Russian history directly the work of Peter the Great and his heirs? It is not, therefore, surprising that that thesis was brilliantly—if hopelessly—propounded by Wladimir Weidlé (Vladimir Veidle), who came out of the Silver Age to become in emigration a remarkable historian of art and culture and a distinguished literary critic. Weidlé wrote in 1949 in *La Russie absente et présente:*

The new culture born as a result of the Petrine revolution constituted in the beginning nothing but a heterogeneous collection of imported articles; but the new elite assimilated them so rapidly that by the end of the eighteenth century there already existed a Russian culture, more homogeneous and more stable than the old one. That culture was Russian in the strictest sense of the word, expressing emotional states and creating values that were properly Russian, and if the people no more than half-understood it, this transpired not because it was not sufficiently national, but because the people were not yet a nation.[229]

Feofan Prokopovich could not have put it better.

---

[228] The two poems, both written in 1913, are in Osip Mandelshtam, *Sobranie sochinenii v dvukh tomakh,* Vol. I (Washington, 1964), pp. 26 and 29–30 respectively. I used the translation in *Complete Poetry of Osip Emilevich Mandelstam* (Albany, 1973), 58–59.

[229] Wladimir Weidlé, *La Russie absente et présente* (Paris, 1949), 69. An English translation came out in 1952. See my review in *Journal of Central European Affairs,* Vol. 12, no. 4 (January 1953), 391–393.

# IV

## The Image of Peter the Great
## in the Soviet Union, 1917–1984

The historical significance of Peter I's reforms was very great. Their total result was the creation of a mighty Russian empire, firmly entrenched on the shores of the Baltic Sea and of the Pacific Ocean. That striking condition of backwardness in the economic, political, and cultural fields, which had been characteristic of the Russian state at the end of the seventeenth century, was overcome to the extent that Russia was no longer immediately threatened with the danger of becoming a colony or a semicolony of any more powerful neighboring Western European state. Russia was transformed, as a result of Peter's reform, into one of the most significant and mighty European states. The Petrine reforms, which had a progressive meaning in the strengthening of the national state of landlords and of the emerging merchant class, came as a strong push toward a further growth of the productive forces of the country, and for that reason they played a major role in the preparation of those conditions within the framework of which there began to appear toward the end of the eighteenth century elements of the capitalist mode of production.

Peter I's progressive reforms were enacted at the expense of the broad masses of population, at the point of collapse at that time under the burden of taxation and of a most cruel feudal exploitation. The class-gentry nature of Petrine reforms, aimed towards strengthening the national state of landlords and merchants, stood out especially prominently in Peter I's administrative reform. That reform had as its purpose the creation, beginning with the organization of the *gubernii* in 1708, of a mighty governing apparatus, with the help of which the state authorities could better and in full realize the class domination of the gentry over the enserfed peasantry, could repress the slightest manifestation of dissatisfaction in the midst of the latter.

Comrade Stalin gave an exhaustive evaluation of the meaning of the Petrine reforms. He wrote: "When Peter the Great, compelled to deal with the more developed countries in the West, feverishly built plants and manufactories to supply the army and strengthen the defenses of the country, that was a singular attempt to jump out of our country's framework of backwardness. It is readily understood, however, that none of the old classes, neither the feudal aristocracy nor the bourgeoisie, could solve the

234

problem of liquidating the backwardness of our country. More than that, these classes not only could not solve that problem, but they were even unable to formulate it in a minimally satisfactory manner. The centuries-old backwardness of our country can be liquidated only on the basis of a successful building of socialism."

G. Novitskii[1]

---

**1**

Marxism, which became the official and dominant ideology in Russia following the revolution of October 1917, was originally little concerned with Peter the Great. Marx and Engels left only a few scattered direct comments on the first Russian emperor, made usually in passing. To be sure, these references were eagerly snapped up and constantly repeated by Soviet scholars. Thus, Professor N. Pavlenko, in a fine recent book on Peter I, used five of these comments as epigraphs for his chapters:[2]

"It is water that Russia wants." These words . . . are inscribed on the title-page of his (that is, Peter's) life.

K. Marx, *Secret Diplomatic History of the Eighteenth Century*[3]

Narva was the first serious defeat of a rising nation, which knew how to turn even defeats into instruments of victory.

K. Marx, *A Retrospective Look at the Crimean Campaign*[4]

. . . Charles XII made an effort to invade Russia; by doing that he ruined Sweden and graphically proved the impregnability of Russia.

F. Engels, *The Foreign Policy of Russian Tsarism*[5]

. . . in one word, Peter, in this quarter, at least, but took hold of what was absolutely necessary for the natural development of his country.

K. Marx, *Secret Diplomatic History of the Eighteenth Century*[6]

This truly great man—not to be compared to Frederick "the Great," an obedient

---

[1] Prof. G. A. Novitskii, *Obrazovanie Rossiiskoi Imperii. Kurs istorii SSSR. Lektsii 22, 23, 24. Stenogramma lektsii, prochitannykh 21, 27 i 29 ianvaria 1940 g.* (Irkutsk, 1947), 54–55.

[2] N. Pavlenko, *Petr Pervyi*, 2d rev. ed. (Moscow, 1976). Very many examples of other Soviet Petrine historians utilizing the quotations from the Marxist classics could be similarly adduced. For a more insistent recourse to them than Pavlenko's, see, e.g., Professor V. Mavrodin's writings, discussed later in this chapter and represented in my bibliography.

[3] Pavlenko, *Petr Pervyi*, 33. I am quoting the original English (Karl Marx, *Secret Diplomatic History of the Eighteenth Century* and *The Story of the Life of Lord Palmerston*, edited and with an introduction and notes by Lester Hutchinson [New York, 1969], 122–123).

[4] Pavlenko, *Petr Pervyi*, 84.

[5] *Ibid.*, 157.

[6] *Ibid.*, 181. The reference is to the Baltic coast and to the early, pre-Poltava period of the Great Northern War (Marx, *Secret Diplomatic History*, 123).

servant of Peter's successor Catherine II—first fully gauged the situation in Europe exceptionally favorable for Russia.

F. Engels, *The Foreign Policy of Russian Tsarism*[7]

Perhaps more surprisingly, Lenin too wrote very little on Peter the Great. Pavlenko culled only two chapter epigraphs from his works to add to the five from those of Marx and Engels. (Pavlenko used no other epigraphs in his book on Peter I than these seven, dispensing with epigraphs for most of his chapters.)

The first, and best-known, declared:

. . . Peter hastened the adoption of Western ways by barbarian Russia, not refraining from barbarian means to fight barbarism.

V. I. Lenin, *About "Left" Infantilism and the Petty Bourgeois Element*[8]

The second selection placed the Petrine reign within a broad historical process:

The development of the Russian state system in the course of the last three centuries shows us that it kept changing its class character in one definite direction. The seventeenth-century monarchy with the boyar *duma* does not resemble the bureaucratic-gentry monarchy of the eighteenth century. The monarchy of the first half of the nineteenth century is not the same thing as the monarchy of the years 1861–1904. In 1908–1910 there appeared clearly the outlines of a new stage, marking one more step in the same direction, which can be described as the direction towards a bourgeois monarchy.

V. I. Lenin, *Those Who Would Eliminate Us (Nashi uprazdniteli)*[9]

The general Marxist approach to history proved to be much more influential in the evolution of the Soviet image of Peter the Great than the specific comments on the subject of the first Russian emperor found in Marxist classics. Marxism, particularly in its Leninist Soviet version, believes in regularities, indeed laws, in history, viewing the historical process as both progressive and inevitable. Based on the history of Europe from the classical world to modern capitalism, the Marxist model is certainly a Westernizer one, immediately and readily adaptable to judging the Russian past and present in terms of "backwardness" or of "catching up" vis-à-vis the West. The Westernization of Russia, usually associated with Peter the Great, although not the embodiment of reason of eigh-

---

[7] Pavlenko, *Petr Pervyi*, 364. Engels's "truly great man" became a favorite quote of the Soviet partisans of Peter the Great.

[8] *Ibid.*, 66. Lenin's fighting barbarism by barbarian means was borrowed from Marx: "If Peter the Great conquered Russian barbarism with barbarism, so Proudhon did everything within his power to conquer French phrase-mongering with phrases" (*Sochineniia*, Vol. XVI [Moscow, 1936], Chapter 2, 29). As Professor Cyril Black noted, Soviet readers are not given Lenin's immediately preceding statement (made in the spring of 1918) of the need to copy German state capitalism and adopt dictatorial methods to speed the copying (C. E. Black, "The Reforms of Peter the Great," *Rewriting Russian History*, edited by Cyril E. Black, 2d rev. ed. [New York, 1962], 232–259, 238).

[9] Pavlenko, *Petr Pervyi*, 298.

teenth-century philosophes or the march of spirit through history of nineteenth-century ideologues, stands out as a major step in the right direction. One is reminded of the fact that both the Enlightenment and German idealistic philosophy were major sources of Marxism.

Yet the view of the historical process changed drastically. The Marxist emphasis on impersonal forces, on the economic basis and class structure of a society, on the immanent dialectic of its evolution, devalued, in effect dismissed, that personal element that had been central to the image of Peter the Great from the days of Feofan Prokopovich to those of Bogoslovskii. In the new scheme of things, the turning points of Russian history were not the young ruler's first journey to the West, not even the battle of Poltava or the Treaty of Nystad, but the rise of the service gentry or the emancipation of the serfs. Eventually, the dominant Soviet historical interpretation classified Russia as feudal from the late Kievan period, that is, from the eleventh or the twelfth centuries, until the abolition of serfdom in 1861, the vast sweep of centuries swallowing the reign of the first emperor as well as much else. Nor could Peter I—"Peter I" replaced "Peter the Great" as the standard Soviet usage—be treated in simple positive terms even in his new, much-reduced role. Because history was a history of class struggle, he could no longer merely represent reason, progress, or the Russian destiny, but had to be linked intrinsically to the exploiting classes whereas the sympathies of Soviet scholars rested with the exploited. Logically, but especially circumstantially, debunking and even denunciation and hatred became prominent elements in the original Soviet image, or rather images, of Peter the Great.

Still, Peter the Great was too important, both in fact and in the Russian intellectual tradition, to be entirely dismissed even from the Marxist point of view, especially when that view extended beyond the immediate pressing issues and was combined with an intellectual and cultural sophistication. If Lenin was too preoccupied with the development of capitalism in Russia, not to mention party ideology and struggles, to evaluate the historical role of the first emperor, that task was performed, at least in part, by his onetime mentor, "the father of Russian Marxism," Georgii Valentinovich Plekhanov (1856–1918).[10]

Plekhanov published no works on Peter the Great or the Petrine reign. His relevant opinions have to be gathered from broader studies, such as his remarkable *History of Russian Social Thought* (*Istoriia russkoi obshchestvennoi mysli*, 1909–1918, with three of the projected seven volumes finished at the time of the author's death), and from articles devoted to literary criticism, philosophy, or idelogical polemics. A paper in my seminar on the subject contained more than eighty references to some fifteen

---

[10] On Plekhanov, see especially Samuel H. Baron, *Plekhanov: The Father of Russian Marxism* (Stanford, Calif., 1963). Professor Baron pays much attention to the nature of Plekhanov's Marxism and to its Marxist "correctness." Cf. my review of his book in *Political Science Quarterly*, Vol. LXXIX, no. 3 (September 1964), 457–59.

pieces. Nevertheless, in spite of the scattered nature of the material, a total picture of the Petrine historical role does emerge. Indeed it is a complex and nuanced evaluation that cannot be rendered full justice in my summary presentation of it.

On the positive side, Plekhanov endorsed wholeheartedly the Westernizer orientation of Marxism and thus the fundamental validity and value of the Petrine course. Moreover, outstanding Marxist theoretician that he was, Plekhanov provided a powerful doctrinal rationale for the importance of the Petrine moment in the Westernization of Russia. He accomplished this by treating Peter the Great not merely as an epiphenomenal representative of this or that governing class but as an heir to a species of Oriental despotism in a society based on the Asiatic mode of production. That mode of production, a possible variant in Marxist historical schemes,[11] led to a crushing dominance of the state, a relative inhibition of the class struggle, and stagnation. Yet, in a triumph of the dialectic, the first Russian emperor used his awesome heritage to promote modernization and thus to cultivate the seeds of the ultimate destruction of the Asiatic Muscovite system itself.

Old Muscovite Russia was distinguished by a completely Asiatic character. Its social manners and customs, its administration, the psychology of its inhabitants—everything in it was completely foreign to Europe and very closely related to China, Persia, ancient Egypt. To that Russia Chaadaev's gloomy characterization indubitably does apply to a large extent. To a European it could not help but appear as some kind of "gap" in the rational order. From the point of view of European progress, of course, it did not constitute and could not constitute a necessary part of humanity, from which it had long isolated itself in its wastes. But that country had the great good fortune of being not in Asia but in Europe, or at least in the neighborhood of Europe. As a result of this geographic peculiarity of its location, Muscovite Russia *was forced* to borrow certain things from its neighbors, simply because of the instinct of self-preservation. Already from the time of Ivan the Terrible it tried to move towards the Baltic Sea. Peter, finally, hewed "a window into Europe." Peter possessed colossal authority and an iron energy. But he could not do more than what was amenable to authority. "On a social base, which went back almost to the eleventh century"— A. Rambaud justly remarks—"there appeared a foreign service, a regular army, a bureaucratic hierarchy, an industry satisfying the taste for luxuries, schools, academies." In one word, Peter merely attached *European limbs to a torso,* which still remained *Asiatic.* However, the new limbs exercised a tremendous influence

---

11 *Re* Russia, consult particularly Samuel H. Baron, "Feudalism or the Asiatic Mode of Production: Alternative Interpretations of Russian History," Samuel H. Baron and Nancy W. Heer, eds., *Windows on the Russian Past* (Columbus, Ohio, 1977), 24–41. An extreme use of the Marxist or quasi-Marxist "Asiatic" approach can be found in: Karl A. Wittfogel, *Oriental Despotism* (New Haven, 1957). See my debate with Professor Wittfogel (Professor Bertold Spuler was the third participant) in *Slavic Review,* Vol. XXII, no. 4 (December 1963), 627–662 (Karl A. Wittfogel, "Russia and the West: A Comparison and Contrast," 627–643; Nicholas V. Riasanovsky, " 'Oriental Despotism' and Russia," 644–649; Bertold Spuler, "Russia and Islam," 650–655; Karl A. Wittfogel, "Reply," 656–659).

on the nature of the old torso. Money was needed to support the post-reform system. The Petrine reform gave a push towards the development of a market economy in Russia. In addition, at least some kind of *manufactory-plant industry* was needed to support the post-reform system. Peter laid the foundations of this industry in our country, and thus threw into the Russian soil the seeds of entirely new economic relations. For a long time the industry, which had been planted by Peter, led a rather miserable existence, apparently in complete obedience to the general tone of Russian social life. It was enserfed to the state and itself became a serf institution, maintained by the compulsory labor of peasants ascribed to factories and plants. Nevertheless, it still continued its work of transforming the Russian social body, with the strong assistance of the same international relations, without which the activity of genius-Peter would also have been unthinkable. The successes of Russian economic development can be seen from the fact that, whereas the Petrine reform demanded a *simplification* of serfdom, the reforms of Alexander II were predicated on its *abolition*. The beginning of the new economic order, "unsympathetic" to the populists and the subjectivists, is usually assigned among us to the nineteenth of February, 1861. We have seen that that beginning had been laid already by Peter the Great. But it is true that the nineteenth of February gave a strong push to the development of that order; it brought out and changed into a mighty current the economic stream which had been hiding underground, only slowly and imperceptibly demolishing the old economic formation. In the course of thirty and more years, which have passed since the abolition of serfdom, that old formation has worn out completely. Now there is no hole, no wild corner in Russia, where the mighty influence of the new economic relations is not felt. The Petrine reform has reached its logical end, at least in the economic domain; the new European arms have fully transformed the old Muscovite torso. And no matter how much anyone may sigh for the old Muscovite *oblomovism,* no force can any longer resurrect it. *Finis Moscoviae! Thou has conquered, Saardam carpenter!*[12]

Or, to make the same point more briefly and with a special emphasis on the Russian proletariat:

In our fatherland, the formation of that class has an even greater significance [than elsewhere in Europe, where its significance was enormous]. The very character of Russian culture changes with its appearance; our old, *Asiatic* economic way of life vanishes, ceding its place to the new way, the *European* one. The working class is destined to complete in our land Peter's great undertaking: to carry the process of *the Europeanization of Russia* to its conclusion. But the working class will give a totally new character to this task, on which the very existence of Russia as a civilized country depends. Begun at one time *from above,* by the iron will of the most *despotic* of Russian *despots,* it will be finished *from below,* by means of a *liberation* movement of the most *revolutionary* of all the classes ever known to history.[13]

Plekhanov's sweeping and resounding endorsement of the Westerniza-

12 G. V. Plekhanov, "Pessimizm kak otrazhenie ekonomichesoi deistvitelnosti (Pessimizm P. Ia. Chaadaeva)," *Sochineniia,* Vol. X, edited by D. Riazanov (Moscow and Petrograd, n.d.), 133–162, quoted from pp. 154–155.

13 G. V. Plekhanov, "Novyi zashchitnik samoderzhaviia, ili gore g. L. Tikhomirova," *Izbrannye filosofskie proizvedeniia,* Vol. I (Moscow, 1956), 382–417, quoted from p. 413.

tion of Russia and of the first emperor's role in that Westernization—an endorsement that included references to Peter's greatness and genius—brought him into a very long sequence of yea-sayers and glorifiers over a period of some two centuries. Within that sequence he was closest to the radical Westernizers, perhaps especially to Belinskii, about whom "the father of Russian Marxism" wrote so perceptively and well. And yet the difference between the two, on the subject of Peter and in general, was also major. In contrast to the critic of the 1840s, the ideologue of the end of that century saw only too clearly "the other side" of the Petrine phenomenon. The Asiatic mode of production and the resulting Oriental despotism, which had given Peter his power, were a frightening legacy. His dialectical break from them was a tour de force, incomplete and precarious. No wonder that the New Russian industries used compulsory labor and that serfs were debased to the level of slaves in Russia precisely when serfdom disappeared in the West. A content analysis would indicate that Plekhanov devoted more space to the failures than to the successes of the Petrine reforms and certainly to their crushing pain than to their glory. He collected his information from the best available sources, such as Kliuchevskii and, especially and explicitly, Miliukov.

But the issue was not simply that of harrowing obstacles and tragic costs in pursuit of a necessary and sublime goal. The pursuit itself raised fundamental questions. Whereas eighteenth-century admirers declared that Peter the Great had brought Russia from nonbeing into being, whereas their counterparts in the first half of the nineteenth century believed that it was through the reforming emperor that Russia entered European history and became a historical entity, and whereas Professor Weidlé could claim in the mid-twentieth century that the emperor, his successors, and the educated elite gave Russia a national culture before Russia had become a nation, Plekhanov, a dedicated Marxist theoretician, had to look at historical change in a different context. And that context informed him that Petrine Russia was economically and socially unprepared for modernization. Hence the repeated failures of the reformer, as well as the superficial nature of those results that were finally achieved. Hence the separation of the educated stratum from the masses and its useless and superficial existence, like a European colony in the midst of barbarians, to cite an acute Slavophile comment. Plekhanov came to the conclusion that it was only after the abolition of serfdom in 1861 that Western ideas acquired relevance to Russian reality.

Yet, as Plekhanov's own life and struggles graphically demonstrated, 1861 was not to mark the solution of Russian problems either. Even the great revolution, when it finally came in October 1917, was, for Plekhanov, a wrong revolution at a wrong time. He died, however, on May 30, 1918, without leaving to us—to the best of my knowledge—any reconsideration of the role and legacy of Peter the Great in Russian history in the light of "Great October."

2

The ten or fifteen years that followed the October Revolution may well be considered a transitional period in the history of Russian culture. The richness, the variety, the high standards of the preceding years remained at least in part, in spite of the devastation of civil war, hunger, typhus, political repressions, and other disasters. Many Russian intellectuals and artists perished, many emigrated, but enough remained in their country to continue the cultural tradition and indeed to score striking new successes in numerous areas. Victorious Marxists were themselves divided, and they engaged in vigorous debates with one another as well as with outside opponents. The party and the government struggled against illiteracy, experimented in education, and left no doubt about their intention to control culture. But the controls were still relatively loose; the party line had not been set on many issues, and it was contested. A truly effective gleichschaltung would come only later.

Study of Peter the Great, like so very much else, declined during the catastrophic years that followed the October Revolution; and indeed little appeared about the first emperor and his reign throughout the 1920s and into the early 1930s. The publication of the fundamental *Letters and Papers of Emperor Peter the Great (Pisma i bumagi Imperatora Petra Velikogo)* was discontinued after 1918, to be resumed only in 1946. Still, for the 1920s, one can refer to a considerable continuity of the Petrine image. A number of scholars, notably Bogoslovskii, who was to die in 1929, continued treating the reformers in their old manner.[14] Others, especially Kliuchevskii, although dead, continued to exercise their influence. Even Miliukov, a political enemy and an émigré, was frequently cited with regard to the devastating results of Petrine policies.

Marxist interpretations, however, rapidly became more prominent. Following Plekhanov's early, sketchy, and scattered analysis of the Petrine phenomenon, Mikhail Nikolaevich Pokrovskii (1869–1932), proceeded to give it a much more massive and explicit Marxist treatment. Strictly speaking, the Pokrovskii version, too, belonged to the prerevolutionary period, for it found its fullest expression in the historian's five-volume *Russian History from the Most Ancient Times,* first published in 1910–1913.[15] But in 1920, Pokrovskii reworked his magnum opus thoroughly

14 In the 1920s M. M. Bogoslovskii published the following Petrine works: *Petr Velikii i ego reforma* (Moscow, 1920); *Russkoe obshchestvo i nauka pri Petre Velikom* (Leningrad, 1926); "Gorodskaia reforma 1699 g. v provintsialnykh gorodakh," *Uchenye zapiski Instituta istorii RANIION* (1927), 219–250; "Palata ob Ulozhenii 1700–1703 gg.," *Izvestiia AN SSSR,* nos. 15–17 (1927), 1347–1474; no. 1 (1928), 81–110; "Administrativnye preobrazovaniia Petra Velikogo, 1699–1700 gg.," Part 1, "Boiarskaia duma," *op. cit.,* nos. 4–7 (1928), 279–298; "Administrativnye preobrazovaniia Petra Velikogo, 1699–1700 gg.," Part 2, "Prikazy i mestnoe upravlenie," *op. cit.,* no. 2 (1929), 97–121.

15 M. N. Pokrovskii, *Russkaia istoriia s drevneishikh vremen* (5 vols., Moscow, 1910–1913). The original edition contained contributions by V. K. Agafonov, N. M. Nikolskii, and V. N. Storozhev later dropped. I shall refer to the recent republication of the four-

into a two-volume *Brief History of Russia;*[16] and it was in the 1920s and the early 1930s that Pokrovskii's writings, in ever-new editions, flooded the Soviet market. It was also during those years that Pokrovskii promoted his historical views most actively, violently attacking his rivals and opponents in polemical print.[17] Moreover, Pokrovskii became much more than an energetic academician:

From 1921 to 1928 Pokrovskii not only extended and disseminated his historical views, he performed as an "organizer of scholarship." This phrase is difficult to define because there is no equivalent responsibility in American society. "Academic bureaucrat" suggests the closest equivalent—the scholar-administrator, possessed of both academic and entrepreneurial skill, who holds positions in private foundations, the government and universities, and who thereby shapes science and educational policy at the state and university levels. Pokrovskii more than anyone else created the "historical front"—the phrase used to describe a hierarchical organization of scholars authorized to work out in full detail the Marxist understanding of the past and to show the falsity of rival theories . . .

As deputy chairman of Narkompros, the Peoples' Commissariat of Education, and chairman of its State Council of Scholars (*GUS*) he was a major voice in policy making in higher education. He was also chairman of the Presidium of the Communist Academy (*KA*), a network of institutes that for a time sought to rival the older and better established Academy of Sciences. He supervised the education of historians and participated directly in the process as rector of the Institute of Red Professors (*IKP*) and as a member of the leadership of the Institute of History, one of the forebears of today's historical institutes of the Academy of Sciences. The Institute existed within several organizations before 1936; through much of the 1920s, it was a branch of the Russian Association of Social Science Research Institutes (*RANION*), which was a network of institutes where non-Marxists worked and taught under the supervision of Marxists. Pokrovskii led the Marxist historians most directly and the non-Marxists indirectly in his capacity as head of the Society of Marxist Historians (*SMH*).[18]

No wonder that Russian historiography, Petrine historiography included, existed for about a decade under the sign of Pokrovskii although one should not fall into an anachronism and exaggerate his authority or his

---

volume version of *History* in M. N. Pokrovskii, *Izbrannye proizvedeniia* (4 vols., Moscow, 1965–1967); *Russkaia istoriia s drevneishikh vremen* occupies vols. 1 and 2 of that publication, with Chapter X, "Petrovskaia reforma," presented on pp. 518–646 of the first volume. For the complex evolution of the text, see Roman Szporluk, "Introduction," M. N. Pokrovskii, *Russia in World History, Selected Essays by M. N. Pokrovskii* (Ann Arbor, 1970), 1–46, especially p. 6, and the editorial note in Pokrovskii, *Izbrannye proizvedeniia*, Vol. I, 649–650.

[16] I am using the standard title of D. S. Mirsky's English translation. The Russian title was *Russkaia istoriia v samom szhatom ocherke.* It composed Vol. III (1967) of the already-cited *Izbrannye proizvedeniia.*

[17] See especially M. N. Pokrovskii, *Istoricheskaia nauka i borba klassov. (Istoriograficheskie ocherki, kriticheskie stati i zametki)* (Moscow and Leningrad, 1933).

[18] George M. Enteen, *The Soviet Scholar-Bureaucrat: M. N. Pokrovskii and the Society of Marxist Historians* (University Park and London, 1978), 3–4. See my review of Professor Enteen's book in *The Russian Review*, Vol XXXVIII, no. 4 (October 1979), 485–486.

power to enforce comformity in what was in many ways still a pluralistic, or at least an uncoordinated, society.

A student of Kliuchevskii, a gifted intellectual, and an early Russian Marxist, Pokrovskii turned with a bitter vengeance against the pre-1917 Russian establishment. In many ways he possessed an ideal temperament and character to lead a cultural revolution. Sarcasm and hate dominated his view of the Russian past, as well as of historians who wrote such nonsense about it. The old, false world had to be torn down to let the new, correct one rise, in historiography as much as in history. Characteristically, Pokrovskii began his chapter on "the Petrine reform" in his *Russian History from the Most Ancient Times* as follows:

In very ancient times that cultural overturn that the Muscovite state experienced at the threshold of the seventeenth-eighteenth centuries [*sic*] was considered exclusively, so to speak, from the pedagogical point of view: Russia "learned," the West "taught," we became "pupils" of Western Europe. What made us pupils was self-evident: love of enlightenment. "Learning is light, ignorance is darkness"; as long as light was hidden from us, as long as Russians had not seen enlightened Europe, they could stagnate as yet in their ignorance. But, look, Russians began to travel abroad (at that point several anecdotes were always told, showing how ludicrous they were then), foreigners began to visit Moscow; because the issue was enlightenment, among the foreigners doctors, druggists, artists and technicians of every kind were moved to the fore; little by little "a cultural interaction" began, which at the time of Peter led safely to the fact that the Muscovite savages, having shaved the hair that had been growing naturally on their chins, increased the supply of hair on their heads by means of a large artificial layer in the form of a curly, wavy wig. At the same time, they built a navy and established, first, elementary schools and later also the Academy of Sciences, after which there began to come to Russia not only druggists and doctors, but also luminaries of European science.[19]

Having thus disposed of the two-hundred-year-old tradition of the Petrine enlightenment, Pokrovskii proved equally contemptuous of idealistic, metaphysical explanations and of the related claim that Russia had to Westernize to save itself from outside enemies. That obligation presupposed a world process and purpose, which there was no reason to assume; Poland, for example, apparently felt no such obligation, for it went down. Indeed, Westernizing in order to survive and surviving in order to Westernize were a mere tautology, reminiscent of Molière's elucidation of how opium puts people to sleep because it has soporific power. Russian historians thus failed to discover what caused the Petrine reform. Yet the answer did exist although it had to include Russia within a broader economic, international framework: "The key to Petrine reform must be sought in the last analysis—the reader will see that below—in the conditions of European trade in the seventeenth century."[20]

19 Pokrovskii, *Russkaia istoriia s drevneishikh vremen,* 518.
20 *Ibid.,* 520.

Pokrovskii's "Petrine reform" became a determined tracing of the rise in Russia of merchant capital, which the historian considered crucial for the understanding of the age. By the beginning of the seventeenth century, a Europewide grain market was being formed, and active Dutch merchants were interested in including Russian resources in its ambit. Though that plan essentially failed, Russian foreign trade increased rapidly, exhibiting its typical form of a state monopoly in furs, silk, grain, vodka, and much else. The tsar was the first and the overwhelmingly important merchant of the realm. Moreover, Russian imports also acquired a mass character. Further:

Seventeenth-century merchant capital exercised an enormous influence on both the foreign and domestic policy of the Muscovite government. Until the conquest of the Ukraine and in part even up to Peter's time, the south was the objective; the colonization of southern borderlands, now fallen undivided into Muscovite hands, provided the immediate reason both for Prince V. V. Golitsyn's Crimean campaigns and for those of Peter aimed at Azov. The change in the orientation of that policy, connected with the Northern War, was evoked mainly by the interests of Russian foreign trade.[21]

That war provided a marvelous demonstration of the primacy of economic, in this case specifically commercial, interests:

The alliance of Russia with Poland, precisely on that basis, was as natural as the attraction on the part of Riga toward the Muscovite state: both states needed for their exports a "free" Baltic Sea, that is, the abolition of the Swedish monopoly there. Denmark was at one with them in this matter if for no other reason than, in the first place, because of Sound dues, not even to mention the ancient rivalry of the two Scandinavian peoples in the Baltic area. Just the opposite, the Dutch, who had escaped from these very Sound dues into the White Sea, had to be very unsympathetic to the Russian-Polish undertaking. The mutual relations between Peter and the Dutch Republic at the time of the Northern War and in connection with that war can serve as the best illustration of how every kind of "cultural" influences cedes its place to economic ones in case of a collision. One would think, what could be stronger than the Dutch influence on the "Saardam carpenter," who even in his signature slavishly copied that country, which was in his eyes the embodiment of European civilization? And just the same, he knew, when he began the war, that his friends were looking at it more than coldly.[22]

Mercantilism formed the foundation of Russian policy. Russia knew both its first stage, concerned entirely with raw materials, and the second, associated with Colbert and zealous to promote and protect native manufacturing. Pokrovskii concentrated on such topics as Athanasius Ordyn-Nashchokin's commercial code of 1667, Pososhkov's highly relevant writings, and the rise of manufacturing in Muscovy in the second half of the

21 *Ibid.,* 542.
22 *Ibid.,* 545.

seventeenth century with foreign entrepreneurs and, as usual, the government playing leading roles.

Thus, there were present in Russia at the end of the seventeenth century conditions necessary for the development of large-scale manufacturing; there was capital, although in part foreign; there was the internal market; there were available factory hands. All this is more than sufficient to negate any comparison between Petrine factories and artificially produced hothouse plants. And still the failure of Petrine large-scale manufacturing is as indubitable a fact as all those cited above. The manufactories founded at the time of Peter collapsed one after another, and barely 10 percent of them eked out an existence until the second half of the eighteenth century. Taking a closer look at this first industrial crisis in Russian history, we see, however, that it, too, was as natural as can be and that it is to be explained precisely by what was formerly frequently used to explain the appearance of large-scale manufacturing at the time of Peter. Totally erroneous is the view that political conditions forced the development of Russian capitalism in the seventeenth to eighteenth centuries; but that the political shell of a gentry state prevented this capitalism from developing—that is entirely correct. Here, too, as in other areas, Peter's autocracy could not create anything, but destroyed much. In this respect, the history of Petrine manufactures forms a perfect parallel to the picture of an administrative devastation so well drawn by Mr. Miliukov in his book.[23]

Disaster resulted from the monarch's addiction to excessive and often senseless regulation, his impatience, and his devotion to compulsion, which, in his opinion, could remedy all things. Forced labor was used to operate Russian factories whereas capital continued to try to escape into trade. Moreover, there developed a whole new exploitative social layer intrinsically linked to Petrine economic policies: "Thus, next to foreign capitalists, there appears before us another social group, which gathered the fruits of 'the reforms': that was a new feudal nobility, which under the name of 'supreme lords' began ruling Russia on the very day following Peter's death."[24]

"The springtime of merchant capitalism" at the turn of the century was reflected even in the administration of the state. Bourgeois elements invaded that typically gentry administration. In fact, the class realignment, albeit temporary, offered the strongest testimony to the significant social shifts of the time.

Nothing can illustrate the revolutionary, catastrophic character of Petrine reforms more strikingly than this replacement, which it has become customary to explain by modest considerations of state convenience. To deprive one class of authority and to hand it over to another for the sole reason of "a more reliable regulation of financial responsibility" (as Miliukov explains the reform of 1699)—that no state in the world ever accomplished because not one could have accomplished it. True, in Petrine Russia, too, it did not succeed for long: in less than thirty years the gentry state took its own. But even to attempt such a

23 *Ibid.*, 560–561.
24 *Ibid.*, 567.

move required a very special correlation of forces; there had to be that alliance of the bourgeoisie with the upper reaches of the landlord class, which we discussed above. When the new feudal aristocracy had used up fully its bourgeois ally, the latter had again to return to its former political nullity. But it became immediately apparent that without its modest support the "supreme lords" themselves were totally unable to maintain their position: finding themselves face-to-face with the gentry, which had been pushed back for a time, they were quickly forced to surrender their position to the latter, and the gentry established themselves once more in the saddle, this time for almost two centuries.[25]

Pokrovskii thus placed an enormous emphasis on the town administration reform of 1699, which was based on a project of 1681 and which empowered Russian merchants, those of the city of Moscow in particular, to manage a very large part of the state finances. Among other things, ". . . the entire financial apparatus of the Petrine army found itself under the supervision of city magistrates: they paid the armed forces on location and checked the use by military authorities of the money they provided. A nobleman with 'an epaulet' had to submit his report obediently to a 'miserable merchant.' "[26] Similarly, a new bureaucracy of special financial agents, the "fiscals," was supplied largely by the merchant class. But the new importance of the Russian bourgeoisie did not last. In particular, the grandees of Peter's reign, led by Menshikov, proceeded to take over the running and the riches of the country, making private satrapies out of the provinces into which Russia was divided in 1708 and dominating such key Petrine central institutions as the colleges and the Senate. Even the leadership of the fiscals passed to the gentry. The monarch was totally unable to stem the wholesale rapacity and corruption around him. When he died early in 1725, he was much more than merely physically worn out,

The conquest of feudal Russia by merchant capital, no matter how transitory and unstable that conquest was, had to be accompanied by major changes in *the way of life* of Russian society. In *that* regard the latter probably had not experienced a sharper change in appearances in the entire course of its thousand-year-old history. The change will strike us especially if we look at that society from the top. At the very pinnacle of the pyramid, there, where only so recently rose something in the nature of a living ikon in the severe Byzantine style, stepping forth slowly and grandly in front of the eyes of a worshipful crowd, stepping forth only for a minute in order immediately to vanish in the dark depth of private quarters, there was now seen a nervous, lively-to-the-point-of-fidgeting figure in a laborer's jacket, always among people, always in the street; moreover, it was impossible to distinguish where it was that the street ended and the tsar's palace began. For both here and there everything was equally disorderly, noisy, and drunk; both here and there roamed an equally mixed and unceremonious crowd, where a tsar's minister in a golden caftan and wearing the band of the Order of St. Andrew was elbowed by a Dutch sailor, arriving hither straight from

25 *Ibid.,* 568.
26 *Ibid.,* 572.

his ship, or by a German shopkeeper coming straight from behind his counter. True, the farther away from the palace, the less was the change felt. Already the serviceman, who had rather willingly donned the German costume and somewhat less willingly shaved his beard, was not averse, as he sat in a collegium established according to a foreign model, to engage in the old manner in *mestnichestvo* squabbling with his neighbor, and at home he kept everything according to the old order, and if he let the street enter his house on some days, he did so only very reluctantly and following a strict ukase of the tsar. Below servicemen extended the thick mass of "Old Believers and bearded people," whom change had not affected even externally and who preserved for another century and a half, up to Pecherskii's novels and Ostrovskii's comedies, their "way of life" in all inviolability. And, finally, no change whatsoever could be noticed in the multimillion peasant mass.[27]

The "Petrine" transformation of Russia was very similar to the earlier, sixteenth-century change in Western Europe, to the Italian and Flemish Renaissance, and for good reason: both, in their respective areas, were the work of the bourgeoisie. One had only to read eyewitness accounts of the fantastic displays of festival gaiety and pageantry, whether at the court of Pope Leo X or of Tsar Peter. Realism and individualism became prominent in court life, literature, and art. Whether or not the Russian monarch's notorious "all-drunken council" was associated, like similar Western pastimes, with serious freethinking, tsarist soldiers were indeed directed not to fast when campaigning, and the Old Believers enjoyed a new degree of tolerance. But the Russian version of the Renaissance was particularly primitive and crude, symbolized by constant physical beatings, from the very top down; and it displayed a militarism typical of a gentry state, with the sovereign devoted, above all, to his noble guards' regiments. "The thin bourgeois veneer changed as little the nature of the Muscovite state as a German caftan the nature of a Muscovite."[28]

Pokrovskii gave a brief and incomplete but devastating description of the last years of Peter's reign. Economic ruin, so effectively documented by Miliukov, was total. Even the armed forces were in a most miserable condition, with the government unable to pay their personnel. The rapacity of the new nobility exceeded all measure. The monarch, in the meantime, started another war. "The same merchant capitalism that compelled Peter to fight twenty years for the Baltic Sea now drove him to the Caspian."[29] The Persian War, although not as disastrous as the earlier Prut campaign against Turkey, resulted in huge losses and costs for very little gain. Peter I's overdue death, when it finally came, was that of a coward, "sufficient to shake the legend about 'iron men' ":[30] terrified, the emperor repented, freed from jail debtors and most other

[27] *Ibid.,* 592. This passage contains marvelous echoes of Pokrovskii's teacher, Kliuchevskii.
[28] *Ibid.,* 614.
[29] *Ibid.,* 617.
[30] *Ibid.,* 620.

categories of criminals, ordered prayers to be said for him in all churches of the empire, partook of Holy Communion thrice in one week, but failed to arrange in time for his succession.

Pokrovskii criticized bitterly not only bourgeois historians but also Plekhanov for assigning too much importance in Russian history to the state. In particular, they lent unwarranted significance and prominence to Peter the Great. Yet history would stand in a clear light if, instead of Plekhanov's ratiocinations about Asiatic despotism and a shift to the European line of development, we recognized the reformer simply as an agent of merchant capital. Or, as Pokrovskii put it in reference to Miliukov's able exposition: "if we replace the symbolic figure of Peter by merchant capital, which precisely by the beginning of the Northern War moved to the center of all affairs."[31] The critic concluded that his own history was too conventional and that a correct presentation demanded stark treatment in Marxist class terms.

Pokrovskii's two-volume *Brief History of Russia,* which won Lenin's special commendation, was, thus, by no means simply a condensation of his *Russian History from the Most Ancient Times.* Rather, it was a fundamental reworking of the earlier five volumes in the direction of Marxist categories and sociological abstraction (Lenin suggested that it be supplemented by a chronological table of facts). In the Petrine period, merchant capital reigned supreme. Peter the Great, by contrast, came out much diminished in prominence. According to one calculation, "Peter" or "Petrine" appeared 225 times on 64 different pages in the earlier history as against only 23 times on 11 pages in the later one.[32] Biographical information vanished almost entirely. Yet Pokrovskii certainly did not grow kinder to the first emperor. He wrote, for example, in *Brief History:*

Peter, whom sycophantic historians called "Great," locked up his wife in a convent in order to marry Catherine, who had earlier served as a maid of a pastor (a Lutheran priest) in Estonia. He tortured with his own hands his son Alexis and after that ordered him to be secretly executed in a casemate of the Peter-and-Paul Fortress. He died (1725) from complications produced by syphilis, after infecting with it his second wife, who outlived him by only two years.[33]

31 *Ibid.,* 574.

32 The counting was done in my seminar. The author of the paper used Jesse D. Clarkson and M. R. M. Griffiths' somewhat abridged translation of Pokrovskii's magnum opus and estimated that it contained 164,307 words compared to 148,680 words in *Brief History:* the discrepancy in the number of Petrine references could not, therefore, be attributed simply to the fact that the later work was shorter than the earlier one (M. N. Pokrovskii, *History of Russia from the Earliest Times to the Rise of Commercial Capitalism,* translated and edited by J. D. Clarkson and M. R. M. Griffiths, reprinted from the 1928 edition [University Prints and Reprints, Indiana, 1966]; M. N. Pokrovskii, *Brief History of Russia,* translated by D. S. Mirsky, reprinted from the two-volume 1933 edition [University Prints and Reprints, Orono, Maine, 1968]).

33 Pokrovskii, *Russkaia istoriia v samon szhatom ocherke,* 112–113. In the Russian academic tradition, Pokrovskii is remembered for, among other things, his references to Peter the Great as "that syphilitic."

However, in one article, published in 1919, Pokrovskii did take a much more sym-

Pokrovskii's venomous, at times vulgar, attack on Peter the Great undeniably contained a strong personal element. But it should not be treated merely as the idiosyncratic outpouring of a bitter intellectual. Rather, it fitted into the Petrine image—"anti-Petrine" might be more exact—that was popular among certain pre-1917 Russian radicals and that became widespread, perhaps even for a time dominant, after the October Revolution. Tsarism and the tsars were denounced in most direct and crude terms, and the first emperor constituted one of the main targets. Violent denunciations permeated belles lettres as well as academic works. In the changed intellectual and emotional climate, the historic Peter the Great proceeded to supply ample material to his detractors, just as he had been supplying it for so long to his admirers.

A case in point is a brief piece by a gifted writer, Boris Andreevich Pilniak (1894–1937, real last name Vogau), entitled *His Majesty Kneeb Piter Komondor* and published in 1919.[34] Modernistic—or, perhaps better, disjointed—rather than traditionally narrative in form, kaleidoscopic and at times difficult to follow, the "novella" nevertheless left no doubt about its author's view of Peter the Great:

A man, the joy of whose soul was in action. A man with the capacities of a genius. An abnormal man, always drunk, a syphilitic, a hypochondriac, who suffered from psychopathic seizures of depression and violence, who with his own hands choked his son to death. A monarch who could never restrain himself in anything, who did not understand that one must control oneself, a despot. A man, who had absolutely no sense of responsibility, who despised everything, who failed to understand to the end of his life either historical logic or the physiology of the life of the people. A maniac. A coward. Frightened by his childhood, he came to hate the old world; blindly he accepted the new; he lived with foreigners, who arrived for easy gain, he obtained a barracks upbringing; he looked up to the ways of a Dutch sailor as his ideal. A man who remained a child to the end of his days, who loved play above all—and who played all his life: at war, at ships, at parades, at councils, at illumination, at Europe. A cynic who despised the human being in himself and in others. An actor, an actor of genius. An emperor who loved debauchery above all, who married a prostitute, Menshikov's concubine—a man with the ideals of the barracks. The body was

---

pathetic view of Peter the Great, emphasizing parallels between the catastrophic changes in contemporary Russia and in the Petrine period and noting that Lenin and Trotsky, like Peter, were declared Antichrists (M. N. Pokrovskii, "Istoriia povtoriaetsia," *Narodnoe Prosveshchenie*, no. 32 [April 26, 1919]). But in general Pokrovskii's reputation as an extreme enemy of Peter the Great was, of course, very well earned.

34 Boris Pilniak, *Ego Velichestvo Kneeb Piter Komondor*. I used the 1922 "Gelikon" edition where "Piter Komondor" was published following Pilniak's other Petrine piece, "SianktPiterBurkh" under the general title of *A Petersburg Tale:* Boris Pilniak, *Povest Peterburgskaia, ili Sviatoi-Kamen-Gorod* (n.p., 1922), 61–126. In contrast to "Piter Komondor," "SianktPiterBurkh" was situated in its author's own days of revolution and civil war, and, in addition, it was concerned with China and the Chinese in the Red Army and otherwise. Still, Peter the Great appeared, both in a direct reminiscence and through his ties to his city and the Russian Revolution, not entirely unlike his role in Belyi's celebrated *St. Petersburg*.

enormous, unclean, very sweaty, awkward, intoed, thin-legged, eaten through and through by alcohol, tobacco, and syphilis. With the years, the cheeks began to hang down on the round, red, old woman's face, the red lips became flaccid, the red—syphilitic—eyelids would not shut tight, and behind them gazed mad, drunken, wild, child's eyes, the same kind of eyes with which a child looks at a cat when he is sticking a needle into it or when he is applying a red-hot iron to the nose of a sleeping pig: it can not be otherwise—Peter did not understand what he was doing when he was choking his son. He fought for thirty years—he played at a mad war—only because his mock soldiers had grown up and his fleet found itself cramped on Moscow River and on the Preobrazhenskii pond. He never walked—always ran, swinging his arms, his thin legs intoed, imitating Dutch sailors in his gait. He dressed dirtily, tastelessly; he did not like to change underwear. He liked to eat much, and he ate with his hands—the enormous hands were greasy and callused.[35]

Specific episodes included the interrogation by Count Peter Tolstoi and the killing of an old man who denounced the monarch and Peter himself arranging the execution of his mistress Mary Hamilton, whose severed head he kissed and used on the spot for an anatomical explanation. The tale ended with an extended description of a Petrine orgy. In addition, and parallel to the horror at court, there was the horror of the exhausted and ravaged countryside, which the officer of the guards, Zotov, saw at least briefly on his assignment. Pilniak's overwhelmingly negative, vulgar, and violent image of Peter the Great could also be found, in its essentials, in other writers of the period, such as the novelist K. G. Shildkret (1896–1965), who published *Our-Savior-on-the-Tallow Church* (*Spas na zhiru*) in 1931 and a trilogy *Subjugated Russia* (*Podiaremnaia Rus*) in 1933–1935, its three volumes devoted respectively to the reformer's childhood, the first decade of his effective reign, and the story of Tsarevich Alexis. Even Alexis N. Tolstoi's treatment of the Petrine theme, which was eventually to constitute an important contribution to Russian literature—and which is to be examined in a later section—began and developed in the early postrevolutionary years, reflecting strikingly the extreme criticism, the stark realism, and the grossness of the time.[36]

Iurii Tynianov and his *Waxen Effigy* deserve special mention. The brilliant modernist writer and literary critic Iurii Nikolaevich Tynianov (1894–1943) made his unique contribution to Petrine literature when he published in 1931 a hundred-page piece entitled *The Waxen Effigy* (*Voskovaia persona*).[37] Difficult to follow, elaborate and ornate in language

[35] Pilniak, "Piter Komondor," 106–108. The emperor's failure to understand either historical logic or the physiology of the life of the people is another tribute to Kliuchevskii.

[36] Traditionalists and admirers of Peter the Great were, of course, scandalized by the sharply negative and vulgar approach, and some violent exchanges resulted. It will be remembered that Platonov's *Peter the Great, Personality and Activity*, discussed in the preceding chapter, was published in 1926 especially against Tolstoi and Pilniak— in that work the great historian became himself an extreme and violent polemicist.

[37] I used Iurii Tynianov, "Voskovaia persona," *Kiukhlia. Rasskazy* (Leningrad, 1973), 360–464.

and style, the *Effigy* gave a sharp impressionistic account of Peter the Great's death and of Menshikov's reaction to it, then concentrated on the celebrated waxen statue of the first emperor and on its location, the famed *Kunstkamera,* the museum of natural history, in particular of natural oddities assembled by the departed monarch. Everything from Mary Hamilton's head to deformed human beings assigned as exhibits to the museum combined to produce an engrossing, eerie, weird, indeed truly macabre, picture. Yet *The Waxen Effigy* was not simply a gothic tale, for it also seemed to make a powerful statement on such issues as the destruction of human dignity and the cruelty of humans. And the picture remained unrelieved, except perhaps by a very bitter humor.

If Plekhanov provided the first Marxist historical interpretation of Peter the Great and Pokrovskii the second, the third was offered by Nikolai Aleksandrovich Rozhkov (1868–1927) in his *A Comparative View of Russian History,* published in twelve volumes in 1919–1926.[38] Not himself a specialist on the Petrine period, Rozhkov gave a derivative and, on the whole, conventional account of the events of the reign although he stressed economic policies and development rather than, for example, military history. And he tried to analyze the Petrine phenomenon in Marxist, class terms. Quite dissatisfied with Pokrovskii's overwhelming stress on merchant capitalism, Rozhkov argued instead that the Petrine reign represented the third and final phase of "the gentry revolution," of the fundamental rise to domination of the gentry class and gentry monarchy at the expense of the boyars and feudal arrangements.

Thus, three moments of the gentry revolution in Russia are to be distinguished: the first, the initial, the second half of the sixteenth century, mainly the reign of Ivan the Terrible; the second, the intermediary, the Time of Troubles, and its results in the first half of the seventeenth century; and, finally, the third, the concluding one, the reform of Peter the Great in the first quarter of the eighteenth century, together with its preparation, which took place in the second half of the seventeenth century.[39]

Moreover, devoted to a sociological, comparativist approach, Rozhkov drew striking and insistent parallels between the Russian gentry revolution and gentry revolutions elsewhere in Europe.

38 N. Rozhkov, *Russkaia istoriia v sravnitelno-istoricheskom osveshchenii (Osnovy sotsialnoi dinamiki)* (12 vols., Moscow and Leningrad, 1919–1926). The fifth volume dealt with the reign of Peter the Great. (It was entitled—the appropriateness of the title will be seen very shortly—*Konets dvorianskoi revoliutsii v Rossii. Ee tretii moment.*)

39 Rozhkov, *Russkaia istoriia,* V, 270.
The references to the Petrine reform as a revolution and to Peter the Great as a revolutionary go back at least to the Decembrist Dmitrii Irinarkhovich Zavalishin (1804–1892) (see his *Zapiski dekabrista* [St. Petersburg, 1906], 121—"in politics a true revolutionary.") They are also to be found in Herzen (cf. my discussion of Herzen in the second chapter earlier), and they acquired more prominence in the Petrine debate in the Soviet period. The Slavophiles, too, had described the reformer's work as a revolution in the strictly negative sense (cf. Chapter 2 earlier).

The reign of Peter the Great, thus, was both organically linked to the past and presented important characteristics of its own, which turned out to be, in general, not at all unfamiliar to readers of Petrine literature:

That preparation, the closest possible connection of Peter the Great's reform with the past, can not be subjected to the slightest doubt. In the economy, there were being prepared not only particular aspects of the development of merchant capitalism, but also its system: mercantilism. In relation to that, native manufacturing was developing; rural economy, homemade and craft production were adapting increasingly to the market; trade monopolies were developing; mercantilist protectionism was expanding. In agriculture the landed wealth of the gentry was increasing whereas that of the clergy and also of the old appanage aristocracy was relatively declining; also, the *pomestie* and the *votchina* holdings were becoming more and more alike. The gentry, organizing itself as a class adapted to merchant capitalism, aimed at complete equality with the boyars in estate terms, an ambition  assisted by the repeal of the *mestnichestvo*. The merchantry began to organize corporatively. The process of merging the entire rural population into a single estate, that of enserfed peasantry, was making progress. In the state structure and functions, new tasks of foreign policy, linked to problems of mercantilism, were projected; a reorganization of the army in the European manner began; financial-mercantilist experiments were attempted; the taxation system was being improved and simplified; the administration, central and regional, was being united and systematized. In spiritual culture, secularization—secular, not church interests—and Westernization were triumphing; types of the new gentry formation were receiving their final shape. In the lower levels the opposition to the future reform was also being prepared.

Peter's reform emerged out of all of that. But it emerged not immediately, but gradually; at first, it was not planned, systematic, fully conscious.

The work of reform began with changes in everyday life appearances, in military and naval matters, with a decisive foreign policy and the outbreak and conduct of the Great Northern War. The war led to changes in finances and administration: the establishment of state control, the appearance of the town office and local agencies, the drawing of the budget of a new type, a series of specific financial measures in the elementary-mercantilist spirit characteristic of the seventeenth century. In the end, there still resulted a financial deficit, which had to be covered. At the same time, under the influence of war and other events connected with it, there formed gradually, almost spontaneously, the first Petrine *gubernii*, which demolished the old administration. Then the Senate was created, and there was projected the necessity of a systematic reform of the organs of government.

The first phase of the reform, up to 1710, transpired in this elemental way. After that its second phase began: the time of a planned and systematic building of the new order.

It had been prepared by a vast literature of projects, and it expressed itself in the economic area in a broad development of mercantilism of the higher, Colbertian type; in finances, in the introduction of the poll tax, and the great growth of the budget; in the organization of society; in a complete replacement of birthright by merit and service; in service and educational burdens for the gentry; in the law of the single heir, with its double, liberational, and enserfing tendency; in the magistracies for the inhabitants of town settlements; in the merging of the rural population into the estate of enserfed peasants. In the state structure, new departures introducing systematization were the reform of the Senate, the establishment of colleges and the *guberniia* reform of 1719–1721, with subsequent changes and additions, as well as reforms in law and the legal process. The church was subjected to the state. Finally, all this was crowned with changes in the spiritual culture in the first half of the eighteenth century: the final making of the new gentry psychology; the rationalization of religion, to a moderate extent, of course; the almost total secularization of literature and science, together with their rather broad development; the first successes of European education, scientific and artistic. And all these reforms are—consistently— gentry reforms; that is precisely why they produced opposition, moderate among the townspeople, extreme among the peasants.

Thus, the gentry revolution in Russia was completed.[40]

Not surprisingly, considering the author's point of view, Peter the Great himself occupied little space in Rozhkov's *History*. The Petrine image proper was confined to a few pages,[41] which offered nothing new or striking to the reader, although an awkward effort was made to connect the monarch's personality with the author's main historical interpretation: "Peter himself combined in his character traits typical of the new gentry, with its spiritual contradictions coexisting peacefully through the power of a stubborn willfulness [*samodurstvo*], and certain peculiarities appropriate to leaders of great overturns."[42] The monarch was rude, ate with his hands, drank, and had others drink enormously; a London landlord itemized the horrid destruction brought to his house by the Russian sovereign and the sovereign's party. Worse still, Peter was "morally rude and lax," writing indecent letters to Catherine, in which he discussed his intimacies with prostitutes. Irritated by the patriarchate, he established his notorious "all-drunken council" and engaged in disgusting revelry, including one occasion when the mock pope, Zotov, was almost drowned in a kettle of beer. The ruler's parsimoniousness went to extremes, reminding one of the Muscovite tsars of the Ivan Kalita line. The accusations of cruelty, however, needed qualification to say the least. The frightening episode with the *streltsy* itself indicated "fanaticism, a deep conviction in one's own rightness, and not personal cruelty."[43] Nartov was justified when he quoted and endorsed Peter's alleged assurance to him that he merely wished the good of the fatherland and fought ignorance, stubbornness, and treachery, rewarding the deserving and correcting the others only as necessary. "In general, moral, ethical impulses were very strong in Peter."[44] Thus, his view of the sovereign as the ser-

[40] Rozhkov, *Russkaia istoriia*, V, 273–274.
[41] *Ibid.*, 224–228.
[42] *Ibid.*, 224.
[43] *Ibid.*, 226.
[44] *Ibid.*, 226.

vant of the common good, or his celebrated words before the battle of Poltava. Kliuchevskii observed correctly that Peter was strict and demanding toward himself and lenient to others. But he underestimated badly the ruler's moral responsiveness to people. For Peter knew how to love, for example, Catherine, Menshikov, or even the blunt and honest Jacob Dolgorukii. "In that sense, too, one should understand the execution of Tsarevich Alexis: Peter loved his son, but he was convinced of the necessity to sacrifice him, and he did it."[45]

Moreover:

It was this moral frame of mind, strength of ethical impulses, power of conviction, daring in ideas, that composed that ethical trait in Peter's character that made him the leader of a revolution, the director of a great overturn. Another trait, necessary to every organizer, also helped him in that respect: a knowledge of people, a skillful selection, and an effective utilization not only of their merits, but also of their demerits—of all their qualities.[46]

But Peter the Great also displayed traits characteristic of the gentry as a whole, and in the first place individualism. He valued power, tolerated no challenge or threat to his authority, and demanded perfect obedience. Even the West was to serve as a model only until Russians had borrowed there what they needed. He loved and valued glory, and for that reason he undertook the production of *The History of the Swedish War*. He loved glory so much that he even accepted base flattery—"Alexander founded Derbend, Peter conquered it."[47] Finally, the emperor exhibited very considerable artistic interests and tastes, illustrated by his decoration of the palace in the Summer Garden, his Hermitage collections, or the remarkable grace of his own handwork.

In reviewing Rozhkov's *History*, Pokrovskii found something to praise and much to criticize.[48] Still, the conclusion was a positive one, even if carefully qualified and measured: Rozhkov—a Marxist but not a Bolshevik—was advancing in the right direction.

As to the third part, dealing with the Soviet period, N. A. Rozhkov, when he finally joins us, will himself, undoubtedly, rewrite it anew. He is moving in that direction, of that fact there can be no doubt, but each step forward costs him a great effort, a greater effort than had appeared to be the case to many observers before the book came out. But his desire to advance to the end, it seems to me, can not be doubted; and I am not losing hope that he will yet give us a work that will actually represent the true "crowning" of his thirty-year-long labor.[49]

45 *Ibid.*, 227.
46 *Ibid.*
47 *Ibid.*, 228. Alexander the Great, of course, was meant. Rozhkov borrowed this illustration, with full acknowledgment, from Miliukov's cultural history of Russia.
48 M. N. Pokrovskii, "Novaia kniga po noveishei istorii (o knige Rozhkova N.—*Russkaia istoriia v sravnitelno-istoricheskom osveshchenii*, t. XIII)," *Istoricheskaia nauka i borba klassov*, 212–223. See also Pokrovskii's obituary of Rozhkov, written soon thereafter: "N. A. Rozhkov," *ibid.*, 224–233.
49 Pokrovskii, "Novaia kniga," 223.

As it turned out, Rozhkov died the following year, 1927. Moreover, before too long the issue in Soviet historiography became not Rozhkov's differences with Pokrovskii, but an all-out attack on Pokrovskii himself.

## 3

Stalin and Stalinism affected the image of Peter the Great as well as everything else in the Soviet Union.

Pokrovskii's fortunes declined precipitously during the last years and months of his life. The historian and leader "on the intellectual front" was accused increasingly of bad Marxism and bad scholarship. Challenged, he fought back, explaining his views and emphasizing Lenin's endorsement of his presentation of Russian history, but, under constant pressure, he also modified and even abandoned some of his former positions. Pokrovskii was in full embattled retreat when he died, of throat cancer, early in 1932.

The charges against Pokrovskii, which increased in scope and vehemence in the years following his death until he became one of the most denounced figures in the Soviet Union, were many and varied. Perhaps his most serious theoretical error, it was claimed, was the emphasis on merchant capitalism in interpreting Russian history: contrary to facts, it was also ideologically incorrect because merchants, mere intermediaries in the economic process, did not own the means of production and thus could not exercise hegemony. Moreover, because even Pokrovskii could not entirely deny the feudal nature of the Russian state and society, his exposition of Russian history became a contradictory tangle of merchant capitalist and feudal elements, an accusation very much applicable to the presentation of the Petrine period, where it was impossible to decipher which of the two forces, to what extent and at what precise time, the new institutions, policies, and even the ruler himself represented. Because of his profoundly erroneous approach, the historian neglected the peasant masses and even the class struggle in its typical-for-the-age form of popular rebellions. Merchant capitalist phantoms replaced feudal reality.[50]

Also, it was argued, Pokrovskii failed to do justice to the more positive aspects of tsarist history, Petrine history certainly included. To put it in measured Marxist terms, he "feared realistically to recognize the relatively progressive nature of Peter's activity."[51] But the attack on Pokrovskii went beyond measured terms and precise Marxist definitions. His de-

---

[50] Criticism of Pokrovskii's scholarship has not, of course, been limited to "the new wave" of Soviet historians and ideologues, such as E. M. Iaroslavskii. My Oxford teacher, B. H. Sumner, once remarked that Pokrovskii, first, based all Russian history on grain prices, and, second, got his grain prices wrong.

[51] The quote is from N. I. Bukharin's article in *Izvestiia* as given in S. Tomsinskii, "Znachenie reform Petra I," *Istorik Marksist*, Book 2 (1936), no. 2 (54), 9–21, 11. Bukharin and references to Bukharin, but not criticism of Pokrovskii, disappeared very soon after in the great purge.

structive, negative approach to Russian history fitted well the spirit—and perhaps the facts—of the October Revolution and its aftermath, when the issue was to sweep away the old world. It did not suit the needs of the construction or reconstruction of society. Perhaps the most important date in Soviet historiography was May 16, 1934, when teaching history, as a separate and important subject, was reintroduced in the schools of the country. Rejecting the nihilism of the intervening years, the authorities decided that history was once again to play a positive role in the education of Russian, more precisely Soviet, men and women although, of course, it was also to be kept within the Marxist-Leninist, and for many years Stalinist, framework.

In the new Soviet climate, Pokrovskii's devastatingly negative image of Peter the Great—drawn along the lines of Daumier's scorching caricatures although without Daumier's supreme artistry—was replaced by a more complicated and strikingly bipolar one. To be sure, it took time for the new image to be fully established and developed. For example, it was affected by a further emphasis on the role of the state and centralized leadership in the late 1930s and by a great rise of patriotism during the Second World War. To be sure, too, the image was many-sided, indeed contradictory, and all its elements cannot be easily defined, classified, and compared. And yet, it is remarkable to what extent this image, introduced in the 1930s, has maintained its continuity and its form, has persisted, and has dominated Soviet Petrine perception and literature to the present day. The image was bipolar, because, in contrast to Pokrovskii or to the Russian Enlightenment and the Slavophiles for that matter, both sides of the Petrine phenomenon were to be sharply etched.

On the negative side, the highly critical Marxist approach to the Petrine state and society remained. Not only was it a fundamentally exploitative, unjust, and immoral social order, but the Petrine reign proper marked a great deterioration in that respect. Stalin was frequently quoted to the effect that Russian peasants were flayed thrice to provide resources for the Petrine reforms. Scholars referred to a fourfold increase in the taxation burden. It was even suggested that Peter the Great succeeded in prolonging feudalism in Russia by a century—a withering criticism for those believing in the progressive march of history. Naturally, Soviet writers sided with popular rebellions, whether in Astrakhan or along the Don, aimed at overthrowing the Petrine rule and system. Moreover, Marxism-Leninism demanded that even the Petrine economic, social, and historical gains be considered "class-bound" and temporary, the final effective solution of all major problems belonging exclusively to the proletariat, the October Revolution, and its aftermath—as stated by G. Novitskii, quoting Stalin, in the passage that served as the epigraph for this chapter, and by uncounted other Soviet scholars and writers. Finally, it would be wrong to consider the Marxist-Leninist critique of Peter the Great as merely ritualistic or archaic; on the contrary, it has remained an effective major force in the Soviet presentation and handling of the Petrine theme.

But, in contrast to Pokrovskii, the positive side also became extremely prominent. Peter I created the Russian navy as well as the modern Russian army. He fought and won the decisive Great Northern War and thus made Russia a major European, even world, power. His diplomatic skill rivaled his military prowess. In fact, Soviet scholars enthusiastically endorsed the entire Petrine foreign policy, the glory of Poltava, the necessity and logic of the acquisitions on the Baltic, the new role of Russia in Europe. At home, too, the monarch achieved important results. The government became more centralized, effective, and modern. Industry boomed, even if some of the industrial achievements proved to be only temporary. Russia was opened to advanced technology and science. And, in general, secular education and progressive Western culture were important acquisitions for the Russians.

It is readily apparent that the complex image allowed for different approaches. One could be wholly sympathetic to the Bulavin rebellion or present a scathing and tragic account of the fiscal oppression of the peasants of the Russian North. On the other hand, one could extoll Peter, the military commander, or rejoice in the rapid Russian acquisition of Western learning. Certain areas, including perhaps the entire major field of the national economy, remained controversial; and indeed there exist very different Soviet assessments of Petrine economic policies. The total picture, however, required a bipolar emphasis, extreme both ways and essentially, if not entirely, contradictory.

The fate of the Petrine image in the narrow sense deserves notice. Soviet Marxist historiography continued to de-emphasize the individual; many books and articles on Petrine subjects paid little or no attention to the reformer himself. Also, the achievements of the reign were attributed especially to the Russian people, not to their ruler or other leaders. Yet if the negative pole of the Petrine complex linked the first emperor to exploitation and serfdom, the positive pole offered ample opportunities for a favorable presentation, and even glorification, of him: as soldier, sailor, or commander, as student or teacher, as an indefatigable worker, as a dedicated patriot, as a truly great man according to Engels, and almost as a quasi-divine figure according to Lomonosov. If Marxist theory played down the significance of rulers, Stalinist practice made them look virtually all-important. And the impact of Stalinism could be found in the Petrine, as in other Soviet, literature of the time, perhaps especially in such an imaginative writer as Alexis N. Tolstoi. In short, after the demise of Pokrovskii, the personal treatment of Peter I acquired considerable flexibility and interest.

Berngard (Boris) Borisovich Kafengauz (1894–1969), a historian educated at the University of Moscow, where he also taught for many years, wrote the Petrine contribution to the remarkable two-volume denunciation of Pokrovskii published in 1940: "The reforms of Peter I in M. N. Pokrovskii's Evaluation."[52] In the very first sentence Kafengauz declared: "The reforms of Peter I moved the country markedly forward, compared to the condition of the Russian state in the seventeenth century."[53] The foreign policy of the reign, its military affairs, the cultural modernization of Russia, even when narrow, were all positive phenomena. Of course, the Petrine regime had two sides. Indeed: "The working masses not only fought heroically in the war, but also rose tempestuously against feudal oppression."[54] After a twelve-page historiographical introduction—one of Kafengauz's special interests—in which he attacked Miliukov particularly for judging Petrine foreign policy premature for backward Russia and, therefore, noxious to it, and where he performed most impressively in milking the Marxist classics, culminating with Stalin, for guidance, Kafengauz turned to the actual subject of Pokrovskii's view of the Petrine reform.

"Pokrovskii's mistake consisted in the fact that he was looking for the economic foundation of society not in production, but in the sphere of exchange."[55] Nor was the historian correct in downgrading industrial development under Peter I, in particular the growth of metallurgy. The erroneous emphasis on merchant capital led to an exaggerated and incorrect presentation of such Petrine institutions as the town administration (the *Ratusha*) and the fiscals as well as to a general confusion in the treatment of the Petrine administration. Moreover, and contrary to Stalin's views:

. . . peasantry almost entirely dropped out of Pokrovskii's field of vision. We do not see in his work either an analysis of the changes in the social-economic conditions of the agricultural population or an elucidation of the bitter struggle of the peasants against the landlords. Together with the feudal economy, to which Pokrovskii paid so little attention, the peasantry and the class struggle also dropped out in his case. This may well be the most astonishing characteristic of Pokrovskii's conception. Having devoted three chapters to merchant capital and industrial policy, he deals in a page and a half with the ruin of the peasantry . . .

Pokrovskii talks about the struggle of merchant capital against industrial capital and leaves completely out of consideration the mass actions of peasants, town-settlement people, and oppressed nationalities.[56]

Pokrovskii, unfortunately, took a one-sided, totally negative view of Peter I. He regarded the Petrine reform as leading to bankruptcy in every respect, economic, military, cultural, even in terms of foreign policy. In

[52] B. B. Kafengauz, "Reformy Petra I v otsenke M. N. Pokrovskogo," *Protiv anti-marksistskoi kontseptsii M. N. Pokrovskogo. Sbornik statei*, Part 2 (Moscow and Leningrad, 1940), 140–176.
[53] *Ibid.*, 140.
[54] *Ibid.*, 141.
[55] *Ibid.*, 154.
[56] *Ibid.*, 165–166.

contrast to all other historians, with the exception of Miliukov, he failed to notice the positive and lasting results of Petrine activity. He treated the person of the reformer, too, in the same one-sided and distorted manner. In actuality:

Peter I had a more complex nature than Pokrovskii thought. Undeniable gifts were combined in him with rude traits, which astonish the investigator. For the historian, it is most important to elucidate the fact that Peter managed to put his gifts, will power, and energy into the historical cause, at the head of which he stood. "Marxism does not at all deny the role of outstanding individuals," says comrade Stalin in his discussion with the German writer Emil Ludwig, "or the fact that people make history. In Marx, in his *Poverty of Philosophy,* and in other works, you can find words to the effect that it is precisely people who make history. But, of course, people make history not as some fantasy might suggest it to them, not in any way that may come into their heads. Each generation encounters certain definite conditions, already present in full when that generation arises. And great individuals are worth something only to the extent that they can understand correctly those conditions, can understand how they can be changed. . . ." Peter I was precisely that kind of protagonist. Engels calls him "a truly great man." Contemporaries and researchers noted in Peter the qualities of a lawgiver, of a worker in his study, of a military commander. Military historians, as they evaluate highly Peter's strategic talents, note his personal role in the Grodno operation, where the Russian army was led out of a trap, and especially in the preparation and conduct of the battle of Poltava. In "the diary of military events" at Poltava there have been preserved striking recollections of Peter's speeches before his commanders on the eve of the battle of Poltava, where Peter explained the political aims of the war.[57]

Kafengauz must be listed among the true Petrine scholars, for very much of his historical work centered on the period and the reign. His contributions to the subject included a massive volume on the economy of the Demidovs in the eighteenth and nineteenth centuries (*Istoriia khoziastva Demidovykh v XVIII–XIX vv.*); shorter treatments of such topics as Petrine foreign policy (*Vneshniaia politika Rossii pri Petre I*) or, more specifically, the Northern War and the Treaty of Nystad (*Severnaia Voina i Nishtadtskii mir, 1700–1721*); much editorial work, ranging from the standard edition of Pososhkov's *Book about Poverty and Wealth* (Kafengauz also wrote a monograph on Pososhkov) to the reformer's own *Letters and Papers,* when their publication was finally resumed; a whole series of historiographical essays; and a variety of articles and reviews. The historian was proud of his favorite subject. As he stated at the end of his survey of "The Epoch of Peter the Great in the Light of Soviet Historical Science," published in a joint volume in 1947:

That progressive epoch and its study evoke the legitimate feeling of Soviet patriotism. The last word about Peter the Great and his reforms has not yet been said; there lies before our historians a wide way for further work. In this area,

[57] *Ibid.,* 173–174.

Soviet historical science reminds one of a magnificent building being built, still surrounded by the scaffolding, with the work going ahead full speed.[58]

Kafengauz presented a summary account of the entire Petrine reign in a slim volume written as a high school history textbook and published in 1948 under the title *Peter I and His Time (Petr I i ego vremia)*. The second, reworked, edition, which came out in 1955, carried significantly the title *Russia at the Time of Peter the First (Rossiia pri Petre Pervom)*. In teaching the Petrine period to high school students, the author offered a fully sympathetic chapter on "popular rebellions," and he indicated clearly that "the Russia of that time was a state of landlords and merchants,"[59] resulting, for example, in government support of the upper, not the lower, classes in the Ukraine. But the bulk of the book was taken up by a highly favorable presentation of Petrine policies, very much including war and diplomacy. Kafengauz emphasized the historically Russian nature of much of the crucial territory that Peter I had won from the Swedes and, on the other hand, both the friendly attitude of and the advantages to non-Russian peoples, such as the population of the Baltic area, who then joined the Russian empire. Euphemisms included a curious reference to the monarch "being away on a trip" *("byl v otezde")*[60] at the precise hour of the Narva debacle, an unusual description of his timely and hasty departure from Narva. The story of Alexis was carefully delineated in a large section of ten pages, with the verdict entirely in the first emperor's favor. "The investigation demonstrated that Alexis occupied the central position in a circle of disaffected individuals, who were dreaming of coming to power with the help of rebelling troops."[61] Indeed:

Tsarevich Alexis served as the banner of reactionary circles; toward him tended a part of the nobility and of the clergy, dissatisfied with the reforms. A transfer of power to Alexis and his adherents threatened to liquidate everything that had already been attained by hard labor, war, and blood. It was necessary to destroy that reactionary nest.[62]

Professor Kafengauz's treatment of the Petrine period and, in particular, his presentation of it to high school students may be usefully compared to Professor G. A. Novitskii's lectures on the subject, delivered at

[58] B. B. Kafengauz, "Epokha Petra Velikogo v osveshchenii sovetskoi istoricheskoi nauki," ed. A. I. Andreev, *Petr Velikii. Sbornik statei* (Moscow and Leningrad, 1947), 334–389, quoted from p. 389. For a bibliography of Kafengauz's publications, see "Spisok trudov B. B. Kafengauza i retsenzii na nikh," *Absoliutizm v Rossi (XVII-XVIII vv.)* (Moscow, 1964), 508–518. The joint volume marked Kafengauz's seventieth birthday and his "forty-fifth anniversary of scholarly and pedagogical activity."

[59] B. B. Kafengauz, *Rossiia pri Petre pervom* (Moscow, 1955), 126.

[60] *Ibid.*, 92.

[61] *Ibid.*, 142.

[62] *Ibid.*, 143.

the Higher Party School attached to the Central Committee of the Party in 1940.[63] Adhering to the same fundamental image, Novitskii, like Kafengauz, emphasized both the positive and the negative, but more sharply and in different proportion. Peter I's reforms, Novitskii stated, did play "a large progressive role in the strengthening of the Russian national state."[64] The Petrine effort was necessitated by the comparative economic and cultural backwardness of Russia, conditioned largely by its isolation. Hence the desperate importance of the struggle for the Baltic. Failure, even delay "threatened Russia with the danger of becoming a colony or semicolony of one of the more powerful Western European states."[65] Marx had a full understanding of the situation and commented perspicaciously on Petrine foreign policy, including the founding of St. Petersburg early in the Great Northern War, in a location that became truly secure only with the acquisition of Finland in 1809. Other Petrine policies also had their rationale. As in the case of Kafengauz, Novitskii stressed the development of industry, most notably metallurgy: ". . . Petrine industry, in particular metallurgy, was not at all an artificial implantation of Peter I, but possessed, because of the preceding evolution of the country, all basic prerequisites for its emergence."[66]

However, neither Peter I's promotion of industry nor the sponsorship of trade, to which the monarch assigned enormous importance, could, or was meant to, change the essentially gentry nature of the Petrine state. Characteristically, merchants were not allowed to own serfs, but only to operate state factories to which "possessional" peasants were attached. Peter I lavishly granted lands and peasants to the gentry, thus creating some 350,000 new serfs—apparently not even counting their children—in the course of the reign. As to the peasants in general:

The strengthening of the class positions of the gentry and the merchants was obtained at the expense of the peasantry. Throughout his entire reign Peter I conducted a merciless policy of increasing the weight of serfdom. Because of the uninterrupted augmentation of taxes and of all possible kinds of obligations in the nature of work assignments in the building of canals, ports, fortresses, and other constructions, the position of the peasantry in the reign of Peter I worsened sharply. Tens of thousands of peasant economies were ruined. A large number of peasant lives perished on construction projects, especially when building Petersburg. Peasant flight became a mass phenomenon. As a result of the ruin and the flight, there was observed a diminution of taxable households. The census of 1710 discovered only 635,412 households, that is, 20% less than the number of households recorded by the census of 1678.[67]

63 Prof. G. A. Novitskii, *Obrazovaniie Rossiiskoi Imperii. Kurs istorii SSSR. Lektsii 22, 23, 24. Stenogramma lektsii, prochitannykh 21, 27 i 29 ianvaria 1940 g. Vysshaia partiinaia shkola pri TsK VKP(b)* (Irkutsk, 1947).
64 *Ibid.*, 3.
65 *Ibid.*
66 *Ibid.*, 26.
67 *Ibid.*, 31–32.

The poll tax of 1718 constituted, in the opinion of contemporaries, two and a half times the burden of all previous direct taxes that it replaced and, in addition, had to be paid for children and the incapacitated, as well as the ablebodied. Appropriately, the new census takers were accompanied by executioners with knouts and gallows. Stalin had every reason to say that the Petrine reforms were purchased by flaying the peasants thrice! The army itself was no different from the rest of the system:

Peter I's army bore the character of a serf society: soldiers' service was lifelong, cruel punishments formed the foundation of military discipline, draftees were branded, soldiers were poorly fed, soldiers' escapes were a chronic phenomenon, only the gravely wounded were given leave.[68]

Native peoples were similarly exploited, and the exploitation increased greatly in the Petrine reign. In the Volga and Ural areas, taxation reform meant a fivefold increase in taxes imposed on the natives, not to mention the extremely burdensome obligation to work in the lumber industry; special exactions even came to include taxes on black and gray eyes; heavy and effective pressure was applied to baptize the natives. The resulting uprisings of the Bashkirs "were a striking expression of the struggle of the oppressed nationalities of the Russian empire against tsarist colonial oppression."[69]

The Petrine reforms and reign received different evaluations in the course of almost 250 years of Russian historiography and intellectual debate. And the author paid some attention to the various opinions. Yet for the correct and encompassing estimate, one had to turn to the words of Comrade Stalin—largely reproduced in the epigraph to this chapter—who stressed sharply both the positive aspect of securing and strengthening the Russian state and the negative one of an increasing and horrendous class exploitation, together with the ultimate inability of tsarist Russia to solve the problem of backwardness. As to Peter the Great himself, to whom very little attention was paid in the lectures, Novitskii, in effect, followed Rozhkov in what became the standard interpretation in Soviet historiography: the monarch possessed remarkable capacities and qualities, such as energy, an extraordinary perspicacity in recognizing the importance of science and education, and, again, in selecting assistants, an ability to work tremendously hard and to participate in everything, but he combined these positive traits "with the rudest habits and ways of a Russian landlord-serfowner."[70]

There were many variants of the bipolar interpretation and image. Professor Vladimir Vasilievich Mavrodin (1908–    ), a longtime teacher and active academic at the University of Leningrad and a specialist on the emergence of the Russian state in the ninth century and on several

68 *Ibid.,* 36.
69 *Ibid.,* 43.
70 *Ibid.,* 51.

other major historical subjects, has not been a dedicated and original Petrine scholar like Bogoslovskii or Kafengauz. He has contributed, nevertheless, a whole series of Petrine pieces, usually of a summary nature, some of which have received very wide currency. Most prominent among them is the book *Peter the First (Petr Pervyi)*, published, in different versions, by the state, Komsomol, and military presses in 1945, 1948, and 1949 respectively.

*Peter the First* began with a long, essentially introductory part, which emphasized such points as the grievous burden of the Mongol invasions and yoke, the determined Russian effort, especially in the seventeenth century, to make up for lost time, and also the old Russian presence and cultural leadership in the Baltic area, "where the Prince of Polotsk was considered the supreme ruler of all the lands along the Dvina up to the sea,"[71] where Russians introduced Christianity and promoted trade, but were careful not to force themselves upon the natives or to oppress them in any manner. Peter I threw his great abilities and celebrated energy into the continuation of the Russian historical task. Mavrodin's Peter, in contrast to the usual Marxist depiction, was in command and control of every situation and did almost all important things himself. In connection with the Great Northern War, the historian even provided one more contrasting estimate of the two chief contenders: "Charles, compared to Peter, was a commonplace commander although not without his virtues; Peter was an outstanding tactician and strategist. Charles was a military commander; Peter—a statesman. Charles would win battles; Peter—wars. Peter did not immediately gain success, but he gained it securely."[72] The heavy costs, too, often had their justification, as in the building of St. Petersburg:

It was not easy to build an enormous city amid forests and swamps in the severe northern climate. Thousands of peasants and "working people," cossacks and convicts, laboring in unheard-of hard conditions, felled forests, drained swamps, dug canals, laid avenues, erected houses and factories. The new capital of the Russian land cost the lives of many laborers. But its growth and development were the growth and development of Russia herself.[73]

And yet, the other, negative, side was always present. Mavrodin explained:

The creation of a centralized government apparatus, of a regular army and navy, had positive significance. It helped to defend the territory of the national Russian state and guarantee the independent existence of the Russian people.

71 V. Mavrodin, *Petr Pervyi* (Leningrad, 1948), 144. All my future references will be also to this, by far the fullest, version of the book. For a different brief summary, see, e.g., V. V. Mavrodin, *Petr I i preobrazovanie Rossii v pervoi chetverti XVIII veka* (Leningrad, 1954).

72 Mavrodin, *Petr Pervyi*, 201.

73 *Ibid.*, 260. Cf. V. Mavrodin, *Osnovanie Peterburga* (Leningrad, 1978).

But, together with that, Peter's state was a state based on serfdom. It kept the people in a condition of oppression and ignorance.[74]

Or, to consider that condition in somewhat greater detail:

Because of taxes and exactions, because of heavy obligations, because of the draft, the quitrent, ·and the landlords' corvée, entire regions were devastated and ruined. Peasants perished in war, died out from starvation and epidemics, passed away from impossible work in the building of roads and canals, in the construction of towns and fortresses, in mines, in factories. Many abandoned native places and escaped by flight. In 1719, in the Orel province, there were 60,223 registered souls; by 1726, 55,845 remained. In the Vologda province, in 1719, there were 86,229 souls; by 1726, 63,180 remained.

They left for the land of the Bashkirs, for the Don, for the Ural river, for the north.

The Russian empire, created by the labor and the sweat of the people, fell as a frightful burden upon its shoulders.[75]

The first emperor's personal qualities and achievements also obviously had their limitations, for, as the always correct Stalin put it, Peter the Great was to Lenin what a drop of water was to an ocean.

The relationship between Russia and the West has almost invariably been both a central and a particularly difficult issue in Petrine studies, but the approach to it in the late Stalinist years was, to say the least, extraordinary; and that approach found full expression in Mavrodin's volume. Its reader is instructed that Russia, overcoming its isolation of the Mongol period, had been developing relations with Europe long before Peter I: Russia acquired knowledge whereas the West, in turn, profited from "the experience of the Russian people and Russian 'book learning' (*knizhnost*)."[76] Moreover:

The seventeenth century was the time when Russia established continuous intercourse with Western Europe, arranged closer-than-before commercial and diplomatic ties with it, utilized its technology and science, was receptive to its culture and its enlightenment. But that was, precisely, intercourse and not influence, and it is impossible to speak of any kind of imitation.[77]

In that setting, Mavrodin's judgment of the first emperor was ambivalent, not to say contradictory. On the one hand, the historian stressed Peter's patriotism and his determination that Russia be independent of the West. Thus, leaving on his celebrated first journey abroad:

Peter went to learn, not at all to receive a new upbringing (*uchitsia, no otniud ne vospityvatsia*); he went to borrow European knowledge and techniques, but only in order that Russia could thereafter develop on its own, independently of Europeans, in all aspects of its industrial, state, and spiritual activity. And on a

[74] Mavrodin, *Petr Pervyi*, 297.
[75] *Ibid.*, 285.
[76] *Ibid.*, 61.
[77] *Ibid.*, 65.

certain occasion, already much later, Peter said: "From now on, may everything in Russia be Russian."[78]

Still, on the other hand: "Exasperated by Moscow, he [Peter] turned to face the foreign German Suburb, deciding time and again too precipitously the argument between the West and Russia in favor of the former, borrowing from the West too indiscriminately, together with the useful, that which was not needed in Russia."[79] And:

From the time of Peter originates that very "obsession with the foreign" (*chuzhebesie*), that worship of everything "from another land," "from beyond the sea," which was received so ironically by the Russian people (about which, as we shall see below, Russian folk creations speak), which ensconced itself so deeply among the Russian nobility, and against which a true son of Slavdom, Iurii Križanić, fought so much in the reign of the Quiet One [Tsar Alexis].

It was this, precisely, that led to the fact that all that was one's own, Russian, appeared crude, "barbarian," "base" whereas everything from "beyond the sea" was looked at with adoration. People treated with revulsion their native language, and they replaced their remarkable, rich, and beautiful Russian speech with "babbling," first Dutch-German, later French; and they allowed incoming foreigners, of doubtful antecedents and with shady biographies, both from "beyond the sea" and their own, "truly-Russian" as they called themselves, German descendants of the Baltic barons, to climb on the back of the common people.[80]

Later historians made matters worse by constantly emphasizing the foreign assistants of Peter I and forgetting the Russian ones, of whom Mavrodin supplied a ready list. By contrast with that fixation on Western Europe, our author noted that even in regard to the new navy: "It is interesting to record that Peter was helped in the creation of the galley fleet not by English and Dutch seamen in Russian service, but by Dalmatian officers, who were Slavs and Greeks."[81]

Whereas Kafengauz, Mavrodin, and a few others tried, in the days of Stalin, to cover the reformer and the reformer's reign single-handedly, a many-sided treatment of the Petrine theme was also offered by a collection of articles edited by Professor A. I. Andreev and published in 1947. Its very title, *Peter the Great,* rather than the usual Soviet "Peter I," attested to the significance of its subject.[82]

*Peter the Great* contained ten contributions. The editor, Andreev, wrote on "Peter the Great in England in 1698," on "The Founding of the Academy of Sciences in Petersburg," and "In Memory of Ivan Afanasievich Bychkov." Related to the first topic, N. A. Baklanova presented

78 *Ibid.,* 102. This probably apocryphal, although not necessarily inappropriate, statement, ascribed to Peter the Great, is usually supposed to refer to some later date in Russian history after the reformer's own reign.

79 *Ibid.,* 78.

80 *Ibid.,* 345. It is not clear how something originating in the reign of Peter the Great could already be bitterly opposed in the reign of Tsar Alexis.

81 *Ibid.,* 367.

82 See the full reference to *Petr Velikii. Sbornik statei* in note 58 earlier.

"The Great Embassy Abroad in 1697–1698 (Its Life and Manners according to the Income-Expense Accounts of the Embassy)." There were two military-diplomatic, and two economic, pieces: the first two consisted of T. K. Krylova's "The Victory of Poltava and Russian Diplomacy" and P. P. Epifanov's "Peter the Great's Military Statutes"; the second, of E. I. Zaozerskaia's "Commerce and Enterprises of the *Gostinaia* Guild (*sotnia*) in the Middle Volga Area at the Turn from the Seventeenth to the Eighteenth Centuries," and V. G. Geiman's "The Petersburg Manufacturing Industry in Peter's Time." Substantive studies of the period were followed by historiographical essays, Kafengauz's already mentioned "The Epoch of Peter the Great in the Light of Soviet Historical Science," and S. A. Feigina's "Foreign Literature About Peter the Great in the Last Quarter of a Century." Rich in interesting material, the volume covered especially—it will be noticed—"positive" aspects of the Petrine phenomenon, and it contained predictable judgments. Krylova praised in a florid language the great successes of Russian diplomacy:

Basing himself on the rising Russian nation [with a reference to Marx and Engels to support that point], skillfully utilizing international contradictions, the daring pilot, assisted by hundreds and thousands of people devoted to him, confidently led the ship of Russia and the Northern Alliance toward the goal he had set—the destruction of the Swedish domination in the Baltic area, the domination that had deprived the neighbors of Sweden of the possibility of a normal economic and political growth.[83]

Epifanov stressed that Petrine military statutes were generally undervalued and insufficiently studied, that, in particular, the emphasis had been on an alleged wholesale borrowing from abroad instead of a proper appreciation of the role of the Russian military practice in the formulation of these statutes, and that the Petrine statutes led directly to Suvorov and the Red Army. Baklanova dealt as follows with the perilous problem of the Petrine relationship with the West, which in her piece could hardly be avoided:

We have seen that, finding itself in the West, the embassy quickly adopted the external traits of the Western European way of life: the dress, the equipage, even details of table manners. It utilized also the achievements of the West in the domain of spiritual culture. But the reception of elements of a foreign culture did not devalue in the eyes of the embassy its own cultural heritage, which was connected to national self-consciousness. The embassy remembered its motherland and, while abroad, retained traits of its own way of life. This was reflected in the internal setting of the domicile, in the habits, and especially in celebrating one's own holidays, both those connected with religious rituals and those evoked by the news of victories scored against the enemies.

These facts testify that the reception of elements of Western European life was not blind imitation, that they were subjected to a serious internal evaluation and

[83] *Petr Velikii. Sbornik statei,* 166.

reworking on the basis of one's own culture. That critical attitude towards the West found a fine expression in the evaluation, given by Peter in one of his first letters to Moscow from abroad, of the facade of Western European culture, the negative traits of which he encountered in Riga: "The trading people here walk in mantles and appear extremely honest, but with our coachmen, when it came to selling a sled, for a kopeck . . . they shout and swear, and they sell for three times the proper price."[84]

Zaozerskaia's and Geiman's economic studies, as well as Andreev's own pieces, however, stayed very close to their rich facts and made no explicit contribution to the current image of Peter the Great.

Andreev's third item, the last one in the volume, served also to demonstrate pointedly, although in its own special way, the connection between past and present Petrine scholarship. It was a touching tribute to Ivan Afanasievich Bychkov, son of a distinguished archivist, scholar, and member of the Academy of Sciences Afanasii Fedorovich Bychkov (1818–1899), who had been foremost in the work with Petrine sources, including the publication of the first seven volumes of the monarch's *Letters and Papers*. The son labored with his father and continued the father's labor after his death, becoming "without doubt, the best specialist on the sources of the epoch of Peter the Great."[85] From 1881 until his death in 1944 at the age of eighty-five, sixty-three years later, he served in the priceless manuscript department of the St. Petersburg-Petrograd-Leningrad Public Library. (His father was put in charge of that department in 1844, moving to the assistant directorship of the entire library in 1868 and to the directorship in 1882—together father and son were associated with the manuscript department and the library for exactly 100 years.) Andreev closed the article and the volume with Kliuchevskii's great praise of A. F. Bychkov on a jubilee occasion, readdressed by Andreev to his son.

*Peter the Great* was not received favorably. It had the misfortune to come out when the demands on Soviet intellectuals had become even more exacting, and it was treated as ideologically incorrect and especially as an example of base servility to the West. To quote from *Voprosy Istorii,* describing a public conference called to criticize the work of the Institute of the Academy of Sciences (October 15–18, 1948):

In the discussion that developed, individual members of the Institute made an effort to reduce the consideration of the issues raised to a formal admission of the mistakes that they had allowed; however, that effort met with a firm rebuff on the part of the majority of those in attendance. No one could be satisfied with the explanations adduced by Prof. Andreev in regard to his thoroughly false, antiscientific, and politically noxious article "The Journey of Peter the Great to England" [*sic*], published in the symposium *Peter the Great.* Kowtowing before the West led the author of this article to the conclusion that all state reforms of Peter the Great were borrowed by him from England. A. I. Andreev

84 *Ibid.,* 62. The break is Baklanova's.
85 *Ibid.,* 432.

tried to justify his incorrect and noxious position in this question by the fact that he was writing his article still in 1942, for Newton's jubilee. At that time it had seemed to him appropriate to push forward the role of England in Peter the Great's reforming activity. Were he to write that article at present, A. I. Andreev asserted, he certainly would not have permitted the mistake for which he is now being reproached. The reference to circumstances of a conjunctural character, which allegedly influenced his scholarly conclusions, reveals the unsteadiness of the author's ideological positions. To this moment A. I. Andreev has not understood or does not want to understand what is the essence of his mistakes, and he limits himself to a formal admission of them.[86]

Feigina's pedestrian classification and brief summary of Western literature on Peter the Great fared no better than Andreev's scholarly factual article (which, incidentally, did not touch at all most of the first emperor's "state reforms"):

Equally unsatisfactory was the "repentant" speech of S. A. Feigina, who had published in the same symposium *Peter the Great,* an article representing a collection of slanderous statements by bourgeois authors, including even Fascists, concerning the Petrine epoch and the Russian people in general. S. S. Feigina explained her lack of discrimination in stringing quotations by the fact that she had meant her article to be a reference aid, prepared for a small group of scholars-specialists. Such an explanation can not, of course, be taken seriously. It is appropriate to ask S. A. Feigina, why does she assume that scholars-specialists had to be interested precisely in the false, slanderous inventions of our enemies. Only a complete methodological helplessness, the lack of the party spirit *(partiinost)* could give birth to such, pardon the expression, "positions" in the author's scholarly work.[87]

Whereas *Peter the Great* reflected well the condition of contemporary Soviet Petrine studies and whereas the criticism that followed its appearance expressed tellingly some of the problems of Soviet historiography at the time, it is noteworthy that the volume did not at all clash with the established bipolar image of Peter the Great. The treatment of the first emperor and his policies, either highly favorable or at least neutral, could be very largely explained by the selection of topics. For the bipolar image, though it prescribed both an extreme positive and an extreme negative emphasis for the total evaluation, permitted, indeed required, a one-sided presentation of many issues. This, to repeat, referred not only to particular articles on specific topics, but to whole vast areas of Petrine research.

One overwhelmingly positive, pro-Petrine, domain was military and naval history, to which a number of scholars applied themselves in the days of Stalin. Building on the works of their prerevolutionary predeces-

86 Z. Mosina, "O rabote Instituta istorii Akademii nauk SSSR," *Voprosy Istorii,* no. 11 (November 1948), 144–149, quoted from p. 144. For other examples of the criticism of *Peter the Great,* see the review by G. Anpilogov in *Voprosy Istorii* (April 1948), no. 4, 120-134; and A. Krotov, "Primirenchestvo i samouspokoennost," *Literaturnaia gazeta,* no. 72 (2455) (September 8, 1948), 2.
87 Mosina, "O rabote Instituta istorii," 144–145.

sors, and, of course, on the Petrine record itself, they proceeded to find ever greater accomplishments and achievements of the emperor, ever brighter glory for Russia. As Professor K. V. Bazilevich explained in an article entitled "Peter I—Founder of Russian Military Art":

Peter I's activity as a military reformer and a military commander played the largest role in the strengthening of the military might of Russia and in the creation of Russian military art. At the time of Peter the Great the Russian army and navy achieved, in less than a quarter of a century, results, to attain which many of the most advanced countries of Western Europe needed decades and centuries. The war against Sweden, which brought glory to Russian arms, propelled the Russian army into the ranks of first-class European armies. Peter laid the foundations of Russian military art that determined its further development at the time of Rumiantsev, Suvorov, Kutuzov.[88]

Overcoming early defeats and establishing an essentially Russian system of military conscription, Peter the Great managed to create a modern Russian army and a first-class navy, which he led personally to decisive victories, including the epoch-making battle of Poltava. In the process, he introduced many important tactical and strategic innovations.

Peter introduced a series of new tactical means and methods, unknown or insufficiently widespread in contemporary foreign armies. These include establishment of close coordination among different branches of the army (infantry, artillery, and cavalry), separate positioning of the reserves, deepening of the linear order of battle, strengthening of the flanks with the help of the cavalry and the grenadiers, distribution of units in a battle order so arranged that they could offer timely assistance to one another, the use of new forms of field fortifications, utilization of maneuvering on the field of battle, counteracting the enemy and seizing the initiative.[89]

Bazilevich also noted the use of the bayonet, as well as the saber and the broadsword, as an offensive weapon, not merely a defensive one to meet an enemy charge; the flexible utilization of opportunities and, in general, improvisation as against routine; and still other tactical achievements of Peter the Great. As to strategy, the first emperor, who read very widely in military history and liked Julius Caesar best, typically preferred a carefully prepared offensive aimed at the complete destruction of his opponent, not at simply winning the field of battle, which was common at the time.

Peter's military art, though essentially original and independent, was at the same time profoundly national, Russian. Peter knew well the characteristics of the Russians, formed by history: love for the motherland, endurance, firmness, patience, courage. Without these characteristics it would have been impossible

88 K. Bazilevich, "Petr I—osnovopolozhnik russkogo voennogo iskusstva," *Bolshevik*, nos. 11–12 (June 1945), 35–48, 35. See also Prof. K. Bazilevich, "Petr Velikii," *Bolshevik*, no. 17 (September 1943), 49–64; and K. Bazilevich, "Petr I kak polkovodets," *Russkoe voenno-morskoe iskusstvo* (Moscow 1951), 40–46.
89 Bazilevich, "Petr I—osnovopolozhnik russkogo voennogo iskusstva," 47.

to overcome the enormous difficulties that faced the Russian army at the beginning of the war against the Swedes. Peter counted on these characteristics as he strove to translate into practice the principles of strategy and tactics that he had advanced, principles permeated with the energy of the offensive. In his system of military education, Peter did not limit himself to utilizing the historically formed traits of the Russian warrior, but tried to develop them in accord with military demands.[90]

Another authority, Colonel of the Guards E. I. Porfiriev, emphasized especially Peter I's penetrating recognition of the importance of the battle itself as contrasted to mere successful maneuvering so popular at the time and his unique and tremendous achievement in combined operations, that is, in coordinating the activities of naval and land forces.[91] As already indicated, the monarch's organizational abilities and achievements were considered equal to his military talents and activities proper, and they too received unstinting praise:

Peter was the founder of the national Russian regular army. With the foresight of a genius, Peter knew how to select and adopt the useful and the progressive, how to throw away the useless.

By creating a regular army, Peter the Great erected an eternal monument to himself in the history of the Russian state.

Peter conducted the grandiose reorganization of the armed forces of Russia as a wise and clear-sighted statesman. In the conditions of the burdensome Northern War, in the conditions of the backwardness of the Russian state, Peter the Great successfully solved that historical problem.[92]

Even more marginal and controversial Petrine military enterprises produced bountiful positive results. Thus, V. P. Lystsov, the author of a book entitled *Peter I's Persian Campaign 1722–1723,* concluded that, although the Russian territorial gains on the Caspian Sea had soon to be abandoned, the war served a good purpose or rather purposes: it secured the safety of the southeastern Russian border; it stimulated the liberation movement of Transcaucasian peoples, and strengthened the links between Russia, on the one hand, and Georgia and Armenia, on the other; and it helped Persia to maintain its independence against Turkey.[93]

90 *Ibid.,* 48.

91 Gvardii polkovnik E. I. Porfiriev, *Petr I—osnovopolozhnik voennogo iskusstva russkoi reguliarnoi armii i flota* (Moscow, 1952).

92 P. Epifanov, "K voprosu o voennoi reforme Petra Velikogo," *Voprosy Istorii,* no. 1 (1945), 33–58, quoted from p. 58.

93 V. P. Lystsov, *Persidskii pokhod Petra, I, 1722–1723* (n.p., 1951), 243.

Even though the broad field of military endeavor was certainly treated most positively by Soviet post-Pokrovskii Petrine scholars, the negative pole of the Petrine image was never really very far away. Typically, Colonel B. S. Telpukhovskii ended his book entitled *The Northern War,* representative of the genre, with the well-known quote from Stalin to the effect that neither the feudal aristocracy nor the bourgeoisie could liquidate Russian backwardness, and a reminder that that could be accomplished only by the party of Lenin-Stalin after the victory of the socialist October Revolution (Polkovnik B. S. Telpukhovskii, *Severnaia voina, 1700–1721. Polkovodcheskaia deiatelnost*

Petrine foreign policy could not be separated from military history, and it also received, as we have already seen, full endorsement. Whether dealing with war and diplomacy equally, as in a popular small book entitled *The Russian Navy and Peter I's Foreign Policy* by a leading Russian and Soviet historian of Europe, Eugene Tarle,[94] or concentrating on foreign relations proper, as in L. A. Nikiforov's volume on *Russian-English Relations at the Time of Peter I*,[95] scholars stressed the first emperor's great skill and success, especially in establishing Russia, against heavy odds, on the Baltic.

Political reforms and administration were more complicated. Positive in the main, they contained major negative aspects. Soviet scholars praised centralization and a certain modernization, a stronger and more effective government. They frequently noted, however, that some of the reforms proved to be extremely oppressive and that they were aimed against the popular masses. The new provincial administration had as one of its main purposes to keep the population down, and the same was even more strikingly true of the overall police arrangements and practices. As a Petrine specialist, V. I. Lebedev, tried to draw the balance at the end of his rather grim summary account of "Peter I's Administrative Reforms":

Peter I's reforms, including the administrative ones, did not constitute a sudden overturn. They were dictated by the growth of the state in the seventeenth century. Increasing the power of the dominant class, the gentry, and assisting the merchants, Peter I enserfed still more the peasantry and promoted the pillaging of oppressed nationalities.

Peter I fought with "barbarian means" the lack of culture of the Russian landlords and merchants. "Peter hastened the adoption of Western ways by barbarian Russia, not refraining from barbarian means to fight barbarism" [Lenin].

At the same time, the progressive character of the Petrine reforms in general and of the administrative reforms in particular is beyond doubt.[96]

---

*Petra I* [Moscow, 1946], 180). More important, the established Soviet view treated very negatively social relations and conditions in the Petrine army in spite of occasional efforts by Bazilevich and others to depict its moral virtues or its consideration for the individual soldier. For the dominant view, see Novitskii and Mavrodin earlier or N. B. Golikova later.

94 E. V. Tarle, *Russkii flot i vneshniaia politika Petra I* (Moscow, 1949).

95 L. A. Nikiforov, *Russko-angliiskie otnosheniia pri Petre I* (Moscow, 1950).

96 V. Lebedev, "Administrativnye reformy Petra I," *Borba Klassov* no. 12 (December 1936), 109–116, quoted from p. 116. Other Petrine works by Vladimir Ivanovich Lebedev (1894–1966) included *Bulavinskoe vosstanie (1707–1708)* (Moscow, 1934), expanded version (Moscow, 1967); "Bashkirskie vosstaniia 1705–1711 gg.," *Istoricheskie Zapiski*, no. 1 (1937), 81–102; *Istoriia SSSR do XIX veka. Lektsii, chitannye na Istoricheskom fakultete MGU. (V szhatom izlozhenii)* (Moscow, 1939), a substantially different version (Moscow, 1945); "Astrakhanskoe vosstanie 1705–1706 gg. (Po pytochnym recham povstantsev v Preobrazhenskom prikaze)," *Uchenye zapiski Moskovskogo gosudarstvennogo pedagogicheskogo instituta imeni V. P. Potemkina* (1941), Vol. II, Part (Vypusk) 1, 3–32; editor, *Reformy Petra I: Sbornik dokumentov* (Moscow, 1937). Cf. G. Anpilogov, "Senat pri Petre I," *Istoricheskii Zhurnal*, no. 4 (1941), 40–49.

The crucial economic and socioeconomic aspects of the Petrine reign and activity created still greater difficulties. It was in that area that such desirable policies as industrialization and the development of natural resources clashed with the oppressive, and indeed "feudal" to use the Soviet terminology, nature of the regime conducting them. The contradictory handling of the resulting situation can be seen strikingly in E. V. Spiridonova's *Peter I's Economic Policy and Views*.[97] Published in 1952, the book also reflected the extreme "antiforeignism" of the period, the mentality we have already encountered when considering the criticism of Andreev's symposium.

After a denunciation of the worship of the West and the denigration of native creativity and achievement, allegedly characteristic of all past treatment of Russian economic history and thought, including notably recent Soviet works, the author turned to the reformer himself:

Peter I is not only one of the major statesmen of Russia at the end of the seventeenth and the beginning of the eighteenth centuries, but also one of the most outstanding economists of his epoch. . . . In the realization of that attempt ["to jump out of the framework of backwardness," Stalin] Peter showed himself as an independent economic statesman and thinker, who played a large role in establishing the lines of development for the Russian state and for Russian economic thought.

Peter I did not leave behind any theoretical works, and his economic views can be traced mainly on the basis of an analysis of his economic policy, his practical activity.[98]

Incorrectly, that policy has usually been interpreted simply in terms of mercantilism, at best of a mercantilism more interested in trade itself than in the acquisition of specie, whereas the actual historical problem, boldly faced by progressive Russian statesmen and economists, was that of preserving the independence of Russia, threatened because of the backwardness of the country. "The economic program advanced by Ordyn-Nashchokin constitutes, so to speak, a prototype of Peter I's economic program."[99] Thus:

It follows that Peter never identified the concept of riches with money. The wealth of a country depended, in the understanding of Peter, on its economic condition and, in the first place, on its industrial development, on the presence of factories and plants, of different "skilled crafts." Peter considered that the source of the wealth of a country resided in the socially useful activity of the people, in their productive labor in the areas of industrial, craft, agricultural, commercial activity.[100]

[97] E. V. Spiridonova, *Ekonomicheskaia politika i ekonomicheskie vzgliady Petra I* (Moscow, 1952).
[98] *Ibid.*, 6.
[99] *Ibid.*, 60.
[100] *Ibid.*, 67.

Hence he promoted industry, crafts, commerce, urging even that some of the members of the gentry dispossessed by his single-heir law enter these occupations. The owner of land with mineral resources had to let others develop them if he would not do so himself. "In the period from 1701 to 1725 the government issued some thirty ukases concerning the protection and planting of forests"[101] while establishing a school of forestry. The state assigned 8 to 10 percent—and occasionally even 20 percent—of the annual budget to the development of industry, a large figure considering the fact that up to 80 percent was consumed by military expenses. Peter I strove indefatigably to introduce advanced technology and to promote invention. Also, he exerted extraordinary efforts to supply Russian manufactures with raw materials and with a labor force. In that last case, however, he did not infringe on serfdom, but found additional labor in marginal social groups, ranging from paupers and convicts to members of the armed forces and Swedish prisoners of war. The monarch himself supervised the translation of relevant Western literature, as attested by his remarkable "Ukase to Those Laboring in the Translation of Books in Economics." In all his ceaseless activity, "Peter believed in the creative abilities of the Russian people, a fact that distinguished him extremely favorably from all of his successors on the Russian throne."[102] The results were impressive. As to industry, "greater results were achieved in a quarter of a century than in all previous centuries of the existence of the Russian state."[103]

But the other side of the coin was also quite real:

A recognition of Peter's progressive role in strengthening the economic condition of Russia of the beginning of the eighteenth century is fully compatible with a recognition of the fact that that progress was achieved at the expense of an extreme increase in exploitation, of a worsening of the situation of the laboring masses, at the expense of a further strengthening of serfdom. It is fully compatible with a recognition of the fact that Peter's entire policy was directed toward strengthening the positions of the dominant class of landlords-serf owners in the conditions of emerging new social relations; and, finally, it is fully compatible with a recognition of the fact that Peter, having secured certain shifts in the economic development of the country, did not solve and could not solve the problem of liquidating the general economic backwardness of Russia because that was beyond the historical possibilities of the class which Peter represented.

The historical and class limitations of Peter expressed themselves precisely in

101 *Ibid.*, 79.
102 *Ibid.*, 143.
In her determination to denounce and expose foreigners, Spiridonova asserted that those then coming to Russia "very frequently" failed to live up to their contracts and that, in particular, they were unwilling to teach their Russian pupils: "Peter even began to wonder whether they were forbidden to do so by their governments or their guild organizations" (*ibid.*, 130). The reference to the Law Code, *Polnoe Sobranie Zakonov*, which Spiridonova cites, however, mentions only guilds, not governments.
103 *Ibid.*, 146.

the fact that, understanding the necessity of reforming Russian reality, he tried to solve the pressing historical problems of the country within the narrow framework of a serfdom-feudal system, *on its foundation, on its base*. More than that, the tsar of the serf owners aimed, as a result of his reforming activity, to achieve a further spread of serf slavery, a greater strengthening and consolidation of the serf system; and in regard to that aim Peter attained more than a little success.[104]

Peter I's commercial and financial policies reflected the emperor's perspicacious understanding of the needs of the country. Typically, Peter I preferred to export products, not raw materials, rope rather than hemp, linseed oil rather than seed. Though attracting foreign merchants, he tried his best to develop a commercial class in Russia and to have it play an increasingly greater role in international trade. The monarch's desperate struggle to obtain precious metals was not at all a form of specie fetishism characteristic of many mercantilists: the purpose was not to store silver and gold, but to use them in foreign trade and even in one's own coinage, which depended on this influx for its existence. The result was again impressive:

By the end of the first quarter of the eighteenth century, exports almost doubled imports. The character of the exports and the imports changed. From a country that exported almost entirely raw materials and imported industrial products, Russia was becoming a country with a prevailing export of industrial goods. Now 52 percent of the Russian export consisted of products; and 48 percent, of raw materials. The first place among the objects of export was occupied by flaxen textiles, iron, leather, and other items of industrial production.[105]

Indeed, in contrast to other states where in the characteristic mercantilist fashion everything was made to serve trade, Peter I made trade serve a many-sided economic development and the strengthening of the country based on industry.

And yet the crushing poll tax, which, in the words of the very officials who translated it into practice, led to "an extreme and complete ruin of the peasants," as well as so many other taxes and exactions, made the costs and the distribution of the costs painfully clear:

A survey of Peter's measures carried out in the field of financial-tax policy gives a clear answer to the question at whose expense these financial successes were attained. They were attained at the expense of the most deprived masses of the multimillion enserfed peasantry and the lowest classes of the suburbs, in effect, the city poor. The class character of Peter's activity revealed itself most strikingly in his financial-tax policy.

Understanding correctly that the source of the wealth of a country, of its economic might can be found in the productive branches of the economy of the people and in the first place the principal branch at that time, argiculture,

104 *Ibid.*, 175.
105 *Ibid.*, 237.

Peter, because of his class orientation, deposited the entire burden of his reforming activity on the shoulders of the popular masses, driving them to extreme ruin and penury, all the while not only not infringing on the property interests of the dominant classes, but, on the contrary, promoting in every way the gathering of riches in the hands of the class of landlords and the emerging class of merchants.[106]

What final conclusion could one reach?

Without doubt, there lay on Peter's progressive activity the stamp of his historical and class limitations. But acting in the interest of strengthening the national state of landlords and the emerging class of merchants, Peter was together with that strengthening the economic might of the country, which fact contributed to the prevention of the danger of the Russian state's becoming a colony of Western European countries. Just that constituted the progressive role of the Petrine reforms.[107]

Although Spiridonova's book was quite representative of the treatment of Peter the Great's economic thought and policy in the years of Stalinism, high Stalinism in particular, some other approaches also found expression. The prominent economist, statistician, and economic historian Academician Stanislav Gustavovich Strumilin (1877–1974), one of the main drafters of the First Five-Year Plan, was concerned with Petrine economics in his volume on industry in the Urals at the time of Peter, in his history of Russian metallurgy, and in a number of other both general and more specialized studies out of a total of some 700 works.[108] Strumilin's criticism of Miliukov, mentioned in the preceding chapter,[109] was central to his Petrine orientation, for the economist denied any excessive burden of Petrine reforms, incorrectly postulated in his opinion by critics ignorant of economics (e.g., calculating taxes in absolute figures without regard for what percentage of the product they represented or for inflation) and otherwise deficient. Strumilin's views of Petrine economics thus stood at the positive extreme although he made it clear that these economics were not to be compared to Soviet achievements.

Whereas Strumilin frequently engaged in sweeping generalizations, most Soviet scholars of Petrine economics—as of so much else—concentrated their attention almost entirely on a detailed study of their specific topics. Usually, they were not concerned with Peter the Great as a person, and their contributions to the larger Petrine image were at best indirect and second- or thirdhand. For several decades pride of place among them belonged to the indefatigable researcher Elizaveta Ivanovna Zaozerskaia

[106] *Ibid.*, 275.
[107] *Ibid.*, 276.
[108] See S. G. Strumilin, *Gornozavodskii Ural petrovskoi epokhi* (Moscow, 1947); S. G. Strumilin, *Istoriia chernoi metallurgii v SSSR*, Vol. I (Moscow, 1954); and other works by Strumilin.
[109] See Chapter 3, note 79 earlier.

(1897–1974).[110] Although Zaozerskaia supported the established interpretations, defending the significance and lasting quality of Petrine manufacturing in one of her books[111] and presenting another as the application to concrete historical material of one of Stalin's postulates,[112] the entire weight of her scholarly work resided in a careful investigation of very substantial but little-known topics. Many other specialists performed likewise, although on a smaller scale, as they dealt with the College of Manufacturing,[113] peasant industry,[114] or "The Role of Peter the Great in the Organization of the Chemical Industry in Russia."[115]

If Petrine diplomacy and war elicited unstinting praise and if Petrine economic policy combined in a complicated manner the good and the bad, the established system was treated entirely negatively by Soviet historians when dealing with popular rebellions. A favorite Soviet theme, the Bashkir, Astrakhan, and Bulavin rebellions, as well as other evidences of mass opposition to the government, were invariably presented as glorious liberation movements against a totally oppressive system. As Lebedev declared in an early book on the Bulavin rebellion: "One must most decisively reject the Lassalean, and later Menshevik, point of view that peasant wars are reactionary. . . . The peasant wars of the seventeenth to eighteenth centuries could not defeat the Russia of feudalism and serfdom, but they shook the feudal-serf order to its foundations; they were clearing the way for the coming revolution."[116] Or as a Soviet specialist explained to me in the autumn of 1979: "We believe in the right of the people to rebel against an unjust system."[117]

Perhaps as a belated result of the victory over Pokrovskii and the firm recognition of the Petrine reign as an important part of Russian history,

---

110 Zaozerskaia made some sixty scholarly contributions, of which I found the following, in chronological order, most important for the Petrine theme: E. I. Zaozerskaia, *Manufaktura pri Petre I* (Moscow, 1947); E. Zaozerskaia, "Moskovskii posad pri Petre I," *Voprosy Istorii*, no. 9 (1947), 19–35; E. Zaozerskaia, "K voprosu o razvitii krupnoi promyshlennosti v Rossii v XVIII veke," *Voprosy Istorii*, no. 12 (1947), 62–73; E. Zaozerskaia, "K voprosu o zarozhdenii kapitalisticheskikh otnoshenii v melkoi promyshlennosti Rossii nachala XVIII veka," *Voprosy Istorii*, no. 6 (1949), 70–84; E. I. Zaozerskaia, *Razvitie legkoi promyshlennosti v Moskve v pervoi chetverti XVIII v* (Moscow, 1953); E. I. Zaozerskaia, *Rabochaia sila i klassovaia borba na tekstilnykh manufakturakh v 20–60 gg. XVIII v* (Moscow, 1960); E. I. Zaozerskaia and L. N. Pushkarev, eds., *Volneniia rabotnykh liudei i pripisnykh krestian na metallurgicheskikh zavodakh Rossii v pervoi polovine XVIII v* (Moscow, 1975). Cf. other contributions by Zaozerskaia discussed earlier and later.

111 Zaozerskaia, *Manufaktura pri Petre I*, esp. 147–149 but also *passim*.

112 Zaozerskaia, *Razvitie legkoi promyshlennosti*, 494.

113 D. Baburin, *Ocherki po istorii "Manufaktur-kollegii" (XVIII v.)* (Moscow, 1939).

114 I. D. Meshalin, ed., *Materialy po istorii krestianskoi promyshlennosti XVIII i pervoi poloviny XIX v* (2 vols., Moscow, 1935–1950).

115 Prof. P. Lukianov, "Rol Petra Velikogo v organizatsii khimicheskogo proizvodstva v Rossii," *Voprosy Istorii*, no. 6 (1947), 79–85.

116 Lebedev, *Bulavinskoe vosstanie*, 69.

117 I asked him whether he wanted Bulavin's victory or the Treaty of Nystad because the two together were out of the question. He said that he would have to think about it.

the publication of Peter the Great's *Letters and Papers* (*Pisma i bumagi imperatora Petra Velikogo*) was resumed in 1946, under the editorship of Andreev and Kafengauz. It advanced from Volume Seven, Part Two, to Volume Nine, Part Two, before Stalin's death and another three volumes since, reaching the end of A.D. 1712. Another remarkable documentary work appeared in 1945: N. A. Voskresenskii's new edition of the *Legislative Acts of Peter I*. By collating all the material available, Voskresenskii was able to trace some of the legislation through its drafts and, in general, to present a much richer view of the Petrine legislative process. But only the first of the proposed four volumes, the one dealing with higher state institutions, ever came out.[118]

It is also noteworthy that the early forties witnessed the publication of the most outstanding study of the Petrine regime since the contributions of Miliukov and Bogoslovskii, B. I. Syromiatnikov's *The "Regular" State of Peter I and Its Ideology*.[119] Boris Ivanovich Syromiatnikov (1874–1947), an able prerevolutionary historian and legal scholar who had published little,[120] presented his unexpected Petrine volume not to confirm the established interpretation, but to offer yet another Marxist solution to the Petrine problem. Where Plekhanov stressed the shift from a species of Oriental despotism to the Western course of development, where Pokrovskii emphasized the commercial bourgeoisie, and Rozhkov, as well as the subsequent dominant view, the gentry, Syromiatnikov came to the conclusion that the Petrine historical moment represented the typical third and last stage of the feudal era (following appanage division and, after that, the formation and evolution of a centralized *Standestaat*, where the estates limited the power of the ruler), the stage of absolute monarchy. Balancing the interests of the landlords against those of the rising middle class, the government acquired at that particular historical moment considerable independence and freedom of action to create a well-organized, "regular," bureaucratic state characteristic of the Enlightenment. Syromiatnikov's scheme proposed to account for both continuity

118 N. A. Voskresenskii, *Zakonodatelnye akty Petra I. Redaktsii i proekty zakonov, zametki, doklady, donosheniia, chelobitia i inostrannye istochniki*, edited and with an introduction by B. I. Syromiatnikov. Vol. I. *Akty o vysshikh gosudarstvennykh ustanovleniiakh* (Moscow and Leningrad, 1945). See Black, "The Reforms of Peter the Great," 248–251, for the circumstances of publication as well as for a very high appraisal of the work. Black makes a special point of the fact that both Voskresenskii's documentary volume and Syromiatnikov's own book on the Petrine reign—to be discussed next—were published not through the regular historical channels but by the Institute of Law of the Academy of Sciences.

119 B. I. Syromiatnikov, *"Reguliarnoe" gosudarstvo Petra Pervogo i ego ideologiia*, Part 1 (Moscow and Leningrad, 1943).

120 I am especially grateful to Professor Terence Emmons of Stanford University for supplying me with a photocopy of Syromiatnikov's valuable unknown and unpublished book "Traditsionnaia teoriia russkogo istoricheskogo razvitiia. (Istoriograficheskii ocherk)" (Moscow, 1911). The work was stopped in the last stage of publication in connection with the Kasso incident. Part of the first chapter, however, had been published as an article in 1906: B. I. Syromiatnikov, "Osnovnye momenty v razvitii istoricheskoi mysli," *Russkaia Mysl*, no. 12 (1906), 71–97.

and change in the relation of the Petrine state to the Russian past and to trace the necessarily limited but real counterimpact of the superstructure on the base as well as the impact of the base on the superstructure.

The Petrine effort was, thus, progressive, particularly in regard to ideology and culture:

Having transformed the Russian Church into "a servant of the state" (*ancilla civitatis*), in contrast to the medieval principle according to which the state was "a servant of the church" (*ancilla ecclesiae*), Peter stands before us as a typical "enlightener," as a propagandist of the joy of life ("the rehabilitation of the flesh"), an enemy of the ascetic ideal of "a life of fasting," a man opening the way to the individual's personal abilities (talent, individual initiative, merit), in contrast to the estate principle of "blood." His "notables" are people of labor, useful to state and society (in the words of one of Peter's resolutions, "distinction is to be measured according to usefulness"), and not "slothful parasites" and "drones": he who does not work, should not have bread to eat! He is a partisan of exact, especially mathematical, sciences and of "natural" sciences, and of the significance of their broad practical application; he is a persecutor and an exposer of all kinds of superstitions (miracles, "pious" deceit). He propagandizes "sociability," a social way of life; he liquidates the Muscovite *terem* [isolated quarters for women]; he organizes public festivals, carnivals, a theater accessible to all. He propagandizes and lays the foundation for the social sciences, especially history and jurisprudence, and so on and so on.[121]

To conclude:

The theory and the practice of the "enlightened" police state and *absolute monarchy* as its perfect expression: such was the ideal and the miracle-working means, with the aid of which the "happiness" of peoples and the "common good" were to be secured. That political utopia was to serve as the highest justification of absolutism . . .

He expected to realize his program and his plan of reform in twenty-five to thirty years, coming to an understanding of the futility of these hopes of his only as he was lying on his deathbed. It was not so much that he overvalued the actual condition of the country, the *backwardness* of which he saw clearly; it was rather that Peter, believing in the miracle-working power of "enlightened" coercion, tried to force the historical process, counting on surpassing, as mentioned earlier, his teachers. But no miracle occurred! If "the superstructure," ideology, does exercise a certain counteraction on the base, the fact that provides for the role of the individual in history, still, in the last analysis, that influence has definite limits set by the objective conditions of the relationships of production . . .

Peter is great precisely because he struggled for a renaissance, for an economic and cultural progress of Russia. Of course, Peter struggled with those means that the age put in his hands; but he looked far beyond, far ahead of his time. That is why he is a truly "great" historical figure and why his image still rivets to itself the attention of his distant progeny.[122]

121 Syromiatnikov, *"Reguliarnoe" gosudarstvo*, 148.
122 *Ibid.*, 151–153.

Historiography was one of Syromiatnikov's specialties, and his brilliantly written book turned largely into a resounding, at times even caricaturing, attack on almost all Petrine literature, very much including recent Soviet contributions. Unfortunately, on the constructive side, it offered an outline at best, frequently mere suggestions, of the important work to be done. And, although labeled "Part One," the volume had no sequel. Nor was Syromiatnikov's lead followed by other Soviet scholars.[123]

The dominant bipolar Petrine interpretation and image was not limited, of course, to history and economics. It was also present, for example, in literary criticism. Thus, with regard to Pushkin's treatment of the Petrine theme in general and *The Bronze Horseman* in particular—a subject discussed in an earlier chapter—Soviet specialists emphasized both the apotheosis of the great emperor by the great poet and, at the same time, Pushkin's perception of the cruelty and oppression intrinsic to the autocrat and the autocratic regime. Indeed, one could well argue that poetry made a much better case for the paradoxical dichotomy than plain historical prose![124]

Writers continued to utilize the Petrine theme in novels, stories, and plays. Even the Petrine anecdote was revived as a genre in V. B. Shklovskii's "Novellas about Peter I."[125] Most of this literature was patriotic and remarkably traditional—Professor Gasiorowska noted that E. A. Fedorov's *The Demidovs*[126] reminded her of Lazhechnikov and that D. I. Petrov's *Bulavin*,[127] with its favorable treatment of Peter the Great, "could have been written a hundred years earlier"—although it readily incorporated such new, or partly new, preferences as the emphasis on the common people and antiforeignism. The main point of Iu. P. German's *Youthful Russia,* which came out, appropriately, in 1953,[128] seemed to have been precisely this superiority of common Russian people to foreigners.

---

123 Not surprisingly, Syromiatnikov's book was received critically. See, e.g., V. Lebedev's and S. Iushkov's review in *Istoricheskii Zhurnal,* nos. 10–11 (1944), 124–131. Kafengauz noted that Syromiatnikov returned to some of Pokrovskii's theses (B. B. Kafengauz, "Epokha Petra Velikogo v osveshchenii sovetskoi istoricheskoi nauki," 378). In any case, the new interpretation was firmly rejected by Soviet mainstream historians.

124 Very many examples of this dominant Soviet approach to Pushkin and Peter the Great could be cited. To link history to literary criticism, see Kafengauz's own venture into the subject: B. B. Kafengauz, "Pushkin o Petre I," *Istoriia SSSR,* no. 3 (1961), 150–160. See also perhaps the best and the most fully integrated example of the approach: P. Mezentsev, "Poema Pushkina 'Mednyi Vsadnik' (k voprosu ob ideinom soderzhanii)," *Russkaia Literatura,* no. 2 (1958), 56–68.

125 V. Shklovskii, "Novelly o Petre I," *Tridstsat dnei,* no. 6 (1941), 25–29.

126 *Demidovy* was first published in 1941. I used the 1950 edition: Evgenii Fedorov, *Kamennyi Poias,* Book 1, *Demidovy* (Moscow and Leningrad, 1950).

127 D. Petrov-Biriuk, *Dikoe pole* (n. p., 1946). Cf. the later version: Dm. Petrov (Biriuk), *Kondrat Bulavin* (Moscow, 1970). The remarks are in Xenia Gasiorowska, *The Image of Peter the Great in Russian Fiction* (Madison, Wis., 1979), pp. 186, 188 respectively.

128 I used the 1976 edition: Iurii German, *Sobranie sochinenii.* Vol. III. *Rossiia molodaia* (Leningrad, 1976).

Yet at least one writer of that period contributed much more to the Petrine literature than mediocre retellings of essentially traditional themes. In the process, he offered a remarkable implicit commentary on his times. Aleksei Nikolaevich Tolstoi (1883–1945) began to write about Peter the Great in 1917 and continued to do so until his death in 1945. Because of the striking changes in subsequent versions of certain works, there is not even agreement as to how many Petrine pieces Tolstoi produced; a careful estimate would include three stories, three plays, two screenplays, and a long unfinished novel in three parts, published originally in *Novyi mir* in 1929–1930, 1933–1934, and 1944–1945 respectively. The novel, *Peter the First,* represented a major fundamental contribution to the Petrine theme whereas the other items had their more limited and disparate value.[129]

Alexis Tolstoi was already mentioned in a preceding section of this chapter, together with Pilniak and others, as an extreme, even vulgar, denigrator of Peter the Great in the years following the revolution of 1917 (and as being assailed, in turn, by Platonov for his efforts). That remained basically the writer's stance from the first two Petrine stories written in 1917 to the first Petrine play, which came out in the beginning of 1929. Peter I was crude, cruel, violent, isolated from his people, and indeed their enemy. His obsessive activity was not only barbarous and costly, but also fruitless. Even shades of Merezhkovskii's Antichrist— an influence Alexis Tolstoi acknowledged—appeared. Popular rebellion seemed to be the obvious response.

But the first part of the novel published later in 1929 already marked the transition to the second phase in Alexis Tolstoi's treatment of Peter the Great. It was a remarkable presentation full of realism and vitality, reminiscent at its best of the greatest Tolstoi himself. Alexis Tolstoi wrote very well about violence and even better about hunger: in his novel the reader is constantly aware of who was fed and who went hungry—a not at all inappropriate slant on the desperately hard times that the author described, as well as on some through which he lived. The brutal, negative vision of the Petrine age, thus, largely remained, but it was modified by a new belief in some virtues in the monarch and some purpose to the events. The last paragraph read:

Torture and executions continued the entire winter. In answer, rebellions would flare up in Archangel, in Astrakhan, on the Don, and in Azov. Torture chambers filled up, and the winter storms swung on the walls of Moscow thousands of new corpses. The entire country was gripped by terror. The old hid in dark

129 A. N. Tolstoi, *Polnoe sobranie sochinenii.* Vol. IX. *Petr Pervyi* (Moscow, 1946). Tolstoi's writings can be best found in the following collected works: A. N. Tolstoi, *Polnoe sobranie sochinenii* (14 vols., Moscow, 1947–1953); and, A. N. Tolstoi, *Sobranie sochinenii* (10 vols., Moscow, 1958–1961). See also the following pieces not included in the above: A. N. Tolstoi, "Petr I," *Novyi mir* (1935), no. 1, 54–80 (the second version of the Petrine play); and Tolstoi, A. N., and Petrov, V., *Petr I: kinostsenarii* (Moscow, 1935) (the first version of the Petrine screenplay).

corners. Byzantine Russia was coming to its end. In the March wind there seemed to appear beyond the Baltic coastline shadows of merchantmen.[130]

This second phase in Alexis Tolstoi's depiction of Peter the Great lasted roughly through 1935 or a little later, finding its further expression in the story "Martha Rabe" (one of the names attached to Catherine I in early life), in the second version of the author's Petrine play, renamed *Peter the First* instead of *On the Rack,* in the first screenplay, and in the second part of the huge novel. Positive elements and interpretations increased although continuously in struggle with the negative setting and factors, a situation that apparently resulted in some of the author's best writing. The change from the first to the second phase has been variously explicated. For one thing, it obviously followed the change in the Soviet intellectual scene. For example, almost as a parody of the rise and fall of Pokrovskii and his emphasis on commercial capitalism, Alexis Tolstoi paid little or no attention to merchants in the beginning, then went on to assign them prominence and a positive role, only to eliminate both once more—unfortunately he was a little late in making both adjustments and was criticized accordingly. The author's main protagonists, Peter, Catherine, Menshikov, and others, were gradually becoming solid characters, even heroes, instead of the desperate and marginal human beings of earlier versions. The tragic element correspondingly declined in favor of optimistic assertion. Social opposition and protest, one of the author's fortes, was reduced in the screenplay to a ubiquitous peasant, Fedka, representing the people in all kinds of circumstances, at the expense of one of Alexis Tolstoi's most effective tools, realism. Still, as perhaps charitable but to me convincing critics have argued, party directives did not constitute the entire story. Also important in the transformation was Alexis Tolstoi's increasing knowledge of the Petrine age, in which he became highly proficient, as well as his own changing appreciation of the reformer and his reforms in the light of contemporary Soviet history.

The third phase of Alexis Tolstoi's treatment of Peter the Great extended from the later thirties until the author's death in 1945. In fact, Alexis Tolstoi died with the novel in the year 1704, though he wanted to continue it at least to 1709 and Poltava, and as he was considering revising the first two parts, to bring them more into line with the last one. The products of the third phase included the third and last version of the Petrine play, the second and last version of the Petrine screenplay, and the third part of the Petrine novel. Of these, many remember best the splendid film, where Peter the Great rose in all his majesty, much larger than life, and which managed to retain, nevertheless, some of Alexis Tolstoi's original realism and vitality. The third part of the novel also reflected its times remarkably well. Peter the Great, once alienated from his people and later linked to them only in part, became their organizer and true leader. Popular protest disappeared entirely. It might be added that the third and last version of the play, that of 1938, had already transformed Tsarevich Alexis, at one time a poignant tragic protagonist much like Merezhkovskii's Alexis, into a conspiratorial collaborator of foreign enemies who deserved death. In the third part of the novel patriotism and antiforeignism, once absent in Alexis Tolstoi, reigned supreme. There even appeared a new emphasis on Russian cultural achievements and cultural competition with the West exemplified by such characters (unusual for the author) as Peter's sister Natalia, writing poetry and active in the theater, and a certain Sanka Brovkina, who emerged from the lower classes to become an aristocrat, compose verses, and dazzle Europe with her beauty and politesse.

Much of Alexis Tolstoi's handling of the Petrine theme indicated very well the intellectual currents of the time and the problems with the Soviet image of Peter the Great, including its difficult bipolarity.[131] Yet the end result might prove misleading, for Tolstoi's Peter became a virtually perfect hero, suggesting, by extension, a simple and total Soviet endorsement of the first emperor. But the extension is not a legitimate one. A novel could not replace formal ideology or even considered historical judgment. Besides, Alexis Tolstoi wrote his late work at the height of patriotic sentiment and a certain wartime permissiveness, both of which were shortly to be brought to order. In any case, the bipolar image of Peter the Great outlived not only the death of Alexis Tolstoi in 1945, but also that of Stalin in 1953.[132]

## 4

The presentation of the age of Peter the Great in the age of Stalin received rich, comprehensive, and, in a sense, final expression in a huge volume entitled *Russia in the First Quarter of the Eighteenth Century. Peter I's Reforms.*[133] Part of a fundamental *Survey of the History of the U.S.S.R.,* the book contained almost 800 large pages of text as well as numerous excellent illustrations, maps, indices, and other aids. Although published in 1954, that is, the year following the death of Stalin, it fully reflected the interpretations, emphases, and ways of the Stalinist period— including profuse quotations from the leader—indeed, a certain split from Stalinism together with the so-called de-Stalinization were to emerge only at the Twentieth Party Congress in 1956. Professor Boris Kafengauz—

---

[131] For transformations in the works of Soviet intellectuals similar to Alexis Tolstoi's, see, e.g., Ann K. Erikson, "E. V. Tarle, the Career of a Historian Under the Soviet Regime," *The American Slavic and East European Review,* Vol. XIX, no. 2 (April 1960), 202–216.

[132] In dealing with Alexis Tolstoi, I want to make a special acknowledgment of my indebtedness to Ms. Lynn Mally's paper presented in my seminar and entitled "A Hero of His Time: Alexei Tolstoi's Changing Image of Peter the Great."

[133] *Ocherki istorii SSSR. Period feodalizma. Rossiia v pervoi chetverti XVIII v. Preobrazovaniia Petra I,* eds. B. B. Kafengauz and N. I. Pavlenko (Moscow, 1954).

discussed in the preceding section of this chapter—and Professor Nicholas Pavlenko—to be discussed in the following—were the editors of the volume, and Kafengauz wrote the lengthy introduction.

The present book has as its task to reveal, on the basis of Marxist-Leninist science, the main aspects of the historical development of our Fatherland at the end of the seventeenth and the first quarter of the eighteenth centuries. The exposition begins with a characterization of the forces of production, the development of agriculture, manufacturing, and trade; after that, the state of the relations of production is analyzed, that is, the condition of the peasants and of the working population in towns, as well as the history of the exploiting classes, the gentry, and the merchants. Following a study of the phenomena of the base, the present "Survey" illuminates the development of the class struggle, the reforms in the organization of the state and in the armed forces, and the brilliant achievements in the foreign policy of that time. Finally, a large place is allotted to the history of culture, the growth of enlightenment, the development of science, literature, and the arts. The "Survey" also shows the connections of the Russian people to other peoples of our country, but the history of individual peoples at that time will be elucidated in more detail in the next book, where the processes that were taking place in the second quarter of the eighteenth century will be studied.[134]

Emphasizing continuity with the past and careful to note both the progressive quality and great success of some parts of Petrine activity, on the one hand, and its overall class-bound, exploitative nature on the other, Kafengauz described the reformer himself also in the usual bipolar manner:

A man of extraordinary talents, strong will, and boundless energy, Peter was a great Russian statesman, an outstanding general, diplomat, and lawgiver. He remained, however, a representative of the dominant class. Peter's activity was based on the idea of the tsar's "service" to the state, of "the common good," which in fact turned out to be, first of all, the good of the gentry and the merchants. It was characteristic of him to reject the religious pomp which had surrounded preceding tsars; he stood before the people in the guise of an officer of the guards endowed with autocratic power. A. S. Pushkin, who valued Peter highly, noted at the same time his gentry class traits, emphasizing that many of his ukazes had been as if "written with a knout" and had "escaped from an impatient despotic landowner."[135]

A peculiar variant of bipolarity was provided by the relationship of the Russian people to the other peoples of the Petrine state. Again, Kafengauz treated that difficult, and even dangerous, topic completely in line with the current ideology:

In the history of the peoples of the Russian empire, there were observed, to a greater or a lesser extent depending on their level of development, phenomena and processes that they had in common with the Russian people: a consolidation

134 *Ibid.*, 5. "Introduction" occupies pp. 5–43.
135 *Ibid.*, 18.

of the dominant feudal class was taking place; commercial relations developed; there was an increase in the exploitation through serfdom of the laboring masses of the peoples who populated our Fatherland. The colonial policy of tsarism manifested itself especially clearly in the increase in the exploitation of the peoples of the Volga area and of Siberia, in the growth of taxes and other obligations. Together with that and despite colonial policy of autocracy, a friendship was being established between the great Russian people and other peoples of our country based on an economic and cultural rapprochement and the community of class interests.[136]

Having emphasized the Marxist approach and classics, given an overview of the Petrine age, and even mentioned non-Russian nationalities, Kafengauz turned to the historiography of his subject.

The differences in the evaluation of the reforms are explained by the class allegiance of those who made the evaluations. The historical and publicistic literature of a rising class gave a positive evaluation of the processes of the first quarter of the eighteenth century. Contrariwise, historians and publicists from the camp of expiring classes and social groups had a hostile attitude to the reforms. The gentry historiography, exactly like the bourgeois, took at different stages in the existence of its class different attitudes toward the transformation: welcomed it at the time of the strengthening of the gentry and the bourgeoisie and condemned it in the period of the decline of these classes.[137]

One could, thus, readily understand the resounding praise of Peter the Great in eighteenth-century Russian gentry historiography, as well as the appearance of serious doubt and criticism with Shcherbatov and, later, Karamzin and the Slavophiles. Or, to take the bourgeois line of development, one could appreciate the positive thrust and the central role of S. Soloviev's writings, together with the collapse of his affirmative position in the works of Kliuchevskii and, especially, Miliukov. But, even at its best, pre-Revolutionary Russian historiography could achieve only a limited grasp of its subject, and it exhibited other defects besides. "Worship of everything foreign and an exaggeration of the role of foreigners in Russian service in the realization of the reforms are characteristic of gentry-bourgeois historiography."[138] Fortunately, the approach finally changed. "In the meantime already at the end of the nineteenth century an overturn, connected with the appearance of the works of Marx, Engels, Lenin, Stalin, had occurred in the historical science."[139] Soviet historians were happy heirs of that overturn. In dealing with Marxist Petrine historiography, Kafengauz sharply criticized, once again, the condemned Pokrovskii, and he pointed out the basic errors of Plekhanov and Rozhkov, as well as of Syromiatnikov, but he took a positive and optimistic

---

[136] *Ibid.*, 18–19.

[137] *Ibid.*, 19. This approach is, of course, basic to Soviet historiography, used perhaps most effectively on a large scale in N. L. Rubinshtein, *Russkaia istoriografiia* (n. p., 1941).

[138] *Rossiia v pervoi chetverti XVIII v.*, 36.

[139] *Ibid.*

view of the recent and current work of many Soviet scholars in the different specific areas of Petrine research. The way was open to further study, to bringing together the results of separate investigations, to creative Marxist historical effort.

The first chapter of almost 200 pages was entitled "The Forces of Production and the Social-Economic Order" and consisted of seven contributions by five authors. Zaozerskaia dealt with "Small-scale Industry" and "Manufacturing," Kafengauz himself treated "Commerce" as well as "The Merchants. The Towns," and three other scholars contributed pieces on "Agriculture," "The Peasants," and "The Gentry."[140] Although Russian economic achievements and advances were carefully noted, even exaggerated on occasion, the narrative was in general strictly factual, and its tone sober and even critical. Zaozerskaia, for example, wrote of a low productivity in agriculture and of frequent conditions of starvation and also remarked that the increase in peasant commerce indicated not only the availability of a surplus to sell but also an increase in the exploitation of peasants.[141] The section on the peasants argued that "the policy of Peter I's government in regard to the peasantry was directed toward strengthening its servile dependence. This manifested itself, in the first place, in the growth of the fuedally dependent contingent of the population of the country and in the increase in the feudal exploitation of it."[142]

The second chapter, of more than fifty pages, presented "The Class Struggle at the End of the Seventeenth–the First Quarter of the Eighteenth Centuries." It contained four sections by six authors: "Uprisings in Siberia at the End of the Seventeenth Century" (by V. A. Aleksandrov), "The Astrakhan Rebellion of 1705–1706" (by A. V. Chernov and N. B. Golikova), "The Rebellion on the Don in 1707–1708" (by V. I. Lebedev—whom we encountered dealing with the same subject earlier—and E. P. Podiapolskaia), and "The Class Struggle in Manufacturing Establishments" (again by E. I. Zaozerskaia).[143] Interestingly, the Bashkir rebellion received only half a page at the end of Golikova's and Chernov's expert narration of the Astrakhan uprising, and that diminutive space was used to stress the feudal nature of the Bashkir leadership and its orientation toward Turkey.[144] The chapter offered appropriately a thoroughly negative view of Petrine Russia, with its wholesale oppression of the masses

[140] "Proizvoditelnye sily i sotsialno-ekonomicheskii stroi," 44–229, subdivided into E. I. Indova, "Selskoe khoziastvo," 44–63; E. I. Zaozerskaia, "Melkaia promyshelnnost," 63–87; E. I. Zaozerskaia, "Manufaktura," 87–126; B. B. Kafengauz, "Torgovlia," 127–152; A. L. Shapiro, "Krestiane," 152–185; E. N. Kusheva, "Dvorianstvo," 185–211; B. B. Kafengauz, "Kupechestvo. Goroda," 211–229.

[141] *Ibid.*, 62–63.

[142] *Ibid.*, 184.

[143] "Vosstaniia v Sibiri v kontse XVII v.," 230–240; "Astrakhanskoe vosstanie 1705–1706 gg.," 240–253; "Vosstanie na Donu 1707–1708 gg.," 253–279; and "Klassovaia borba na manufaktorakh," 279–285 respectively.

[144] *Ibid.*, 252–253. But refer back to the last sentence of the first paragraph of the "Introduction" quoted earlier.

and its class "justice." By contrast, the rebellions, although unsuccessful, were positive phenomena, for they served "as an important means of counteracting the proclivity of the class of landlords and of the absolute state toward an unlimited exploitation of the peasantry."[145] And, in spite of merciless repression, the popular struggle was to continue in the years following.

The third chapter, some 150 pages long and entitled "The Formation of the Gentry-Bureaucratic Empire. The Consolidation of Absolutism in Russia," dealt with a huge subject or rather a cluster of subjects. Seven sections by seven authors followed Pavlenko's brief but pregnant programmatic introduction: "Reform of the Higher and Central Organs of the State Government" (by D. S. Baburin), "Reforms of the Local Government" (by B. G. Slitsan), "Reform of the Army and the Creation of the Navy" (by L. G. Beskrovnyi), "Reform of the Church Administration" (again by B. G. Slitsan), "Financial Reform and the State Budget" (Kafengauz's fourth contribution), "Law and the Courts" (by B. M. Kuritsyn), and "The Struggle Against Reactionary Opposition" (by T. K. Krylova and V. A. Aleksandrov).[146]

Pavlenko stated the main issue in the very first sentence: "In Russia, in the first quarter of the eighteenth century, there came to its culmination the process of the formation of a new political form of domination of the feudal class: absolute monarchy."[147] In Western Europe absolutism resulted from the rise of the bourgeoisie, which enabled government to balance its interests against those of the old class of landlords, to rely on a bureaucracy, to acquire a considerable independence of action, and to promote Enlightenment. In Russia, it would seem—a crucial point not crystal clear either in Pavlenko's exposition or in Soviet theory in general—the landlords remained dominant; yet there, too, a bourgeoisie appeared and proceeded to develop, at least through its early stages, the entire historical process resembling that in the West:

Cruel governmental measures against class actions of the popular masses were interwoven with a demagogic phraseology about "the common good." A partial secularization of monastic lands, the subordination of the Church to the state, a certain religious tolerance, the establishment of schools and of the Academy of Sciences—all that testifies to the fact that the state power in Russia at that time was partly permeated by elements of "enlightened despotism."[148]

145 *Ibid.*, 279.

146 "Obrazovanie dvoriansko-chinovnichei imperii. Utverzhdenie absoliutisma v Rossii.," 286–431, subdivided into: "Vvedenie," 286–291; "Reforma vysshikh i tsentralnykh organov gosudarstvennogo upravleniia," 291–317; "Reformy mestnogo upravleniia," 318–342; "Reforma armii i sozdanie voenno-morskogo flota," 342–371; "Reforma tserkovnogo upravleniia," 371–381; "Finansovaia reforma i gosudarstvennyi biudzhet," 381–395; "Pravo i sud," 395–412; "Borba s reaktsionnoi oppositsiei," 412–431.

147 *Ibid.*, 286.

148 *Ibid.*, 290. I translated *prosveshchennyi absoliutizm* with the conventional English "enlightened despotism." Pavlenko quoted the Marxist classics very abundantly in his "Introduction." That such quotation has its dangers can be seen from the extended

Contributors to the chapter were, thus, left to elucidate as best they could the exact class nature of the particular reforms they were discussing as well as to deal with the perennial problem of evaluating correctly measures that were progressive and desirable but also exploitative and class-bound. Baburin, writing on central institutions, concluded as follows in regard to their social content: "The reformed state apparatus was called upon to strengthen gentry domination. At the same time absolutism contributed to the development of new relations of production, to the growth of industry, commerce, and of the emerging bourgeoisie, keeping the bourgeoisie, however, on the second plane, compared to the gentry."[149] The historian even paid considerable attention to the monarch himself, ending a summary account of his personality and life as follows: "Peter I was a representative of the dominant gentry class; and, together with that, he belongs among the outstanding statesmen who know how to understand complex historical conditions and who find ways to change them."[150] Kuritsyn came to a similar judgment in his study of the legal state organs:

The judicial system as a whole served the interests of the gentry, strengthened its dictatorship. Together with that, absolute monarchy was forced to take into account the rising merchantry, to create the minimum of legal conditions necessary for its activity. The development of commercial-monetary relations determined also the appearance and development of the legal norms, which regulated these relations. In the depths of feudal law appear and develop elements of bourgeois law.[151]

The issue was taken up once more on the very last page of the chapter:

The absolute gentry-bureaucratic state strengthened the position of the gentry, protecting it from peasant mass actions. Russian foreign policy was successfully carried out by the personnel of the reorganized apparatus; that same bureaucratic apparatus contributed to the development of the bourgeoisie.[152]

Still, in the words of the final sentence: "In reality state administrative reforms did not at all change the purpose of the feudal-absolute state: to

---

reference to Lenin, which links bureaucracy most emphatically to the bourgeoisie and thus, it would seem, puts in question the fundamentally gentry nature of any state based on a bureaucracy (*ibid.*, 289).

149 *Ibid.*, 312.

150 *Ibid.*, 317.

151 *Ibid.*, 412.

152 *Ibid.*, 431. Technically speaking, this quoted statement and the next belonged to Krylova's and Aleksandrov's section on "The Struggle Against Reactionary Opposition," but, because its last two pages followed a break in the text and were of a general summary nature, they might have been the work of the editors of the volume. Krylova and Aleksandrov, it may be added, of course, condemned "the reactionary opposition," i.e., the *streltsy* and the circle centered on Tsarevich Alexis, remarking in the latter case: "Sedition and treason were the main means of struggle of the reaction at the time of the affair of Tsarevich Alexis" (*ibid.*, 429).

defend in the first place the interests of the dominant class, the gentry."[153]

As to achievements and progress, Professor Beskrovnyi, writing about the army and the navy, was predictably most affirmative and enthusiastic. In fact, he gave a glowing account not only of weapons and tactics but also of the education of the Russian soldier: "Peter assigned enormous importance to the business of educating the troops. In contrast to the Prussian school, based on a bastinado drill, the Russian system placed at the foundation of education the formation of high moral qualities: courage, daring, mutual rescue in combat."[154] But even Beskrovnyi added that:

the army and the navy constituted an integral part of the absolutist state, were a means of strengthening the class domination of the gentry and the emerging merchantry . . .

The creation of the regular army and of the navy was a progressive phenomenon; however, it was realized at the cost of an increase in the oppression of the laboring masses, who carried the burden of the draft and of augmented obligations to the state.[155]

The difficulty and the ambivalence in separating the good from the bad in the Soviet Petrine image established in the 1930s found striking expression in Kafengauz's own conclusion to his expert study of financial reform and the state budget:

The financial measures of Peter I's government were successful from the fiscal point of view. They tripled the state budget, helped Russian military and diplomatic victories, materially secured the new measures of the government, the reform of the army, the building of the navy, the creation of manufacturing establishments, and so on. The financial reforms had been prepared by the entire preceding economic development of the country. The growth of direct taxation, in its turn, raised the marketability of the national economy. Robbing the people by means of a taxation system served as one of the sources of primary accumulation in Russia.

But the growth of the state budget was utilized in the interests of the gentry and the merchantry. The structure of the budget testified to the fact that it was subordinated to the solution of the two main state functions: "to keep the exploited majority bridled" and "to broaden the territory of its own dominant class at the expense of the territory of other states or to defend the territory of its state from attacks on the part of other states." The realization of the budget led to a tense exertion of peasant strength, to a ruin of the laboring masses; and, together with that, it led to an increase in the incomes of the gentry and the emerging bourgeoisie.[156]

153 My emphasis earlier and later on ideological issues relevant to the image of Peter the Great is not meant to obscure the fact that the great bulk of the volume was factual in content and narrative in style and that analytic and evaluative passages frequently seemed to be tacked on rather artlessly to the body of the text.

154 *Ibid.*, 356.

155 *Ibid.*, 371.

156 *Ibid.*, 395. The quotations are from Stalin.

The fourth chapter, devoted to "Foreign Policy," was almost 200 pages long, but it had fewer—if any—fundamental problems to resolve than the preceding chapters. Nikiforov, Kafengauz again, and other specialists emphasized the continuity of Petrine foreign policy with the past as well as its complete congruity with the Russian needs at the time; and they rejoiced in its resounding success. The positive pole of the bipolar image held sway. To be sure, the exploitative nature of the Petrine state was mentioned repeatedly even in this chapter, but it did not intrude upon the actual presentation of events and issues.[157]

The fifth and last chapter, some 130 pages on "Russian Culture," again provided much information on many subjects, including cultural activities of the masses as well as of the educated public. It also managed to devote less than minimal attention to foreign influences,[158] endorse both Petrine reformers and reforms, on the one hand, and leaders and publicists of popular rebellions who were trying to destroy them on the other, and quote the Marxist classics at every turn. It, too, punctuated effectively the age of Stalin.[159]

Pavlenko wrote the "Conclusion" to the volume.[160]

In the first quarter of the eighteenth century, the forces of production developed at an accelerated tempo, and the economic and political independence of our Fatherland was strengthened. This was a struggle against backwardness in economic life, as well as in regard to military matters, state administration, and culture. But, together with that, one must keep in mind the class limitations of these achievements, which increased gentry domination and oppression through serfdom—the successes were purchased at a high price.[161]

The Petrine state had its distinct characteristics:

[157] The contents read as follows: "Vneshniia politika" ("Foreign Policy"), 432–628, subdivided into B. B. Kafengauz, "Vvedenie" ("Introduction"), 432–435; S. A. Feigina, "Azovskie pokhody i vneshniaia politika 1695–1699 gg." ("The Azov Campaigns and the Foreign Policy of the Years 1695–1699"), 435–459; T. K. Krylova, Iu. R. Klokman, "Pervye gody Severnoi voiny i Poltavskaia bitva (1700–1709 gg.)" ("The First Years of the Northern War and the Battle of Poltava, 1700–1709"), 459–510; N. I. Kazakov, Iu. R. Klokman, T. K. Krylova, L. A. Nikiforov, "Voennye deistviia i diplomatiia v 1709–1716 gg." ("War and Diplomacy in the Years 1709–1716"), 510–573; L. A. Nikiforov, "Poslednie gody Severnoi voiny i Nishtadtskii mir" ("The Last Years of the Northern War and the Treaty of Nystadt"), 573–598; V. P. Lystsov, V. A. Aleksandrov, "Persidskii pokhod i otnosheniia Rossii s Kitaem" ("The Persian Campaign and the Relations of Russia with China"), 598–623; L. A. Nikiforov, "Itogi vneshnei politiki" ("The Results of Foreign Policy"), 623–628.

[158] Characteristically, the brief introduction underlined "the basis of Russian experience" and mentioned only one foreign name (not counting a reference to Engels), Copernicus.

[159] "Russkaia kultura" ("Russian Culture"), 629–765, subdivided into B. B. Kafengauz, N. I. Pavlenko, "Vvedenie" ("Introduction"), 629–631; B. B. Kafengauz, "Obshchestvenno-politicheskaia mysl" ("Social-Political Thought"), 631–655; N. A. Baklanova, "Shkola i prosveshchenie" ("Schools and Enlightenment"), 655–681; N. A. Baklanova, "Nauka" ("Science"), 681–702; A. V. Kokorev, "Literatura i teatr" ("Literature and Theater"), 702–728; M. A. Ilin, "Iskusstvo" ("Art"), 728–765.

[160] N. I. Pavlenko, "Zakliuchenie," 766–774.

[161] *Ibid.*, 766.

The Russian empire of the first quarter of the eighteenth century represents an absolutist state of landlords and the emerging class of merchants with bureaucratic institutions. The bureaucratic Senate replaced the aristocratic Boyar Duma; a few colleges took the place of the obsolete *prkazy*. Instead of a patriarch, the Church was ruled by a "spiritual college," or Synod, on a par with the other colleges and the Senate, subject to the emperor. Two *oblast* reforms, the creation of the division into *gubernii* and of the "provinces," with a whole system of local institutions, completed the formation of the gentry-bureaucratic apparatus of the empire.[162]

Yet Pavlenko's able discussion of the appearance of the Petrine state and of its nature and activity led to a familiar conclusion:

The feudal-serf system proved still capable of securing a certain rise of the forces of production; but serf relations limited its scope; the dominant class, the gentry, could not overcome the backwardness of the country any more than the bourgeoisie could. Only two centuries later the proletariat, having accomplished the Great October Socialist Revolution and having seized power, created conditions for an unheard-of cultural and material rise of the popular masses.[163]

## 5

The death of Stalin in 1953 and, especially, the de-Stalinization that emerged in 1956 affected the Soviet treatment of the Petrine theme as well as other Soviet intellectual—and not only intellectual—efforts. Quotation and citation of the Marxist classics, especially quotation out of context or quotation of the perfectly obvious, was sharply reduced whereas Stalin's name and writings simply vanished from Soviet scholarship. To illustrate the point, it is sufficient to compare, for example, the Petrine anthology published in 1973[164] with the 1954 volume discussed in the preceding section of this chapter. Nationalism, exaggerated patriotism, and even a certain xenophobia remained, but at least they were diminished in size, with a greater freedom in the matter exercised by individual authors: in any case, such tours de force as presenting Petrine cultural history almost without foreign influences or Petrine reforms entirely without foreign models, as in the 1954 textbook, were no longer in vogue. Moreover, Soviet historical scholarship, Petrine scholarship included, gained overall in nuance, sophistication, and general quality. Doubters should carefully compare post-1956 Soviet historical works with those written in the age of Stalin, not with Western scholarship.

Still, the dominant Soviet Petrine image established in the 1930s survived essentially intact. Its persistence testifies, no doubt, at least to some

[162] *Ibid.*, 769.

[163] *Ibid.*, 774.

[164] *Rossiia v period reform Petra I*, eds. N. I. Pavlenko, L. A. Nikiforov, and M. Ia. Volkov (Moscow, 1973).

extent, to its comprehensiveness and its general intrinsic strength, not only to its fitness for the Soviet scene. That image, to repeat, covered all aspects of the Petrine phenomenon and allowed for rich historical research and different and disparate analyses and evaluation in various discrete fields although the judgments involved were frequently controversial, to say the least, and the total synthesis did not necessarily carry conviction. After 1956, Soviet Petrine scholars, thus, continued on the whole their previous work under somewhat improved conditions.

At the negative pole of the Petrine image, popular rebellions remained a favorite subject of the Soviet students of the reign of the reforming emperor. Books on the topic included reworked editions of earlier studies, for example, Lebedev's 1967 version of *The Bulavin Rebellion (1707–1708)*,[165] first published in 1934, but also new monographs, such as E. P. Podiapolskaia's *The Bulavin Rebellion,* which came out also in 1967,[166] and N. B. Golikova's *The Astrakhan Rebellion, 1705–1706,* which appeared in 1975.[167] But, old or new, these pieces carried the same message. As Golikova concluded:

The Astrakhan rebellion of 1705–1706 occupies a prominent place among the class battles of the feudal period. Its participants, who stubbornly refused to reconcile themselves to exploitation and want of justice, who gave to the struggle not only their entire strength but also their lives, enter of right into the ranks of people who, speaking in V. I. Lenin's words, "struggled as best they knew how and as best they could."[168]

That endorsing popular uprisings has broader implications can be seen strikingly in the work of Nina Borisovna Golikova. An indefatigable student of the Petrine period, whose interests have ranged from the Astrakhan rebellion to workers, soldiers, merchants, industry, and aspects of government, her entire oeuvre can be considered, in one of its main aspects, a sweeping condemnation of Petrine Russia from the standpoint of the lower, exploited, classes. Appropriately, Golikova's best-known book is her *Political Processes at the Time of Peter I. Based on the Materials of the Preobrazhenskii Office*.[169] An archival, largely case, study of the Petrine system of law enforcement, the investigation led to definite conclusions:

165 V. I. Lebedev, *Bulavinskoe vosstanie (1707–1708)* (Moscow, 1967).

166 E. P. Podiapolskaia, *Vosstanie Bulavina* (1967). See also: N. A. Zadonskii, *Kondratii Bulavin* (Moscow, 1959), published in a large edition.

167 N. B. Golikova, *Astrakhanskoe vosstanie 1705–1706 gg.* (Moscow, 1975).

168 *Ibid.,* 315. Golikova had been studying the Astrakhan rebellion for many years. See her earlier N. B. Golikova, "Istoriia sostavleniia obrashchenii uchastnikami Astrakhanskogo vosstaniia 1705–1706 gg.," *Istoriia SSSR,* no. 6 (1971), 158–169; N. B. Golikova, "K istorii Astrakhanskogo vosstaniia 1705–1706 gg. (sotsialnaia politika i organy upravleniia vosstavshikh)," *Rossiia v period reform Petra I,* 249–288; as well as her joint contribution to the 1954 volume.

169 N. B. Golikova, *Politicheskie protsessy pri Petre I. Po materialam Preobrazhenskogo prikaza* (Moscow, 1957).

The number of examples of this kind [of peasants punished for legally inform-
ing on landlords], as well as of the instances of peasants criticizing the government and denouncing landlords, could be increased considerably. But they
would not change our conception of the character and the class nature of
peasant political cases handled in the Preobrazhenskii office. All of them convincingly testify to one and the same thing: the growth of peasant dissatisfaction
with the increase of feudal-serf oppression by the landlords and also with the
augmentation of taxes and state obligations, which fell as a heavy burden on
the popular masses.[170]

One of Golikova's fortes was her depiction of the grossly unfair, class
nature of Petrine justice, an unexceptionable point in itself, which, however, the historian developed skillfully to inform and inspire much of
her narrative. For example, in the case of torture commonly used in the
judicial process:

If the accuser was a peasant, a slave, a soldier, and the accused a boyar, a member of the gentry, an officer, or a representative of the higher clergy, the accused
was subjected to torture only after the accuser and the witnesses confirmed the
accusation at the questioning, at face to face confrontations, and under torture.
If the witnesses did not confirm the accusation, the accuser was tortured no less
than three times, and only after that was the accused sent to the torture cham-
ber. Even then he was not as yet tortured, but only questioned "next to torture,"
that is, questioned next to the instruments of torture. If the accused continued
to deny his guilt, the accuser was again tortured, and only after a new con-
firmation of the accusation by him was the accused tortured. Such a system of
questioning led, as a rule, to an exoneration of the accused, because the accuser,
unable to bear the torture, withdrew his accusation.

But, if the accused belonged to the lower social classes, he was subjected to torture after simple testimonies of the witnesses and face-to-face confrontation with
the accuser and the witnesses. The accuser and the witnesses were sent to torture
after the accused had withstood it.[171]

Similarly, whereas members of the gentry received some three to seven
strokes of the knout, peasants had to suffer from fifteen to thirty-five or
forty at a single session. Also, the former were usually considered innocent if they withstood torture thrice, but the latter were tortured six and
more times.[172] Statistics as well as procedures confirmed judicial partiality:

The investigative and judicial practice of the Preobrazhenskii office convincingly
testifies to the class, serfdom character of its activity. This is graphically demonstrated by the results of the judicial processes, which show that from 1697 to
1709 the acquittals went as follows: of the peasants 7.1%, of the suburban people 8.6%, of the soldiers 2.2%, of the landlords 54%, of the officers 81%. The
same is indicated by the measures of punishment applied to the common people.
Peasants, soldiers, and suburban inhabitants were punished for "unbecoming

170 *Ibid.*, 198.
171 *Ibid.*, 67–68.
172 *Ibid.*, 182.

talk" by corporal punishment, maiming, and exile to hard labor, whereas members of the gentry suffered for the same crime only corporal punishment.[173]

However, although deeply concerned with the crushing cruelty of the system, Golikova—in contrast to many writers of other orientations—was not interested in Peter the Great's personal cruelty. In fact, she traced how the reforming monarch acted to reduce the application of capital punishment[174] and quoted him to the effect that though "it is incumbent to impose punishments for disturbances and crimes, one should still try to preserve the lives of one's subjects as much as possible."[175] Throughout Golikova's book the reader could see not only individual cases of injustice and protest, but also the rising tide of popular opposition to Petrine reforms and Petrine Russia. The historian's findings included a greater role of the lower Orthodox clergy in that opposition—but a lesser role of the Old Believers than the one generally assigned them—and the fact that even some "reactionary" and "privileged" enemies of the regime, namely, the *streltsy* and, once more, the lower Orthodox clergy, had considerable rapport with the masses.

Golikova's striking piece under the heading "From the History of Class Contradictions in the Russian Army (1700–1709)," published in 1959 in an anthology entitled *Poltava*,[176] could be considered, in a sense, an addendum to the book on the Preobrazhenskii office. It dealt with class justice and class exploitation in the Russian armed forces, where officers frequently utilized their position and their power over their men for personal gain, and it noted considerable dissatisfaction in the Petrine army. "It is extremely indicative that soldiers took an active part in such leading movements of the first quarter of the eighteenth century as the Astrakhan city rebellion of 1705–1706 and the Bulavin rebellion of 1707–1708."[177] Very sharply different in tone and content from the usual military glorification of Peter the Great—including many articles in the same anthology—Golikova's contribution fitted well, nevertheless, as we had occasion to see in other similar instances, the established bipolar image of the first emperor and his Russia.

Writers on peasants also frequently took a negative view of the Petrine reign. A case in point is E. N. Baklanova and her study of *The Peasant Household and Commune in the Russian North. The End of the Seventeenth—the Beginning of the Eighteenth Centuries*,[178] published in 1976. A thorough statistical investigation of three districts of the later Vologda

---

173 *Ibid.*, 291.

174 *Ibid.*, 52–54.

175 *Ibid.*, 41.

176 N. B. Golikova, "Iz istorii klassovykh protivorechii v russkoi armii (1700–1709 gg.)," *Poltava. K 250-litiiu Poltavskogo srazheniia*, eds. L. G. Beskrovnyi, B. B. Kafengauz, V. A. Diadichenko, N. I. Pavlenko (Moscow, 1959), 269–285.

177 *Ibid.*, 283.

178 E. N. Baklanova, *Krestianskii dvor i obshchina na russkom Severe. Konets XVII-nachalo XVIII v.* (Moscow, 1976).

province, an area that represented the northernmost extention of gentry estates and that bordered on the entirely peasant far north, it depicted the growth of the peasant economy in the last quarter of the seventeenth century. Then the situation changed:

In the first quarter of the eighteenth century the productive forces of the peasant household were brought entirely into the service of the state and the landlord patrimony. The state tax burden, increased by a factor of two, accompanied by feudal exploitation augmented in the same manner, exhausted the working capabilities of the peasant household. If in the last quarter of the seventeenth century a peasant household cultivated 2.25–4.5 *desiatiny* of allotment land in three fields and one third of a *desiatina* of the landlord's plough-land a year, and, in 1702, 1.6 of a *desiatina,* then in the first quarter of the eighteenth century, with its own allotment remaining the same, it had to cultivate as corvée already 3.5 *desiatiny.* This burden was worsened by the state mobilization of men of the most active working age. Everything taken together undermined peasant economy. The differentiation in property reaches the extreme: pauperization and ruin of peasant households and also the abandonment of some half of them, registered in the 1678 census. It became the lot of the households that had retained their ability to function to carry the burden of both the state and the landlord obligations of the households that had disappeared. The peasant economy could meet all these obligations by utilizing labor reserves, which had been reduced to a minimum and, apparently, by intensifying the labor.

In that connection, the following circumstance must be certainly noted. During the period under investigation, the number of peasant households declined by half as a result of the ebb of population in the first quarter of the eighteenth century. The remaining households retained their basic economic characteristics: the number of male workers (one to three full-time and one part-time), the size of the allotment (2.25–4.5 *desiatiny* in three fields), and the number of heads of work animals (one to two horses). Thus what occurred, in the conditions of the Northern War and the undoubtedly augmented private feudal exploitation, was not only a general overall weakening of the economic possibilities of the peasant population under investigation, but also the complete ruin of one part of the peasantry, while the other retained the necessary economic level to secure a simple reproduction of itself.[179]

In other words, Peter the Great's reign was a catastrophe for the peasants of the Russian north.

Still, the positive pole of the Petrine image and reign remained at least as prominent as the negative. Military and naval historians, unaffected by Khrushchev's revelations about Stalin and other recent developments, continued to glorify the victor of Poltava and the creator of the Russian navy.[180] Related Petrine subjects included even the Russian penetration

---

179 *Ibid.,* 193–194. Cf., for the broader picture, the most recent Soviet account: E. V. Anisimov, *Podatnaia reforma Petra I. Vvedenie podushnoi podati v Rossii, 1719–1728 gg.* (Leningrad, 1982).

180 See notably and also representatively L. G. Beskrovnyi, *Russkaia armiia i flot v XVIII veke (Ocherki)* ("The Russian Army and Navy in the Eighteenth Century, a Survey") (Moscow, 1958); A. I. Dubrovin, "Korabelnyi master Petr Mikhailov. K 300-

of the distant southern seas, which originated, again, with the first emperor.[181] Specialists in diplomacy, building on the work of Nikiforov and other predecessors, developed their investigations of that rich Petrine (and immediately post-Petrine) field. Thus, Professor G. A. Nekrasov contributed learned monographs, based on archival research, on *Russian-Swedish Relations and the Great Power Politics, 1721–1726* and on *The Role of Russia in International European Politics, 1725–1739*.[182] Nekrasov emphasized not only the skill and success of Russian diplomacy but also Peter I's personal role in it. Numerous scholars of different aspects of Russian culture showed interest in the Petrine period and generally praised Petrine initiatives and legacy. The variety and the high quality of their work can be perhaps most readily seen in such anthologies as *The Problems of the Russian Enlightenment in Eighteenth-Century Literature* and *The Problems of the Literary Development of Russia in the First Third of the Eighteenth Century*, both used extensively in the first chapter of this study.[183]

And, in general, joint Petrine volumes, though few in number, reflected especially well the state of Soviet Petrine scholarship. In 1959, *Poltava. For the Two-Hundred-Fiftieth Anniversary of the Battle of Poltava. A Collection of Articles* came out.[184] The twenty-five contributions, which followed a historiographical introduction, began with Besk-

---

letiiu so dnia rozhdeniia Petra I" ("Shipwright Petr Mikhailov. For the Three-Hundred-Year Anniversary of the Day of Peter I's Birth"), *Sudostroenie*, no. 6 (1972), 66–72; A. I. Dubrovin, "Ledovye pokhody Petra I. K 300-letiiu so dnia rozhdeniia Petra I" ("Peter I's Ice Expeditions. For the Three-Hundred-Year Anniversary of the Day of Peter I's Birth"), *ibid.*, no. 5, 58–64; I. V. Girs and B. N. Favorov, " 'Poteshnaia' flotiliia Petra" ("Peter's 'Mock' Flotilla"), *ibid.*, no. 6, 72–74; A. M. Ivanov, "V chest pervykh pobed russkogo flota" ("In Honor of the First Victories of the Russian Navy"), *ibid.*, no. 8 (1966), 70–71; A. Kozev, "Petr I—osnovatel russkogo flota" ("Peter I: The Founder of the Russian Navy"), *Rechnoi transport*, no. 9 (1972), 53–54; E. I. Porfirev, *Poltavskoe srazhenie. 27 iiunia 1709 g.* ("The Battle of Poltava. June 27, 1709") (Moscow, 1959); L. A. Shimkevich, "Osnovatel reguliarnogo russkogo flota" ("The Founder of the Regular Russian Navy"), *Sudostroenie*, no. 1 (1972), 40–43; V. E. Shutoi, *Borba narodnykh mass protiv nashestviia armii Karla XII, 1700–1709* ("The Struggle of the Popular Masses against Charles XII's Invading Army, 1700–1709") (Moscow, 1970); V. E. Shutoi, *Severnaia voina (1700–1721 gg.)* ("The Northern War, 1700–1721") (Moscow, 1970); *Voprosy voennoi istorii Rossii. XVIII i pervaia polovina XIX vekov* ("Problems of Russian Military History. The Eighteenth and the First Half of the Nineteenth Centuries") (Moscow, 1969).

181 A. B. Davidson and V. A. Makhrushin, *Zov dalnikh morei* ("The Call of Distant Seas") (Moscow, 1979).

182 G. A. Nekrasov, *Russko-shvedskie otnosheniia i politika velikikh derzhav v 1721–1726 gg.* (Moscow, 1964); G. A. Nekrasov. *Rol Rossii v evropeiskoi mezhdunarodnoi politike. 1725–1739 gg.* (Moscow, 1976).

183 *Problemy russkogo prosveshcheniia v literature XVIII veka* (Moscow and Leningrad, 1961); and *Problemy literaturnogo razvitiia v Rossii pervoi treti XVIII veka* (Leningrad, 1974). The first book was edited by P. N. Berkov; the second, by G. P. Makogonenko and G. N. Moiseeva; both were produced under the auspices of Pushkinskii Dom (The Institute of Russian Literature of the Academy of Sciences of the U.S.S.R.). See also Iu. K. Begunov, "Izuchenie literatury petrovskoi epokhi za poslednee desiatiletie," *Russkaia literatura*, no. 4 (1980), 208–225.

184 For full reference to *Poltava*, see note 176 earlier.

rovnyi's "The Strategy and Tactics of the Russian Army in the Poltava Period of the Northern War" and ended with "The Memorials of the Battle of Poltava in the Hermitage Museum (Leningrad)" (no author given).[185] They were divided into three parts: the immediate circumstances of the battle as well as military and diplomatic developments closely related to it, with such specific topics as the use of artillery in the battle, the military councils of 1708–1709, and the victory of Poltava and Russian-French relations; a section on the Russian army and Petrine reforms, with most of the pieces concerned with Russian economic development and with such particulars as the supply of powder, clothing, and ammunition to the army; and a final part on "The Materials and Memorials of the Victory of Poltava," which, however, also included A. I. Kozachenko's critique of "Ukrainian gentry-bourgeois historiography" of the events in question.[186] Although the first part of the volume fitted neatly into the continuing investigation and glorification of the battle of Poltava and the third contained much interesting bibliographical and museum material, the second offered a few pieces of a broader scope. To refer to the ones we have already encountered, it was in *Poltava* that Strumilin gave a particularly sanguine account of the Petrine economy, but, to repeat, it was also in *Poltava*—reminding us of the bipolar nature of the Petrine image—that Golikova presented her devastating picture "from the history of class contradictions in the Russian army (1700–1709)."

Fourteen years later, in a less thematically restricted anthology entitled *Russia in the Period of Peter I's Reform,* a dozen Soviet scholars offered their contribution to Petrine studies.[187] N. I. Palvenko, L. A. Nikiforov, and M. Ia. Volkov edited the volume. In adiditon to one of Golikova's already-mentioned pieces on the Astrakhan rebellion and Pavlenko's major investigation of Peter I's social and political views, to be discussed later with the historian's other works, the authors and their topics were as follows: L. A. Nikiforov, "Russia in the System of European States in the First Quarter of the Eighteenth Century"; T. S. Maikova, "Peter I and 'The History of the Swedish War,'"—cited in my first chapter— M. D.. Riabinovich, "The Social Origin and the Ownership of Property of the Officers of the Regular Russian Army at the End of the Northern War"—based on a statistical study of 2245 officers—A. I. Zaozerskii, "Field Marshal Sheremetev and the Government Milieu of Petrine Time"; Iu. A. Tikhonov, "Feudal Rent on the Landlord Estates in Central Rus-

185 L. G. Beskrovnyi, "Strategiia i taktika russkoi armii v poltavskii period Severnoi voiny," *ibid.*, 21–62; and, "Pamiatniki Poltavskoi pobedy v Ermitazhe (Leningrad)," *ibid.*, 419–435.

186 A. I. Kozachenko, "Sobytiia 1708–1709 gg. na Ukraine v osveshchenii ukrainskoi dvoriansko-burzhuasnoi istoriografii," *ibid.*, 323–350.

187 For full reference to *Rossiia v period reform Petra I,* see note 164 earlier. Cf. James Cracraft, "The Tercentenary of Peter the Great in Russia," *Canadian-American Slavic Studies,* Vol. VIII, no. 2 (Summer 1974), 319–326.

sia at the End of the Seventeenth—the First Quarter of the Eighteenth Centuries (Obligations to the Landlord and State Taxes)"; S. M. Troitskii, "The Economy of a Major Russian Statesman in the First Quarter of the Eighteenth Century (according to Prince A. D. Menshikov's Archive)"; N. F. Demidova, "From the History of the Conclusion of the Treaty of Nerchinsk of 1689"; M. Ia. Volkov, "The Monk Avraamii and His 'Message to Peter I' "; M. A. Alekseeva, "Brothers Ivan and Alexis Zubov and Prints in Petrine Time"; M. P. Pavlova-Silvanskaia, "An Annotated Bibliography of Foreign Literature about Peter I (1947–1970)"— Pavlova-Silvanskaia continued Feigina's work published in the 1947 joint volume considered earlier in this chapter.[188] Apparently relatively little concerned with ideological injunctions, the 1973 anthology represented a series of expert, usually archival studies of different Petrine subjects. Repeatedly it dealt skillfully with the interplay of political, social, and economic factors whether the particular topic was Menshikov's estates or the Astrakhan rebellion. And, in the case of Zaozerskii's splendid posthumous article on Sheremetev, it displayed a fine feeling for the nuances and a general sensitivity to its subject.

The positive pole of the Petrine image, powerfully presented by Soviet scholars, has received, no doubt, an even greater emphasis at lower academic levels. Conversation with Soviet men and women who went to school after the mid-1930s indicates that Peter I was generally treated by their teachers as a hero. Whereas textbooks, such as Kafengauz's *Peter I and His Time* analyzed earlier, dutifully expounded both poles in the classroom, somehow the positive one prevailed. Although Bulavin and the oppression of the peasants did form part of the curriculum, they were not as prominent or as memorable as the creation of the Russian navy, the battle of Poltava, or the Treaty of Nystad. I have come across no exception to this rule. As to the contradiction between the two views, I was told repeatedly that the negative elements were in different chapters, which did not interfere with the main glowing exposition. More interestingly, I was occasionally informed that school teachers labeled the Bulavin rebellion as "premature" and even "anarchist" and "incorrect," a step that formal academic scholarship has refused, as we have seen, to take. It should be added that most of the Soviet teachers, at all levels, whom I have met had positive feelings about Peter the Great and be-

---

[188] "Rossiia v sisteme evropeiskikh derzhav v pervoi chetverti XVIII v.," 9–39; "Petr I i 'Gistoria Sveiskoi voiny,' " 103–132; "Sotsialnoe proiskhozhdenie i imushchestvennoe polozhenie ofitserov reguliarnoi russkoi armii v kontse Severnoi voiny," 133–171; "Feldmarshal Sheremetev i pravitelstvennaia sreda Petrovskogo vremeni," 172–198; Feodalnaia renta v pomeshchichikh imeniiakh Tsentralnoi Rossii v kontse XVII—pervoi chetverti XVIII v. (vladelcheskie povinnosti i gosudarstvennye nalogi)," 199–214; "Khoziaistvo krupnogo sanovnika Rossii v pervoi chetverti XVIII v. (po arkhivu kniazia A. D. Menshikova)," 215–248; "Iz istorii zakliucheniia Nerchinskogo dogovora 1689 g.," 289–310; "Monakh Avraamii i ego 'Poslanie Petru I,' " 311–336; "Bratia Ivan i Aleksei Zubovy i graviura Petrovskogo vremeni," 337–361; "Annotirovannaia bibliografiia inostrannoi literatury o Petre I (1947–1970 gg.)," 362–382, respectively.

lieved that they were presenting his case sympathetically. They frequently referred to the years immediately following the October Revolution and to Pokrovskii to put their own views into a proper focus.

Post-Stalinist Petrine fiction continued on the whole to endorse and glorify the first emperor, although no talent comparable to Alexis Tolstoi's emerged. Whether meant for children and covering the most striking events of the reign, as in A. M. Volkov's *Two Brothers;*[189] pietistic in the manner of K. I. Konichev's *Peter the First in the North. A Narration About Peter the First, About His Deeds and Companions in the North, Written According to Documents and Tradition;*[190] yet another justification of the destruction of Tsarevich Alexis, as in the case of "Tsar Peter's Night" by V. N. Ivanov;[191] or simply entitled by G. P. Shtorm "Poltava,"[192] Soviet belles lettres in recent decades have given abiding and popular support to a positive Petrine image. As Konichev concluded his Petrine book:

Finishing the narration about the deeds of Peter the First connected with our North, let us make the qualification that, naturally, the author could not mention all the sides of Peter's activity and indeed had not proposed to do so. These are only fragments of the biography of an outstanding person who felt correctly the imperatives of the time and who managed to do more than a little for the development and the strengthening of the Russian state.[193]

Other media have supported the Petrine message of scholarly, pedagogic, and artistic literature. Magnificent Petrine holdings and special exhibits in Soviet museums in Leningrad and elsewhere must be allotted a major, if incalculable, role.[194] A still greater role should probably be assigned to the city of Leningrad itself and to its environs. In the films, Alexis Tolstoi's superb Peter can still be considered the dominant image, not seriously challenged. Recently A. P. Petrov's opera, *Peter I,* appeared. Making up in good intentions what it lacked in artistry, it offered, in ten "frescoes," a naively enthusiastic version of Peter I's life and labors from the boyhood in Preobrazhenskoe through the victory at Poltava. Popular opposition—one of the opponents dies crushed by a church bell that sol-

189 A. M. Volkov, *Dva brata. Roman* (Moscow, 1961).

190 Konstantin Konichev, *Petr Pervyi na Severe. Povestvovanie o Petre Pervom, o delakh ego i spodvizhnikakh na Severe, po dokumentam i predaniiam napisano* (Leningrad, 1973).

191 V. N. Ivanov, "Noch tsaria Petra," in *Imperatritsa Fike* (Moscow, 1968).

192 G. P. Shtorm, "Poltava," *Deti dobroi nadezhdy. Istoricheskie povesti i rasskazy* (Moscow, 1962), 145–165.

193 Konichev, *Petr Pervyi na Severe,* 287.

194 As two examples of such exhibits, see a catalog and a booklet: Gosudarstvennyi Russkii Musei, *Feierverki i illiuminatsii v grafike XVIII veka. Katalog vystavki* ("Fireworks and Illuminations in the Graphic Arts of the Eighteenth Century. A Catalog of the Exhibition") (Leningrad, 1978); and Gosudarstvennyi Ermitazh, *Russkaia kultura pervoi poloviny XVIII veka* ("Russian Culture of the First Half of the Eighteenth Century") (Leningrad, 1979).

diers had cut down to melt into cannon—resulted from the agitation of the religious Old Believer fanatics, and in time the people learn better to celebrate, in a kind of apotheosis, the victory at Poltava and to sing and work exuberantly for their beloved monarch.[195]

Although the opera *Peter I* should not be overvalued, the general claim of Soviet glorification of Peter the Great is impressive. Soviet schools and general cultural environment, as well as much specific historical writing, present an extremely and emphatically favorable picture of the first Russian emperor. Nor is it likely that Soviet citizens fail to understand that powerful message or respond to it.[196] It has even been suggested, therefore, that the established Soviet image of Peter I should be considered unequivocally and strongly positive and that its "other side" could be ascribed to formulaic and archaic Marxism or irrelevant theorizing in general. That is surely, however, a short view of the matter. Class exploitation and class struggle remain at least as much part of Soviet thought and teaching as the Russian need for the Baltic. There is no apparent reason to pay less attention and respect to the writings of a Golikova or a Baklanova than to those of a Beskrovnyi or a Nekrasov. It bears reminding that, in pre-Revolutionary Russia, Constantine Aksakov held his Petrine views with the same sincerity and passion as Belinskii held their opposite. Also in pre-Revolutionary Russia such leading Petrine scholars as S. Soloviev, Miliukov, and Bogoslovskii came to vastly different conclusions. Nor is Pushkin's unforgettable legacy in the matter at all clear after a century and a half of explication. Moreover, and to repeat, the Soviet Petrine image, established in the 1930s and still dominant, allows, nay, requires both strikingly positive and strikingly negative evaluations, depending on the exact subject under discussion. It also contains areas of ambivalence and divided opinion, as well as room for straight scholarly research relatively unimpeded by ideological considerations. But the total picture remains the bipolar picture—to me at least unresolved. The best way to take leave of Soviet Petrine historiography is, then, to take one more look at the present state of that bipolar image, as painted by its most distinguished practitioner, Professor Nikolai Ivanovich Pavlenko.

Professor Pavlenko has earned his prominence in the scholarship on the first emperor. A specialist on Russian eighteenth-century economic

195 I saw the forty-eighth performance of *Petr I* on the night of November 1, 1979, in the Kirov Theater in Leningrad.

196 They respond to it, of course, in the Soviet manner. Thus, they were quick to notice in the increased praise of Peter the Great and especially in Tolstoi's film of him not only the return of Russian historical heroes but also the parallel between the monarch and Stalin and between Petrine and Soviet history. As one boy—so the Soviet story goes—asked his father after the film: "What other tsars were Communists?" As another link between nationalism and Soviet Marxism, I was told that some schoolteachers commended Peter the Great especially for creating the industrial labor class in Russia—a more difficult point to make at a high academic level.

and social history,[197] he developed into an expert on the facts of Peter the Great's life and activities of a quality unequaled since Bogoslovskii. It was Pavlenko who gathered all the information available on the first emperor's illness and death and presented it (without naming the patient) to the Soviet medical Academy to obtain a definitive verdict of uremia. It was also Pavlenko who destroyed a number of persistent Petrine myths, including the universally accepted one of the speechless dying monarch writing, "Give everything to . . ." and then being unable to continue.[198] Firsthand study has left the historian with an impressive and generally positive but rather severe image of the reformer, who wanted military discipline and obedience in everything. In fact, instead of praising him in the usual manner for his ability to find the right assistants and to get the most out of them, Pavlenko came to the conclusion that the despotic ways of the monarch stifled talent and initiative in his entourage. It should be added that Pavlenko became a leading specialist on that entourage, as attested by his studies of Raguzinskii and, most recently, of Menshikov.[199]

Of the historian's many Petrine pieces—a number of which I found very useful in the writing of the present work—his "Peter I. (A Contribution to the Study of His Social-Political Views)"[200] deserves special attention. It is a remarkably clear and sober presentation of the monarch's fundamental ideology, based on the concept of reason, of the idea of service to "the common good," which also meant service to the state, and of ranking according to merit. Pavlenko added to it an evaluation of Peter I as a historical figure, in the time-hallowed form of a contrast with his opponent, Charles XII of Sweden:

The talents of the Swedish King, Charles XII, manifested themselves in full measure in only one sphere: the military. A madly courageous warrior, a magnificent tactician, a sullen ambitious man, he considered it unworthy of himself to be occupied with all that was not connected with campaigns, bloody battles, daring raids, gunfire, the clanging of sabers, and the cannonade of artillery. All

---

[197] His recent contributions to this field include N. I. Pavlenko, "O rostovshchichestve dvorian v XVIII v. (k postanovke voprosa)" ("Concerning Gentry Usury in the Eighteenth Century, Toward the Formulation of the Problem"), *Dvorianstvo i krepostnoi stroi Rossii XVI–XVIII vv.* ("The Gentry and the System of Serfdom in Russia in the Sixteenth to Eighteenth Centuries"), eds., N. I. Pavlenko, I. A. Bulygin, A. A. Preobrazhenskii, S. M. Troitskii (Moscow, 1975), 265–271; and N. I. Pavlenko, "Torgovo-promyshlennaia politika pravitelstva Rossii v pervoi chetverti XVIII veka" ("The Commercial-Industrial Policy of the Russian Government in the First Quarter of the Eighteenth Century"), *Istoriia SSSR*, no. 3 (1978), 49–69.

[198] N. I. Pavlenko, "Tri tak nazyvaemykh zaveshchaniia Petra I" ("The Three So-called Testaments of Peter I"), *Voprosy Istorii*, no. 2 (1979), 131–144.

[199] N. Pavlenko, "Savva Lukich Vladislavich-Raguzinskii," *Sibirskie ogni*, no. 3 (1978), 156–168; N. I. Pavlenko, *Aleksandr Danilovich Menshikov* (Moscow, 1981).

[200] N. I. Pavlenko, "Petr I (k izucheniiu sotsialno-politicheskikh vzgliadov)," *Rossiia v period reform Petra I*, 40–102. Pavlenko also served as the editor in chief (Soviet "responsible editor") of the entire volume, discussed earlier.

his short life he was destroying cities, storming fortresses, shedding blood. He built only redoubts.

Peter's talents were immeasurably broader. He knew how to hold a sword in a firm hand, but he had mastered the pen with equal success, and he willingly took a chisel and an ax. Diplomacy and military affairs, state building and enlightenment, industry and trade, the way of life and the mores—this is a far from complete list of the spheres of existence of the country in which Peter authoritatively intervened and upon which he left his mark, which struck the eye not only of descendants but also of contemporaries.[201]

Diametrically opposed results followed: under Charles XII, Sweden lost the position of a great power; under Peter I, Russia gained it.

Appropriately, already in 1954 Pavlenko edited, with Kafengauz, and made several contributions to the huge fundamental volume on Russian history in the first quarter of the eighteenth century, which formed the subject of the preceding section of this chapter. But the historian's own fullest and most comprehensive presentation of Peter the Great came some two decades later in a book entitled *Peter the First* and given wide circulation.[202]

Forcefully written and strong in detail and anecdote, as well as in such Pavlenko specialties as the social-political views and attitudes of the monarch, the volume presented effectively the established judgments on the Petrine reign. The author did not conceal in the least the extreme brutality of the suppression of the *streltsy,* but he considered it as essentially inevitable because of the head-on collision of the new and the old. Similarly, Tsarevich Alexis was unhesitatingly condemned, though his case was presented in an expert manner. The Astrakhan rebellion, by contrast, it was claimed, had a popular quality, and its achievements included a temporary check to some of the Petrine oppression of the masses. Pavlenko noted that the reform of local government had as its main aim a more thorough control of the people, but on the whole he was favorable to the Petrine political and administrative change. The greatest prominence and praise was given to the saga of war and international success.

But the bipolar nature of the Petrine image remained as pronounced as ever and unresolved. Pavlenko explained in the beginning: "Evaluating positively the significance of Peter's reforms in the history of our Motherland, one must remember that Peter's policy had a class character. The reforms of that epoch were realized at the cost of enormous sacrifices of laboring population."[203] And, to explicate the matter further:

Peter's policy was directed toward raising the gentry. His reforms strengthened the dominant position of the gentry in feudal society. The gentry estate became more monolithic and better educated; its role in the army and in the apparatus

201 *Ibid.*, 101.
202 I used the second, revised edition: N. Pavlenko, *Petr Pervyi* (Moscow, 1976).
203 *Ibid.*, 6.

of the state increased; its rights to the labor of enserfed peasants broadened. Newly acquired seaports guaranteed to the landlords and the rich merchants advantageous conditions for selling the produce of an economy of serfdom.

The class direction of the reforms does not preclude their enormous pannational significance. They led Russia onto the road of accelerated economic, political, and cultural development; and they inscribed the name of Peter, the initiator of these reforms, in the Pleiad of outstanding statesmen of our country.[204]

There were two sides to Peter I's activity:

It would appear that Peter the lawgiver was possessed by two mutually exclusive passions: to teach, educate and to punish, threaten. That provided the ground for great Pushkin to remark that Peter in some cases displayed a broad mind, full of benevolence and wisdom, and in others, cruelty and willfulness. Some of Peter's ukases, said the poet, "were, it would seem, written with a knout."[205]

Moreover, considered in their historic setting, the positive Petrine measures were woefully weak and inadequate:

Life in an antagonistic society, based on a most cruel exploitation, arbitrariness, and class oppression, developed according to its laws and laughed cruelly at the ukases explaining how to obtain best and in the simplest possible manner the blessedness and prosperity of all subjects. Instead of "harmony," new social contradictions were born; instead of a general accord, class struggle, which could not be either overcome or stopped by new institutions, new ukases, new reglaments.[206]

Nevertheless, the historian concluded:

Peter is an autocratic tsar, who expressed the interests of his class, who planted the new and cleared away the old by barbarian means. He was a son of his age. But he was truly great because he cared about the fate of his country, about the growth of its power. What Peter accomplished, together with the people and against the people, exercised an enormous influence not only on the subsequent historical destinies of Russia, but also in part of Europe.

Peter was and remains one of the great statesmen whose name belongs forever to his country and to history.[207]

204 *Ibid.*

205 *Ibid.*, 317. Elsewhere Pavlenko commented even more devastatingly: "Possibly, Pushkin, continuing to think about the character of Peter's legislative activity, would have changed the evaluation cited above and would have discovered that not only 'temporary' but also permanent ukases 'were written with a knout.'" Pavlenko, "Petr I (k izucheniiu sotsialno-politicheskikh vzgliadov)," 97.

206 Pavlenko, *Petr Pervyi*, 317.

207 *Ibid.*, 377.

# Conclusion

> The figure of Peter the Great has dominated the development of Russian social and political thought, as well as Russian historical writing. As a matter of fact, the historiography of Peter the Great provides an almost perfect mirror for the Russian intelligentsia's views on the past and future of Russia, their relationship to the West, and the nature of the social and political problems confronting their country.
>
> Marc Raeff[1]

Peter the Great left a remarkable impress on Russian history and thought. The original image of him and his role, drawn by the reformer himself as well as by such members of his admiring entourage as Feofan Prokopovich, blended wonderfully well with the concept of the enlightened despot of the Age of Reason. The first emperor brought light into darkness, converted barbarism into civilization, even created a rational state and society ex nihilo. The new Russian power and international significance confirmed brilliantly his accomplishment. The Russian educated public, itself a product of the Petrine reform, kept believing in this overwhelming image of its originator and kept mounting his praises, without a fundamental change in the point of view, for some 125 years. Catherine the Great made the claim that she represented a still higher stage of the Russian Enlightenment, and different Russian intellectuals, reflecting personal tastes or the ideological currents of the moment, placed different emphases on the first emperor's many virtues and achievements, but they did not question his primacy or his supreme significance. Criticism was limited to an occasional mention of costs, to some aristocratic unease, to an infrequent sentimental regret of things past, and, only toward the end of the long period, in the cases of Radishchev and certain Decembrists, to a more radical reading of the Enlightenment than the established Petrine image allowed for. Much more common was an absolute endorsement of the reformer and an enthusiastic defense of him and his activity, character trait by character trait and incident by incident, in the generally accepted terms of the Age of Reason. The identification of the modern Russian educated public, between the years of 1700 and 1825 or

[1] Marc Raeff, ed., *Peter the Great Changes Russia*, 2d ed. (Lexington, Mass.; Toronto; London, 1972), 195.

thereabouts, with the modern Russian monarchy found splendid expression in the Russian Enlightenment image of Peter the Great.

A new situation emerged only in the 1830s. The Russian government had lost all its liberal promise, having consciously chosen extremely conservative policies. The world, after the French Revolution, Napoleon, the Congress of Vienna, and repeated disturbances, was divided and seemed threatening. Inside Russia, too, the simple Enlightenment beliefs in education and progress appeared to bear little relationship to reality. Moreover, the ideology of the Age of Reason itself had been challenged and, in part, replaced by traditionalist doctrines and by German idealistic philosophy and Romanticism in general. In these circumstances, three basic images of Peter the Great arose in Russia. The Enlightenment image split in two. The government and its supporters retained faith in Peter the Great, the victorious creator of the Russian empire and its might, the sage organizer of the state, the lawgiver of modern Russia. But they rejected any further imitation of the West, dynamic development, progress. The Westernizers, by contrast, hypostasized precisely that other part of the original Petrine image as the true aim and hope of their country and their people. In addition, a third Petrine image, the first full-scale negative one to emerge in the midst of the Russian educated public, was postulated by the Slavophiles. They declared the entire Petrine reform a perversion and a disaster and clamored for a return to the true Russian principles, reflecting, one may surmise, the difficulty—some would say the failure—of the Russian adjustment to the modern world that followed the Petrine turn Westward. The unity between the government and the educated public, as well as the unity within the educated public itself, were no more. The celebrated debate between the Westernizers and the Slavophiles was carried on not in the quasi-empirical framework of the Age of Reason, but in a metaphysical one, that of German idealism to be more exact: for both schools of thought, Peter the Great possessed transcendent power and importance; only the first endowed him with a plus, and the second with a minus, sign.

The third period in the history of the Russian image of the reformer, from about 1860 to 1917, exhibited less unity than the second, not to mention the first. Utilitarianism, pragmatism, positivism, scientism, and an emphasis on precise scholarship were less favorable to overarching schemes than earlier weltanschauungs. Also, Russian society and culture were becoming more pluralistic, and that led to a greater differentiation of attitudes toward Peter the Great as toward other topics under discussion. Still, certain trends in regard to the Perine image should be noted. The decline of metaphysics and the new vogue of "scientific history" led to S. Soloviev's outstanding treatment of the Petrine reign: the original Westernizer metaphysical structure was used to render meaning, pace, and power to an extensive and thoroughly scholarly factual exposition. With the eventual disappearance of that structure, the way was opened to Miliukov's presentation of the reign as catastrophe and confusion worse confounded and to Bogoslovskii's supreme devotion to detail. Furthermore, whereas the new Petrine scholarship surpassed by far in quantity and quality earlier contributions, it also became evident for the first time that important modern Russian history could be focused on other subjects than the first emperor, such as the gentry or serfdom. The ideologues also provided different approaches. The government continued to uphold its statist image of Peter the Great although with less emotional commitment and enthusiasm than before. Most liberals sailed in the wake of the original Westernizers. On the radical Left, opinions split: one could follow Belinskii and consider the reformer, cruelty and all, as the true Enlightener; or one could agree with the late Herzen (and indeed already some Decembrists) and emphasize Petrine autocratic oppression. Some anarchists and populists were not only inimical to the first emperor, but also little concerned with him. Finally, the Petrine theme was revived in the so-called Silver Age (strictly speaking, a separate intellectual period): its ramifications, like the age itself, pointed in different directions and await further study.

The October Revolution was followed by a denunciation and denigration of Peter the Great together with other Romanovs. The first dominant school to emerge, that of Pokrovskii, took a strikingly negative, as well as personally hostile view, of the reformer and his historical role. Yet when Stalin came to power and the Soviet system received its definitive form in the 1930s, Pokrovskii's schema was replaced by a much more complex bipolar Petrine image, which remains the established Petrine image in the Soviet Union today (even if it is at present less xenophobic and less insistently linked to the Marxist classics than formerly). That image emphasizes both the positive and the negative in the reformer and the reform in an extreme and contradictory manner: positive in strengthening the state, in war, diplomacy, industrial development, education, organization and administration; negative in its furtherance of gentry domination and in the increasing oppression of the people. Although the parts are disparate, the totality exhibits a striking bipolar symmetry. An outstanding example of conflict between a national and a class interpretation, the image has other aspects besides. Thus, contemporaries quickly noticed parallels between Peter the Great and Stalin as to leadership, methods, and costs, as well as the international setting and the alleged primacy of the struggle for survival. Such critics of the Soviet system as Alexander Solzhenitsyn and Alexander Yanov censured not only Stalin but also Peter the Great, the first essentially for the emperor's betrayal of Russian principles, the second for his having been a fine example of the recurrent autocratic blight in Russian history. Yet, at the age of about fifty, the dominant Soviet Petrine image is clearly second in duration only to the Petrine image of the Russian Enlightenment.

What will the next Russian image of Peter the Great be like?

# Bibliography

The bibliography is limited to the items, almost all of them published, mentioned specifically in the present work.

Akademiia nauk SSSR. Institut istorii. *Protiv istoricheskoi kontseptsii M. N. Pokrovskogo; sbornik statei* [Red. kollegiia: B. Grekov i dr.]. 2 vols. Moscow, 1939–1940. [Title varies, v. 2: *Protiv antimarksistskoi kontseptsii M. N. Pokrovskogo*]

Aksakov, I. S. *Sochineniia*. Vol. V. *Gosudarstvennyi i zemskii vopros. Stati o nekotorykh istoricheskikh sobytiiakh*. Moscow, 1887.

Aksakov, K. S. "O sovremennom literaturnom spore." *Rus.* 1883, No. 7.

———. *Polnoe sobranie sochinenii*. Vol. I. Moscow, 1861.

Alekseeva, M. A. "Bratia Ivan i Aleksei Zubovy i graviura Petrovskogo vremeni." *Rossia v period reform Petra I.* 337–361.

E. V. Anisimov. *Podatnaia reforma Petra I. Vvedenie podushnoi podati v Rossii, 1719–1728 gg*. Leningrad, 1982.

Annenskii, Innokentii. *Posmertnye stikhi*. St. Petersburg, 1923.

Anpilogov, G. Review of *Petr Velikii. Sbornik statei*, edited by A. I. Andreev. *Voprosy Istorii*. 1948 (April): 120–134.

———. "Senat pri Petre I." *Istoricheskii Zhurnal*. 1941. No. 4: 40–49.

Antonovich, M. A. "Opyt istoricheskogo opravdaniia Petra I-go, protiv obvineniia nekotorykh sovremennykh pisatelei. Karla Zadlera. S.-Peterburg. 1861 g." *Sovremennik. Literaturnyi zhurnal*. Vol. 78: 161–172.

Atreshkov, N. "Nekotorye vozrazheniia kritiku nashchet izmenenii Petrom Velikim natsionalnosti russkikh." *Severnaia Pchela*. Nos. 7, 8 (January 10–11, 1833).

Baburin, D. *Ocherki po istorii "Manufaktur-kollegii" (XVIII v.)*. Moscow, 1939.

Baehr, Stephen L. "From History to National Myth: *Translatio imperii* in Eighteenth-Century Russia." *The Russian Review*. Vol. 37, no. 1. January 1978, pp. 1–13.

———. "In the Re-beginning: Rebirth, Renewal and *Renovatio* in Eighteenth-Century Russia." *Russia and the West in the Eighteenth Century*. Edited by A. G. Cross. Newtonville, Mass., 1983, pp. 152–166.

———. "In the Image and Likeness: The 'Political Icon' in Seventeenth and Eighteenth Century Russia." Manuscript.

von Baer, K. M. *Peter's des Grossen Verdienste um die Erweiterung der geographischen Kenntnisse*. St. Petersburg, 1872.

Baiov, A. K. *Istoriia russkoi armii: kurs voennykh uchilishch*. St. Petersburg, 1912.

Baklanova, E. N. *Krestianskii dvor i obshchina na russkom Severe. Konets XVII–nachalo XVIII v*. Moscow, 1976.

Bakunin, M. A. *Sobranie sochinenii i pisem, 1828–1876*. Edited by Iu. M. Steklov. Vols. III, IV, Moscow, 1935.

Baron, Samuel H. "Feudalism or the Asiatic Mode of Production: Alternate Interpretations of Russian History." *Windows on the Russian Past.* Edited by Samuel H. Baron and Nancy W. Heer. Columbus, Ohio, 1977. 24–41.

———. *Plekhanov: the Father of Russian Marxism.* Stanford, California, 1963.

Barsukov, N. P. *Zhizn i trudy M. P. Pogodina.* 22 vols. St. Petersburg, 1888–1910.

Basnin, P. P. "Raskolnichi legendy o Petre Velikom." *Istoricheskii Vestnik.* St. Petersburg, Vol. XCIII (1903): 513–548.

Bazilevich, K. "Petr I kak polkovodets." *Russkoe voenno-morskoe iskusstvo.* Moscow, 1951, 40–46.

———. "Petr I—osnovopolozhnik russkogo voennogo iskusstva." *Bolshevik.* 1945. Nos. 11–12 (June): 35–48.

———. "Petr Velikii." *Bolshevik.* 1943. No. 17 (September): 49–64.

Begunov, Iu. K. "Izuchenie literatury petrovskoi epokhi za poslednee desiatiletie." *Russkaia literatura.* 1 (1980): 208–225.

Belinskii, V. G. "*Deianiia Petra Velikogo, mudrogo preobrazovatelia Rossii,* sobrannye iz dostovernykh istochnikov i raspolozhennye po godam. Sochinenie I. I. Golikova. Izdanie vtoroe. Moskva. 1837–1840. Tomy I–XIII. *Istoriia Petra Velikogo.* Sochinenie Veniamina Bergmana. Perevel s nemetskogo Egor Aladin. Vtoroe, szhatoe (kompaktnoe) izdanie, ispravlennoe i umnozhennoe. S.-Peterburg. 1840. Tri toma. *O Rossii v tsarstvovanie Aleksiia Mikhailovicha.* Sovremennoe sochinenie Grigoriia Koshikhina. S.-Peterburg. 1840." *Polnoe sobranie sochinenii.* Edited by S. A. Vengerov. Vol. VI. St. Petersburg, 1903, 118–143, 179–198, 573–575, 585–586.

———. "Peterburg i Moskva." *Sobranie sochinenii v trekh tomakh.* General editor, F. M. Golovenchenko. Vol. II. Moscow, 1948, 763–791.

———. *Pisma.* Edited by E. A. Liatskii. 3 vols. St. Petersburg, 1914.

———. *Sobranie sochinenii v trekh tomakh.* General editor, F. M. Golovenchenko. 3 vols. Moscow, 1948.

Berkov, P. N. "Osnovnye voprosy izucheniia russkogo prosvetitelstva." *Problemy russkogo Prosveshcheniia v literature XVIII veka.* Moscow–Leningrad, 1961, 5–27.

Beskrovnyi, L. G. *Russkaia armiia i flot v XVIII veke (Ocherki).* Moscow, 1958.

———. "Strategiia i taktika russkoi armii v poltavskii period Severnoi voiny." *Poltava. K 250-letiiu Poltavskogo srazheniia,* 21–62.

Bestuzhev-Riumin, K. *Biografii i kharakteristiki.* St. Petersburg, 1882.

———. "Prichiny razlichnykh vzgliadov na Petra Velikogo v russkoi nauke i russkom obshchestve." *Zhurnal Ministerstva Narodnogo Prosveshcheniia.* CLXI. 1872 (5–6): 149–156.

Black, Cyril E. "The Reforms of Peter the Great." *Rewriting Russian History.* Edited by Cyril E. Black. New York, 1962, 232–259.

Blok, A. "Petr." *Gorod moi . . . Stikhi o Peterburge-Petrograde.* Leningrad, 1957, 72–75.

Bobrovskii, P. O. *Voennoe pravo v Rossii pri Petre Velikom.* St. Petersburg, 1886.

Bogoslovskii, M. M. "Administrativnye preobrazovaniia Petra Velikogo, 1699–1700 gg." Part I. "Boiarskaia duma." *Izvestiia AN SSSR.* Nos. 4–7 (1928): 279–298.

————. "Administrativnye preobrazovaniia Petra Velikogo, 1699–1700 gg." Part 2. "Prikazy i mestnoe upravlenie." *Izvestiia AN SSSR.* No. 2 (1929): 97–121.

————. "Gorodskaia reforma 1699 g. v provintsionalnykh gorodakh." *Uchenye zapiski Instituta istorii RANIION* (1927): 210–250.

————. *Oblastnaia reforma Petra Velikogo. Provintsiia 1719–27 gg.* Moscow, 1902.

————. "Palata ob Ulozhenii 1700–1703 gg." *Izvestiia AN SSSR.* Nos. 15–17 (1927): 1347–1474; No. 1 (1928): 81–110.

————. *Petr I. Materialy dlia biografii.* 5 vols. (*n.p.*), 1940–1948.

————. *Petr Velikii i ego reforma.* Moscow, 1920.

————. "Petr Velikii (Opyt kharakteristiki)." *Tri veka. Rossiia ot Smuty do nashego vremeni.* Edited by V. V. Kallash. Vol. III. *XVIII vek. Pervaia polovina.* Moscow, 1912–1913, 15–33.

————. "Petr Velikii po ego pismam." *Sbornik statei v chest Matveia Kuzmicha Liubavskogo.* Petrograd, 1917, 216–250. Slavica-Reprint No. 57. Düsseldorf–Vaduz, 1970.

————. *Russkoe obshchestvo i nauka pri Petre Velikom.* Leningrad, 1926.

Boltin, Ivan. *Primechaniia na Istoriiu drevniia i nyneshniia Rossii g. Leklerka.* 2 vols. St. Petersburg, 1788.

Briusov, Valerii. "Mednyi Vsadnik." *Pushkin.* Edited by S. A. Vengerov. St. Petersburg, 1909. Vol. III, 456–472.

Brown, Edward J. *Stankevich and His Moscow Circle.* Stanford, California, 1966.

Brückner, A. *Geschichte Russlands biz zum Ende des 18. Jahrhunderts.* Vol. I. *Die Europäisierung Russlands. Land und Volk.* Gotha, 1888. Vol. II. C. Mettig. *Die Europäisierung Russlands in 18. Jahrhunderte.* Gotha, 1913.

————. *Istoriia Petra Velikogo.* St. Petersburg, 1882.

————. *Peter der Grosse.* Berlin, 1879.

Bulgarin, F. *Vospominaniia.* Vol. I. St. Petersburg, 1846.

Buzhinskii, Gavriil. *Polnoe sobranie pouchitelnykh slov, skazyvannykh v vysochaishem prisutstvii gosudaria imperatora Petra Velikogo.* Moscow, 1784.

————. "V pokhvalu Sanktpeterburga i ego Osnovatelia, Gosudaria Imperatora Petra Velikogo." *Polnoe sobranie pouchitelnykh slov. Moscow,* 1784, 1–36.

Byrnes, Robert F. *Pobedonostsev, His Life and Thought.* Bloomington–London, 1968.

Cherniavsky, Michael. "The Old Believers and the New Religion." *Slavic Review.* XV (March, 1966): 1–39.

————. *Tsar and People.* New Haven, 1961.

Chernyshevskii, N. G. "Apologiia sumashedshego." *Polnoe sobranie sochinenii v piatnadtsati tomakh.* Vol. VII. *Stati i retsenzii 1860–1861.* Moscow, 1950, 592–618, 1033–1034.

————. *Ocherki gogolevskogo perioda russkoi literatury.* Moscow, 1953.

————. *Polnoe sobranie sochinenii v piatnadtsati tomakh.* Vol. V. *Stati 1858–1859.* Moscow, 1950.

————. "(Zametki o Nekrasove) Zametki pri chtenii 'Biograficheskikh svedenii' o Nekrasove, pomeshchennykh v I tome 'Posmertnogo izdaniia' ego 'stikhotvorenii.' SPb. 1879." *Polnoe sobranie sochinenii v piatnadtsati tomakh.* Vol. I. Moscow, 1939, 742–754, 814–816.

Chicherin, B. N. *Vospominaniia. Moskva sorokovykh godov.* Moscow, 1929.

Chizhevskii, D. I. *Gegel v Rossii.* Paris, 1939.

Chistov. K. V. *Russkie narodnye sotsialnoutopicheskie legendy XVIII–XIX vekov.* Moscow, 1967.

Cracraft, James, ed. *For God and Peter the Great: The Works of Thomas Consett, 1723–1729.* Boulder, 1982.

Cracraft, James. "Did Feofan Prokopovich Really Write *Pravda Voli Monarshei?*" *Slavic Review,* Vol. 40, No. 2 (Summer 1981), 173–193.

―――. "The Tercenary of Peter the Great in Russia." *Canadian-American Slavic Studies.* Vol. VIII, No. 2 (Summer 1974): 319–326.

Crummey, Robert O. *The Old Believers and the World of Antichrist: The Vyg Community and the Russian State, 1694–1855.* Madison, Milwaukee, and London, 1970.

Custine, Astolphe Marquis de. *La Russie en 1839.* 4 vols. Brussels: Société Belge de Librairie, 1843.

Dashkova, E. R. "Mon histoire." *Bumagi kniagini E. R. Dashkovoi. Arkhiv kniazia Vorontsova.* Vol. XXI. Moscow, 1881, 1–365.

Davidson, A. B., and V. A. Makhrushin. *Zov dalnikh morei.* Moscow, 1979.

Demidova, N. F. "Iz istorii zakliucheniia Nerchinskogo dogovora 1689 v." *Rossiia v period reform Petra I,* 289–310.

Derzhavin, G. R. "Monument Petra Velikago." *Sochineniia Derzhavina s obiasnitelnymi primechaniiami.* Vol. I, 13–14.

―――. "Petru Velikomu." *Sochineniia Derzhavina s obiasnitelnymi primechaniiami.* Vol. I, 10–12.

―――. *Sochineniia Derzavina s obiasnitelnymi primechaniiami.* 4 vols. St. Petersburg, 1895.

Ditiatin, I. *Ustroistvo i upravlenie gorodov Rossii.* Vol. I. *Vvedenie. Goroda Rossii v XVIII stoletii.* St. Petersburg, 1875.

Dobroliubov, N. A. "Pervye gody tsarstvovaniia Petra Velikogo (Istoriia tsarstvovaniia Petra Velikogo. N. Ustrialova. SPb. 1858, tri toma)." *Sochineniia.* Vol. II. 6th edition. St. Petersburg (n.d.), 60–180.

Dostoevskii, F. M. "Peterburgskaia letopis." *Polnoe sobranie sochinenii v tridtsati tomakh.* Vol. XVIII. *Stati i zametki, 1845–1861.* Leningrad, 1978: 11–34, 216–229 (notes).

Druzhinin, N. M. "Prosveshchennyi absoliutizm v Rossii." *Absoliutizm v Rossii (XVII–XVIII vv.).* Edited by N. M. Druzhinin, N. I. Pavlenko, and L. V. Cherepnin. Moscow, 1964, 428–459.

Dubrovin, A. I. "Korabelnyi master Petr Mikhailov. K 300-letiiu so dnia rozhdeniia Petra I." *Sudostroenie,* 1972. No. 6: 66–72.

―――. "Ledovye pokhody Petra I. K 300-letiiu so dnia rozhdennia Petra I." *Sudostroenie,* 1972. No. 5: 58–64.

Enteen, George M. *The Soviet Scholar-Bureaucrat: M. N. Pokrovskii and the Society of Marxist Historians.* University Park and London, 1978.

Epifanov, P. "K voprosu o voennoi reforme Petra Velikogo." *Voprosy Istorii,* 1945, No. 1: 33–58.

Erhard, M. "La Satire 'De l'éducation' de A. D. Kantemir," *Revue des études slaves,* Vol. 38 (1961), 73–79.

Erikson, Ann K. "E. V. Tarle, the Career of a Historian under the Soviet Regime." *The American Slavic and East European Review,* Vol. XIX, No. 2 (April 1960): 202–216.

Fedorov, Evgenii. *Kamennyi poias.* Book I. *Demidovy.* Moscow–Leningrad, 1950.

Feinberg, Ilia. "Istoriia Petra I." *Nezavershennye raboty Pushkina.* Third, enlarged edition. Moscow, 1962, 13–242.

Filippov, Aleksandr. *O nakazanii po zakonodatelstvu Petra Velikogo, v sviazi s reformoiu.* Moscow, 1891.

Firsov, N. N. *Petr I Velikii, Moskovskii tsar i imperator vserossiiskii.* Moscow, 1916.

Gasiorowska, Xenia. *The Image of Peter the Great in Russian Fiction.* Madison, Wisconsin, 1979.

Gerbstman, A. "O siuzhete i obrazakh 'Mednogo Vsadnika.' " *Russkaia literatura,* 1963, No. 4: 77–88.

Gere, Vladimir. *Otnosheniia Leibnitsa k Rossii i Petru Velikomu. Po nieizdannym bumagam Leibnitsa v Gannoverskoi biblioteke.* St. Petersburg, 1871.

German, Iurii. *Sobranie sochinenii.* Vol. III. *Rossiia molodaia.* Leningrad, 1976.

Gershkovich, Z. I. "O metodologicheskikh printsipakh izucheniia russkogo prosvetitelstva," in *Problemy russkogo Prosveshcheniia v literature XVIII veka.* Moscow–Leningrad, 1961, 151–157.

Girs, I. V., and B. N. Favorov. " 'Poteshnaia' flotiliia Petra." *Sudostroenie,* 1972, No. 6: 72–74.

Gogol, N. V. *Polnoe sobranie sochinenii.* Vol. VIII. *Stati.* Leningrad, 1952.

Golikov, Ivan. *Deianiia Petra Velikogo, mudrogo preobrazovatelia Rossii, sobrannye iz dostovernykh istochnikov i raspolozhennye po godam.* 12 vols. Moscow, 1788–1789.

———. *Dopolnenie k Deianiiam Petra Velikogo, mudrogo preobrazovatelia Rossii.* 18 vols. Moscow, 1790–1797.

———. *Sravnenie svoistv i del Konstantina Velikogo, pervogo iz rimskikh khristianskogo imperatora, s svoistvami i delami Petra Velikogo, pervogo vserossiskogo imperatora, i proizshestvii, v tsarstvovanie oboikh sikh monarkhov sluchivshikhsia.* 2 vols. in 1. Moscow, 1810.

Golikova, N. B. *Astrakhanskoe vosstanie 1705–1706 gg.* Moscow, 1975.

———. "Istoriia sostavleniia obrashchenii uchastnikami Astrakhanskogo vosstaniia 1705–1706 gg." *Istoriia SSSR,* 1971. No. 6: 158–169.

———. "Iz istorii klassovykh protivorechii v russkoi armii (1700–1709 gg.)." *Poltava. K 250-letiiu Poltavskogo srazheniia.* 269–285.

———. "K istorii Astrakhanskogo vosstaniia 1705–1706 gg. (sotsialnaia politika i organy upravleniia vosstavshikh)." *Rossiia v period reform Petra I.* 249–288.

———. *Politicheskie protsessy pri Petre I. Po materialam Preobrazhenskogo prikaza.* Moscow, 1957.

Goltsev, V. "K voprosu o petrovskoi reforme." *Russkaia Mysl.* VII (1886), August: 170–175.

———. *Zakonodatelstvo i nravy Rossii XVIII veka.* Moscow, 1886.

Golyshev, I. *Lubochnaia starinnaia kartinka: "Myshi kota pogrebaiut" i nekatorye prezhnie narodnye graviury.* Vladimir, 1878.

"Gosudarstvennye idei Petra Velikogo i ikh sudba." *Vestnik Evropy.* 1872 (No. 6): 770–796.

Gosudarstvennyi Ermitazh. *Russkaia kultura pervoi poloviny XVIII veka.* Leningrad, 1979.

Gosudarstvennyi Russkii Musei. *Feierverki i illiuminatsii v grafike XVIII veka. Katalog vystavki.* Leningrad, 1978.

Gote, Iu. V. *Istoriia Oblastnogo upravleniia v Rossii ot Petra I do Ekateriny II.* Vol. I. Moscow, 1913. Vol. II. Moscow–Leningrad, 1941.

Gradovskii, A. D. "Vysshaia administratsiia Rossii XVIII st. i general-prokurory." *Sobranie sochinenii.* Vol. I. St. Petersburg, 1899, 37–297.

Granovskii, T. N. *T. N. Granovskii i ego perepiska.* Vol. II. *Perepiska T. N. Granovskogo.* Moscow, 1897.

Grech, N. I. *Examen de l'ouvrage de M. le Marquis de Custine intitulé la Russie en 1839.* Paris, 1844.

Grot, Ia. "Petr Velikii, kak prosvetitel Rossii." *Zapiski Imperatorskoi Akademii Nauk.* Vol. XXI. St. Petersburg, 1872, 31–86.

Herzen, A. I. *Byloe i dumy, Chasti I–II. Sobranie sochinenii v tridtsati tomakh.* Vol. VIII. Moscow, 1956.

———. "Dvadtsat osmoe ianvaria." *Sobranie sochinenii v tridtsati tomakh.* Vol. I. *Proizvedeniia 1829–1841 godov.* Moscow, 1954, 29–35, 463–464, 482–483.

———. "Moskva i Peterburg." *Sobranie sochinenii v tridtsati tomakh.* Vol. II. *Stati i feletony, 1841–1846. Dnevnik, 1842–1845.* Moscow, 1954, 33–42, 426–428, 439–440.

———. "Panslavisme muscovite et européisme russe." *Sobranie sochinenii v tridtsati tomakh.* Vol. VII. *O razvitii revoliutsionnykh idei v Rossii, Proizvedeniia 1851–1852 godov.* Moscow, 1945, 101–118.

———. "Pierre Ier." *Sobranie sochinenii v tridtsati tomakh.* Vol. VII. *O razvitii revoliutsionnykh idei v Rossii, Proizvedeniia 1851–1852 godov.* Moscow, 1956, 40–62, 396–398.

———. "Pisma ob izuchenii prirody." *Sobranie sochinenii v tridtsati tomakh.* Vol. III. *Diletantizm v nauke, Pisma ob izuchenii prirody, 1842–1846.* Moscow, 1954, 89–315, 319–330.

———. "Revoliutsiia v Rossii." *Sobranie sochinenii v tridtsati tomakh.* Vol. XIII. *Stati iz 'Kolokola' i drugie proizvedeniia 1857–1858 godov.* Moscow, 1958, 21–29.

———. "La Russie." *Sobranie sochinenii v tridtsati tomakh.* Vol. VI. *S togo berega, Stati, Dolg prezhde vsego, 1847–1851.* Moscow, 1955, 150–186, 476–477, 514–519.

———. *Sobranie sochinenii v tridtsati tomakh.* 30 vols. Academy of Sciences edition. Moscow, 1954–1966.

Iarosh, K. *Psikhologicheskaia parallel, Ioann Groznyi i Petr Velikii.* Kharkov, 1898.

"Istoricheskaia khronika." *Istoricheskoe Obozrenie.* Vol. V. St. Petersburg, 1892: 175–248.

*Istoriia russkogo iskusstva.* Edited by E. E. Grabar, V. S. Kamenev, and V. N. Lazarev. Vol. V. Moscow, 1960.

Iunakov, N. L. *Severnaia voina.* 2 vols. St. Petersburg, 1909.

*Iunosti chestnoe zertsalo ili pokazanie k zhiteiskomu obkhozhdeniiu. Sobrannoe ot raznykh Avtorov. Napechatasia poveleniem Tsarskago Velichestva, v Sankt-piterburkhe Leta Gospodnia 1717, Febralia 4 dnia.* Facsimile edition. Moscow, 1976.

Ivanov, A. M. "V chest pervykh pobed russkogo flota." *Sudostroenie,* 1966. No. 8: 70–71.

Ivanov, V. N. "Noch tsaria Petra." *Imperatritsa Fike.* Moscow, 1968.

Kafengauz, B. B. "Epokha Petra Velikogo v osveshchenii sovetskoi istoricheskoi nauki." *Petr Velikii. Sbornik statei.* Edited By A. I. Andreev. Moscow–Leningrad, 1947: 334–389.

———. "Pushkin o Petre I." *Istoriia SSSR,* 1961, No. 3: 150–160.

———. "Reformy Petra I v otsenke M. N. Pokrovskogo." *Protiv antimarksistskoi kontseptsii M. N. Pokrovskogo. Sbornik statei.* Part II. Moscow–Leningrad, 1940: 140–176.

———. *Rossiia pri Petre pervom.* Moscow, 1955.

Kantemir, Antiokh. "Petrida ili opisanie stikhotvornoe smerti Petra Velikogo, *Sobranie stikhotvorenii.* Leningrad, 1956: 241–247.

Karamzin, N. M. *Letters of a Russian Traveler, 1789–1790.* Translated and abridged by Florence Jonas. New York, 1957.

———. "Oda na sluchai prisiagi moskovskikh zhitelei Ego Imperatorskomu Velichestvu Pavlu Pervomu, Samoderzhtsu Vserossiiskomu." *Polnoe sobranie stikhotvorenii.* Moscow–Leningrad, 1966: 185–190.

———. "Rech, proiznesennaia na torzestvennom sobranii Imperatorskoi Rossiiskoi Akademii 5 dekabria 1818 goda." *Izbrannye sochineniia.* Vol. 2. Moscow–Leningrad, 1964: 233–242.

*Karamzin's Memoir on Ancient and Modern Russia.* Translation and analysis by Richard Pipes. New York, 1966.

*Kartiny iz deianii Petra Velikogo na severe.* St. Petersburg, 1872.

Kavelin, K. "Mysli i zametki o russkoi istorii." *Vestnik Evropy.* Year One. Volume II (June 1866): 325–404.

Kharlap, M. "O 'Mednom Vsadnike' Pushkina." *Voprosy literatury.* No. 7 (July, 1961): 87–101.

[Kheraskov, Mikhail Matveevich] "Stikhi ot izdatelia." *Numa ili Protsvetaiushchii Rim.* Moscow, 1768, 177–180.

Khodorov, A. E. "Ukrainskie siuzhety poezii K. F. Ryleeva." *Literaturnoe nasledie dekabristov.* Edited by V. G. Bazanov and V. E. Vatsuro. Leningrad, 1975, 121–141.

Khomiakov, A. S. *Polnoe sobranie sochinenii.* Vol. III. Moscow, 1900.

Kireevskii, I. V. *Polnoe sobranie sochinenii.* Edited by M. O. Gershenzon. Vol. I. Moscow, 1911.

Kizevetter, A. A. *Posadskaia obshchina v Rossii XVIII st.* Moscow, 1903.

Klinger, Hartmut. *Konstantin Nikolaevič Bestužev-Rjumins Stellung in der russischen Historiographie und seine gesellschaftliche Tätigkeit. Ein Beitrag zur russischen Geistesgeschichte des 19. Jahrhunderts.* Frankfurt am Main, 1980.

Kliuchevskii, V. O. "Evgenii Onegin i ego predki." *Ocherki i rechi. Vtoroi sbornik statei.* Petrograd, 1918, 66–87.

———. *Istoriia soslovii v Rossii.* 3d edition. Petrograd, 1918.

———. *Kurs russkoi istorii.* Part IV. 2d edition. Moscow, 1915.

———. "Otzyv o issledovanii P. N. Miliukova 'Gosudarstvennoe khoziastvo Rossii v pervuiu chetvert XVIII v. i reforma Petra Velikogo.'" *Sochineniia.* Vol. VIII. *Issledovaniia, retsenzii, rechi: 1890–1905.* Moscow, 1959: 177–183.

———. "Pamiati S. M. Solovieva." *Ocherki i rechi. Vtoroi sbornik statei.* Petrograd, 1918, 37–56.

———. *Peter the Great.* New York, 1959.

———. "Petr Velikii sredi svoikh sotrudnikov." *Ocherki i rechi. Vtoroi sbornik statei.* Petrograd, 1918, 454–495.

———. "Podushnaia podat i otmena kholopstva v Rossii." *Opyty i issledovaniia. Pervyi sbornik statei.* Moscow (n.d.), 311–416.

———. "Russkii rubl XVI–XVIII vv. v ego otnoshenii k nyneshnemu." *Opyty i issledovaniia. Pervyi sbornik statei.* Moscow (n.d.), 123–211.

———. "S. M. Soloviev, kak prepodavatel." *Ocherki i rechi. Vtoroi sbornik statei.* Petrograd, 1918, 26–36.

———. "Sergei Mikhailovich Soloviev." *Ocherki i rechi. Vtoroi sbornik statei.* Petrograd, 1918, 5–25.

Klochkov, M. *Naselenie Rossii pri Petre Velikom po perepisiam togo vremeni.* Vol. I. *Perepisi dvorov i naseleniia (1678–1721).* St. Petersburg, 1911.

Klokman, Iu. R. "Neizdannyi tom 'Istorii tsarstvovaniia Petra Velikogo' N. G. Ustrialova." *Poltava. K 250-letiiu poltavskogo srazheniia. Sbornik statei.* Moscow, 1959, 311–322.

Konichev, Konstantin. *Petr Pervyi na Severe. Povestovanie o Petre Pervom, o delakh ego i spodvizhnikakh na Severe, po dokumentam i predaniiam napisano.* Leningrad, 1973.

Kornilovich, A. O. *Sochineniia i pisma.* Moscow–Leningrad, 1957, 148–203.

———. "Zhizneopisanie Mazepy." *Sochineniia i pisma.* Moscow–Leningrad, 1957, 203–207.

Kovalevskii, P. I. *Petr Velikii i ego genii.* St. Petersburg, 1900.

Kozachenko, A. I. "Sobytiia 1708–1709 gg. na Ukraine v osveshchenii ukrainskoi dvoriansko-burzhuaznoi istoriografii." *Poltava. K 250-letiiu Poltavskogo srazheniia.* 323–350.

Kozev, A. "Petr I—osnovatel russkogo flota." *Rechnoi transport,* 1972. No. 9: 53–54.

[Krekshin, Petr Nikiforovich] *Kratkoie opisanie slavnykh i dostopamiatnykh del Imperatora Petra Velikogo, ego znamenitykh pobed i puteshestvii v raznye Evropeiskie Gosudarstva so mnogimi vazhnymi i liubopytnymi dostoinymi proizshestviiami, predstavlennoe razgovorami v tsarstve mertvykh General-Feldmarshala i kavalera Rossiiskikh i Maltiiskikh ordenov Grafa Borisa Petrovicha Sheremeteva, Boiarina Fedora Alekseevicha Golovina i samogo sego Velikogo Imperatora s Rossiiskim Tsarem Ioannom Vasilevichem, s Shvedskim Korolem Karlom XII, Izrailskim Tsarem Solomonom i Grecheskim Tsarem Aleksandrom.* St. Petersburg, 1788.

Kropotkin, Peter. *Memoirs of a Revolutionist.* New York, 1962.

Krotov, A. "Primirenchestvo i samouspokoennost." *Literaturnaia gazeta.* 72 (2455). September 8, 1948, p. 2.

Kukolnik, N. V. "Denshchik." *Sochineniia dramaticheskie. Sochineniia.* Vol. III. St. Petersburg, 1852, 189–330.

Kuleshov, V. I. "Slavianofily i romantizm." *K istorii russkogo romantizma.* Moscow, 1973, 305–344.

Labriolle, F. de. "Le prosveščenie russe et les lumières en France (1760–1798)." *Revue des études slaves,* Vol. 45 (1966), 75–91.

Lappo-Danilevskii, A. S. "Ideia gosudarstva i glavneishye momenty ee razvitiia v Rossii so vremeni smuty i do epokhi preobrazovanii." *Golos Minuvshego.* No. 12, 1914 (December): 5–38.

———. "Petr Velikii, osnovatel Imperatorskoi Akademii Nauk v S. Peterburge." *Rechi, proiznesennye na torzhestvennom sobranii Imperatorskoi Akademii*

*Nauk po sluchaiu trekhsotletiia tsarstvovaniia doma Romanovykh.* Petrograd, 1915, 33–88.

—————. *Russkie promyshlennye i torgovye kompanii v pervoi polovine XVIII veka.* St. Petersburg, 1898–1899.

Lebedev, V. "Administrativnye reformy Petra I." *Borba Klassov,* 1936. No. 12 (December): 109–116.

—————. "Astrakhanskoe vosstanie 1705–1706 gg. (Po pytochnym recham povstantsev v Preobrazhenskom prikaze.)" *Uchenye zapiski Moskovskogo gosudarstvennogo pedagogicheskogo instituta imeni V. P. Potemkina.* 1941. Vol. II. Part 1: 3–32.

—————. "Bashkirskie vosstaniia 1705–1711 gg." *Istoricheskie Zapiski.* 1937. No. 1: 81–102.

—————. *Bulavinskoe vosstanie (1707–1708).* Moscow, 1934 [and expanded version: Moscow, 1967].

—————. *Istoriia SSSR do XIX veka. Lektsii, chitannye na Istoricheskom fakultete MGU. (V szhatom izlozhenii).* Moscow, 1939 [and substantially different 1945 version].

—————, ed. *Reformy Petra I: Sbornik dokumentov.* Moscow, 1937.

Lebedev, V., and S. Iushkov. Review of *"Reguliarnoe" gosudarstvo Petra Pervogo i ego ideologiia,* by B. I. Syromiatnikov. *Istoricheskii Zhurnal.* 1944. Nos. 10–11: 124–131.

Lednicki, W. A. *Pushkin's Bronze Horseman: The Story of a Masterpiece.* Berkeley and Los Angeles, 1955.

Leer, G. A., ed. *Obzor voin Rossii ot Petra Velikogo do nashikh dnei: Posobie dlia izucheniia voennoi istorii v voennykh uchilishchakh.* 2d edition. St. Petersburg, 1893.

Leer, G. A. "Petr Velikii kak voennyi genii." *Voenno-istoricheskii sbornik.* 1865. Nos. 3 and 4.

Lenin, V. I. *Sochineniia.* Vol. XVI. Moscow, 1936.

*Literaturnoe nasledie dekabristov.* Edited by V. G. Bazanov and V. E. Vatsuro. Leningrad, 1975.

Lomonosov, M. V. "Oda na den tezoimenitstva Ego Imperatorskogo Vysochestva Gosudaria Velikago Kniazia Petra Feodorovicha 1743 goda." *Polnoe sobranie sochinenii.* Vol. VIII. Moscow–Leningrad, 1959, 103–110.

—————. *Polnoe sobranie sochinenii.* Vol. VI. *Trudy po russkoi istorii, obshchestvenno-ekonomicheskim voprosam i geografii, 1747–1765 gg.* Moscow–Leningrad, 1952. Vol. VII. *Trudy po filologii, 1739–1758 gg.* Moscow–Leningrad, 1952. Vol. VIII. *Poeziia, oratorskaia proza, nadpisi, 1732–1764 gg.* Moscow–Leningrad, 1959.

Lopatinskii, Feofilakt. "Slovo o bogodarovannom mire." *Panegiricheskaia literatura petrovskogo vremeni.* Moscow, 1979, 255–264.

Lortholary, A. *Le Mirage russe en France au XVIIIᵉ siècle.* Paris (n.d.).

Lukianov, P. "Rol Petra Velikogo v organizatsii khimicheskogo proizvodstva v Rossii." *Voprosy Istorii.* 1947. No. 6: 79–85.

Lystsov, V. P. *Persidskii pokhod Petra I, 1722–1723* (n.p.), 1951.

M. D. "Golitsyn, Dmitrii Mikhailovich," in *Entsiklopedicheskii Slovar* (Brochhaus-Efron). Vol. IX, Book 17 (St. Petersburg, 1893), 48–49.

McNally, Raymond T. *Chaadaev and His Friends. An Intellectual History of Peter Chaadayev and His Russian Contemporaries.* Tallahassee, 1971.

————. "Chaadaev's Evaluation of Peter the Great." *Slavic Review,* XXIII (1964): 31–44.

————, trans. and commentator. *The Major Works of Peter Chaadaev.* Notre Dame and London, 1969.

Maikova, T. S. "Petr I i 'Gistoriia Sveiskoi voiny,' " in *Rossiia v period reform Petra I.* Edited by N. I. Pavlenko, L. A. Nikiforov, M. Ia. Volkov. Moscow, 1973, 103–132.

Makogonenko, G. P. *Radishchev i ego vremia.* Moscow, 1956.

Malia, M. *Alexander Herzen and the Birth of Russian Socialism, 1812–1855.* Cambridge, Massachusetts, 1961.

Mandelstam, Osip. *Complete Poetry of Osip Emilevich Mandelstam.* Albany, 1973.

————. *Sobranie sochinenii v dvukh tomakh. Vol. I.* Washington, D.C., 1964.

Marx, Karl. *Secret Diplomatic History of the Eighteenth Century* and *The Story of the Life of Lord Palmerston.* Edited and with an introduction and notes by Lester Hutchinson. New York, 1969.

Mashinskii, S. "Stankevich i ego kruzhok." *Istoriia literatury.* 1964. No. 5: 125–148.

Mavrodin, V. *Osnovanie Peterburga.* Leningrad, 1978.

Mavrodin, V. V. *Petr Pervyi.* Leningrad, 1948.

————. *Petr I i preobrazovanie Rossii v pervoi chetverti XVIII veka.* Leningrad, 1954.

*Medals and Coins of the Age of Peter the Great. From the Hermitage Collection./Medali i monety Petrovskogo vremeni. Iz kollektsii Gosudarstvennogo Ermitazha.* Leningrad, 1974.

Merezhkovskii, D. S. *Antikhrist. Petr i Aleksei.* 2 vols. Berlin, 1922.

Meshalin, I. D., ed. *Materialy po istorii krestianskoi promyshlennosti XVIII i pervoi poloviny XIX v.* 2 vols. Moscow, 1935–1950.

Mezentsev, P. "Poema Pushkina 'Mednyi vsadnik' (k voporsu ob ideinom soderzhanii)." *Russkaia literatura.* 1958. No. 2: 56–68.

Mezhov, V. I. *Iubilei Petra Velikogo. Bibliograficheskii ukazatel literatury Petrovskogo iubileia 1872 g. s pribavleniem knig i statei o Petre i voobshche, iavivshikhsia v svet s 1865 do 1876 g. vkliuchitelno.* St. Petersburg, 1881.

Mikhailovskii, N. K. "Iz literaturnykh i zhurnalnykh zametok 1872 goda." *Sochineniia.* Vol. I. St. Petersburg, 1896, col. 634–810.

Miliukov, P. *Gosudarstvennoe khoziaistvo Rossii v pervoi chetverti XVIII stoletiia i reforma Petra Velikogo.* 2d edition. St. Petersburg, 1905.

————. "Gosudarstvennoe khoziaistvo Rossii v pervoi polovine XVIII veka i reforma Petra Velikogo." *Russkaia Mysl.* July 1892: 57–66.

————. "Petr Velikii i ego reforma (K dvukhsotletnei godovshchine)." *Na Chuzhoi Storone.* X (Prague, 1925): 11–28.

Miliukov, P. N. (Milioukov, Paul); Ch. Seignobos; L. Eisenman; *et al. Historie de Russie.* Vol. I. Paris, 1932.

Miliukov, P. *Ocherki po istorii russkoi kultury.* 3 vols. in 4. Paris, 1930–1937.

————. *Ocherki po istorii russkoi kultury.* Vol. I, Part 2. The Hague, 1964.

Miliukov, P. N. (Milioukov, P.). "Pierre le Grand et sa réforme (Pour le deuxième centenaire de la mort de Pierre)." *Le Monde Slave* (February 1925): 157–185.

Miliukov, P. "Stikhiinaia reforma Petra i stikhiinaia oppositsiia ei." *Ocherki po istorii russkoi kultury.* Vol. III. *Natsionalizm i evropeism.* Paris, 1930, 157–217.

Mosina, Z. "O rabote Instituta istorii Akademii nauk SSSR." *Voprosy Istorii.* 1948 (November): 144–149.

Myshlaevskii, A. Z. *Petr Velikii. Voina v Finlandii v 1712–1714 g. Sovmestnaia operatsiia armii, galernogo i korabelnogo flotov.* St. Petersburg, 1896.

N. Ch. "Shevyrev, Stepan Petrovich." *Russkii biograficheskii slovar.* St. Petersburg, 1911, 19–29.

Nechkina, M. V. *Vasilii Osipovich Kliuchevskii. Istoriia zhinzi i tvorchestva.* Moscow, 1974.

[Nekhachin, Ivan Vasilievich] *Iadro istorii gosudaria Petra Velikogo pervogo Imperatora Vserossiskogo s prisovokupleniem opisaniia Monumenta, vozdvignutogo v pamiat semu Ottsu Otechestva Ekaterinoiu II Velikoiu i s kratkoiu Istorieiu syna Ego, tsarevicha Alekseia Petrovicha.* Moscow, 1794.

Nekrasov, G. A. *Rol Rossii v evropeiskoi mezhdunarodnoi politike. 1725–1739 gg.* Moscow, 1976.

———. *Russko-shvedskie otnosheniia i politika velikikh derzhav v 1721–1726 gg.* Moscow, 1964.

Nekrylova, A. F. "Predaniia i legendy, otrazivshie voennye sobytiia petrovskogo vremeni." *Russkaia narodnaia proza. Russkii folklor.* Vol. XIII. Leningrad, 1972, 103–110.

Nikiforov, L. A. "Rossiia v sisteme evropeiskikh derzhav v pervoi chetverti XVIII v." *Rossiia v period reform Petra I.* 9–39.

———. *Russko-angliiskie otnosheniia pri Petre I.* Moscow, 1950.

Nikitenko, A. *Pokhvalnoe slovo Petru Velikomu, imperatoru i samoderzhtsu vserossiiskomu, ottsu otechestva, proiznesennoe v torzestvennom sobranii Imperatorskogo S.-Pb. universiteta, marta 25-go dnia 1838 goda.* St. Petersburg, 1838. Presented in Shmurlo. *Petr Velikii v russkoi literature (Opyt istoriko-bibliograficheskogo obzora).* St. Petersburg, 1889, 48–53.

Novitskii, G. A. *Obrazovanie Rossiiskoi Imperii. Kurs istorii SSSR. Lekstii 22, 23, 24. Stenogramma lektsii, prochitannykh 21, 27 i 29 ianvaria 1940 g. Vysshaia partiinaia shkola pri TsK VKP(b).* Irkutsk, 1947.

*Ocherki istorii SSSR. Period feodalizma. Rossiia v pervoi chetverti XVIII v. Preobrazovaniia Petra I.* Edited by B. B. Kafengauz and N. I. Pavlenko. Moscow, 1954. For detail on authorship and content, see pp. 282–290.

Odoevskii, V. F. *Russkie nochi.* Moscow, 1913.

Ogarev, N. P. "Chto by sdelal Petr Velikii?" Published by S. Pereselenkov. *Literaturnoe Nasledstvo.* 39–40 (1941): 317–322.

Orlovsky, Daniel T. *The Limits of Reform: The Ministry of Internal Affairs in Imperial Russia, 1802–1881.* Cambridge, Massachusetts, 1981.

*O Vysochaishikh prishestviiakh Velikogo Gosudaria, Tsaria i Velikogo Kniazia Petra Alekseevicha, vseia Velikiia i Malyia i Belyia Rossii Samoderzhtsa.* Moscow, 1783.

Panchenko, A. M. "O smene pisatelskogo tipa v petrovskuiu epokhu." *Problemy literaturnogo razvitiia v Rossii pervoi treti XVIII veka. XVIII vek,* Sbornik 9. Leningrad, 1974, 112–128.

*Panegiricheskaia literatura petrovskogo vremeni.* Moscow, 1979.

Pavlenko, N. I. *Aleksandr Danilovich Menshikov.* Moscow, 1981.

———. "O rostovshchichestve dvorian v XVIII v. (k postanovke voprosa)." *Dvorianstvo i krepostnoi stroi Rossii XVI–XVIII vv.* Edited by N. I. Pavlenko, I. A. Bulygin, A. A. Preobrazhenskii, S. M. Troitskii. Moscow, 1975, 265–271.

————. "Petr I. (K izucheniiu sotsialnopoliticheskikh vzgliadov)." *Rossiia v period reform Petra I.* Edited by N. I. Pavlenko, L. A. Nikiforov, M. Ia. Volkov. Moscow, 1973, 40–102.

————. *Petr Pervyi.* 2d revised edition. Moscow, 1976.

————. "Sava Lukich Vladislavich-Raguzinskii." *Sibirskie ogni.* 1978. No. 3: 156–168.

————. "Torgovo-promyshlennaia politika pravitelstva Rossii v pervoi chetverti XVIII veka." *Istoriia SSSR.* 1978. No. 3: 49–69.

————. "Tri tak nazyvaemykh zaveshchaniia Petra I." *Voprosy Istorii.* 1979. No. 2: 131–144.

Pavlova-Silvanskaia, M. P. "Annotirovannaia bibliografiia inostrannoi literatury o Petre I (1947–1970 gg.)." *Rossiia v period reform Petra I.* 362–382.

Pavlov-Silvanskii, N. P. *Feodalizm v drevnei Rusi.* Petrograd, 1924.

————. "Mneniia verkhovnikov o reformakh Petra Velikogo," in *Ocherki po russkoi istorii XVIII–XIX vv.* St. Petersburg, 1910, 373–401.

Pekarskii, P. *Nauka i literatura v Rossii pri Petre Velikom.* Vol. I. *Vvedenie v istoriiu prosveshcheniia v Rossii XVIII stoletiia.* Vol. II. *Opisanie slaviano-russkikh knig i tipografii 1698–1725 godov.* St. Petersburg, 1862.

*Petr Velikii. Sbornik statei.* Edited by A. I. Andreev. Moscow-Leningrad, 1947.

Petrov, P. N. *Petr Velikii, poslednii tsar moskovskii i pervyi imperator vserossiskii.* St. Petersburg, 1872.

Petrov, S. *Russkii istoricheskii roman XIX veka.* Moscow, 1964.

Petrov-Biriuk, D. *Dikoe pole.* (n.p.) 1946.

Petrov-Biriuk, D. *Kondrat Bulavin.* Moscow, 1970.

Petrovich, Michael B. "V. I. Semevskii (1848–1916): Russian Social Historian." *Essays in Russian and Soviet History in Honor of Geroid Tanquary Robinson.* Edited by John Shelton Curtis. Leiden, 1963, 63–84.

Pilniak, Boris. "Ego Velichestvo Kneeb Piter Komondor." *Povest Peterburgskaia, ili Sviatoi-Kamen-Gorod.* (n.p.) 1922, 61–126.

————. "SianktPiterBurkh." *Povest Peterburgskaia, ili Sviatoi-Kamen-Gorod.* (n.p.) 1922, 1–60.

Pipes, Richard. "The Background and Growth of Karamzin's Political Ideas down to 1810." *Karamzin's Memoir on Ancient and Modern Russia.* New York, 1966, 3–92.

————. *Struve: Liberal on the Left, 1870–1905.* Cambridge, Massachusetts, 1970.

————. *Struve: Liberal on the Right, 1905–1944.* Cambridge, Massachusetts and London, England, 1980.

*Pisma i bumagi Imperatora Petra Velikogo.* 12 vols. Moscow–Leningrad, 1887–1977.

Platonov, S. F. *Lektsii po russkoi istorii.* St. Petersburg, 1904.

————. *Petr Velikii, lichnost i deiatelnost.* Leningrad, 1926.

Plekhanov, G. V. "Novyi zashchitnik samoderzaviia, ili gore g. L. Tikhomirova." *Izbrannye filosofskie proizvedeniia.* Vol. I. Moscow, 1956, 382–417.

————. "Pessimizm kak otrazhenie ekonomicheskoi deistvitelnosti (Pessimizm P. Ia. Chaadaeva)." *Sochineniia.* Vol. X. Edited by D. Riazanov. Moscow–Petrograd (n.d.), 133–162.

Podiapolskaia, E. P. *Vosstanie Bulavina.* 1967.

Pogodin, M. P. *God v chuzhikh kraiakh, 1839.* 4 vols. Moscow, 1844.

————. "Petr Velikii." *Istoriko-kriticheskie otryvki.* Vol. I. Moscow, 1846, 333–363.

————. "Sud nad tsarevichem Alekseem Petrovichem." *Russkaia Beseda.* 1860: 1–84.

Pokrovskii, M. N. *Brief History of Russia.* Translated by D. S. Nirsky. Reprinted from the 2-volume 1933 edition. University Prints and Reprints, Orono, Maine, 1968.

————. *History of Russia from the Earliest Times to the Rise of Commercial Capitalism.* Translated and edited by J. D. Clarkson and M. R. Griffiths. Reprinted from the 1928 edition. University Prints and Reprints, Indiana, 1966.

————. *Istoricheskaia nauka i borba klassov. (Istoriograficheskie ocherki, kriticheskie stati i zametki).* Moscow–Leningrad, 1933.

————. "Istoriia povtoriaetsia." *Narodnoe Prosveschchenie.* No. 32 (April 26, 1919).

————. *Izbrannye proizvedeniia.* 4 vols. Moscow, 1965–1967.

————. "N. A. Rozhkov." *Istoricheskaia nauka i borba klassov.* Moscow–Leningrad, 1933, 224–233.

————. "Novaia kniga po noveishei istorii (o knige Rozhkova N.—*Russkaia istoriia v sravnitelno-istoricheskom osveshchenii,* t. XII). *Istoricheskaia nauka i borba klassov.* Moscow–Leningrad, 1933, 212–223.

————. *Russkaia istoriia s drevneishikh vremen.* 5 vols. Moscow, 1910–1913.

————. *Russkaia istoriia s drevneishikh vremen.* Vols. I, II. *Izbrannye proizvedeniia.* Vols. I, II. Moscow, 1965–1967.

————. *Russkaia istoriia v samom szhatom ocherke. Izbrannye proizvedeniia.* Vol. III. Moscow, 1965–1967.

Pokrovskii, S. A. *Gosudarstvennopravovye vzgliady Radishcheva.* Moscow, 1956.

Polevoi, Nikolai. *Istoriia Petra Velikogo.* 4 vols. St. Petersburg, 1843.

Polievktov, M. *Baltiiskii vopros v russkoi politike posle Nishtadskogo mira (1721–1725).* St. Petersburg, 1907.

————. *Nikolai I. Biografiia i obzor tsarstvovaniia.* Moscow, 1918.

*Polnoe sobranie zakonov Rossiskoi imperii.* XVIII. No. 12.957 (August 11, 1767), 292, column 1.

*Poltava. K 250-letiiu Poltavskogo srazheniia.* Edited by L. G. Beskrovnyi, B. B. Kafengauz, V. A. Diadichenko, N. I. Pavlenko. Moscow, 1959.

Porfirev, E. I. *Petr I—osnovopolozhnik voennogo iskusstva russkoi reguliarnoi armii i flota.* Moscow, 1952.

————. *Poltavskoe srazhenie. 27 iiunia 1709 g.* Moscow, 1959.

Pososhkov, Ivan. *Sochineniia.* Moscow, 1842.

*Pravda Voli Monarshei.* In Fedor Tumanskii. *Sobranie raznykh zapisok i sochinenii, sluzhashchikh k dostavleniiu polnogo svedeniia o zhizni i deianiiakh Gosudaria Imperatora Petra Velikogo.* Part 10. St. Petersburg, 1788, 123–243.

*Problemy literaturnogo razvitiia v Rossii pervoi treti XVIII veka.* Edited by G. P. Makogonenko and G. N. Moiseeva. Leningrad, 1974.

*Problemy russkogo prosveshcheniia v literature XVIII veka.* Edited by P. N. Berkov. Moscow–Leningrad, 1961.

Prokopovich, Feofan. *Istoriia Petra Velikogo ot rozhdeniia ego do Poltavskoi batalii i vziatiia v plen ostalnykh shvedskikh voisk pri Perevolochne vkliuchitelno.* St. Petersburg, 1773.

[————] *Kratkaia povest o smerti Petra Velikogo Imperatora Rossiiskogo.* St. Petersburg, 1819.

————. *Sochineniia.* Moscow–Leningrad, 1961.

Pushkin, A. S. "Arap Petra Velikogo." *Izbrannye proizvedeniia.* Vol. I. Leningrad, 1961, 383–517.

————. "The Bronze Horseman." Translated by Oliver Elton. *Verse from Pushkin and Others.* London, 1935, 152–167.

————. "Istoriia Petra." *Polnoe sobranie sochinenii.* Vol. X. Moscow, 1950, 1–292.

————. *Izbrannye proizvedeniia.* Leningrad, 1961.

————. "Poltava." *Izbrannye proizvedeniia.* Vol. I. Leningrad, 1961, 498–543.

————. "Stansy." *Izbrannye proizvedennia.* Vol. I. Leningrad, 1961, 189.

Puzyrevskii, A. K. *Razvitie postoiannykh reguliarnykh armii i sostoianie voennogo iskusstva v veke Liudovika XIV i Petra Velikogo.* St. Petersburg, 1889.

Pypin, A. "Novyi vopros o Petre Velikom." *Vestnik Evropy.* XXI (1886). No. 5 (May): 317–350.

————. "Petr Velikii v narodnom predanii." *Vestnik Evropy.* St. Petersburg, Year XXXII, Book 8 (August 1897): 640–690.

————. "Russkaia nauka i natsionalnyi vopros v XVIII-m veke." *Vestnik Evropy.* XIX (1884). No. 5 (May): 212–256; No. 6 (June): 548–600; No. 7 (July): 72–117.

Quénet, Charles. *Tchaadaev et les lettres philosophiques. Contribution à l'étude du mouvement des idées en Russie.* Paris, 1931.

Radishchev, A. N. "Osmnadtsatoe stoletie." *Polnoe sobranie sochinenii.* Vol. I. Moscow, 1907, 462–464.

————. "Pismo k drugu, zhitelstvuiushchemu v Tobolske, po dolgu zvaniia svoego." *Polnoe sobranie sochinenii.* Vol. I. Moscow, 1907, 67–75.

Raeff, Marc, ed. *Peter the Great Changes Russia.* 2d edition. Lexington, Massachusetts; Toronto; London, 1972.

Raeff, Marc. *Plans for Political Reform in Imperial Russia, 1730–1905.* Englewood Cliffs, N.J., 1966.

————. "State and Nobility in the Ideology of M. M. Shcherbatov." *The American Slavic and East European Review.* XIX (October 1960), 363–379.

Ragsdale, Hugh. *Détente in the Napoleonic Era: Bonaparte and the Russians.* Lawrence, Kansas, 1980.

Ransel, David. *The Politics of Catherinian Russia: The Panin Party.* New Haven, 1975.

Rasmussen, Karen. "Catherine II and the Image of Peter I." *Slavic Review,* Vol. 37, No. 1 (March 1978), 57–69.

————. "Catherine II and Peter I: The Idea of a Just Monarch." Ph.D. dissertation, University of California, Berkeley, 1973.

Reddaway, W. F., ed. *Documents of Catherine the Great: The Correspondence with Voltaire and the "Instruction" of 1767 in the English Text of 1768.* Cambridge, 1931.

Riabinovich, M. D. "Sotsialnoe proiskhozhdenie i imushchestvennoe polozhenie ofitserov reguliarnoi russkoi armii v kontse Severnoi voiny." *Rossiia v period reform Petra I.* 133–171.

Riasanovsky, Nicholas V. "Afterword: The Problem of the Peasant." *The*

*Peasant in Nineteenth-Century Russia.* Edited by Wayne S. Vucinich. Stanford, California, 1968, 263–284, 306–307.

———. *Nicholas I and Official Nationality in Russia, 1825–1855.* Berkeley and Los Angeles, 1959.

———. "Oriental Despotism and Russia." *Slavic Review,* XXII (December 1963): 644–649.

———. *A Parting of Ways: Government and the Educated Public in Russia, 1801–1855.* Oxford, 1976.

———. "Pogodin and Ševyrëv in Russian Intellectual History." *Harvard Slavic Studies,* IV (1957): 149–167.

———. Review of *Letters of a Russian Traveler, 1789–1790,* by N. M. Karamzin (Florence Jonas translation). *The American Slavic and East European Review,* XVII (December 1958): 545–546.

———. Review of *La Russie absente et présente,* by Wladimir Weidlé. *Journal of Central European Affairs,* XII (January 1953): 391–393.

———. Review of *Plekhanov: the Father of Russian Marxism,* by Samuel H. Baron. *Political Science Quarterly,* LXXIX (September 1964): 457–459.

———. Review of *The Soviet Scholar-Bureaucrat: M. N. Pokrovskii and the Society of Marxist Historians,* by George M. Enteen. *The Russian Review,* XXXVIII (October 1979): 485–486.

———. *Russia and the West in the Teaching of the Slavophiles: A Study of Romantic Ideology.* Cambridge, Massachusetts, 1952.

Riasanovsky, V. A. *Obzor russkoi kultury.* Part II. Issue I. New York, 1947.

Rogger, Hans. *National Consciousness in Eighteenth-Century Russia.* Cambridge, Massachusetts, 1960.

Romanovich-Slavatinskii, A. *Dvorianstvo v Rossii ot nachala XVIII veka do otmeny krepostnogo prava.* St. Petersburg, 1870.

*Rossiia v period reform Petra I.* Edited by N. I. Pavlenko, L. A. Nikiforov, M. Ia. Volkov. Moscow, 1973.

Rovinskii, D. A. *Russkie narodnye kartinki.* Vol. I. St. Petersburg, 1900.

Rozhdestvenskii, S. V. *Ocherki po istorii sistem narodnogo prosveshcheniia v Rossii v XVIII-XIX vekakh.* Vol. I. St. Petersburg, 1912.

Rozhkov, N. *Konets dvorianskoi revoliutsii v Rossii. Ee tretii moment. Russkaia istoriia v sravnitelno-istoricheskom osveshchenii.* Vol. V.

———. *Russkaia istoriia v sravnitelno-istoricheskom osveshchenii (Osnovy sotsialnoi dinamiki).* 12 vols. Moscow–Leningrad, 1919–1926.

Ruban [Vasilii Grigorievich]. *Nachertanie, podaiushchee poniatie o dostoslavnom tsarstvovanii Petra Velikogo, s priobshcheniem khronologicheskoi rospisi glavneishikh del i prikliuchenii zhizni sego velikogo gosudaria.* St. Petersburg, 1778.

———. *Nadpisi k Kamniu Gromu, nakhodiashchemusia v Sanktpeterburge, v podnozhii konnogo, vylitogo litsepodobiia dostoslavnogo imperatora Petra Velikogo.* St. Petersburg, 1782.

Rubinshtein, N. "Istoricheskaia teoriia slavianofilov i ee klassovye korni." *Trudy Instituta Krasnoi Professury. Russkaia istoricheskaia literatura v klassovom osveshchenii. Sbornik statei.* Edited by M. N. Pokrovskii. Moscow, 1927. Vol. I, 53–118.

Rubinshtein, N. L. *Russkaia istoriografiia.* (n.p.) 1941.

Sadler, C. *Peter der Grosse als Mensch und Regent.* St. Petersburg, 1872.

Sakulin, P. N. *Iz istorii russkogo idealizma. Kniaz V. Odoevskii.* Moscow, 1913.

Schiemann, Theodor. *Geschichte Russlands unter Kaiser Nikolaus I.* Vol. III. Berlin, 1913.

Schilder, N. K. *Imperator Aleksandr pervyi, ego zhizn i tsarstvovanie.* Vol. II. St. Petersburg, 1904.

————. "Imperator Nikolai I v 1848 i 1849 godakh." *Imperator Nikolai Pervyi, ego zhizn i tsarstvovanie.* Vol. II. St. Petersburg, 1903, 619–639.

Schmemann, Serge. "Deep in Siberia, Three Centuries of Faith in God." *The New York Times.* November 30, 1982.

Sementkovskii, R. "Kantemir (kn. Antiokh Dmitrievich)," *Entsiklopedicheskii Slovar* (Brockhaus-Efron). Vol. XIV, Book 27 (St. Petersburg, 1895), 314–317.

Semevskii, M. I. *Ocherki i rasskazy iz russkoi istorii XVIII v. Slovo i delo! 1700–1725.* 2d revised edition. St. Petersburg, 1884.

————. *Ocherki i rasskazy iz russkoi istorii XVIII v. Tsaritsa Ekaterina Alekseevna, Anna i Villim Mons, 1692–1724.* 2d revised and enlarged edition. St. Petersburg, 1884.

Semevskii, V. I. *Krestianskii vopros v Rossii v XVIII i pervoi polovine XIX veka.* 2 vols. St. Petersburg, 1888.

Serman, I. Z. "Aleksandr Kornilovich kak istorik i pisatel." *Literaturnoe nasledie dekabristov.* Edited by V. G. Bazanov and V. E. Vatsuro. Leningrad, 1975, 142–164.

————. "Prosvetitelstvo i russkaia literatura pervoi poloviny XVIII veka," in *Problemy russkogo Prosveschcheniia v literature XVIII veka.* Moscow–Leningrad, 1961, 28–44.

*Severnaia Pchela.* No. 78 (April 9, 1852).

Shashkov, S. S. "Vsenarodnoi pamiati tsaria-rabotnika." *Delo.* 1872. No. 7 (Section I): 291–324.

Shcherbatov, M. M., Prince. "O povrezhdenii nravov v Rossii." *Russkaia Starina.* Vol. II (1870): 13–56, 99–116; Vol. III (1871): 673–688.

————. "Otvet grazhdanina na rech, govorennuiu E. I. V. Ober-Prokuratorom Senata Nekliudovym, po prichine torzhestva Shvedskogo mira, 1790 sentiabria, 5 chisla." *Chteniia v Imperatorskom Obshchestve Istorii i Drevnostei Rossiiskikh pri Moskovskom universitete.* Moscow, 1860, Vol. III, Part 5: 41–49.

————. "Primernoe vremiaischislitelnoe polozhenie, vo skolko by let, pri blagopoluchneishikh obstoiatelstvakh, mogla Rossiia sama soboiu, bez samovlastiia Petra Velikogo, doiti do togo sostoianiia, v kakom ona nyne est, v rassuzhdenii proshveshcheniia i slavy." *Chteniia v Imperatorskom Obshchestve Istorii i Drevnostei Rossiiskikh pri Moskovskom universitete.* Moscow, January–March 1860, Vol. I, Part 1: 23–28.

————. "Rassmotrenie o porokakh i samovlastii Petra Velikogo. Beseda." *Chteniia v Imperatorskom Obshchestve Istorii i Drevnostei Rossiiskikh pri Moskovskom universitete.* Moscow, January–March 1860, Vol. I: 5–22.

Shimkevich, L. A. "Osnovatel reguliarnogo russkogo flota." *Sudostroenie.* 1972. No. 1: 40–43.

Shishkin, I. "Panegiristy i poritsateli Petra Velikogo. (Opyt istoricheskogo opravdaniia Petra I-go protiv obvinenii nekotorykh sovremennykh pisatelei. Karla Zadlera. S. Peterburg. 1861)." *Russkoe Slovo. Literaturno-uchenyi zhurnal.* 1861, No. 8.

Shklovskii, V. "Novelly o Petre I." *Tridtsat dnei*. 1941, No. 6: 25–29.

Shmurlo, E. F. "Kriticheskie zametki po istorii Petra Velikogo." *Zhurnal Ministerstva Narodnogo Prosveshcheniia*. *Vol. 329* (May–June 1900): 54–95; *Vol. 330* (July–August 1900): 193–234; *Vol. 331* (September– October 1900): 335–366; *Vol. 338* (November–December 1901): 237–249; *Vol. 340* (March–April 1902): 421–439; *Vol. 341* (May–June 1902): 233–256.

———. *Petr Velikii v otsenke sovremnnikov i potomstva*. St. Petersburg, 1912. (Also in *Zhurnal Ministerstva Narodnogo Prosveshcheniia* for 1911–1912.)

———. *Petr Velikii v russkoi literature*. St. Petersburg, 1889. (Also in *Zhurnal Ministerstva Narodnogo Prosveshcheniia* for the same year.)

———, ed. *Sbornik dokumentov, otnosiashchikhsia k istorii tsarstvovaniia imperatora Petra Velikogo*. Vol. I. *1693–1700*. Iuriev. 1903.

———. *Volter i ego kniga o Petre Velikom*. Prague, 1929.

Shtorm, G. P. "Poltava." *Deti dobroi nadezhdy. Istoricheskie povesti i rasskazy*. Moscow, 1962, 145–165.

Shutoi, V. E. *Borba narodynkh mass protiv nashestviia armii Karla XII, 1700–1709*. Moscow, 1958.

———. *Severnaia voina (1700–1721 gg.)*. Moscow, 1970.

Smirnyw, Walter. "Lev Tolstoi's Unfinished Novel on the Epoch of Peter I: The Enigma of Russia in an Enchanted Circle." *Russian Literary Triquarterly*. 17 (1982): 102–116.

Sokolovskii, I. V. *Petr Velikii, kak vospitatel i uchitel naroda*. Kazan, 1873.

Soloviev, S. M. *Istoriia Rossii s drevneishikh vremen*. Vols. XIII–XVIII. St. Petersburg (n.d.).

———. *Moi zapiski dlia detei moikh, a, esli mozhno, i dlia drugikh*. Petrograd (n.d.).

———. *Publichnye chteniia o Petre Velikom*. Moscow, 1872.

Soloviev, V. S. "Neskolko slov v zashchitu Petra Velikogo." *Sobranie sochinenii*. (n.p., n.d.) Vol. V, 161–180.

———. "Ocherki iz istorii russkogo soznaniia." *Vestnik Evropy. Zhurnal istorii, politiki, literatury*. 24. Book 5 (May, 1889): 290–303.

Spirodonova, E. V. *Ekonomicheskaia politika i ekonomicheskie vzgliady Petra I*. Moscow, 1952.

"Spisok trudov B. B. Kafengauza i retsenzii na nikh." *Absoliutizm v Rossii (XVII–XVIII vv.)*. Moscow, 1974, 508–518.

Spuler, Bertold. "Russia and Islam." *Slavic Review*, XXII (December 1963): 650–655.

Stankevich, N. V. *Perepiska: 1830–1840*. Moscow, 1914.

Strumilin, S. G. *Gornozavodskii Ural petrovskoi epokhi*. Moscow, 1947.

———. *Istoriia chernoi metallurgii v SSSR*. Vol. I. Moscow, 1954.

———. "K voprosu ob ekonomike Petrovskoi epokhi." *Poltava. K 250-Letiiu poltavskogo srazheniia. Sbornik statei*. Moscow, 1959, 179–189.

Struve, O. V. "Ob uslugakh, okazannykh Petrom Velikim matematicheskoi geografii Rossii." *Zapiski Imperatorskoi Akademii Nauk*. Vol. XXI. St. Petersburg, 1872, 1–19.

Sumarokov, Aleksandr P. "Na pobedy Gosudaria Imperatora Petra Velikogo," *Polnoe sobranie vsekh sochinenii*. Vol. II. Moscow, 1787, 3–12.

———. "Nadpisi." *Polnoe sobranie vsekh sochinenii*. Vol. I. Moscow, 1787, 265–284.

————. "Rossiiskii Vifleem." *Polnoe sobranie vsekh sochinenii.* Vol. VI. Moscow, 1787, 302–303.

————. "Slovo Pokhvalnoe o Gosudare Imperatore Petre Velikom, sochinennoe ko dniu Tezoimenitstva Eia Imperatorskogo Velichestva 1759 goda." *Polnoe sobranie vsekh sochinenii.* Vol. II. Moscow, 1787, 219–228.

Sumner, B. H. *Peter the Great and the Emergence of Russia.* London, 1950.

Syromiatnikov, B. I. "Osnovnye momenty v razvitii istoricheskoi mysli." *Russkaia Mysl.* 1906. No. 12: 71–97.

————. *"Reguliarnoe" gosudarstvo Petra Pervogo i ego ideologiia.* Part I. Moscow–Leningrad, 1943.

————. "Traditsionnaia teoriia russkogo istoricheskogo razvitiia. (Istoriograficheskii ocherk)." Moscow, 1911. Produced for publication, but not released.

Szporluk, Roman. "Introduction." M. N. Pokrovskii. *Russia in World History: Selected Essays by M. N. Pokrovskii.* Ann Arbor, 1970, 1–46.

Tarle, E. V. *Russkii flot i vneshniaia politika Petra I.* Moscow, 1949.

Tatishchev, V. N. *Istoriia Rossiiskaia.* Vol. I. Moscow-Leningrad, 1962.

Telpukhovskii, B. S. *Severnaia voina, 1700–1721. Polkovodcheskaia deiatelnost Petra I.* Moscow, 1946.

Tikhomirov, N. *Sbornik literaturnykh proizvedenii, otnosiashchikhsia k Petru Velikomu.* St. Petersburg, 1872.

Tikhonov, Iu. A. "Feodalnaia renta v pomeshchichikh imeniiakh Tsentralnoi Rossii v kontse XVII–pervoi chetverti XVIII v. (vladelcheskie povinnosti i gosudarstvennye nalogi)." *Rossiia v period reform Petra I.* 199–214.

Tkhorzhevskii, S. "V. O. Kliuchevskii, kak sotsiolog i politicheskii myslitel." *Dela i Dni.* 1921, Book 2: 152–179.

Togawa, Tsuguo. *Pierre Tchadaev: Fragments et pensés diverses (inédits).* Surabu Kenkyū. 23. Supplement (Sapporo, 1979): 23–36.

Tolstoi, A. N., and V. Petrov. *Petr I: kinostsenarii.* Moscow, 1935.

————. "Petr I." *Novyi mir, 1935.* No. 1: 54–80.

————. *Polnoe sobranie sochinenii.* Vol. IX. *Petr Pervyi.* Moscow, 1946.

Tomsinskii, S. "Znachenie reform Petra I." *Istorik Marksist.* Book II (1936), No. 2 (54): 9–21.

Troitskii, S. M. "Khoziaistvo krupnogo sanovnika Rossii v pervoi chetverti XVIII v. (po arkhivu kniazia A. D. Menshikova)." *Rossiia v period reform Petra I.* 215–248.

Tumanskii, F. *Polnoe opisanie deianii Ego Velichestva Gosudaria Imperatora Petra Velikogo.* Vol. I. St. Petersburg, 1788.

————. *Sobranie raznykh zapisok i sochinenii sluzhashchikh k dostavleniiu polnogo svedeniia o zhizni i deianiiakh Gosudaria Imperatora Petra Velikogo.* 10 vols. St. Petersburg, 1787–1788.

Tynianov, Iurii. "Voskovaia persona." *Kiukhlia. Rasskazy.* Leningrad, 1973, 360–464.

Uspenskii, B. A. "Historia sub specie semioticae." *Kulturnoe nasledie drevnei Rusi. Istoki, stanovlenie, traditsii.* Moscow, 1976, 286–292.

Ustrialov, N. *Istoriia tsarstvovaniia Petra Velikogo.* Vols. I–IV, VI. St. Petersburg, 1858–1864.

————. *Russkaia istoriia.* 5th edition. Vol. II. St. Petersburg, 1855.

Uvarov, S. S. "Tsirkuliarnoe predlozhenie G. Upravliaiushchego Ministerstvom Narodnogo Prosveshcheniia Nachalstvam Uchebnykh Okrugov 'o vstuplenii v upravlenie Ministerstvom.'" *Zhurnal Ministerstva Narodnogo Prosvesh-cheniia*. 1834, Part I, 1.

V. R-v. "Nepliuev (Ivan Ivanovich)." *Entsiklopedicheskii Slovar* (Brockhaus-Efron). Vol. XXA, Book 40 (St. Petersburg, 1897), 887.

Valdenberg, V. E. *Shcherbatov o Petre Velikom*. St. Petersburg, 1903.

Vasilchikov, A. A. *O portretakh Petra*. Moscow, 1872.

Veretennikov, V. I. *Istoriia Tainoi kantseliarii petrovskogo vremeni*. Kharkov, 1910.

———. *Ocherki istorii general-prokuratury v Rossii do-ekaterinskogo vremeni*. Kharkov, 1915.

Verkhovskoi, P. V. *Uchrezhdenie Dukhovnoi kollegii i Dukhovnyi Reglament. K voprosu ob otnoshenii Tserkvi i gosudarstva v Rossii. Issledovanie v oblasti istorii russkogo tserkovnogo prava*. Vol. I. *Issledovanie*. Rostov-on-Don, 1916.

Veselovskii, K. S. "Petr Velikii kak uchreditel Akademii nauk." *Zapiski Imperatorskoi Akademii Nauk*. Vol. XXI. St. Petersburg, 1872, 20–30.

Vilinbakhov, G. V. "Emblema na rotnom znameni Sankt-Peterburgskogo Polka 1712 goda." *Soobshcheniia Gosudarstvennogo Ermitazha*. XLIV, Leningrad, 1979, 32–34.

———. "K istorii uchrezhdeniia ordena Andreia Pervozvannogo i evoliutsii ego znaka." *Sbornik russkoi kultury i iskusstva petrovskogo vremeni*. Leningrad, 1977, 144–158.

Vilinbakhov, V. B. "Gosudarevo synoubiistvo." Manuscript.

———. "Pir byl gotov, no. . . ." Manuscript.

Vladimirskii-Budanov, M. *Gosudarstvo i narodnoe obrazovanie v Rossii XVIII-go veka*. Part I. *Sistema professionalnogo obrazovaniia (ot Petra do Ekateriny II)*. Iaroslavl, 1874.

Volk, S. S. "Dekabristy o Petre I i ego preobrazovaniiakh. Otsenka osnovynkh sobytii russkoi istorii XVIII veka." *Istoricheskie vzgliady dekabristov*. Moscow-Leningrad, 1958, 395–421.

Volkov, A. M. *Dva brata. Roman*. Moscow, 1961.

Volkov, M. Ia. "Monakh Avramii i ego 'Poslanie Petru I.'" *Rossiia v period reform Petra I*. 311–336.

[Voltaire]. *Histoire de l'empire de Russie sous Pierre le Grand*. Par l'Auteur de l'histoire de Charles XII. Tome premier MDCCLIX. Tome second MDCCLXIII.

*Voprosy voennoi istorii Rossii. XVIII i pervaia polovnia XIX vekov*. Moscow, 1969.

Voskrensenskii, N. A. *Zakonodatelnye akty Petra I. Redaktsii i proekty zakonov, zametki, doklady, donosheniia, chelobitia i inostrannye istochniki*. Edited and with an introduction by B. I. Syromiatnikov. Vol. I. *Akty o vysshikh gosudarstvennykh ustanovleniiakh*. Moscow–Leningrad, 1945.

Wada, Haruki. "The Inner World of Russian Peasants." *Annals of the Institute of Social Science*. No. 20. University of Tokyo, 1979, 61–94.

Walicki, Andrzej. *A History of Russian Thought from the Enlightenment to Marxism*. Stanford, 1979.

———. "Personality and Society in the Ideology of Russian Slavophiles: A Study in the Sociology of Knowledge." *California Slavic Studies*. II (1963): 1–20.

———. *The Slavophile Controversy: History of a Conservative Utopia in Nineteenth Century Russian Thought*. Oxford, 1975.

Weidlé, Wladimir. *La Russie absente et présente.* Paris, 1949.

Wittfogel, Karl A. *Oriental Despotism.* New Haven, 1957.

———. "Russia and the East: a Comparison and Contrast." *Slavic Review,* XXII (December, 1963): 627–643, 656–661.

Zadonskii, N. A. *Kondratii Bulavin.* Moscow, 1959.

Zaozerskaia, E. I. "K voprosu o razvitii krupnoi promyshlennosti v Rossii v XVIII veke." *Voprosy Istorii.* 1947. No. 12: 62–73.

———. "K voprosu o zarozhdenii kapitalisticheskikh otnoshenii v melkoi promyshlennosti Rossii nachala XVIII veka." *Voprosy Istorii.* 1949. No. 6: 70–84.

———. *Manufactura pri Petre I.* Moscow, 1947.

———. "Moskovskii posad pri Petre I." *Voprosy Istorii.* 1947. No. 9: 19–35.

———. *Rabochaia sila i klassovaia borba na tekstilnykh manufakturakh v 20–60 gg. XVIII v.* Moscow, 1960.

———. *Razvitie legkoi promyshlennosti v Moskve v pervoi chetverti XVIII v.* Moscow, 1953.

———, and L. N. Pushkarev, eds. *Volneniia rabotnykh liudei i pripisnykh krestian na metallurgicheskikh zavodakh Rossii v pervoi polovine XVIII v.* Moscow, 1975.

Zaozerskii, A. I. "Feldmarshal Sheremetev i pravitelstvennaia sreda Petrovskogo vremeni." *Rossiia v period reform Petra I,* 172–198.

Zavalishin, D. I. *Zapiski dekabrista.* St. Petersburg, 1906.

Zimin, A. A. "Formirovanie istoricheskikh vzgliadov V. O. Kliuchevskogo v 60-e gody XIX v." *Istoricheskie Zapiski.* 69 (1961): 178–196.

Zotov, R. M. *Tridtsatiletie Evropy v tsarstvovanie Imperatora Nikolaia I.* 2 vols. St. Petersburg, 1857.

## Papers Presented in My Seminar on "The Image of Peter the Great in Russian History and Thought"

Bernstein, Laurie. "Plekhanov's Image of Peter the Great."

Goldberg, Esther S. "A Man of His Time: M. N. Pokrovskii and His Image of Peter the Great."

Hinshaw, Christine Ruane. "Kliuchevskii's Image of Peter the Great."

Hollingsworth, Paul. "The 'All-Drunken, All-Joking Synod': Carnival and Rulership in the Reign of Peter the Great."

Malley, Lynn. "A Hero of His Time: Alexei Tolstoi's Changing Image of Peter the Great."

Sedik, David J. "Paul Miliukov's Image of Peter the Great: State and Society in His Early Historical Works."

Steinberg, Mark. "Autocracy and Reform: The Image of Peter the Great in the Writings of Nikolai Ivanovich Turgenev."

# Index